WAY TO GO!

WAY TO GO!

("Jesus answered, 'I am the way.' ")

Corrine Vanderwerff

Review and Herald® Publishing Association
Hagerstown, MD 21740

This book was
Edited by Richard W. Coffen
Designed by Bill Kirstein
Cover art by Helcio Deslandes
Typeset: Clearface 9.5/10.5

PRINTED IN U.S.A.

98 97 96 95 94 93 10 9 8 7 6 5 4 3 2 1

R&H Cataloging Service
Vanderwerff, Corrine
Way to go!

1. Teenagers—Prayer books and devotions—English.
2. Devotional calendars—Juvenile literature. I. Title.

242.82

ISBN 0-8280-0699-7

Dedicated

with love to Matthew.

"Jesus answered,
'I am the way and
the truth
and the life' " (John 14:6).
" 'Follow me,' he told him,
and Matthew got up
and followed him" (Matt. 9:9).

Acknowledgments

This book would not have been without Date, my most patient husband, who cheerfully puts up with my writing; Dianne and Pete Watts, who not only gave me a place to write but who've been real friends and encouragers; Linda, Dean, and Jeff Rogers, who not only open their home to our comings and goings but also manage to get us to and from airports at the most unfriendly hours of day or night; Geri and Werner Seidel, who shared stories and experiences; Jean, Carole, and Ralph Fletcher, who made it possible to include stories with a British touch; Cherie Kirk, who generously shared resource materials; and our children—Joann and Richard Chabaylo and Jon Vanderwerff, who always take excellent care of their parents, and, of course, little Matthew, who was learning to walk and to talk and helped Grandma see the world in a new way when she was there writing this book. And the folks at the Review and Herald, particularly Penny Estes Wheeler, who's not only full of good advice about writing but a friend, and Jack Calkins, who unwittingly gave me a most valuable help when, for another small project I was doing, he let me have a study Bible with many good helps in which he'd added his personal notes. I'm also very grateful for the support and prayers of the ladies of the Lubumbashi Bible study group—particularly Glynis Bradfield and Gillian Raymond.

Meet Corrine Vanderwerff

Corrine grew up in southwestern Washington State, attended Columbia Academy and Canadian Union College (and a host of other colleges), lived in western Canada after graduating from academy until in 1981 her husband, Date, was called to be director of Gitwe College in Rwanda. They later moved to Zaire, where he has developed the ADRA work and has become a specialist in integrated village development, including school-health-agriculture and other area-appropriate projects.

Corrine and Date met at Canadian Union College and for several years were a principal-teacher team. She taught elementary school, then secondary English at Fraser Valley Academy, in British Columbia; at Okanagan Academy, also in British Columbia; at Gitwe College, in Rwanda; and at Songa Secondary School, in Zaire. Corrine has also been a newspaper reporter and columnist and now writes full-time—her first love.

Education, though, remains very much a part of her life, and her deep-down commitment is to help kids have the best future possible. She's very involved with—in fact, manages—the REACH (International/Italy/Canada) child sponsorship programs in Zaire, which have more than 2,500 kids. With cooperation between REACH, ADRA, and private funders, they've built more than a dozen schools for kids who had no schools, and have helped establish churches in villages which had no churches.

In addition, Corrine is vice president of the administrative board of The English-Speaking School of Lubumbashi (TESOL), which serves the children of mission, diplomatic, and business families from English-speaking countries. She is also active in a women's Bible study group.

Corrine's hobbies are studying the Bible, visiting with family and friends, and traveling. Some of her favorite places are the Oregon beaches; the Catacombs in Rome; Victoria Falls, Zimbabwe; West Edmonton Mall, Canada; Wookey

Hole (caves), England; the church in Echten, the Netherlands; and the Vancouver (Canada) Aquarium. She likes biking, doing casual photography, and putting together photo albums about their missionary work in Zaire.

Oh, yes, Corrine and Date have a cat—very spoiled—and a red Mercedes jeep.

Some Notes About Writing This Book

One of my biggest burdens has been to try to share ideas about God and about being His friend—ideas that I wish I'd known when I was a kid, or even when my kids were kids. I've known about God for a long time. But something was always missing, and I kept waiting for that magic day when somehow I'd suddenly be a good Christian. Then one day as we were grinding along one of our long and tedious African roads and I was on the jump seat of our old Nissan 4 x 4, reading (yes, that is sometimes possible!), a paragraph suddenly broke through my thinking—the secret to having Christ in my life lay in my will—in my power of choice. I could choose right then and there to have Christ in my life, and I did. That was the beginning.

About that time I'd also had the opportunity to fulfill a longtime wish to become a full-time free-lance writer. I handed the opportunity over to God, and He opened the way for me to have this—and other—assignments.

When military and political unrest forced our evacuation from Zaire, the devotional was hardly half-written and the deadline close enough that my husband and I decided that I should go to North America, where I'd try to find a quiet place to finish the book while he, as ADRA director, would stay close to the border and reenter the country as soon as possible to set up relief aid. (I believe he and a nurse from another mission were the first Protestant missionaries to return to our area on a permanent basis.)

God opened the way. My friend Dianne Watts had just taken over temporary management of a hotel property, and she gave me a quiet, comfortable room for a month. It was an ideal place to write, but having been evacuated by air in a hurry, all I had with me besides a sleeping bag and a few clothes were my little notebook computer, some disks I'd saved, and a Bible. The reference books I'd counted on using and my notes were all back in Lubumbashi, and when I'd left, the looters were moving toward our street with threats that they'd ransack the mission.

With no telephone, fax, telex, or even telegraph operating into our part of the country, I had no way of staying in contact with Date once he went back. I had my place to write, but faced with an empty computer screen, I felt very alone without the notes and books I'd counted on using, and I worried, of course, about my husband's safety.

I didn't know how I could possibly get the job done. Deep down I knew that I could count on God's help, but I felt very much in need of some tangible evidence and told God so one morning.

Now, I'm not in the habit of just opening my Bible and letting my finger fall on some text and taking that as my message for the day, but at that moment I did open my Bible at random and began scanning the right-hand column and found myself reading in Acts 26 about Paul, who was telling his story to King Agrippa. The words of verse 16 caught and held my attention.

"Now get up and stand on your feet. I have appeared to you to appoint you as a servant and as a witness of what you have seen of me and what I will show you."

As I read those words, they translated as a direct command: "Start writing. Tell what you know about Me. I'll show you the rest."

And I went to work. Writing 365 devotional readings is no small task, but with the Lord's help, you now have the book. Each day as I wrote, I continued to claim the promise of Acts 26:16, and the Lord helped. My prayer for each page is that in some way it will speak a special spiritual message to at least one youngster somewhere, and my prayer for each youngster who picks up this book is that he or she will find at least one helpful spiritual thought.

After four months in North America—from Virginia I went to stay in Edmonton with our children and continued writing—I was able to rejoin Date in Zaire, where I put the finishing touches on the book. So in a sense this book comes from an international perspective—besides the major sections that were written in Zaire, the United States, and Canada, other parts were written in Europe, when we were there on leave shortly before the rioting forced our evacuation. During these travels I've learned firsthand that no matter where in the world I am or how ugly the circumstances, God is always there, and He prompts other people to help us carry our burdens.

While I've written directly to juniors, I know from experience that a junior devotional often becomes a family or classroom worship tool, and as I've written I've tried to look over the kids' shoulders to those others who are no longer juniors, and some of the searching-out-God activities are intended for them too. No matter how old we become, the biggest truths are best told in simple words and illustrations, and those truths are best retained as we become involved in meaningful activity that will help fix them in our minds.

Corrine Vanderwerff
Lubumbashi, Zaire

JANUARY

1

The Broken Vase

Then you will know the truth, and the truth will set you free. John 8:32.

Josh looked down at his hands, feeling like the culprit in the middle of one of those famous old-time *Bedtime Stories*. He held the broken pieces of his mother's favorite vase. The Nerf® football lay where it had ricocheted in a wild spin. And not another person was in the house. He wanted to drop the pieces where they had first crashed, disappear, and let his mother happen onto the scene.

Then she'd probably blame it on the cat, he told himself.

His conscience suggested that he find a better idea.

Glue! Glue them together, and Mom'll never see the difference . . . He took three steps. . . . *till later.*

Leaving the evidence to implicate the cat did seem better. He stepped backward and bent to put the pieces back on the floor.

A brave man is not afraid of the truth—or its consequences. Why did that saying his dad often repeated have to pop into his mind just then?

The family rules defined acceptable and unacceptable behavior. Keep the rules and keep out of trouble; break the rules—and pay.

Pay for a vase like this, though? Thinking of what that would do to his savings, Josh shook his head.

If you were Josh, what would you have done?

When Jesus said, "The truth will set you free," He was talking to those who believed in Him and chose to follow His teachings. When Josh betrayed his mother's trust in him not to throw things in the living room, he suddenly faced new—and difficult—choices.

Sin always brings about choices, and making the right choices still brings eternal freedom.

This book deals with knowing the truth about Jesus and God and about choices you can make so that the truth *can* set you free.

By the way, after struggling over his choices, Josh decided to confess. He and his mother did try to glue the vase, but they couldn't get it to look right, so they agreed on a plan that let Josh work off the price of a new one. Even though it cost him, he found that telling the truth did make him free—free from the feelings of guilt.

JANUARY

2

Real Friends

I no longer call you servants, because a servant does not know his master's business. Instead, I have called you friends, for everything that I learned from my Father I have made known to you. John 15:15.

"Welcome to the Hall of Wonders!" The lady at the reception desk seemed to be smiling. "We're so glad you could visit us. And what are your names?"

"I'm Lana, and this is . . ."

"Sshh!" hissed Alycia. "That's not a real person."

"But she's talking," Lana whispered back.

"She's a dummy that's been programmed to trick us."

"Then why are you whispering?"

"Because . . ." Alycia suddenly realized what she was doing. "Because she looks so real," she finished, feeling foolish.

The two girls looked at each other, then burst out laughing. Visiting the wax museum offered more surprises than they'd expected. That afternoon they saw the likenesses of many famous people. From a distance, they all looked real, but up close they looked like what they really were—lifeless models. Even with implanted electronic chips that could give them natural human movements and voices and the ability to respond to spoken commands, the models could never be real, breathing people with minds of their own. They could never be anything more than what they were programmed to be.

God created us in His image, not as programmed models but as independent beings with the ability to think and do as we choose. Even so, some Christians act as though they've been programmed. Like the wax model that fooled the girls, they say—even do—the right things. They're like servants who obey commands because that's their job.

God wants us to be His friends. That's why He gave each of us a will, or in other words, the power of choice. Two friends choose to be friends—both of them. In order to have real friendship, though, each person must choose to be friends with the other. How can you tell that two people are really friends?

____

____

____

You likely suggested ideas such as talking, doing things, and going places together, even acting and talking like each other.

God has chosen you to be His friend. Have you chosen to be friends with Him? Can others tell by the way you act?

JANUARY

Zach's Airplane

Do not be like the horse or the mule, which have no understanding but must be controlled by bit and bridle. Psalm 32:9.

I'm gonna make an airplane with it, and no one's gonna stop me!" Zach looked up, his blue eyes full of a 7-year-old's determination.

His mother raised an eyebrow. "Oh?" Her one-word question was voiced in that certain special motherly tone.

"Yeah!" In his eagerness he ignored the warning in her voice. "I'm gonna nail on boards for wings. Then put a 'peller in front. Then I'll pedal hard . . ." He swept his hand in a huge arc as he imagined himself zooming up and over the house and looping around the neighborhood.

"Are you sure Uncle James wants you nailing things on his grindstone?" Mother looked at Zach's intended airplane—an old sawhorse with a stone wheel and pedals. The operator straddled it and pedaled—hard—to turn the heavy grinding wheel. It was gray with age, an antique that had been in the family for generations.

"It'll be a good plane." Zach's head was full of pictures of him sitting astride his four-legged craft, peddling full tilt, diving above his friends' heads. "Soon's I find the right boards, I'm gonna fly." He slapped his hands onto his hips. "And no one's gonna stop me."

"Zachery!"

His mother's voice caught him full-force—as if he'd been hit across the stomach with a board. He'd been sure she'd like his airplane idea.

"But I *want* to fly."

His mother put her hand on his shoulder. "Even if that sawhorse would make the best airplane in the world, should you just take it and nail things on it without asking permission?"

When you were younger did you, like Zach, ever let your ideas run ahead of good sense? God created us so that as we grow, we gain understanding and learn to think things through and make good decisions. He also gave us a built-in freedom to make choices—and that includes making choices about Him and His way.

Zach can look back now and laugh at his childish idea of building an airplane. Looking back on wrong choices about God, though, will never be a laughing matter.

JANUARY

4

The Way of Life

How can we know the way? John 14:5.

"Don't you understand what's happening?" Muteb asked as he leaned forward and looked at his friend. "On Monday two of your next-door children fell ill with a sudden fever and had to be taken to the hospital, and the lady two doors down had her money stolen in the market. Then on Tuesday the boy across from her had his leg broken when he was hit by that motorcycle. Yesterday the ceiling fell down in the house next to his, three more children on this street had to go to the hospital with the fever, and your corner neighbor lost his job. Today, already . . ."

Ngoy understood the warning in what Muteb was saying. He understood, but he was not afraid as he once would have been.

"I'm telling you, it's that woman across from you. She's jealous, and she has power. Your family'll be next. You and your wife have good jobs, your children go to good schools, and you have nice clothes. She's jealous of all that, and if you don't have very strong medicine, you can't escape the evil of her spells."

Ngoy nodded. "Our neighborhood's having more than its share of problems," he agreed, "but we have strong medicine." He glanced at the table where his Bible lay.

Muteb laughed. "You Christians!" he exclaimed. "You say that your God is more powerful than the spirits and that your Bible is stronger than any charm, but I see that you get sick and lose your jobs and have accidents . . ."

As his friend talked, Ngoy wished for a way to help him understand.

"If your God is more powerful, then why do those things still happen to you?"

Ahh, thought Ngoy, *so that's his real question.* He prayed silently for the right words before he spoke. "Our world is full of sickness and misfortune, even death. God's Book shows that this is the way of sin, that sin hurts everyone. But it also teaches us the secret of having the protection of God's power—and that's the way of life."

"That's what I've never been able to see—that 'way of life.' "

At last, Ngoy thought to himself. *After all these years, it seems he's ready to listen.* To Muteb he said, "That way begins with believing in God."

JANUARY

5

The Good Way

This is what the Lord says: "Stand at the crossroads and look; ask for the ancient paths, ask where the good way is, and walk in it." Jeremiah 6:16.

"I used to worry day and night about what the spirits might do," Ngoy confessed to Muteb. "I bought charms and paid for protection and still was so afraid that often I couldn't even sleep. Remember how at mission school they taught us that we must choose God's way *or* the other way, that we couldn't have both?"

Muteb nodded but didn't say anything—he'd been at the same mission school at the same time as Ngoy.

"Well, I wanted both. I wanted the peace that they talked about, yet I was afraid to give up our traditions because the spirits might get me if I did. But following the traditions did not make me feel safe." Ngoy looked at his friend. "You know how it is?"

Muteb nodded again but still didn't speak.

"I kept looking for stronger and stronger charms, but nothing worked. So I went to see a pastor. We talked, and I decided to follow God. He burned all my charms, but he warned me that wasn't enough. He said that I must give myself completely to following God's way, which included replacing my old worries with God thoughts. That's why you always see my Bible here—I read it every day, and it is strong medicine. It tells me about God's way and keeps my mind filled with God thoughts.

"The Bible's a wonderful book about a wonderful God." A happiness radiated from Ngoy's face as he spoke. "You should try it," he added, sensing that his friend was at a crossroads and was looking for a better way.

Muteb nodded.

In the weeks that followed, Ngoy was happy to see Muteb use the five-point plan in today's verse and also choose to follow God's way. The verse uses four different verbs—one twice—to make five commands. List the five one-word commands then explain each in your own words. (Answers are on page 380.)

1. ______________________________
2. ______________________________
3. ______________________________
4. ______________________________
5. ______________________________

JANUARY

6

One of Those Days

He humbled you, causing you to hunger and then feeding you with manna, which neither you nor your fathers had known, to teach you that man does not live on bread alone but on every word that comes from the mouth of the Lord. Deuteronomy 8:3.

Let's imagine that it's one of those mornings. You know the sort—the alarm doesn't go off, and everyone in the family oversleeps. You splash your way hurriedly through the bathroom, pull on some clothes, grab a piece of bread, dash for the door. In your scramble to get to school on time, you don't bother to take a lunch, thinking that you'll buy something at noon.

About halfway through the morning your stomach begins to tell you that lunchtime had better hurry. At last the clock drags its hands to that magic minute, and you're about to dash off for something to eat when you make a discovery. In your hurry to get to school, you forgot to bring lunch money.

Oh, well, you tell yourself, *that's what friends are for.* You slide into a chair and just sit there watching your best friend eat.

"Didn't you bring a lunch today?" your friend asks.

"Naw," you say. "Didn't have time."

"Aren't you going to eat?"

"Naw. Forgot my lunch money."

"Here! Share a sandwich. It's one of my mom's super whole-wheat whammies."

"Naw," you say. "It looks good. You eat it and just tell me how it tastes. That's good enough."

"What?" your friend asks, looking at you strangely.

"Eat your lunch," you reply. "Just tell me how it tastes and how it makes you feel full. That'll be good enough to keep me going until I have a chance to eat later."

By this time your friend would have every reason to question your state of mind. It's impossible for someone else to eat for you. You must feed your own body.

How often do you feed your spiritual body? Just as your physical life depends upon the food you eat, your spiritual life depends upon the Word of God. You can't depend on someone else to "eat" for you. You must "eat" it for yourself.

JANUARY

7

The Waiting Table

In my Father's house are many rooms; if it were not so, I would have told you. I am going there to prepare a place for you.
John 14:2.

Bor-ing!" Janyce muttered as she stuffed her hands into her coat pockets and trailed after her parents. Being a missionary kid was OK—furlough travels had taken her through more countries than some of her cousins back in America could even name. But Janyce had wanted excitement, not a visit to another big old English house.

Just one family with two kids, in a house like this? she asked herself as the guide led them through what seemed to be miles of drawing rooms and salons to library to breakfast room to . . . bedroom? For the daughter? Janyce forgot about being bored and gaped at the huge delicately canopied bed, the many pieces of pretty furniture, the giant marble fireplace, the collection of antique dolls. *With side rooms? It's as big as our whole house!*

As the guide hurried them on to more rooms, past family paintings and more fancy furniture, Jesus' words about going to prepare a house with many rooms flitted through Janyce's thoughts.

They entered a second dining room—even larger than the first—with a long table set for dinner. Janyce stepped closer to the table. She'd never before seen so much silver and crystal. She counted the places. Eighteen. *Eighteen settings—with silver plates!*

"This room is used only when royalty visits," the guide explained. "Queen Elizabeth I was the first royal guest to dine at this table. The settings are of solid silver—the plates, the candlesticks, even the centerpiece. The artist used 62 pounds of fine silver to sculpt this moment of victory of one of England's famous battles."

Janyce imagined being a princess, being invited to dine, seated by a handsome, witty prince, and eating rich and exotic food from silver plates . . .

"But this room hasn't been used for 50 years."

As the guide led them to another room, Janyce looked back at the waiting table. Other than those who dusted and polished and kept the room in readiness, no one ever visited except for the tourists who paid to come and look. She thought again of Jesus' promise.

JANUARY

8

A Jewel of Great Value

A rainbow, resembling an emerald, encircled the throne. Revelation 4:3.

A man in a dark coat stood at the gate. He looked quickly about before he spoke. "I have something that will interest you." He spoke in a low, nervous voice.

Businessman Brown waited for him to continue.

"My brother has just brought this from the diggings." The man reached into his pocket, pulled out a wad of paper, turned back the corners, and held out his hand. Among the rumples lay a bright, transparent green stone.

Mr. Brown's eyes met the man's. "Emerald?"

"Yes. Very good." The man spoke quickly. "I sell it very good price. You take it out of country. Be rich."

Mr. Brown shook his head. "I'm a Christian," he replied. "I'm not interested in smuggling."

"Very good price," the man repeated.

"No!" Mr. Brown repeated and turned away.

Emeralds are usually considered to be worth more than diamonds and are second in value only to rubies. To understand their price, think about this. One million single dollar bills would weigh approximately one ton. A gold brick worth $1 million (at $400 an ounce) would weigh about 200 pounds. A million-dollar emerald for sale in New York City in 1990 weighed just one tenth of an *ounce*. Mr. Brown had just refused the possibility of making a fortune.

When the Spanish first plundered gold and silver in South America, they also found emeralds, and soon royalty in India, Persia, and Egypt wore the giant green jewels. Today South America and certain African countries remain the major producers of emeralds, and their rare beauty continues to make them big business. Smuggling and profiteering and other illegal, get-rich-quick schemes, though, stalk the search for them and other precious stones and often lead to violence and death. The value and beauty of such gems don't make them dangerous business, but the greed to own them does.

The biblical prophets describe the glory around God that they had seen in vision as being like emeralds and other beautiful gems. Jesus said the good news of the gospel is like a valuable jewel—a pearl. Finding it brings peace and life.

Mr. Brown, the businessman, understood this, and in all his dealings he upheld the way of honesty, which would give him this pearl of great price.

JANUARY

Beyond Imagination

No eye has seen, no ear has heard, no mind has conceived what God has prepared for those who love him.
1 Corinthians 2:9.

Bob stared at all the jewels on display, and for a moment he pretended that he had enough money to buy them all. The museum guide pointed to a clear, green stone. "That's an emerald," she said, "but it's synthetic, not natural. Scientists create synthetic emeralds by mixing the same chemicals found in natural stones and then putting them in a furnace at 1,800 degrees Fahrenheit. It takes at least a year at that heat to grow a good one. The process is highly technical, but it pays to manufacture them." She smiled at Bob. "Even though it's synthetic, this one's valued at more than I'd ever be able to pay, but a natural emerald the same size would cost 10 times as much."

"Wow!" Bob exclaimed. "Whoever buys them?"

"Only the very, very rich."

Bob smiled mischievously. "That'll be me—someday."

And someday Bob will be able to have an entire collection of emeralds—or other precious jewels—if he wishes. So will you.

Have you ever pretended, as he did, to be rich enough to buy anything you could possibly want? or of being invited to eat at a table set for royalty such as the one Janyce saw? Yesterday we talked about how greed for such riches can lead to death. On the other hand, the Bible describes the wonderful riches that we'll be able to have in heaven and the new earth.

List at least 10 wonderful things that you're looking forward to having or doing when you get to heaven.

1. ________________	6. ________________
2. ________________	7. ________________
3. ________________	8. ________________
4. ________________	9. ________________
5. ________________	10. ________________

Even the most elegant, the most exquisite, the most exciting, and the most powerful things we can imagine will be nothing compared to the wonders that God is preparing for us. Focusing on God does lead to the magnificent. Even though we may always be poor here, God still gives us beauty to enjoy on this earth.

What are 10 beautiful things you have?

1. ________________	6. ________________
2. ________________	7. ________________
3. ________________	8. ________________
4. ________________	9. ________________
5. ________________	10. ________________

JANUARY

10

Hostage!

Again, the kingdom of heaven is like a merchant looking for fine pearls. When he found one of great value, he went away and sold everything he had and bought it. Matthew 13: 45, 46.

A tiny relative of the sand flea of the Pacific coast beaches lives under the ice packs of Antarctica. This amphipod, as such creatures are called, is a favorite food for many fish, and being less than a quarter inch long, it can't defend itself. Among its neighbors are even smaller sea creatures—the pteropods, or sea butterflies, which get their name from the winglike extensions of their feet, which they use for swimming. Now an amphipod-eating fish would never swallow a sea butterfly. That's not because sea butterflies are too small, or because their wings tickle, but because they taste terrible. They contain certain chemicals that the fish can't stand.

Amphipods seem to know this; therefore, a sea butterfly swimming about enjoying life as usual may suddenly find itself being carried off in a different direction because an amphipod has slipped up behind it, grabbed it, and clamped it onto its back. For several days the amphipod swims about, holding the sea butterfly hostage. Now it can feed in safety because it's protected by its unwilling passenger. In a few days it lets the sea butterfly go, and then goes off to find another.

Even though the sea butterfly can't eat while it's being held by the amphipod, it swims away to carry on life as usual and seems to suffer no ill effects from having been kidnapped.

We're helpless against sin, and no one else can protect us from it like the pteropod can protect the amphipod. Our only hope is to find the Pearl of great price, to give up our wills to Jesus and take Him into our hearts.

Research for the Scientists: (Answers are on page 380.)

1. Amphipods and pteropods are all marine invertebrates, but one group are mollusks and the other are crustaceans. Which is which, and what are their differences?

2. Can you find any reference in the Bible to any relatives to either of these tiny creatures?

3. What scientific connection does Matthew 13:45, 46 have to today's story?

JANUARY

The Contract

Not everyone who says to me, "Lord, Lord," will enter the kingdom of heaven, but only he who does the will of my Father who is in heaven. Matthew 7:21.

Lyndi found the exact pair of boots she needed. They were tall, leather-lined, and excellent for the cold weather. Besides that, they were beautiful. And she found a coat that was a perfect cut and a perfect fit. If only she could have them, she . . . Well, she thought nothing could make her happier.

"Mom," she pleaded. "Dad . . ."

Their answers hinged around not really having enough money right then.

"But I'll help more in the house. And you could take money from my allowance. I *need* a new coat and boots."

Her parents agreed about the need, but the price of the outfit she wanted?

At last her father relented. "But this is going to be a business deal," he warned, "with a proper contract." The two of them discussed the terms. They agreed on the amount to subtract from her allowance until half the price of the outfit would be paid. For the other half, Lyndi agreed to do supper dishes without complaint until everything was completely paid for. They all signed the contract—she and her parents—and then they went to make the purchase.

Lyndi was ecstatic. Wearing her new outfit made her feel so good about herself! Honoring her contract, though, took more effort and self-discipline—especially the not complaining part—than she had realized. But she did it.

Have you ever tried to make a contract with God—and promise to do good deeds so that He'll take you to heaven? If so, you probably wondered at times if such a bargain would really work.

Jesus says that not everyone who says "Lord, Lord" can go to heaven, and He's talking about people who *do good things*. Then He adds that the only people who can go to heaven are those who do God's will. For the rest, He says He'll tell them, "I never knew you."

Do you know what God wills for you when it comes to your salvation? You will not be saved by doing good things but by having faith in Jesus. It is not that doing good things is unimportant, but it is a matter of what God wants. He does not want works without faith; He wants faith that results in good deeds.

JANUARY

12

Learning to Skate

For by the grace given me I say to every one of you: Do not think of yourself more highly than you ought, but rather think of yourself with sober judgment, in accordance with the measure of faith God has given you. Romans 12:3.

Eric's dad had been transferred north. Not far outside the city they found a nice house on a small property that had easy freeway access to his parents' work and was close to his school. The place had several fruit trees and a good garden, and best of all, it had a pond.

"Just wait till winter," Dad said. "That'll make a beautiful rink." Winter came, the pond froze, and Eric's friends were delighted when he invited them over to skate. Eric himself had never skated.

"No problem," his friends said. "We'll teach you."

That afternoon Eric stood uncertainly at the edge of the ice, trying to get the feel of blades under his feet. "Just push off," John called to him. "Take gliding steps . . ."

"Like this," Pollo explained. "I'll show you. Start with short steps."

Eric tried. But he felt all stiff and awkward.

"You're doing great!" Barney yelled. "Keep it up!"

"Relax," John warned. "The stiffer you are, the harder you fall."

"OK, everyone," Josh waved for all to gather round. "Let's get organized. If we . . . Hey, Marty! Are you coming?"

"Soon as I straighten the shoes so we can find things easier when we're done."

"Watch it, Eric!"

John's warning came too late. Eric snagged his skate blade on a rough spot and pitched to the ice. Sam and Dory rushed to him. "Are you hurt?" they both asked.

Eric shook his head no, but gladly let them help him up. Ab skated over. "Just found this stick of gum in a pocket." He held it out to Eric. "Chew it." He grinned. "Might make skating easier."

With the help of his friends, Eric did learn to skate. Though none of them realized it, they were practicing today's text by being themselves and using the talents God had given them. In the first part of Romans 12 Paul talks about doing God's will by accepting ourselves as we are and using our talents to help others. Tomorrow we'll talk about those talents.

JANUARY

13

The Helpers

There are different kinds of gifts, but the same Spirit. 1 Corinthians 12:4.

In yesterday's story eight of Eric's friends were helping him learn to ice skate. As the story progressed, we could see that each was behaving in a different way, yet they all helped.

Paul says that we all have different gifts. He names seven in Romans 12 that are sometimes called the *motivational gifts*—talents that help cause us to behave the way we behave and that influence the kind of personality we have. Nearly everyone has a little bit of each of these gifts, but there is often one that is stronger than all the others. These gifts are:

1. Prophesying—which means more than foretelling the future. In the Bible, it usually applies to a preacher or a person who has insight and understanding about why things happen.
2. Serving or helping.
3. Teaching.
4. Encouraging.
5. Contributing or giving.
6. Leading or governing.
7. Showing mercy.

The Bible offers many good examples of people with these gifts.

John the Baptist was a prophet, a man of insight; Martha was a server, a helper; Apollos was a teacher; Barnabas, an encourager; Abraham, a giver; Nehemiah and Joshua were leaders; and Dorcas and the good Samaritan were merciful.

Each of these traits causes individuals to do things differently and to react differently when something happens. Think back to yesterday's story. Which gift does each of Eric's friends have?

A. Josh ______________ E. Sam ______________
B. Pollo ______________ F. Barney ______________
C. Dory ______________ G. Marty ______________
D. John ______________ H. Ab ______________

(Answers are on page 380.)

If you are tempted to criticize a friend's way of doing things, take a moment to think. Which gift does he or she have that causes him or her to act in that way?

Which gifts do you have?

JANUARY

14

Elijah and the Widow, Part 1

Go at once to Zarephath of Sidon and stay there. I have commanded a widow in that place to supply you with food. 1 Kings 17:9.

Today and tomorrow we'll be reading the story of Elijah and the widow as told in 1 Kings 17:8-16. To make it even more interesting, it's been divided into a dramatic (group) reading. There are parts for three readers: Elijah, the widow, and the narrator. If you want to use more than three readers, have more than one narrator. Skip the words in brackets. One person could also read the entire story, including the words in brackets.

(This story is divided into two parts and has discussion questions at the end. You may want to read both parts today and do the questions tomorrow. As you read, try to make your voices convey how both the widow and Elijah must have felt.)

NARRATOR: Then the word of the Lord came to [Elijah]. "Go at once to Zarephath of Sidon and stay there. I have commanded a widow in that place to supply you with food." So he went to Zarephath. When he came to the town gate, a widow was there gathering sticks. He called to her and asked,

ELIJAH: Would you bring me a little water in a jar so I may have a drink?

NARRATOR: As she was going to get it, he called,

ELIJAH: And bring me, please, a piece of bread.

WIDOW: As surely as the Lord your God lives [she replied], I don't have any bread—only a handful of flour in a jar and a little oil in a jug. I am gathering a few sticks to take home and make a meal for myself and my son, that we may eat it—and die.

NARRATOR: Elijah said to her,

ELIJAH: Don't be afraid. Go home and do as you have said. But first make a small cake for me from what you have and bring it to me, and then make something for yourself and your son. For this is what the Lord, the God of Israel, says: "The jar of flour will not be used up and the jug of oil will not run dry until the day the Lord gives rain on the land."

NARRATOR: She went away and did as Elijah had told her. So there was food every day for Elijah and for the woman and her family. For the jar of flour was not used up and the jug of oil did not run dry in keeping with the word of the Lord spoken by Elijah.

JANUARY

15

Elijah and the Widow, Part 2

Then the woman said to Elijah, "Now I know that you are a man of God and that the word of the Lord from your mouth is the truth." 1 Kings 17:24.

NARRATOR: Some time later the son of the woman who owned the house became ill. He grew worse and worse, and finally stopped breathing. She said to Elijah,

WIDOW: What do you have against me, man of God? Did you come to remind me of my sin and kill my son?

ELIJAH: Give me your son.

NARRATOR: He took him from her arms, carried him to the upper room where he was staying, and laid him on his bed. Then he cried out to the Lord,

ELIJAH: O Lord my God, have you brought tragedy also upon this widow I am staying with, by causing her son to die?

NARRATOR: Then he stretched himself out on the boy three times and cried to the Lord,

ELIJAH: O Lord my God, let this boy's life return to him!

NARRATOR: The Lord heard Elijah's cry, and the boy's life returned to him, and he lived. Elijah picked up the child and carried him down from the room into the house. He gave him to his mother and said,

ELIJAH: Look, your son is alive!

NARRATOR: Then the woman said to Elijah,

WIDOW: Now I know that you are a man of God and that the word of the Lord from you mouth is the truth.

✦ ✦ ✦

What do you think?

1. Find all the examples of faith in both parts of this story—both on the widow's and on Elijah's part. Now, which was the greatest act of faith? Why?

2. If you were the widow, what words would describe how you felt when Elijah asked you to make him some bread?

3. After the miracle of having food for so long, why did the widow accuse Elijah of having something against her? What would you have done under the same circumstances?

4. Describe the picture (idea) of God that you think the woman likely had by the time Elijah left her place.

JANUARY

16

Prince Baymond, Part 1

The Lord is my strength and my shield; my heart trusts in him, and I am helped. Psalm 28:7.

Young Prince Baymond lived in a beautiful castle atop a high hill. His kingdom stretched as far as he could see. He was very rich and had everything a young prince could want.

"You have a good kingdom," his father had told him on the day that he was crowned. "All will go well as long as you reign wisely. We have lived in peace for many, many years, but there is an enemy, a very sly enemy, who will cause trouble if he can." The old king lowered his voice. "There is also a very wise man who lives beyond the boundaries of the kingdom. He visits me often, and his counsel has kept us safe. He has promised to help you, too, but on one condition."

"And what is that, Father?" young Prince Baymond asked.

"He will come only if you invite him in. What he tells you to do will work only if you believe that it will."

"That sounds very simple."

"It is very simple and yet very difficult," said the old king.

"Tell him to come see me," said the prince.

"He'll come."

The young prince felt secure in his castle. His system of locks and guards made it so no one could enter without his permission. He passed his time playing the complicated game of straights and corners, which he'd invented by himself.

One day as he was about to finish with an even higher score than ever, he heard a quiet knock. He ignored it and continued to play. A few minutes later a guard called.

"Sir, an old man wishes to see you."

"Tell him that I'm very busy," the prince replied.

"But he says that it is urgent."

"Umm." The prince continued his game.

"Sir, he says that your father said you would see him."

"Very well." The prince sighed and set aside his game pieces. "Prepare to usher him in."

When Jesus knocks at the door of your heart, are you bothered by the interruption and tell Him to wait? Or do you recognize Him and hurry to let Him in?

JANUARY

17

Prince Baymond, Part 2

The world and its desires pass away, but the man who does the will of God lives forever. 1 John 2:17.

I thought you'd never let me in." The old man spoke quietly. "But good, you've opened the door. I have an important message for you."

"Come in. Come in," the prince invited quickly, recognizing immediately that this was the man his father had told him about. He showed him into his audience chamber, where they settled into comfortable chairs. "What is the message?"

"Your enemy, Prince Dribold, is moving toward your kingdom. He's keeping his troops well hidden and has a very deadly plan."

"What shall we do?"

The old man suggested a plan.

"But I feel we should . . ." The prince started to argue.

"You're the prince. You can do anything you like. I've come only to tell you what I know."

"How can I be sure of your plan?"

"What did your father say?"

"That your advice is good, but that your plans would work only if I believed in them. I want to keep my kingdom safe."

"Then follow the plan I have just given you. It will work if you want it to."

"I don't understand," Prince Baymond said. "What do you mean when you say that it will work only if I want it to?"

The old man smiled. "Suppose you decide to do as I say and then someone else comes with an idea that seems better. No matter how good it may seem, remember that you promised to do things my way. That's the only way you can be sure to protect your kingdom."

"Then let's make the kingdom safe," said Prince Baymond. "Where do we begin?"

As the old man talked, the prince made notes in the secret book of his kingdom so he would be sure to remember everything he must do.

God has a plan that will protect the kingdom of your heart. Following that plan will lead to eternal life. It is up to you to choose whether or not to follow it. Many other choices will come along, but you will be safe only as long as you continue to choose God's way. Remember, the choice will always be up to you.

JANUARY

18

The Battle of the Hairbrush

"Follow me," he told him, and Matthew got up and followed him.
Matthew 9:9.

"I gave my heart to Jesus during Week of Prayer and promised to follow Him." Sarena spoke quietly. "But I don't feel any different. How can I tell if Jesus has really come into my heart?"

"Yeah," interjected Gill. "I know what she's saying. I've heard people talk about this fantastic feeling that came when they gave their hearts to God, but I've never felt anything special. How do you know that Jesus is in your heart?"

"Has anyone else wondered about that?" Nelda said and looked around the circle.

Several heads nodded.

"I used to wonder the same thing," she admitted. "I wondered why I didn't 'feel' Christian. Then I realized that our feelings depend on things like whether or not we've had enough sleep or if someone's been yelling at us. Feelings aren't the *real* us."

"My feelings *feel* very real!" Teddy said with a grin.

"They *are* very real," Nelda agreed. "It's what we do with them that counts—and that depends on the part of us called the will."

"No problem then," Teddy replied. "Mom's always saying that I've got a very strong will."

Nelda chuckled with the others. "Strong enough to choose to do what Jesus would do even when you don't feel like it?"

Complete stillness fell over the group.

"When I invited Jesus into my heart," Nelda continued, "I promised I'd follow Him no matter what. I meant it. The next morning, though . . ." She paused and smiled. "You see, my younger sister used to help herself to my things whenever. My hairbrush was missing. She had it—and I'd had enough. I told her what I thought. We both got red-faced and started screaming. Then I remembered my promise.

"At the moment, my feelings wanted me to pound some sense into that girl. But . . . I had chosen to follow Jesus. I didn't *feel* like it right then. I didn't *want* to. But I made myself step back and stop screaming. I thought a little prayer heavenward, asking for a few calm words. All I said was 'OK, sis, the silly brush isn't worth this commotion.'

"It took more of the morning for my feelings to settle, but that was my first step in really following Jesus. I knew I had Him in my heart because I had chosen to act His way rather than to follow my feelings."

JANUARY

Getting Up

[Epaphras] is always wrestling in prayer for you, that you may stand firm in all the will of God, mature and fully assured.
Colossians 4:12.

After Nelda shared her story about the hairbrush, several of the other young people told about times when they also chose to go against their feelings.

"Following Jesus must be a lot like getting up in the morning," Teddy finally said.

"How can you say that?" Gill asked.

"Well, I never feel like getting up when my alarm rings, so lots of times I don't. Sometimes Dad comes, and I hear little sermons about how lying in bed after I've had enough sleep will make me feel more tired. Or about turning off my light at the right time instead of reading. Or about self-discipline." Teddy shrugged.

"I guess it's the self-discipline part—like my parents have this thing about forming good habits. They say I should make up my mind that I'm going to jump out of bed the moment I hear the alarm. Then each morning I must make myself do just that when the alarm does ring. They say that after a while my body will become so used to getting up at that time that I'll automatically wake up and feel like getting out of bed."

"Are you saying that's like getting to be like Jesus?" Nelda asked.

Teddy nodded.

"Except for one thing," Sarena added. "Teddy also said his dad scolds him for reading too late."

"Well, that could fit in too." Alex spoke for the first time. "The Christian life's like growing. You don't do everything at once. But once Teddy decides he's going to get up when his alarm rings, he might find that turning off his light earlier will help."

Everyone in the group nodded agreement.

"You've made an important point," Nelda said. "As we follow Jesus and choose to do things His way instead of following our feelings, we find that we need to make other choices. Once we start, He helps us see more and more choices we need to make. It's up to us, though. We need to pray for each other that we'll each continue to choose God's will."

JANUARY

20

What Did They Do?

Have you ever had anything happen similar to what either Randy or Alysia faced?

They've both decided to be Christians. They've given their lives to God and want to have the new heart and the new spirit that He has promised, but they both find that doing things God's way is not always easy.

One day they each found themselves faced with a tough decision. The story beginning below gives the settings. If you were in their places, what would you *feel* like doing? What would *Jesus* want you to do? What would *you* do? How would you end the stories?

1. Randy specializes in getting good grades. He wants to be a doctor, and he knows that anyone getting into medical school must have top grades. So he's decided that, even now, the most important thing for him to do is to have as near perfect grades as possible.

During a history quiz one day, he couldn't remember two dates. He just happened to see the answers that the person across the aisle was writing down. He immediately knew that that person was correct, and . . .

2. Alysia and Cynthanne are in the same class. Cynthanne is pretty and has a talent for wearing the right clothes and fixing her hair just so. But Alysia can't stand the way Cynthanne behaves. She thinks Cynthanne's a show-off who just wants to attract the boys' attention.

It was a blustery day, and overnight several inches of snow had fallen. As Cynthanne walked into class, her leather-soled boot came down on a tiny slab of ice someone had carelessly tracked in. The ice shot ahead, throwing her off balance. She went down with a crash, sprawling ridiculously.

Alysia . . .

Have you asked Jesus for a new heart and a new spirit?

Rid yourselves of all the offenses you have committed, and get a new heart and a new spirit. Ezekiel 18:31.

Remember the Sabbath

Remember the Sabbath day by keeping it holy. Exodus 20:8.

War! Revolutionary forces had invaded the country and were trying to overthrow the government. Afraid for their lives, people ran and hid. One Friday afternoon a band of men, loyal to the government, roamed the hills. They had a list of homes of families suspected of helping the revolutionaries, but since the people had all fled, they had to be satisfied with slaughtering livestock, destroying crops, and tearing down buildings.

"Hurry!" they yelled to each other. Their shouts mixed with the screams of animals. "We've got to get this finished."

Flames crackled as one set fire to a shed.

"Hurry! See how low the sun is!"

The men rushed to finish their work of destruction. Then, just before the sun slid behind the ridge of the hills, they stopped. "Have a good Sabbath!" they called to each other as they went their separate ways, hurrying in order to be home before sunset. The next morning they were all in their places at church, in respect of the Sabbath day of the commandment.

The men had kept the first word of the commandment. They had remembered the Sabbath and had finished their work before God's holy day began. But what sort of thoughts and feelings do you think filled their minds and hearts? When God looked into their hearts that Sabbath, what do you suppose He saw?

Today is Friday, the day we call the preparation day, the day on which we get ready for the Sabbath. What tasks do you have planned for today? Will you have to rush to finish them before the sun sets? What sort of thoughts and feelings will be in your mind and in your heart when the Sabbath begins?

The first word of the Sabbath commandment is "remember," but the sentence goes on to tell us to remember it by "keeping it holy." Isaiah 58 gives some good ideas of what God means by "holy": "To share your food with the hungry and to provide the poor wanderer with shelter—when you see the naked, to clothe him, and not to turn away from your own flesh and blood. . . . If you keep your feet from breaking the Sabbath . . . then you will find your joy in the Lord" (verses 7-14).

JANUARY

22

A Psalm for the Sabbath

One day a poet, looking at all the wonderful things God had created and thinking of God's great power and goodness, was inspired to write this psalm. It is a song for the Sabbath day. As you read it, see how many different references to music and nature there are.

"It is good to praise the Lord
and make music to your name, O Most High,
to proclaim your love in the morning
and your faithfulness at night,
to the music of the ten-stringed lyre
and the melody of the harp.
For you make me glad by your deeds, O Lord;
I sing for joy at the works of your hands.
How great are your works, O Lord,
how profound your thoughts!
The senseless man does not know,
fools do not understand,
that though the wicked spring up like grass
and all evildoers flourish,
they will be forever destroyed.

But you, O Lord, are exalted forever.
For surely your enemies, O Lord,
surely your enemies will perish;
all evildoers will be scattered.
You have exalted my horn like that of a wild ox;
fine oils have been poured upon me.
My eyes have seen the defeat of my adversaries;
my ears have heard the rout of my wicked foes.

The righteous will flourish like a palm tree,
they will grow like a cedar of Lebanon;
planted in the house of the Lord,
they will flourish in the courts of our God.
They will still bear fruit in old age,
they will stay fresh and green,
proclaiming, "The Lord is upright;
he is my Rock,
and there is no wickedness in him" (Psalm 92).

God speaks to us through all the wonderful things He has created. By taking time on the Sabbath to enjoy nature—whether by hiking in the wilderness or visiting the zoo or walking through beautiful gardens—we give God an opportunity to speak to us.

Just now, look out your window. Name everything you see that is a reminder of God.

JANUARY

23

Fluffy

Therefore let us stop passing judgment on one another. Romans 14:13.

Fluffy the cat scrambled crazily across the kitchen linoleum, batting at the bouncing table tennis ball. The ball hit the wall and spun back past her. Fluffy hunched, clawed for a grip on the waxed surface, then sprawled into a heap of black-and-white fur, while the ball rolled across the room. Determined to get that ball, she lurched back onto her feet, her claws slipping. But it disappeared under the edge of the folding doors of the broom closet before she could grab it. She sprawled flat—legs spraddled, tail flicking in disgust—and scooted against the door.

She pushed her nose under its edge as if willing herself to squish through the narrow opening. That didn't work. She pulled out her nose and shook her head to rearrange her whiskers, then reached a front leg in, paw curled in an attempt to hook the ball. For several minutes she tried—first reaching under, then clawing and pulling at the door in an effort to get her plaything. At last she gave up.

She stretched slowly to her feet, twitching her sides as if to say "Well, I really didn't want to chase that old ball anymore anyway."

Even though she was an excellent mouser, able to maneuver at high speeds across the yard, and could whisk quickly up trees—or scamper up and over the furniture if no one were watching—her clawed and smooth-padded feet did not provide traction for moving across slippery surfaces at high speeds or for securely trapping smooth, round objects. Yet this handicap did not stop her from trying. In fact, she seemed to enjoy the challenge of chasing a ball in the kitchen.

Like Fluffy, we each have skills. But like Fluff's smooth-padded feet and claws, which make her a good mouser, the very talents that make us good at one thing unfit us for performing other feats with perfect form. Sometimes we may end up sprawling clumsily. This is true for each of us.

If someone makes a mess of things you find easy—think before you criticize. The very handicaps that cause the problem may actually be talents that will enable that person to excel at things you can't do.

JANUARY

24

Thieves?

But the Lord said to Samuel, "Do not consider his appearance or his height, for I have rejected him. The Lord does not look at the things man looks at. Man looks at the outward appearance, but the Lord looks at the heart."
1 Samuel 16:7.

A long, dark line—a narrow trail of tiny, black bodies—curved across the dining room and into the kitchen.

"Not again!" I stamped my foot in disgust. I was tired of sharing our house with ants. Since we had lived in Africa, they seemed to come and go as they pleased, showing no respect for our privacy—or our food. I just knew they were climbing into the cupboard again and getting into our food.

"Enough is enough!" I sputtered, thinking of kerosene. A dousing of it means death to ants. I was about to get some when something prompted me to look more closely.

Their line flowed with definite two-way traffic. Ants coming in were empty-handed. Ants going out each carried a white piece of something. Heavy-headed soldiers patrolled the way. I was fascinated by their discipline and organization. At the same time I wondered what they were stealing.

Just then a dime-sized disk of the same whitish something slid toward me from the kitchen. It was ringed by at least 20 ants—some pushing, some pulling. I had to know what they were getting into, so I followed them to the far corner of the kitchen. There the trail stopped. No ants were going into the cupboard, and no ants were getting into the food. They simply marched toward a white chunk lying on the floor. Each took a piece and carried it back the way it had come. They worked with the precision of a living conveyor belt—coming, cutting, carrying away.

"Go to the ant; . . . consider its ways." The words from Proverbs needled my conscience. I had been ready to kill the entire troop because of what I thought they were doing.

"Sorry, guys," I said as though they could understand me. I smiled. A crumb of cake, mountain size in comparison with their tiny bodies, lay where it had been missed during after-lunch cleanup.

I left them to continue their task. An hour later I looked again. The ants had disappeared. The kitchen corner was clean.

JANUARY

Gilbert, Part 1

Do not say, "I'll do to him as he has done to me; I'll pay that man back for what he did." Proverbs 24:29.

B*oy! Wouldn't it be great to jet through water like that! Or just appear to disappear!* Gilbert looked up from the science magazine he was reading, a smirk playing on his face. *But it would be even neater to have those tentacles to shoot out and catch prey.*

He pictured a squid floating in the dim underwater world, its plump body pulsating, its cascade of arms trailing, its large eyes seeing everything. Suddenly, alerted to an intruder, its body begins to flash a series of colored patterns. Then it disappears. In a split second there is nothing to see but sand and rocks and some sea plants. Then, slowly, there it is again—right where it was. It had perfectly camouflaged itself by assuming the texture, color, and feature of its surroundings, and then reappeared.

"Awesome!" Gilbert exclaimed.

He especially liked the report of what happens if the intruder moves close. The squid suddenly appears to have turned black. Then the dark shape slowly dissolves. It has ejected a black liquid, and while the intruder watches the cloud, the squid jets away at incredible speed—gone, not to be found.

Gilbert wished he could sometimes disappear and escape that quickly. He was sick and tired of being picked on. Not having any friends wouldn't be so bad—he had his books and his computer—but being teased and laughed at all the time hurt, and that hurt was growing bigger. But he could see no way of just disappearing, so he wished for some way, as sneaky as that of the squid, of shooting out tentacles and trapping his persecutors. He wanted to trap all of them and make them hurt for every unkind word they had ever said.

Gilbert did not realize how much anger he had inside or how his thoughts of revenge were making him hurt more. Nor did his church school classmates realize how their teasing was affecting him or how much he wanted to hurt them back. All of them—Gilbert and those who teased him—knew about the Bible and God and prayer, but they each had a problem.

What are the problems? What solutions do you suggest? Tomorrow we'll talk about some.

JANUARY

26

Gilbert, Part 2

Do not let any unwholesome talk come out of your mouths, but only what is helpful for building others up according to their needs, that it may benefit those who listen. Ephesians 4:29.

Gilbert, the young scientist, as yesterday's story showed, wished he could be like the squid that he read about. Because he didn't fit in well, his classmates teased him, and he wanted to get even with them and make them hurt for their unkindness. Yet yesterday's text says that it's not good to pay people back for the wrong they do to us.

There are several reasons for this. Getting even usually causes more mean feelings on the other side. Even worse, when we carry thoughts of paying back, they smother our good and happy thoughts. We can't think mean thoughts and be happy at the same time. Our minds don't function that way.

Sad to say, Gilbert's problem was happening at a Christian school, where everyone is expected to behave in a "Christian" way. Today's text tells us to say only things that will "build others up according to their needs." What should the children do to solve the problem?

The answer that comes quickly to mind is for all to do what the Bible says. Right! But that's easier to say than to do. Here are some specific things to do. See if you can add others.

1. Learn to pray honestly. Tell God exactly how you feel, then ask Him to help you have positive thoughts.

2. Think of Jesus as a friend. What would He do if He were in your place? How would you treat Him?

3. Ask for courage to be strong. If your friends tease one of your classmates, don't be afraid to try to stop them. If you are teased, ask God to help you find ways to cope.

4. Remember the story of Fluffy the cat. We all have different talents. Look for the abilities of others, and compliment them for things they do well. This will not only encourage them, but help you appreciate them more.

A New Name

And I will also write on him my new name. Revelation 3:12.

What's in a name?

Different countries have different customs for giving names. Some names have special meanings. Some names tell where a person was born; others name the family to which he or she belongs. Sometimes when people move to a new country and take out citizenship, they choose to change their names.

When Great-grandfather Kantola came to America from Finland, he couldn't speak English. He studied hard so that he could become an American citizen, and at last the day arrived that he could go before the judge and take the oath of allegiance to his new country. When the judge handed Great-grandfather his citizenship papers, Great-grandfather saw that there was a mistake. His family name had been misspelled. It was misspelled so badly that it was actually an entirely new name—a name that he had neither heard nor seen before.

Great-grandfather still spoke English with a very heavy accent, and he made many mistakes when he spoke. He wanted to tell the judge that his name was spelled wrong, but he was afraid to say anything. He was afraid his English would sound so terrible and be so full of mistakes that the judge would think he shouldn't be an American and therefore take away his citizenship paper. So Great-grandfather didn't say a word. He knew that the name on his citizenship paper was now his legal name and that was the name he would have to use. So instead of being Mr. Kantola, he was now Mr. Kandoll. To this day, that is a unique family name, and all people with that name are descendants of Great-grandfather Kantola.

What is your family name? Does it have a special meaning? Do you know anything about its history?

Some people make a business of tracing the history of names. Family names can often tell us who our ancestors were, where they came from, what occupations they had, and other details of our family's history. They identify who we are.

Jesus has promised to give us a new name—His new name—when we get to heaven. This new name will show that we belong to His family—the family of God—and that we have chosen to be like Him.

JANUARY

28

Tad's Journal of Blessings

In the thirtieth year, in the fourth month on the fifth day, while I was among the exiles by the Kebar River, the heavens were opened and I saw visions of God. Ezekiel 1:1.

January 1. I turned 12 yesterday. Next year I'll be a real teenager. Dad says that when Jewish boys turn 13 they're considered adults and ready to have religious responsibility. They have a ceremony called a *bar mitzvah*. Most Christian churches have confirmation, but I guess the nearest ours has is baptism. Dad says baptism is more than having our past sins washed away. It's a sign that we've decided to be God's person and a responsible church member. I want to be a responsible person. I think I'll be baptized when I'm 13.

January 7. Grandma told me that when we pray, God likes us to remind Him about the good things He's done for us and then to ask Him for even better blessings. She also said it's good to write down the exact day and place when good things happen—like Ezekiel did in the Bible for his visions. I'll try that, but I don't want anyone to think I keep a diary. I don't. I just like to write things in my secret journal.

January 28. Aunt Jessie had a big operation last week. It was bad. Everyone was worried and praying for her. Today the doctor told Mom that Aunt Jessie's going to be OK. I'm so glad.

March 7. Wow! An A in history. Learning all those countries and their capitals and those dates is the most boring! Mom asked why I didn't ask God to help me concentrate, and then settle down and claim His promise of help. It worked!

May 25. We just had the greatest weekend—camping. Mom and Dad and Cyndi and I. I prayed for good weather and good fishing. We had both. I caught four big ones.

June 5. A good report card!

August 27. It'd take a whole book to tell about our past six weeks. Europe. Windmills and castles and the Alps and riding around London on a red double-decker. History's fun when you can travel. And to think—Grandpa and Grandma could get us free tickets because they fly so much for their work! I want to go again. Maybe I'll be a missionary. Missionaries travel lots.

October 15. Week of Prayer. I've joined the baptismal class. New Year's Eve's on Sabbath this year. The pastor says I can be baptized then. I'll be 13.

December 25. For Christmas our family got a big Bible encyclopedia set. It has super illustrations. And good stories. It'll be fun to read. Cyndi and I both got new skis and season passes to Big Top. We go tomorrow. I can hardly wait.

JANUARY

29

What You See

Write down what you have seen. Revelation 1:19, Phillips.

"I don't want anyone to think I keep a diary," Tad wrote after his grandmother suggested that he keep a record of his blessings. "I don't. I just like to write things in my secret journal."

Many people like to journal—to write things down—because it helps them remember, and what they write shows something about them. You see, what we focus on and think and even write about determines the kind of person we are.

Ellen White wrote some interesting ideas that apply to this. Here are some that I have taken from *The Ministry of Healing*, pages 487-492.

"We need not keep our own record of trials and difficulties, griefs, and sorrows. All these things are written in the books and heaven will take care of them. While we are counting up the disagreeable things, many things that are pleasant to reflect upon are passing from memory."

"Let your thoughts be directed to the evidences of the great love of God for you."

"The very act of looking for evil in others develops evil in those who look. By dwelling upon the faults of others, we are changed into the same image."

"Cultivate the habit of speaking well of others. Dwell upon the good qualities of those with whom you associate. . . . When tempted to complain of what someone has said or done, praise something in that person's life or character."

"Cultivate thankfulness."

"By beholding Jesus, talking of His love and perfection of character, we become changed into His image."

If you don't already keep a journal, try writing down blessings and other interesting things that happen to you. As our text says: "Write down what you have seen." But be sure to look for the good.

JANUARY

30

Smiles

A cheerful heart is good medicine, but a crushed spirit dries up the bones. Proverbs 17:22.

Tonya studied the crystal miniatures on display—a graceful giraffe; a darling, chubby elephant; a cute little mouse. "Mom's birthday's coming. I wonder . . ."

"Look!" Shayna tugged on her arm. "The big fish are jumping!"

"Dolphins," Tonya corrected.

"Let's watch."

Before she could answer, Shayna dashed away, ducked through people, and pushed her way to the railing. Tonya followed her little sister—shopping with her was always an adventure, but she didn't mind the excuse to watch the dolphins. It was fun living close to West Edmonton Mall; people came to Canada—to Edmonton—from all over the world just to see their mall. In addition to all the shops and stores and the daily dolphin shows, it has a roller coaster and fun rides, a water slide, a wave pool, an ice skating rink, submarine rides, miniature golf, lots of places to eat, and even its own hotel.

"I'm thirsty!" Shayna exclaimed when the show ended. "Why aren't these people smiling?"

"Because . . ."

"This is a fun place. Everyone should look happy. Let's buy some juice and sit by the jumping water."

Tonya laughed. When Shayna got excited, her thoughts bounced out any old way. But she was right—hardly any of the passers-by wore smiles.

"When I grow up I'm always going to smile. I'd like some red raspberry juice."

I hope she keeps her smiles—like Mrs. Rathers, Tonya thought. *I want to, too.*

Mrs. Rathers had told Tonya how once she'd been a very grumpy person. Then one day while looking in the mirror she was horrified at how sour she looked. *I can't call myself a Christian and go around looking like this,* she told herself. Then and there she gave her face to the Lord and asked Him to give her smiles.

It must've worked, Tonya thought. *She's one of the smilingest, kindest people I know. Just being around her makes me feel good. Mom says her smiles are like medicine.*

"Do you want red raspberry too?" Shayna took her big sister's hand.

"Yes, ma'am!" Tonya replied, smiling. "And then let's go shopping for Mom's birthday present."

JANUARY

31

Joy Here and Now

Say (write) the first word that pops into your mind when you hear these words:

1. Happy ______________________
2. Glad ______________________
3. Joyful ______________________
4. Trial ______________________
5. Trouble ______________________

"Happy," "glad," and "joyful" are often used to mean the same thing, to describe good feelings we have, and "trial" and "trouble" belong on the opposite side of our feelings.

Now, in your own words, explain the word "joy."

____

____

This doesn't mean, of course, that we have only a hope of future joys—we can be full of joy here and now even in our trials and troubles. Romans 5:3, Phillips.

Our text says that "we can be full of joy here and now even in our trials and troubles." Does your explanation allow for that kind of joy—the joy that is more than a feeling, the joy that comes from having confidence in and being sure about God? We can say it this way: *Happiness* depends on what happens to us, but *joy* depends on what we are like on the inside. We can have joy now because we know that no matter what happens, we do have a future, a happy future—in Jesus Christ.

Are you ever afraid of being sad or unhappy? Most of us are, but nowhere in the Bible does Jesus promise that we'll never hurt or feel sad or unhappy. Instead He promises that He'll be with us. As Christian writer Tim Hensel says, "we don't get a free detour around problems when we become a Christian; we get a guided tour through them."

How, then, could you have joy if any of these should happen?

A. You have no money for new clothes.

B. An earthquake damages your home.

C. Your parents divorce, and you're sent to a foster home.

D. Your big brother has AIDS.

E. Everyone teases you, and you feel you have no friends.

All are unhappy situations, but with Jesus "we can be full of joy here and now."

FEBRUARY

1

The Drawing

Stop judging by mere appearances, and make a right judgment. John 7:24.

On Monday morning the children found a new picture centered on the bulletin board—a large black-and-white drawing. It certainly wasn't pretty, but something about it captured their attention.

"It's an old woman!" Ahmad insisted.

"No, it isn't," argued Vimala. "She's young!"

"She's old!" Lacey sided with Ahmad.

More children gathered. The argument swung back and forth. Some insisted that the woman in the drawing was young, and others argued that she was old. All sounded certain about what they were seeing. Then Vimala began to laugh.

The picture below shows the drawing. You may have seen a similar picture. If you have, what did you see when you first looked at it? If not, what do you see now? Do you see an old lady with a big nose and a firm mouth? Or do you see a young, smooth-cheeked woman? Or do you perhaps see *two* people—one old, one young? Vimala did after she had been looking at the picture for a long while, and that's why she started to laugh.

If you're not sure about what you see, try covering the bottom section of the picture diagonally from the top right-hand corner to the bottom left-hand corner. Do you see a drawing of a young woman? Then cover the top diagonal. Do you see an older person? Now look at the entire picture. Do you see it differently than you did at first? Can you see that it is actually a drawing of two people?

It's said that the most exercise some people get is from jumping to conclusions. They see—or hear—something about someone and immediately begin to criticize. They don't stop to check the facts or even to consider that there may be more to the "picture."

If you're ever tempted to criticize, remember what Ellen White says: "Evilspeaking is a two-fold curse, falling more heavily on the speaker than on the hearer."

Ask yourself if you can see the entire picture. Think of the drawing of the two ladies, and make a right judgment.

FEBRUARY

2

Grass Fire

In quietness and trust is your strength. Isaiah 30:15.

Flames leaped into the air with long, searing streamers of fire, shooting rocketlike from one side of the road to the other. I stood well back. On the other side of the fire stood the mission truck . . . waiting . . . for me. I didn't move. A lone figure, head down, ran in my direction.

"Come," Mazozo called.

I shook my head.

"You'll be safe," he assured me. "I understand these fires."

I believed him, but not quite enough to want to run under the flames.

"The others are waiting."

I knew that. I had watched them go in small groups, heads down and running. I had even watched him drive the truck under the flames, but still I didn't want to take the risk. I didn't trust the fire. It tore headlong, roaring angrily through the tall, brittle grass stalks that stretched in every direction over the African savanna. It threw long uneven flares in hot breaths of orange up and over the dusty road. No, I didn't trust that fire. Neither did I trust myself. I'd never been able to run fast. What if . . . ?

"Trust me," Mazozo said. "I've grown up with these dry-season fires. I promise that it won't hurt you."

Reason told me that he knew what he was talking about, that the flames were high enough and scattered enough. Still . . .

He reached for my hand. "Come. Run with me."

At last I let myself be hurried along—head down—under the flames, feeling the heat but not being hurt. We reached the truck and continued our journey back to the mission.

Have you ever been afraid that you won't make it safely to heaven? Afraid that you're not good enough? Afraid of problems? Afraid that you'll make a mistake? Afraid even to say, "Jesus loves me and died to save me!" So you stop and just stand there—afraid.

Jesus calls us to come. He understands. He holds out His hand and promises to lead us. It is up to us to put our hands in His and to trust Him.

FEBRUARY

3

Let Your Light Shine

The light of the righteous shines brightly, but the lamp of the wicked is snuffed out. Proverbs 13:9.

Light shines. That's a known fact. The sun is a gaseous sphere that shines, giving light, heat, and energy to our earth. The moon is a dense sphere that appears to shine. It doesn't shine by itself, though, but simply reflects the light of the sun. A candle, on the other hand, shines when it is lighted, and a light bulb shines when electric current passes through it. Both are useful to light dark places.

Jesus said, "Let your light shine before men, that they may see your good deeds and praise your Father in heaven" (Matthew 5:16). He didn't say, "*Try* to make your light shine." Nor did He say, "*Work hard* and your light will shine." He simply said, "*Let* your light shine."

A candle or a light bulb can't shine by itself. In order to shine, it must first be connected to a power that creates light. We can't *make* our "lights" shine either. We must first be connected to Jesus; then our lights will shine.

Today's text says, "The light of the righteous shines brightly." Put a checkmark by the following things that will help keep a connection with Jesus so that your light will shine.

____ 1. Letting Jesus speak to my heart by reading my Bible.

____ 2. Giving an offering at church.

____ 3. Praying.

____ 4. Watching a hummingbird and thinking of the fantastic way in which Jesus created not only that one little bird, but the whole universe.

____ 5. Taking out the garbage.

____ 6. Singing in the youth choir.

____ 7. Listening to the explosive roar of thunder and remembering that God's power is greater than that of any storm.

____ 8. Talking to Jesus honestly, telling Him how you really feel about everything.

Remember, we become like those we look up to, think about, and spend time with. Thus to become like Jesus, to keep a connection with Him and shine for Him, we must spend time reading the Bible, talking to Him, and thinking about the wonderful things He can do. So numbers 1, 3, 4, 7, 8 are the best answers. Numbers 2, 5, 6 are good things that Christians—and even others—do, but they won't make our lights shine.

FEBRUARY

The Fruit of Righ-teousness

Filled with the fruit of righteousness that comes through Jesus Christ—to the glory and praise of God. Philippians 1:11.

Alex blocked the title at the top of the page: THE FRUITS OF RIGHTEOUSNESS. Then he stopped. He couldn't think of a word to write. He let his pencil wander over the paper, and, as usual, he found himself drawing. He made a banana, some grapes, and an apple. Drawing was always easier for him than writing. "Not exactly what the teacher wants, though." He sighed then remembered what Aunt Susan had suggested.

"If you have trouble writing," she'd said, "pretend that you're talking to a friend. Then write what you'd say."

"If James were here, I'd . . ." Alex added a strawberry to his collection and pecked all sorts of little dots on it. ". . . I'd tell him that . . ."

Suddenly Alex had an idea. ". . . that the fruits of righteousness are like our favorite fruits." He shaded the banana with the side of his pencil lead and then began to write.

"The fruits of righteousness are like the best fruits. My favorite fruits are bananas, apples, grapes, strawberries, and pineapples. They all taste good. They're also good for us. Lots of times, though, I prefer the taste of candy. I go by a store on my way home from school, and it's easy to stop and buy a candy bar. Even though I like fruit and know it's much better for me to eat, I still buy a candy bar. Being filled with the fruits of righteousness is something like that."

Alex stopped to read what he'd written. "That last sentence doesn't make much sense," he told himself. "I'd better explain." He started writing again.

"God's fruits are good things, like being kind and obeying the rules. Like Jessica, who was in our class last year. She got on everyone's nerves. We knew we should be kind to her, but it was easy to make fun of her and call her names. That was like buying candy instead of fruit. We did what we wanted, and called her names.

"To have the fruits of righteousness, we need to choose to do what God wants, not what we feel like doing. To be filled, we're going to have to keep choosing and choosing. Maybe if we do it long enough, choosing to do good things will become a habit."

If you were Alex's teacher, what grade would you have given his essay? Why? What comment would you have written on his paper?

FEBRUARY

5

Sabbath-keeping—a Fruit of Righteousness

Then Jesus said to them, "I ask you, which is lawful on the Sabbath: to do good or to do evil, to save life or to destroy it?" Luke 6:9.

The following is a dramatic reading from Luke 6:1-10. (Instructions are on page 33.) Characters: Narrator, Pharisees, and Jesus.

NARRATOR: One Sabbath Jesus was going through the grainfields, and his disciples began to pick some heads of grain, rub them in their hands, and eat the kernels. Some of the Pharisees asked,

PHARISEES: Why are you doing what is unlawful on the Sabbath?

JESUS: Have you never read what David did when he and his companions were hungry? He entered the house of God, and taking the consecrated bread, he ate what is lawful only for priests to eat. And he also gave some to his companions.

NARRATOR: Then Jesus said to them,

JESUS: The Son of Man is Lord of the Sabbath.

NARRATOR: On another Sabbath he went into the synagogue and was teaching, and a man was there whose right hand was shriveled. The Pharisees and the teachers of the law were looking for a reason to accuse Jesus, so they watched him closely to see if he would heal on the Sabbath. But Jesus knew what they were thinking and said to the man with the shriveled hand,

JESUS: Get up and stand in front of everyone.

NARRATOR: So he got up and stood there. Then Jesus said to them,

JESUS: I ask you, which is lawful on the Sabbath: to do good or to do evil, to save life or to destroy it?

NARRATOR: He looked around at them all, and then said to the man,

JESUS: Stretch out your hand.

NARRATOR: He did so, and his hand was completely restored.

✦ ✦ ✦

In his essay Alex said that "God's fruits are good things, like being kind and obeying the rules." The disciples broke two rules about the Sabbath—by picking a few heads of grain, they were guilty of reaping, and by rubbing the kernels together in their hands, they were guilty of threshing.

Jesus' question frustrated the leaders because they believed that *not* doing good when there was an opportunity was the same as doing evil. They kept the rules so carefully that they had become mean and couldn't accept Jesus' way of keeping God's law by being kind and doing good.

FEBRUARY

6

Why Am I So Ugly?

But who are you, O man, to talk back to God? "Shall what is formed say to him who formed it, 'Why did you make me like this?' " Romans 9:20.

Brooke scowled into the mirror and poked at the loose wave slanting across her forehead. "Oh, why do I have to look so terrible?" she demanded. "Puffy cheeks. Squinty eyes. Mousy hair that won't stay where it belongs. Ugly!" She grabbed a lipstick tube and pounded its top on the counter. "Nothing but ugly! No wonder no one likes me!"

"True beauty comes from the inside." Echoes from one of her mother's favorite sayings tried to push themselves through the unhappiness that filled her mind. *"God has given you the talent of a friendly smile. Thank Him by using it."*

Brooke didn't feel like smiling, much less like being thankful. "Mom just says that to try to make me feel good." She stuck her tongue out at her reflection. "Ugly!"

Pretend that you know Brooke and that you've tried to be her friend, but that she always seems to want to keep to herself. It also appears that the most important thing to her is to be studying her face in the mirror and fixing her hair. She doesn't smile much, and you suspect that she's not very happy. You think she could be happier if she didn't worry so much about how she looked, so you decide to help her.

Now, what will you do? What advice will you give her? Think about/discuss this. At the same time, ask yourself this question: How would I react if someone told me the same thing that I'm planning to tell Brooke?

Does the following paragraph talk about Brooke's problem?

"Many who profess to be Christ's followers have an anxious, troubled heart because they are afraid to trust themselves with God. They do not make a complete surrender to Him, for they shrink from the consequences that such a surrender may involve. Unless they do make this surrender they cannot find peace" (Ellen G. White, *The Ministry of Healing*, pp. 480, 481).

What prayer would you pray for Brooke?

If you know someone who has a problem similar to Brooke's, why not pray that prayer for that person right now?

FEBRUARY

7

You—An Average Christian Kid

Everything that belongs to the world—what the sinful self desires, what people see and want, and everything in this world that people are so proud of—none of this comes from the Father; it all comes from the world.
1 John 2:16, TEV.

YOU is an average Christian kid. He wants to be good, but he has a problem. He goes to Pastor Perry.

"How can I know if I really have Jesus in my heart?"

"What do YOU mean?"

"Well, Christians are supposed to be like Jesus, right?"

"Yes."

"Then why do so many of us do mean things?"

Pastor Perry waits for YOU to go on.

"For example, my sister. She gets to me. Always bossing 'n' getting in the way." YOU hitches himself around on his chair. "She's a terror. But, you know, if I can sneak a pinch on her, she'll yell and start pounding on me. Then Mom'll get after her, and . . ."

". . . YOU get away," the pastor finishes for him, "and she gets the scolding—or more."

YOU nod. "But if I have Jesus in my heart, I won't do things like that, huh?" His eyes meet the pastor's.

"I think God must be talking to YOU, otherwise YOU wouldn't have bothered to ask."

"Really, if Jesus is in my heart I won't want to be mean to my sister, will I?"

"No," Pastor Perry said.

"Then how can I have Jesus in my heart?"

"YOU have come for advice. Right?"

YOU nod.

"That shows YOU want to do things God's way, but YOU need some help, right?"

YOU nod again.

"The best way to start is by talking to God—tell Him exactly how YOU feel. That's the easy part. The hard part comes when YOU have to choose between your feelings and God's way. YOU cannot change your feelings, but YOU can choose God's way. That's called giving Him your will. Here, I'll make a thought ladder so YOU can see how it works."

As Pastor Perry blocks off some lines on a sheet of paper, they talk about the choices that God wants us to make. What are some of the choices God wants YOU to make?

FEBRUARY

YOU's Thought Ladder

Let's imagine you're talking to God about your problem with your sister," Pastor Perry say.

As he and YOU talk he makes notes, and this is what the thought ladder says. If possible, use two readers—one for YOU; one for God.

YOU	I let Mom think sis started the fight we had yesterday.
GOD	Why?
YOU	Sis makes me so mad. But that's not Your way, I know.
GOD	No. I want YOU to become more like Me.
YOU	But how? I want to have Jesus in my heart, so why does sis get on my nerves? Why do I feel so angry? Why do I want to hurt her?
GOD	Because sin's like that. It's the opposite of real love. When YOU feel angry or picked on, the normal human way is to want to hurt the other person back. That's what most people choose to do.
YOU	I want to do things Your way. It's just that when I get so mad, it's easy to be mean. Can't You help me?
GOD	Certainly. But do YOU want to change so much that next time YOU feel like hurting your sister, YOU won't? No matter how angry YOU feel? Or how much YOU feel like getting even?
YOU	I want to change. *I really do.* That's a promise!
GOD	Good! The test'll be the next time YOU start to feel angry with your sister and want to get even. Then YOU will need to remember the promise YOU made, and choose a good way to act. YOU can start now, though. Ask for ideas on how to cope with problem sisters. Read a book about kids getting along with kids. That'll give YOU ideas to use when things start to go wrong. Remember, I want to help, but I'll never force YOU to do things My way.
YOU	I need Your help, and I'll ask the pastor for some ideas.
GOD	Keep in touch. The more we talk, the stronger YOU will become, and the more YOU will want to choose My way. Remember, the choice is always up to YOU.

It is God who arms me with strength and makes my way perfect.
2 Samuel 22:33.

FEBRUARY

9

Washing Up

Who can discern his errors? Forgive my hidden faults. Psalm 19:12.

For a long time I had looked forward to visiting my friend Jean in England. Through letters we'd become close friends, and now we'd be meeting for the first time. We spoke the same language, but I knew that our accents would be different and that certain words would mean something different to each of us. For instance, if she'd say "boot," I knew she wouldn't be thinking of footwear for rainy weather, but of that place for carrying things in the back of the car. And "bonnet" wouldn't mean a baby's hat, but rather the covering over a car's engine. We'd become such good friend through our letters, though, that I didn't worry about our misunderstanding each other.

After the first evening meal at her place, I waited politely, reading her newspaper. She'd promised to call me when she was ready for help with the dishes.

"I'm going to wash up now," she announced, coming into the room.

"Oh?" I wasn't sure what to say. *Odd!* I thought to myself as she left the room. *Why's she telling me that she's going to wash her hands and face?* I waited for her to come back and get me.

The minutes dragged by. I began to feel uncomfortable. Finally, invited or not, I went into the kitchen. There she was up to her elbows in a sudsy dishpan.

"But you said . . ." I scolded, taking up a tea towel.

With her generous English politeness she quickly turned my question to other topics.

The days whisked by. Just for fun, we bought a British-American word book. Looking through it, I began to feel a little less sure of myself. "Oh!" I exclaimed, not able to keep from speaking. "When you say 'washing up' you mean . . ."

"Doing the dishes!" Ralph, Jean's son, broke in.

"And not washing your hands and face?" My voice squeaked. "And . . ." I looked at Jean. ". . . that first night!"

Our eyes met, and we began to laugh.

We were good friends, but I needed to know her and her way of life much better before I could be certain of not making more of the same kind of mistakes.

It's the same in our friendship with God. In order to see our faults and become like Him, we need to know Him better.

FEBRUARY

The Pangolin

Brothers, stop thinking like children. In regard to evil be infants, but in your thinking be adults. 1 Corinthians 14:20.

Bill held out a brown rolled-up something. "Wanna buy this?" he asked.

Vicki wrinkled her nose as she asked, "What is it?"

"A pangolin." He dumped it carefully onto the patio bricks.

"Ooh!" Vicki drew a quick breath and jumped back as the "thing" unrolled into a four-legged, long-snouted, long-tailed, leathery-looking animal. It took a few slow steps. "What is it?" she demanded again.

"A *pangolin*. A kind of anteater. Wanna buy it?"

"Whatever for?"

"A pet. Some village boys caught it."

"I don't need an anteater!"

Bill shrugged. He and the other mission boys were always getting pets of one kind or another—monkeys, parrots, even an antelope. He picked up the pangolin, and immediately it wrapped itself back into a tight roll and clamped its two tiny front feet over its eyes.

"Oh, isn't that cute!" In spite of herself, Vicki reached to stroke the layering of large, leathery scales that covered its body. They felt smooth, comfortable.

"It eats termites." Bill, as a missionary kid, had learned all sorts of things about the local animals and about customs. "They say it goes into termite hills, lifts its scales, lets the termites crawl in, then clamps down its scales and goes away with lunch." He laughed. "I don't know if that's true, but I do know that a woman who's going to have a baby isn't supposed to look at one. They say the baby will be born shy if its mother sees such a timid animal."

Vicki laughed. Even though she was now a student missionary, she knew by experience that it was no fun being shy. "What are you going to do with it?" she asked.

"Give it back." Bill grinned. "It's too shy. With my monkey and my parrot and my dog . . ."

Vicki laughed again. Bill and his pets made life at the mission more fun. His monkey, parrot, and dog were like a miniature circus, but they could have worried the pangolin to death with their teasing. She appreciated Bill's caring enough to let the pangolin go. That was the sort of grown-up thinking she admired.

FEBRUARY

11

Choices

Good and upright is the Lord; therefore he instructs sinners in his ways. He guides the humble in what is right and teaches them his way. Psalm 25:8, 9.

Each day we're faced with many choices. Most are easy, but some can be very difficult.

When you hear (or read) each of the following phrases, what is the first idea that enters your mind? Does it have anything to do with making a choice?

—reading an exciting book
—getting out of bed in the morning
—eating a candy bar
—playing a computer game
—arguing with your sister or brother
—drinking a bottle of pop
—copying a friend's homework
—watching a good movie
—playing baseball
—going shopping

Now, answer the following questions:

1. Are any of these 10 things always wrong? Which? Why?
2. Are any always right? Which? Why?
3. Are any of these always wrong on Sabbath? Which? Why?
4. Give an example of a situation in which you might have to choose whether or not to do one of them.
5. When might one of these become a choice of doing things your way or God's way? Would it be difficult to choose His way? Why?

God wants to teach you His way. Are you ready to learn?

FEBRUARY

12

Breakings or Blessings

You are looking only on the surface of things. 2 Corinthians 10:7.

Have you ever visited an international airport and watched the planes land and take off? It's interesting, but if you'd judge the city or its people by what you see at the airport in one hour, you could come up with several ridiculous ideas. For example, let's suppose you're visiting Vancouver International Airport in Canada just after a big blue-and-white KLM (Royal Dutch Airlines) jumbo jet lands. You stand near the exit gate as people stream from the customs hall. You can't understand anything anyone says. They're all speaking Dutch, and you feel lost.

Suddenly you find yourself thinking that everyone at the airport speaks Dutch, that no one in all Vancouver will understand you. Your thoughts continue to run wild. You think all Canadians speak Dutch. Then your common sense returns, and you realize that you're simply among a group of Dutch-speaking people who just got off a plane from Holland. But none of the ladies are wearing billowing long skirts with striped aprons, and none of the men have on baggy black trousers. No one even wears wooden shoes. You begin to wonder if the travel posters showing Dutch people in their colorful clothes are true.

You know better, though, than to judge an area by the people you see and the languages you hear at an airport. By asking a few questions, you learn that a number of people of Dutch heritage live in the Vancouver area, but that nearly everyone speaks English. You also learn that in Holland some villagers wear traditional costumes for tourists and that many Dutch country folk still wear wooden shoes, but only for work or play.

How often, though, do we make judgments by just looking on the surface of things? When Jesus was on earth, the people had big hang-ups about Sabbathbreaking. They looked at the surface and saw "sins" rather than "blessings." When Jesus healed someone on the Sabbath, they condemned Him for breaking the law because the work that they saw blinded them to the blessing it brought.

God's Sabbath is a special sign of His power, His love, and His care. He wants us to look for its blessings, not its "breakings."

FEBRUARY

13

Never on Sunday

For the kingdom of God is not a matter of eating and drinking, but of righteousness, peace and joy in the Holy Spirit. Romans 14:17.

Talk about being superstitious!" Sarah Mae exclaimed. "My great aunt Hannah never cuts her fingernails on Sunday."

"Why ever not?"

"Well, her folks were very strict Sundaykeepers, and one of their rules was 'Don't cut your fingernails on Sunday.' When Hannah was little, her mother warned her that if she did, then when she dies she'll have to go around and find every piece of fingernail that she ever cut on a Sunday before she'll be allowed to go into heaven. She never goes to church anymore, but she still won't cut her fingernails on Sunday."

"That's stupid," Carolyn broke in.

"If you were taught that when you were little, you'd believe it," Sarah Mae said quickly. "If your mom said that cutting your fingernails on Sabbath is a sin and that Jesus would make you go around and pick up every piece you've ever cut on Sabbath in your whole life before He'd let you into heaven, you wouldn't want to cut your nails either."

"But that's not true. There aren't rules like that in the Bible!"

"No, but when you're little you believe everything adults teach you. We're lucky that we have moms and dads who know their Bibles and teach us the truth about God. My mom keeps saying how important it is for me to read my Bible for myself. She says that being ready for heaven isn't just keeping rules—it's getting to know God and learning to do things His way."

"But God gave us the Ten Commandments," said Carolyn. "We've got to keep them."

"Sure we do," agreed Sarah Mae. "That's part of getting to know God. If we're good friends with Him, we'll want to be like Him, and being like Him is keeping the Ten Commandments. You know, I feel sorry for people like Great-aunt Hannah who grew up thinking that God gives us a bunch of crabby rules and then makes us suffer if we break them. I keep praying that somehow she'll find out how happy she could be if she just knew what God is really like."

FEBRUARY

A Valentine Day History

Cupid, according to ancient myths, went around shooting arrows at people to make them fall in love. His mother became very jealous of a beautiful young princess named Psyche and ordered him to make Psyche fall in love with someone horribly ugly. When Cupid went to obey, he found that Psyche was so beautiful that he pricked himself with one of his own arrows. They were married and, according to the story, were eventually able to live happily ever after.

The Romans and the Greeks celebrated a lovers' festival for young people on February 15 in honor of Cupid and Psyche. They drew names for partners and exchanged gifts, and often this resulted in courtship that led to marriage. Centuries later, when Christianity spread to Rome, the church tried to give meaning to this pagan festival. The pope changed the date from February 15 to February 14, which was already St. Valentine's Day. Valentine was a common name among early Christians who had died for their faith, and at least two had been put to death on February 14. One was credited with having cured his jailer's daughter of blindness, and on the day of his execution he's said to have written a farewell letter to the girl, signing it "From your Valentine."

Valentine's Day continued as a lovers' day with many traditions and superstitions, and it equaled Christmas as a time of gift-giving. One of the oldest beliefs is that the birds always choose their mates on February 14. In many places girls supposed that the first fellow they would see on Valentine's Day would be their husband-to-be, or at least look like him, and some would keep their eyes closed until they sensed that Mr. Right was coming into view. Exchanging Valentine's cards became popular in the 1800s. Many are still decorated with pictures of Cupid and his arrows, and they are still signed "From your Valentine."

In the Bible God often uses the deep love of a husband for his bride to symbolize the love He has for His people. How do you love Him?

Love does not delight in evil but rejoices with the truth. It always protects, always trusts, always hopes, always perseveres.
1 Corinthians 13:6, 7.

FEBRUARY

15

Dear Lord Beetle

You shall have no other gods before me. Exodus 20:3.

Beetles form the largest order of insects in the animal kingdom and range from tiny specks only one hundredth of an inch long to giants eight inches long. The Hercules beetle of Central America and the Goliath beetle of Africa are among the world's largest insects. From a human viewpoint some beetles are good (such as the ladybug, which helps control other insect pests) and some are bad (such as the boll weevil, which destroys cotton crops). And some are gods!

Can you imagine anyone praying "Dear Lord Beetle"?

Well, the Egyptians worshiped a cousin of the June bug, the black-winged dung beetle. To them its circular shape and bright golden tints suggested the shape and luster of the sun. They believed that it was one of the shapes in which the sun god appeared.

Dung beetles have a habit of forming round pellets from bits of animal dung and are frequently seen in different parts of Africa. Tilted back, these beetles push the pellets along with their front legs. They take these pellets to underground burrows and lay their eggs in them. The pellets then provide food for the larvae when they hatch.

Because of their habit of entering the ground, then reappearing, the Egyptians thought these insects symbolized resurrection and eternal life—after all, only a few beetles went into the ground, but many came out. The pellets, they thought, symbolized the world, and the projectiles on the beetles' heads were emblems of the sun's rays.

The Egyptians made images of these beetles—or scarabs, as they are also called—from metal or stone. Many were larger than life and jewelled. Often they would remove the heart of a dead person and put a large carved scarab, an emblem of eternal life, in its place when the body was embalmed.

It is often said that we become like what we worship or admire—but who would want to become like a dung beetle?

What are some of the special things that you treasure? Who are your heroes? In what ways do you try to be like them?

Our behavior often shows whom we admire.

What or who are your real gods? Think about it.

FEBRUARY

16

Praise the Lord

Praise the Lord. Praise the name of the Lord; praise him, you servants of the Lord. Psalm 135:1.

Praise the Lord!" Elder Jensen said as he stared at us with that principal's look he had. "It's good to praise the Lord and to thank Him for His goodness!" He pounded his fist on the pulpit.

Here it comes, I thought. My knees began to feel shaky. Back then at Adventist boarding schools it was fashionable during Friday evening vespers to give the students "opportunity to stand and speak a few words for the Lord." Somehow I got the idea that I had to do this to prove that I was a good Christian, and when it came the turn for our row I'd force myself to my feet. I was scared. I guess most of us were, because we all said about the same thing.

Since then I've sometimes wondered if that's the kind of praise I'd want if I were God—a testimony meeting in which all the people are so scared they can hardly think of a real thing to say.

If you were God, how would *you* want to be praised? Perhaps you'd prefer a huge choir singing praises in full voice with trumpet fanfare and the majestic chords of a pipe organ. Maybe you'd want the homage of military troops, rank after rank marching in perfect step, volleys of artillery firing in the background, jets sweeping overhead in tight formation, and the salutes of generals and princes.

"Praise the Lord!" The Bible repeats the command many times. The dictionary says that praise is an expression of esteem or admiration. Choirs and shows of honor and testimonies are all forms of praise. Isaiah adds another idea: "Is not this the kind of fasting I have chosen: to loosen the chains of injustice and untie the cords of the yoke, to set the oppressed free and break every yoke? Is it not to share your food with hungry and to provide the poor wanderer with shelter—when you see the naked, to clothe him, and not to turn away from your own flesh and blood?" (Isaiah 58:6, 7).

If you were God, how would you want to be praised?
In what ways do you praise God?

FEBRUARY

17

Talking on Paper

I, Paul, write this greeting in my own hand, which is the distinguishing mark in all my letters. This is how I write.
2 Thessalonians 3:17.

Little Susan, not quite 5 years old, sat on the front steps, watching. Her blonde hair waved back from a very somber face. Moisture rimmed her eyes. She kept her hands folded and still in her lap and just watched while her daddy helped Aunty Arlene put her suitcases in the car. "What is it?" Aunty Arlene sat down beside her.

"You're going away."

Aunty Arlene nodded. "But I'll come to see you again next year."

"But that's a long time."

Aunty Arlene slipped her arm around Susan. "Yes, it is," she agreed.

"I don't want you to go."

Aunty Arlene gave her a squeeze. "And I don't want to leave you."

"You can write me a letter?" Susan's voice was very small.

"Yes."

"And put my name on it?"

"Yes."

"And I'll get it tomorrow?"

Aunty Arlene gave her another squeeze. "Maybe not tomorrow. It takes lots of days for a letter to come from my home. But soon."

It's fun to write to and receive letters from people we care about—it's like talking on paper. The Bible is often called God's letter to us, and most of the New Testament books are actual letters. In fact, four of them are personal letters from Paul to close friends—Timothy, Titus, and Philemon. He wrote when he couldn't visit in person.

IDEAS FOR A TALKING-ON-PAPER PROJECT:

1. Letters can be another way of sharing God's love, and people close by often appreciate letters as well as those who are far away. Think of five people who might enjoy receiving a cheerful note. Write to at least two of them, thanking them for the everyday nice things they do. Let them know you care—and that God cares.

2. Writing letters can also be a way of making new friends—the pen pal column in *Guide* magazine has addresses of young people who like to write and get letters. Missionaries and shut-ins also enjoy receiving letters. Ask your teacher and pastor if they know where you can get addresses.

3. Write a letter to God. He's chosen you as His friend, and He wants to hear from you.

FEBRUARY

18

David and His Brothers

See how your brothers are and bring back some assurance from them.
1 Samuel 17:18.

The following is a dramatic reading from 1 Samuel 17:17-31. (Instructions are on page 28.)

JESSE: Take this ephah of roasted grain and these ten loaves of bread for your brothers and hurry to their camp. Take along these ten cheeses to the commander of their unit. See how your brothers are and bring back some assurance from them. They are with Saul and all the men of Israel in the Valley of Elah, fighting against the Philistines.

NARRATOR: Early in the morning David left the flock with a shepherd, loaded up and set out, as Jesse had directed. He reached the camp as the army was going out to its battle positions, shouting the war cry. Israel and the Philistines were drawing up their lines facing each other. David left his things with the keeper of supplies, ran to the battle lines and greeted his brothers. As he was talking to them, Goliath, the Philistine champion from Gath, stepped out from his lines and shouted his usual defiance, and David heard it. When the Israelites saw the man, they all ran from him in great fear. Now the Israelites had been saying,

ISRAELITES: Do you see how this man keeps coming out? He comes out to defy Israel. The king will give great wealth to the man who kills him. He will also give him his daughter in marriage and will exempt his father's family from taxes in Israel.

NARRATOR: David asked the men standing near him,

DAVID: What will be done for the man who kills this Philistine and removes this disgrace from Israel? . . .

NARRATOR: They repeated to him what they had been saying and told him.

ISRAELITES: This is what will be done for the man who kills him.

NARRATOR: When Eliab, David's oldest brother, heard him speaking with the men, he burned with anger at him and asked,

ELIAB: Why have you come down here? And with whom did you leave those few sheep in the desert? . . . You came down only to watch the battle.

DAVID: Now what have I done? Can't I even speak?

NARRATOR: He then turned away to someone else and brought up the same matter, and the men answered him as before. What David said was overheard and reported to Saul, and Saul sent for him.

FEBRUARY

19

Elizabeth and the Cat

How good and pleasant it is when brothers live together in unity! Psalm 133:1.

Elizabeth and the cat!" Jon's words exploded with disgust, as he stood, hands on hips, in the center of his railroad layout and stared. A whirling tornado couldn't have made more of a mess—tracks twisted, cars overturned, buildings broken and scattered. "I don't know which is worse! I want them both locked out of the basement!"

A 3-year-old and a cat—unsupervised—can be equally destructive to an 11-year-old's engineering feats. Have you ever felt like Jon—wanting to lock out a younger brother or sister? Yesterday we read about Eliab's reaction to his kid brother David's pushiness to learn all the details about the giant. Eliab wanted David out of the way, back with his sheep, not embarrassing him by bothering the officers with all his questions.

In some cultures when someone is unkind to a child, another may tell that person to be careful, because that child may one day be president. In other words, he or she may one day have the power to really pay someone back.

Jesus, on the other hand, said, "Whatever you did for one of the least of these brothers of mine, you did for me" (Matthew 25:40). He wasn't suggesting that we buy favors. Rather, He meant that we should treat each human being with the respect of real love.

Later, when he was fleeing from King Saul, David's entire family joined him. His brothers had become convinced of what most of Israel already knew—God had chosen their little brother as the next king. Psalm 133 expresses David's joy at having his family's support.

"How good and pleasant it is when brothers live together in unity!" How would you feel if your baby brother or sister were to become president of your country?

FEBRUARY

20

Lies

Keep your tongue from evil and your lips from speaking lies. Psalm 34:13.

David was scared, scared frantic. King Saul wanted to kill him, so he ran to High Priest Ahimelech for help. "I'm on a secret mission for the king," he lied, afraid to admit that he was running for his life. Doeg, Saul's head shepherd, happened to be there and saw Ahimelech give David food and a sword, the same sword he'd used to kill Goliath.

From the high priest's David ran to the king of Gath. Still afraid, he pretended to be crazy and staggered around Gath, drooling and scribbling on the walls.

This was the same David who had become the hero of all Israel for killing the giant Goliath, the one who had been anointed by the prophet Samuel as God's choice to be next king of Israel! Now, afraid of Saul, David took things into his own hands. Instead of relying on the Lord, he lied and acted like a fool.

Doeg reported what he'd seen to King Saul. "Ahimelech helped David!"

Saul called in the priests and ordered their execution. Eighty-five priests, their wives, and all their children and livestock were killed. Only one priest survived. He fled to David and told him what had happened. Horrified at the massacre, David invited the escaping priest to stay with him for protection.

David's one lie had caused the death of 85 families, and it was with deep feeling that he wrote: "Keep your tongue from evil and your lips from speaking lies."

David did not let his sins keep him from turning back to God. Each time that he realized the results of his own willfulness he repented. "The Lord redeems his servants; no one will be condemned who takes refuge in him," he wrote in the same psalm (verse 22).

No sin is too big for God to forgive—if the sinner wants forgiveness. David wanted forgiveness, and God called him a man after His own heart.

Let God make you a person after His own heart. Take refuge in Him.

FEBRUARY

21

Heroes

Come, my children, listen to me; I will teach you the fear of the Lord. Psalm 34:11.

David became one of the greatest military commanders of all time—a good strategist, a brave soldier, an efficient leader, a man of God who inspired confidence. Yet he tended to let a cowardly streak get between Him and God. Fear for his life caused him to lie, and 85 families died as a result. Fear for his reputation caused him to arrange the death of one of his best officers, and God punished him (see 2 Samuel 11; 12). Yet when he realized his sins, he always turned back to God, and his example of repentance gives us a good pattern to follow.

Who is your favorite Bible hero? Whom would you most want to be like? David? Joseph? Dorcas? Esther? Rahab? Paul? Someone else?

"The example of good and noble men of sacred history is to be imitated by us only where they followed the footsteps of the Lord," wrote Ellen White.

Who are your other heroes? George Washington's famous statement "I cannot tell a lie" gives us a good example to follow. As the commander of the American Revolutionary troops and as the first president of the United States, he earned his place as one of the great men of history. We like to identify with such heroes, and Reggie proudly repeats his grandmother's claim that his great-great-great-granddaddy was standing by and saw George Washington throw that silver dollar across the Potomac River.

Abraham Lincoln is another hero, a great man because he believed that all people are created equal and should be treated with dignity.

Who are your real heroes, the ones you most admire and want to be like? What is it about them that you want to copy and make part of your own life? Does admiring them make you want to know God better?

Do you know anyone who by his or her actions says, "Come, my child, listen to me; I will teach you the fear of the Lord"? If you have someone like that, you have been given one of the greatest blessings that God can give to anyone. If you don't and if you feel lonely, turn to Jesus. Talk to Him. Read the Bible. He wants to be your hero.

FEBRUARY

22

The Wasp

Sunlight glistened on the filmy wings of the lone wasp as it hovered beside the new egg cone it was building. Then it whirred away, its slender blue-black body cutting neatly through the air. It seemed to be a loner—from time to time others like it flew into the house but never bothered anyone. I saw no need to disturb this one—even if it was building a nest by the front porch light above our door.

For several days the wasp worked, shaping its tiny nest to satisfaction. We came and went, and the wasp seemed to ignore us. Then one afternoon when I came in from school, I balanced my books in one arm while I jangled my key ring in the other hand, trying to seperate the front door key from the others. I found the key and was just pushing it into the lock when—whamo! A searing pain pierced my cheek. I flicked my hand upward and connected with the wasp's jointed body.

Suddenly I no longer felt toleration and good will toward it and its filmy-winged, blue-black kind. I dropped my books and hurried to get a broom and some insect spray. The nest came down, and the wasp paid with its life.

"Why didn't you take the nest down when it first started building?" Laurie's question came from good common sense.

I shrugged. "I thought these wasps never bothered anyone."

"Even when they're right by the door, where folks are always coming and going?"

We can develop a similar false confidence in our Christian lives. Going to church each week, attending a Christian school, having worship each morning, can make us feel safe. Because we are surrounded with religious things and participate in religious activities, we can feel we're doing everything necessary for being a Christian. But sin, like the wasp, builds nearby. Just when we feel safe, it can catch us off guard.

To stand firm, to be a real Christian, we need more than just to do religious things. We need to have Jesus in our hearts.

So, if you think you are standing firm, be careful that you don't fall!
1 Corinthians 10:12.

FEBRUARY

23

The Chief's Goats

For I take no pleasure in the death of anyone, declares the Sovereign Lord. Repent and live! Ezekiel 18:32.

They've found the thief who stole the chief's goats," Jeanne announced one morning.

"Really?" Mrs. Warner asked. "Who?"

"The chief's daughter."

"His daughter?" Surprise sounded in Mrs. Warner's voice.

"That's right."

"But why would she steal from her own father?"

Jeanne looked at her missionary boss and grinned. "That's easy," she replied, knowing that new missionaries don't always understand why village people do things the way they do. "If she steals from her father and he catches her, he won't punish her very hard because she's his daughter. Now, if she stole from someone else, then it could be very bad."

"How did he catch her?" Mrs. Warner sounded curious.

"By threatening to go to the lightning lancer." Jeanne spoke of things that were ordinary for her. In her part of Africa, whether in villages or in the cities, people use witchcraft for every kind of problem, even to catch thieves. "When the chief's goats disappeared, he let everyone know that he was going to take the matter to the witch doctor—the one who has power to call down lightning. When his daughter heard her father talking, she became very frightened. Her father did not speak lightly—he *would* go to the lightning lancer. Then they would hire someone to go up and down the village streets and call out their plans so that everyone would be warned."

Jeanne paused for a moment in her story. "I have heard those men," she finally continued. "For three days they'll call out the same message. They tell what has been stolen and warn that if the thief does not confess within four days, lightning will be called down. I know people who've been struck dead by lightning that the witch doctor claims to have called down."

"So what happened?" Mrs. Warner asked.

"Nothing. The chief's daughter confessed."

Satan wants us to be afraid of God and to think He's like the lightning lancer, ready to strike us dead because of our sins. Jesus came to show us the way to God and to let us know that we don't need to be afraid.

FEBRUARY

Tarbaby

Does not the potter have the right to make out of the same lump of clay some pottery for noble purposes and some for common use?
Romans 9:21.

Help!" yelled Vonnie. "We're going to swamp!"

I laughed and shook my head and motioned her toward the center. "You can trust *Tarbaby*," I bragged as I called for the others to climb in. "It's the most reliable boat on the river. It won't sink."

The *Tarbaby*, with its square bow and stern, looked more like a flat, black box than a boat. Its paint job of creosote, that smelly, dark stuff derived from tar, which protects wood, gave it its name. Maybe it didn't look sleek, but it was strong and stable and handled easily. Technically it was a miniature scow—a small copy of those large, flat, square-ended boats that can be heaped with heavy loads and pulled behind tugs. The *Tarbaby*, though, was just the right size to be rowed with oars, and it was mine to use when Dad didn't need it for ferrying fishing nets and supplies between our dock and the warehouse.

Before they were allowed on the water alone, my little brothers—Doug and Wes—used to come out in the *Tarbaby* with me. We explored the river, and they learned to row, handle a boat, and feel at home on water. Sometimes I'd go alone and drift with the tide along that stretch of river where there wasn't a house or a person to be seen, and there from the security of the *Tarbaby* I'd think about the future and where life might take me. Sometimes I'd take friends for a ride. Some, like Vonnie, didn't care much for boats and water, and they doubted the security of the *Tarbaby* because of its looks.

Since that time, we've had other boats—all bigger and faster and more beautiful—but none will ever take the place of the *Tarbaby*—it served well the purpose for which it was built.

We may feel cheated because we don't have the looks or the talents that others might have, but no one else can take our place in God's creation.

FEBRUARY

25

The Rock of Ages

But the Lord has become my fortress, and my God the rock in whom I take refuge. Psalm 94:22.

Huge stone blocks wedged naturally into a rough-walled effect, making the face of the rocky outcropping in the southwest of England look much like the bare rock cliffs in many other parts of the world. A shallow crevice angled upward, knifing a long slash on its face.

"That's it," Jean said. "The cleft in the Rock of Ages."

I stood at the base of the cliff and gazed upward. A few spatters of rain indicated that a shower might be gathering. The crevice wasn't very deep, but big enough that if a squall broke we could scramble up and flatten ourselves into it for shelter. That's how it got its name.

One afternoon more than 200 years ago Augustus Toplady was passing the rock on his way home. As he neared it, a blustery rain stormed in. He clambered upward into the crevice and, pressing against its side, let the rocky wall protect him. Sheltering against the rock reminded him how David had described God as being the Rock in whom he took refuge. Thoughts from other texts added more ideas, and while he waited for the storm to slacken, words for a poem began to form in his mind. That poem has become a favorite gospel song—"Rock of Ages." And later the rocky outcropping was named for the hymn it inspired.

"Rock of Ages" is hymn 300 in *The Seventh-day Adventist Hymnal*. If you look to your left at the top of the music, you'll see Pastor Toplady's name along with the date he wrote the words and the dates of his birth and death. On the right-hand side you'll see that Thomas Hasting composed the music more than 50 years later. If you use the indexes in the back of the hymnal, you can learn more about the "Rock of Ages," as well as about other hymns. For instance, the index called "Scriptural Allusions in Hymns" lists the texts that contain certain ideas for the words. The section "Indexed by Hymn Number" gives two texts—Deuteronomy 32:4 and John 19:34.

God still offers His protection. It is up to us to press close to Him.

FEBRUARY

26

Reflections on Psalm 23

The Lord is my shepherd; I shall not want. Psalm 23:1, KJV.

He maketh me to lie down in green pastures: he leadeth me beside the still waters.

"He restoreth my soul: he leadeth me in the paths of righteousness for his name's sake.

"Yea, though I walk though the valley of the shadow of death, I will fear no evil: for thou art with me; thy rod and thy staff they comfort me.

"Thou preparest a table before me in the presence of mine enemies: thou anointest my head with oil; my cup runneth over.

"Surely goodness and mercy shall follow me all the days of my life; and I will dwell in the house of the Lord for ever" (verses 2-6, KJV).

REFLECTIONS: This psalm is one of the best known, most memorized passages in the Bible. It has been set to music, and a number of familiar hymns are based on it. Entire books have been written about it and photo collections made for it. Take a few minutes to reflect on and/or discuss the reasons you think it is so popular. The following activities may give you some ideas.

1. Psalm 23 contains many word pictures. What pictures do the following phrases create in your mind? "My shepherd." "Lie down in green pastures." "Beside still waters." "Valley of the shadow of death." "A table." What other pictures do you "see" in it?

2. Draw or paint a picture or write a poem or descriptive essay for one of the "pictures" in number 1.

3. Arrange a collection of pictures to illustrate the psalm. You could cut the pictures from magazines or even plan and take a series of photos yourself.

4. A number of hymns are based on Psalm 23. To find them, use the index in your hymnal giving the scriptural allusions of hymns. Sing or play some of them for worship.

5. Psalm 23 also works nicely as a responsive reading. Use the index to see if it has been included in the responsive readings section of your hymnal—you might enjoy reading it responsively for your family or group worship.

FEBRUARY

27

Kicking Against the Goads

We all fell to the ground, and I heard a voice saying to me in Aramaic, "Saul, Saul, why do you persecute me? It is hard for you to kick against the goads." Acts 26:14.

Oxen are known for being strong and steady. In Bible times—and even now—they're used to pull carts and plows and to thresh. Because they can work so hard they're valuable animals, but they've never been known to go anywhere quickly. On the contrary, their plodding pace is slow—extremely slow—and that's why those who plow carry goads. In order to get the oxen to move just a little faster, they give them quick jabs with these sharp-pointed sticks. Of course that hurts, and the natural reaction is to kick the pest, but those bulky beasts, hampered by yoke and harness, find themselves kicking out at empty air. A wise ox soon learns that kicking is useless. If it wants to stay ahead of the pricks, it must simply pick up its feet and move faster.

Saul was dedicated to his work. He was on his way to "convert" the followers of Jesus in Damascus, and he was angry, very angry. Those people claimed that the Messiah had come, and they were causing trouble in the synagogues. They must be made to see that they were wrong. The only way to change their mind, Paul thought, was to have them beaten and thrown in prison, even killed—like Stephen—if necessary.

Saul's conscience must have been bothering him about his methods of evangelism, because when Jesus appeared to him, He said very pointedly, "It is hard for you to kick against the goads."

As you know, that was the turning point in Saul's life. He became the apostle Paul.

Christians these days usually don't have people thrown into jail to make them change. But have you ever heard of them speaking unkindly or criticizing other Christians? Have you ever done that yourself?

God won't come down in a blinding flash to make you change, but He may goad your conscience. Will you kick against the goads? Or will you ask Him to help you think of something kind to say when you're tempted to tease or criticize?

FEBRUARY

28

The Blessing of Reading

Blessed is the one who reads the words of this prophecy, and blessed are those who hear it and take to heart what is written in it, because the time is near. Revelation 1:3.

I can remember my mother reading the first and the last of a book, then skimming through the rest to see if it would be a good story for me to read. By doing this, she could find out who the main characters were, learn something about them, and also get an idea about the plot.

It's interesting to do this with the Bible, too. The first sentence says: "In the beginning God created the heavens and the earth." The last says: "The grace of the Lord Jesus be with God's people." The first chapter of the Bible tells about Creation and how good everything was; the last describes the new (re-created) earth and the second coming of Jesus. From this we see that God and Jesus are the main characters and that something happened to make it necessary to re-create the world for God's people. The in-between parts tell about that.

But the Bible is much more than a storybook about God. It tells us how we can be His people. Since sin became part of the world's story way back near the beginning, God had His commandments written down so that we could know the difference between sin and His way of happiness. And He had the stories of many people recorded so that we could understand that Satan has many ways of deceiving us.

Reading the first and last chapters and skimming the rest will never give us the whole story of a book. We need to read the entire story for ourselves. When I studied literature, I realized that in order to really know and understand the characters of a book, I needed to read and reread certain passages and to make comparisons. With the Bible this is even more important. It's our main source of knowledge about God. In order to really know Him and to understand His commandments and how to become one of His people, we need to read and reread it and study and compare. Reading is still not enough. Putting into practice is what counts.

MARCH

1

Having Joy in Sadness

Though the fig tree does not bud and there are no grapes on the vines, though the olive crop fails and the fields produce no food, though there are no sheep in the pen and no cattle in the stalls, yet I will rejoice in the Lord, I will be joyful in God my Savior. Habakkuk 3:17, 18.

Sher rolled over at the sound of the alarm and started to slide out of bed as usual, but the firmness of the mattress was not right, nor was the soft grain of the wood paneling she found herself staring at. And . . . Suddenly everything whooshed back into her thoughts. She felt that terrible, horrible numbness as if something were wrapped around her middle, trying to squeeze all the feeling out of her. She didn't know if the world would ever be right again. Yesterday, even before Mom had sat them down in the living room to talk, she knew something terrible was wrong.

"It'll be easier for you. It'll be easier for all of us if you spend the next few days with Grandma," Mom had explained. She had tears in her eyes.

Sher felt tears stinging behind her own eyes. In her mind she could understand that maybe there was some good reason for what was happening, but that didn't make it feel any better. Besides, things like this happened only to other kids—not to her and her little sister.

Someone tapped on the door. Then it opened a crack. "Are you awake, Sher?" It was Grandma. "May I come in?"

Sher nodded. Then Grandma was beside her on the bed. Sher snuggled against her just like she had when she was little, and felt Grandma's arm slip around her. "Why?" Sher asked as she pushed back a sob. "Why does Daddy have to go away? Why does there have to be a divorce?"

Grandma squeezed Sher tight. "There aren't any good answers," she said. "In this world sad things just happen—even to good kids. Let's talk to Jesus and ask Him to help us carry this hurt."

The children of Israel relied on their fields and flocks for a living. Figs and olives were especially valuable. Today's text tells of their saddest experience—the Babylonians had destroyed their homes and taken them captive—yet Habakkuk said, "I will be joyful in God."

Can anyone hurt as badly as Sher and still have joy? How can you be "joyful in God" when you are sad?

MARCH

2

Clothed With Christ

For all of you who were baptized into Christ have clothed yourselves with Christ. Galatians 3:27.

Laughter erupted across the assembly as Bobby hurried onto the stage. The way he held his head, the way he walked, the sweater he wore—everyone knew immediately whose part he played—our home ec teacher! He even talked like her.

Role-playing, pretending to be someone else and acting out how he or she would behave in certain situations, gives us an opportunity to behave in different ways. We can surprise ourselves with the positive, self-confident manners we assume for talking and behaving while pretending to be someone else.

Dressing in new clothes that we feel good about can also help us assume a new manner of self-confidence. Perhaps you've read the story about the girl who bought a hair ribbon that she thought did wonders for her looks. She put it on, and walked out of the store feeling that she looked great. She met a boy she never before would have had the nerve to talk to, but because of the ribbon and the confidence it gave her, she was able to talk easily with him. Later she discovered that the ribbon had fallen out of her hair before she left the store—the only difference had been her inside feelings about herself.

Putting on nice clothes, having a new hairstyle, or pretending to be someone else doesn't change who we are, although it affects how we feel about ourselves and shows us that we can change how we act.

Experiment with pretending to be someone else by saying "Where are you going?" as if you are

1. A police officer who has just stopped a speeding driver.
2. A doctor talking to a deaf person.
3. A teacher who has just caught a student sneaking out of class.
4. A first-grader just learning to read.
5. A person talking to a friend who is going on vacation.
6. A frightened 3-year-old replying to his mother.
7. Jesus speaking to someone who is tempted.

Being "clothed with Christ" is a choice that changes us from the inside out. It makes us want to be like Him.

MARCH

3

The Green Curtains

Before they call I will answer; while they are still speaking I will hear. Isaiah 65:24.

Everyone sat under the large mango tree, enjoying its shade. Since Elder and Mrs. Lange had last visited, the Mbayo family had almost finished building their new house. Its neat bricks, metal roof, and large windows contrasted with the mud-and-thatch house they'd lived in before.

"I see you have some nice curtains," Elder Lange said as he pointed to a corner window.

"That's my room," replied Maloba, the eldest daughter, pleased that he'd noticed.

"But what about the windows in the other rooms?"

"You know how it is. If God wishes, we'll have curtains for them too."

"Of course God wants you to have curtains. Don't you pray for them?"

"But I already pray for so much. We don't yet have enough glass for all the windows."

"God cares about little things."

"But there's so much. Every morning when I pray, first I ask God that my father'll have strength to care for our family and to complete the house. Then I pray about my future, that I'll choose the right way."

"But God cares about the little things too," Elder Lange persisted.

"Don't you see," suggested Mrs. Lange, "that when she prays about her father and family and house, she knows that God understands about all the little things also?"

"That's it," Maloba added, smiling. "Even if I don't mention every item every day, God knows about all our needs."

Mrs. Lange turned to Maloba's mother. "Are curtains included in your prayers?" she asked.

Maloba's mother nodded.

"What color would you like?"

"Green." The reply came without hesitation.

On their way back to the apartment where they were staying, Elder Lange slipped his arm around his wife. "You know," he said, "I used that long piece of green material that came boxed with ADRA clothes to pack around the medicines I brought for the hospital. Do you think it would make good curtains?"

His wife nodded. "Very good curtains," she said. "It would make very pretty green curtains."

Has God ever used you to help answer someone else's prayer? What special answers to prayer have you yourself had?

MARCH

The Snowball Tree

It will be a shelter and shade from the heat of the day, and a refuge and hiding place from the storm and rain. Isaiah 4:6.

This text reminds me of Grandma's snowball tree—an old tree with many low branches reaching out and up umbrella-like so that in summer it looked almost like a huge green snowball, shaped like the globs of white blossoms that hung from it. Its thick layer of leaves made a neat canopy, and I loved to climb into it and sit hidden away. It felt particularly snug during summer squalls. I'd pull on a rain slicker and slip away to the snowball tree. Its leaves sheltered me from the wind and rain, making me feel cozy and secure.

A few years ago a heavy storm ravaged the west coast of England, tearing off roofs, hurling up rock, mud, and debris from the beach, and shattering windows. A series of photos showed waves awash, with spray flying and water billowing over the sea wall. But the photographer had not faced into the gale; rather, he had sheltered behind an opposite point that broke the fury of the gale, and from there he had pointed the camera toward the dramatic scene that swept away from him.

The shelter and shade Isaiah writes about reminds us of Jesus. He is like a shelter, a shade, a refuge, and a hiding place. Think of the Bible stories you have read. Think of missionary stories you have heard. Think of what God—Jesus—has done for you.

In what ways is He a shelter?

____

____

a shade? ______________________________

____

a refuge? ______________________________

____

a hiding place? ______________________________

____

Do you have a special place where you go to feel snug and secure? Does it make you think of God's care for you?

MARCH

5

The Black Spot

Praise the Lord, O my soul, and forget not all his benefits. Psalm 103:2.

Preacher Brown held up a blank piece of white cardboard. "What do you see?" he asked his congregation.

"Nothing," someone quickly replied.

"OK," he said, putting the cardboard down. Then he took out a big, fat marking pen, scribbled a black smudge across the center, and held the cardboard up again. "Now what do you see?"

"A big black spot," someone from the back answered.

"What else do you see?" Preacher Brown asked.

No one said anything.

"Don't you see anything else?"

No one spoke.

"I'm surprised," the preacher said at last. "You have missed the most important thing." He paused, still waiting for someone to respond. Everyone seemed puzzled. "The piece of cardboard!" he exclaimed. "The piece of cardboard is the most important."

What do you see in your life? Do you focus on the black spots—the problems, the unpleasant things? Or do you see the white sheet of God's love? If our minds are occupied with all the bad things that happen to us, we won't even notice the good things. What we think about affects our disposition. If we think about problems, about unkind things people have said, we generally frown and feel in a bad mood. If we look for the good things, it's easier to smile and be cheerful.

Mrs. Metcalf had been attending the same Sabbath school class for 20 years. Suddenly one Sabbath she realized what had been happening. "For the past 20 years we've been talking about our problems," she told the others. "What good has it done? We're still talking about the same problems. It's time we change. We need to start praising the Lord for His blessings."

Why not try some blessing experiments too?

1. Each time you have an unhappy thought or begin to worry about a problem, stop and think of one of the blessings God has given you and say a silent thank-You prayer.

2. Make a list of blessings you have each day that, like the sheet of cardboard with the black spot, you never notice. Now add 10 nice things that other people did for you yesterday.

3. Since one of the nicest ways God gives us blessings is through things other people do, how are you going to be a blessing to someone today?

MARCH

The Winners

It is better to take refuge in the Lord than to trust in man. It is better to take refuge in the Lord than to trust in princes. Psalm 118:8, 9.

In 1990 United States president George Bush met with Soviet president Mikhail Gorbachev in Finland just after all the amazing changes had occurred in the Communist countries of Europe. People in that part of the world were getting a new freedom. At their meeting President Gorbachev presented a gift to President Bush in front of the TV cameras.

When he opened the gift, George Bush chuckled, then held it up. It was a framed picture, an enlargement of a cartoon with both him and Gorbachev shown as boxers. They were pictured as having fought together to knock out their common enemy—the cold war. It lay senseless on the ring floor. Between them, holding up their arms in victory, posed the world, acting as their referee and proclaiming them both winners.

The two presidents were credited with setting a new order for world peace and with changing the way the world had run for many, many years. They had stopped the cold war—that unfriendliness and mistrust that had existed for so many years between the Western countries and the Communist countries. People looked to those two men, leaders of the world's two most powerful countries, for a better, more peaceful, and happier world.

As important and powerful as presidents might be, they cannot keep peace forever. Other leaders of less-powerful countries have access to powerful weapons. In their greed for more riches and more power, they have the ability to start a war any time they want, and the most powerful leaders would have difficulty stopping them.

Even when life is scary—or especially when life is scary—we can have joy and peace inside. No person can give this to us, though. It can come only from God. He has promised to be our refuge.

In our devotionals so far this year, we have talked about several different ways to have God's peace—to have Jesus in our hearts. What are some of them?

____

____

____

Do you have God's peace?

MARCH

7

One in One With a Million Zeros

He has . . . set eternity in the hearts of men; yet they cannot fathom what God has done from beginning to end. Ecclesiastes 3:11.

One with a million zeros. That's a big number—much too big to have a simple name and so big that if it were typed, it would fill a book about this size.

Now, let's talk about monkeys.

Suppose we take an average monkey named Joe who just happens to have one outstanding talent—he's a superwhiz at typing. He's so good that he can type a book this size in just one day. To be exact, he can do it in 12 hours if he types steadily at the rate of 191 words a minute. Now that's fast—much faster than a regular typist can type.

But never mind, we've already said that Joe's a super-whiz typist, and, fortunately for our experiment, there's nothing he enjoys more than typing.

So we let Joe sit at a desk and type.

He can hit any key in any order that he wants, as long as he types his 191 words a minute for 12 hours. We'll let him continue doing this day after day after day.

Since Joe's an average monkey who loves to type, he might wonder why we let him enjoy his favorite pastime for 12 hours each day. Well, we want to know if, on one of these days, he'll accidentally happen to type an exact copy of the contents of this book. How long do you think it might be before he manages to do that? __________

If you say such a thing could never ever happen, you're very close to being correct—at least it probably wouldn't happen in your lifetime or even by the time your great-great-grandchildren are adults. Even if he'd started typing on the day of the big bang that evolutionists say might have brought our universe into being a few billion years ago, he'd still have to type every day for another one-with-a-million-zeros years before he'd have typed long enough to have the chance to accidentally write this book just once. For a mathematician that's almost the same as saying it could never happen.

The universe—even the interior universe of our bodies—is many, many times more complex than the simple combinations of 26 letters, 10 numerals, a few punctuation marks, and spaces needed to write this book. Yet all God had to do was to speak, and the heavens and the earth came into being.

God's workings are beyond our understanding, but He gives us enough evidence so we can believe that what He says is true.

MARCH

Willie and the Roses

And we pray this in order that you may live a life worthy of the Lord and may please him in every way: bearing fruit in every good work, growing in the knowledge of God. Colossians 1:10.

Willie was a good worker—he kept the yard clean and tidy, weeded the flower beds, watered the garden, clipped the hedge, and ran errands. He did his best to please Mrs. Smith, and with his careful work, the yard around the Smiths' mission house began to look better and better.

One day Mrs. Smith had an errand for Willie. She'd borrowed a paper cutter from the mission office and wanted him to return it. "Please take this to Rose in the business office," she said, handing the paper cutter to Willie.

Willie took the paper cutter and looked at it. He tried the blade. "Rose?" he asked.

Mrs. Smith nodded. "Yes. It's a paper cutter," she explained. "Please give it to Rose." She spoke carefully. Willie understood some English and she spoke only a little Swahili, his language. "Bring to Rose." She repeated the words she could in Swahili.

"Rose?" Willie asked again.

"Yes, Rose," Mrs. Smith replied.

Willie tried the cutter again, then left. Mrs. Smith went back to her work. About a half hour later Willie was back at the door and handed Mrs. Smith a large bouquet of roses.

Mrs. Smith smiled. "Why, thank you, Willie!" she exclaimed. Then she saw the paper cutter leaning against the porch wall. Suddenly she understood that Willie had misunderstood. Realizing that he'd done his best to please her, Mrs. Smith asked someone to translate what she wanted into Swahili. Then, with a big smile, Willie took the paper cutter to the mission office.

Learning a foreign language does help us understand other people better. Willie speaks Swahili. Here are a few Swahili words and what they mean in English:

Jambo!	Hello!
Habari?	How are you?
Mzuri sana	Very well
Asante	Thank you
Ndio	Yes
Hapana	No
Mungu	God

Do you ever misunderstand what Jesus wants you to do? In your prayer time today, ask Him to help you grow in your knowledge and understanding of His will.

MARCH

9

Learning by Experience

After he was raised from the dead, his disciples recalled what he had said. Then they believed the Scripture and the words that Jesus had spoken.
John 2:22.

"Today we're going to learn how to divide fractions."

Todd rested his chin on his hand as he listened.

"It's really quite easy. All you have to do is invert the divisor and multiply."

"Huh?" Todd heard himself saying.

The teacher smiled. She wrote some fractions on the board. "See! One half divided by two equals one fourth."

Todd stared at the board.

"I don't think you understand what I mean."

Todd and all his classmates shook their heads.

"Then let's do some hands-on fractions. Take out your scissors, please." The monitor gave a duplicated sheet to each student. "Now, cut carefully around the circle."

Todd and the others cut. Soon each had a circle. The teacher held up a circle just like theirs. "This is a traditional fraction pie," she continued. "We're going to divide it in two by cutting along the heavy line that marks the diameter. All right, divide your pie in two."

Everyone snipped across their circles.

The teacher held up her pieces. "See? We have two halves."

Simple, Todd thought. *Anyone knows that.*

"Now we are going to divide one half by two." She wrote 1/2 ÷ 2 on the board. "Cut each of your halves along the line. How many pieces do you have?"

Four, of course, Todd said to himself. *We've cut the pie into quarters.*

The teacher held a piece in each hand, then put them together to form a half again. "See. One-half divided by two . . ." She moved the pieces apart. "Makes one quarter." She held one of the quarters up to emphasize what had happened.

"Oh!" exclaimed Todd. "I understand." He looked at the pieces he had cut. He looked at the fractions on the board. And he nodded his head.

Experience, they say, is the best teacher. In school, explanations with experiments make learning easier. Jesus had tried to tell His disciples what was going to happen. But it made no sense to them. They expected things to go differently. After Jesus was raised from the dead, they remembered what He had said. Then they understood and believed.

MARCH

10

The Ornate Moth

Like newborn babies, crave pure spiritual milk, so that by it you may grow up in your salvation. 1 Peter 2:2.

The ornate moth was flying happily along when *pluff*, it was stopped midwing and found itself upended, suspended, wings outstretched in midair.

It tried to pull its left wing free, but a sticky something looped around it. The moth tried to lift its right wing, but it felt as if someone had tied it fast. It kicked its legs, frantic for a foothold to get some leverage to wrench itself free, but its legs only beat the air. The moth struggled this way and that, but the harder it tried, the more trapped it became.

At last, winded, it let itself relax and hang. It rolled its eyes, trying to assess what had happened, and with a shudder discovered that it hung in the lower left quadrant of a spider's web. There in the distance at eye level, the ornate moth saw the many legs of the squatty arachnid picking quickly across the webbing. The moth panicked and heaved its body from side to side, desperate to get free.

The spider moved closer, and the moth could just see itself on the spider's dinner menu. The many legs padded up until the first set was almost touching the moth's head. The moth froze, waiting for the next move. The spider stopped. Its glazed eyes stared at the moth. The moth stared back. The spider's many legs turned and carried it in a slow, deliberate circle around the moth. Then they stopped again.

The moth felt the threads of the web tremble, then one by one they began to snap. Through the corner of its eye it saw the spider cutting the strands. Then the moth felt itself dropping away from the web—free.

The spider had sensed danger and, fearful, had cut the moth out of the web.

Ornate moths feed on plants that contain a poison. The poison doesn't hurt them, but it stays in their bodies and is deadly to spiders. Scientists have raised these moths, making sure they eat only nonpoisonous food. If trapped, with no protective poison, those moths became the spiders' victims.

Satan is out to trap everyone in his web of sin.

God's Spirit is deadly to sin, but in order to have His protection we must feed on the right things. The Bible is the best food.

MARCH

11

The Storm

And I said, "Here am I. Send me!"
Isaiah 6:8.

The clouds boiled about the plane, tossing it from one turbulent current to the next. Stan tensed. Huge raindrops splattered against the windshield so fast and hard that all he could see was a dark-gray wavy blur. The plane bucked and bounced, and Stan strained to hold it to its bearings. From experience he knew that the clouds sagged to the treetops below, pouring down torrents of rain onto the already-soggy earth. He also knew that it was useless to urge his little craft upward. The rainy season cumulus built into towers that reached far above his range. *God, protect us,* he prayed. *Help me bring my passengers safely to land.*

Stan had always wanted to be a pilot. He'd taken Jesus into his heart when he was a boy, and when he had the opportunity to become a missionary pilot, he gladly accepted, saying, "Lord, here I am. Send me." Flying over remote areas of Africa beyond the reach of beacons and signals became an everyday occurrence for Stan. It was dangerous but exciting. Besides, he'd given his flying skills to God to use in taking other missionaries from one distant post to another.

The turbulence continued to toss the plane as the fat raindrops pounded the windshield. Stan had flown through many storms—this was definitely the wildest. Minutes dragged. He had to see the ground, to know where they were. They'd logged enough time to be over the mission. He'd tried to correct for the drift of the storm, but he needed to see landmarks. They didn't have fuel to keep flying forever. He continued to pray.

Suddenly the angry darkness fell behind them as the plane broke into a clear spot. Stan almost gasped. A double rainbow circled the plane, outlining the gap in the storm. Below lay the mission airstrip. "Thank You, God," he whispered, setting the plane into a quick bank and nosing toward the ground.

It has been said that the safest place to be is where God wants you to be. Have you ever had a frightening experience when something special has happened to make you realize that God really does care?

MARCH

12

Carry Each Other's Burdens

Carry each other's burdens, and in this way you will fulfill the law of Christ. Galatians 6:2.

Bicycles are wonderful inventions." Grandpa's clear blue eyes twinkled. "You're a lucky boy!"

Mark grinned. He'd worked hard for his new bike. He leaned against the workbench beside his grandfather and admired the two-wheeler.

"I remember our first bicycles—Father's and mine—in the old country." Grandpa's voice sounded far away. "We could go farther and faster than we'd ever gone before, peddling miles across the flat country, sailing along, with the wind at our backs." He paused and chuckled. "Or struggling when we had to ride into it."

"In Holland?" Mark asked.

His grandfather nodded. "Ja. Years ago. Hardly anyone had cars yet. My father and I worked together—carpenters. Most of the jobs needed two people, and with our bicycles we could take contracts where we could never go before.

"Father was getting older, but he'd always been strong, and I took for granted he'd work with me until the day he retired. Then he started complaining about being tired.

" 'You have a bicycle now,' I'd tell him. 'You don't have to walk anymore.' And I'd hurry him along. He complained more and more often, but we had lots to do, and I needed his help. Besides, I had growing kids and needed the money. He could afford to take time off, but I insisted he work.

"Then one day he was really sick, and I knew he needed to see the doctor. I'll never forget that day." Grandpa paused and pushed back that unruly wave that always insisted on sliding down over his forehead. "My father was too sick. Too sick. He'd pushed himself to keep working because I needed him, and now I had no choice but to hire someone else.

"I wish I knew then what I know now. I never understood how my father felt until I started to get older myself. He never did get well. I wish . . . I wish I'd told him to take time off before it was too late.

"Mark," he said as he laid his hand gently on Mark's shoulder, "take good care of your dad. Help him. Parents need their kids just as much as kids need their parents."

Do others help you carry your burdens? Do you help them carry theirs? How?

MARCH

13

False Accusations

For it is commendable if a man bears up under the pain of unjust suffering because he is conscious of God. 1 Peter 2:19.

Lindy Chamberlain, an Australian Seventh-day Adventist pastor's wife, was convicted of murdering their baby girl back in the early 1980s and served time in prison before new evidence exonerated her. The movie *A Cry in the Dark,* TV appearances, and several books telling the story and showing the unjustness of her treatment have brought her a certain fame. But can this make up for what happened? For having her baby stolen by a dingo? For having to wait through the long search and then having to give up hope that her baby would ever be found alive? And then, after all that, to be accused, convicted, and sent to prison for killing her baby, a crime she did not commit?

No one can ever erase the bad effects of such things in this life. It's only in heaven that complete healing can happen.

Mandy Lee's best friend SueAnne suddenly became cool and distant, obviously angry about something. "Why?" Mandy Lee asked.

"After what you did that night!"

"What night?" Mandy Lee didn't understand.

"That night you came down to my room and threatened me."

Mandy Lee's mouth dropped in shock. "Threatened you?"

"I saw you. In the door. You said . . ."

The look in SueAnne's eyes, the tone of her voice, told Mandy Lee that she believed what she was saying. Mandy Lee felt a cold worry blanket her body. "Are you sure you didn't see someone else? Or maybe have a bad dream?" she asked, hoping SueAnne would suddenly start to laugh and say she was just pulling a sick joke. "I didn't . . . I wouldn't . . . I . . ."

"Don't try to lie. I saw you!"

Mandy Lee's shoulders sagged. Whatever had happened, obviously SueAnne believed what she thought she had seen. Mandy Lee had no way to prove otherwise, and her denials were useless. Sadly she watched her best friend turn away from her, and she understood that all she could do was pray and hope that one day she could win back her friend's trust. She would just have to wait for that time—even if she had to wait until Jesus comes.

MARCH

14

I Didn't Know

Jord closed his eyes and forced himself to take the last three steps toward the railing. He wanted to look—to see the water rushing through the spillway of the dam. He opened his eyes a slit—and gasped and staggered backward.

"What'sa matter? Scared you're gonna fall?"

Jord turned and hunched his shoulders. Six-feet-two, strong—and scared, scared frantic of high places. He couldn't look down from any place more than five feet off the ground without getting a panicky dizziness.

"C'mon. Let's make the wimp look over the edge."

Jord dodged as Michael lunged to grab him. And field trips were supposed to be fun? It was bad enough to be scared without being tormented.

Back at school the next day, the English teacher announced speeches—three-minute prepared talks. "Gonna talk about high-climbing?" Michael taunted on the way out of class.

Jord said nothing. On speech day Jord was first. He didn't like getting up front, but he'd prepared well and did his best. Toward the end of the period, Michael was called.

Jord watched as Michael hesitated. His face was white, and he shifted his weight from one foot to another. He stuffed his hands into his pockets, then pulled them out. At last he opened his mouth, and his voice squished out high-pitched and quivery. He paused and cleared his throat. He tried to say something more. His voice developed a definite shake. The room became deathly quiet. This was Michael? Big, blustering Michael?

Michael stopped again, cleared his throat twice, then kind of gulped his words out in bunches. Finally he just sat down.

After class Jord waited for Michael. "Getting up front can be tough," he said quietly.

Michael looked at the floor and didn't say anything.

"It's not fun to get so scared of something. I know."

Michael nodded. "I didn't know it'd be like that till I got up there." He didn't look at Jord. "I just didn't know."

You, therefore, have no excuse, you who pass judgment on someone else, for at whatever point you judge the other, you are condemning yourself, because you who pass judgment do the same things.
Romans 2:1.

MARCH

15

Everest!

Bear with each other and forgive whatever grievances you may have against one another. Forgive as the Lord forgave you. Colossians 3:13.

"Everest! Mount Everest! They named that mountain for your nose—it's so huge. And your mouth . . ." Lindsay looked across at the other girls standing in a half-circle in the aisle around Everest's desk. Several nods encouraged her. "It's as big as the Grand Canyon. You're not only ugly, you're . . . you're . . ."

Lindsay paused, waiting for the others to add more insults. Everest stared back at her, his brown eyes unblinking. Frail, even for a fifth-grader, his jeans bagged around his body. He said nothing. Just then the classroom door opened.

"Lindsay, would you come here for a moment?"

Lindsay felt her face stiffen; then a terrible warmth rushed up her neck. *Had Miss Yale heard everything?* she wondered. Her steps felt wooden as she headed for the door. When she was in the hall, Miss Yale closed the door and looked down at her. "I expected so much more of you." She shook her head slowly. "I thought you'd be more understanding than the others."

Lindsay looked at the floor and bit her lip. She loved Miss Yale. Miss Yale was the one person she could count on to be kind to her. And now . . . She felt a tightness choking up through her chest. She wanted to explain, to say how it felt good to have the others on her side for once. How it felt good to be the one to do the teasing instead of being teased.

"I was hoping to ask you to help Everest not be so shy. He's finding it difficult to fit back in to school after being sick for so long."

"I'm sorry," Lindsay mumbled at last. "I know how terrible it feels." Echoes of the "Fatty-Fatty" she'd heard as long as she could remember flickered through her mind. She hated those words. "I . . . I . . ."

Miss Yale slipped an arm around her. "I think Everest is the one who should know that you're sorry. I'm sure you can find a way to show him you really mean it. And maybe that'll help you find a way to forgive those who've teased you too."

MARCH

16

Tell God the Truth

Save me, O God, for the waters have come up to my neck. . . . I am worn out calling for help; my throat is parched. My eyes fail, looking for my God.
Psalm 69:1-3.

Jasmin shoved her face deep into her pillow, trying to block the sound of her sobs. "Nobody cares," she told herself over and over. "Nobody."

Landy slumped into the far corner of the very back seat on the school bus. The sharpness of the teacher's voice when he'd broken another blade in shop class still burned in his ears. "Can't you do anything right? Anything?"

I tried! he told himself, slouching down so no one could see him. *I tried, but I can't do anything right, so what's the use?*

Have you ever felt like Jasmin or Landy? Have you ever felt like giving up because you were up to your neck in problems? Have you felt that no one cares, not even God? Everyone has probably felt that way at some time. David did when he wrote the beginning of Psalm 69, and he told God how he felt.

Have you ever tried telling God how you feel when you think He's not listening to you? Have you ever told God that you think He doesn't even care about helping you?

Some people think feelings like that aren't right, so they try to shove them away and hide them—even from God. They're afraid it would be a sin to tell God the truth and admit that they think He doesn't care. But God knows "everything," and that includes the feelings we try to hide. He even knows why we hide them.

David is a good example of someone who is honest with God. We also need to tell God the truth about how we feel, and about how we feel about how we feel, and about how we'd like to change how we feel.

God asks us to give Him everything that bothers us or that hurts our feelings. We can do that, though, only when we are completely honest with Him in our prayers. He may not take our problems away. He may not even take away our hurt and sadness. When we talk to Him honestly, though, just like we'd talk to any best friend, and ask Him to help us carry our burdens of hurt feelings and sadness, He'll do just that.

By the time David got very far into writing the sixty-ninth psalm, he began to feel a lot better. Parts of the psalm even prophesy about how Jesus would suffer. At the end of the psalm, David is able to praise God and to say, "The Lord hears the needy."

MARCH

17

The Mouse

A series of black dashes suddenly staggered toward every corner of the screen, arranging themselves into a dizzying pattern on the blue surface. I suppose an artist would have liked it. I didn't. I wanted to see words, white words, lots of them—not crazy black marks. Beside me sat the culprit—a mouse, a smooth sleek white device, super intelligent, able to work on any hard surface, whose only purpose in being there was, I thought, to help me use my computer better and more easily. I clicked and double-clicked all the right buttons. I keyed in commands. The black marks still continued to skate about.

With a sigh I turned to the stack of instruction books beside me—somewhere, on one of those thousands of pages about my new system and its resident mouse and the mouse-happy programs, there had to be something that could tell me what to do. With time and a lot of looking, I did find the right page and learned there was no shortcut. I'd have to start all over again.

My problems began when I rushed ahead without learning how to activate the mouse. I knew the computer had the power to make it work. I'd heard about things the mouse could do, but that wasn't enough. I was in error because I hadn't taken time to learn the proper order of commands to make it work.

There's no shortcut to knowing God, either. He has two manuals for us. The main instruction book is the Bible, and His second is the book of nature. The Bible *tells* us about God; nature *shows* us about God. We need to study them both. In the book of nature, what can you learn about God in

1. a flash of lightning? ____________
2. a baby kitten? ____________
3. leaves turning color in autumn? ____________
4. a waterfall? ____________
5. a bouquet of flowers? ____________

What do you think is the most interesting thing God has created? ____________

What does it show you about Him? ____________

____

Jesus replied, "You are in error because you do not know the Scriptures or the power of God." Matthew 22:29.

MARCH

18

About Love

A very smart Pharisee, a teacher of law, wanted to see how much Jesus really knew about the law, so he gave Him a one-question test. "Which is the greatest commandment?"

Jesus quoted two commandments that Moses had given the children of Israel—love God with all your heart (Deuteronomy 6:5), and love your neighbor as yourself (Leviticus 19:18). "The whole law of Moses and the teachings of the prophets depend on these two commandments," He said.

Jesus came to show us how to live this kind of love—and because of that, He died on the cross. Think how the cross also represents love—the up-and-down pole shows His love for God, and the crossbar with His hands reaching out shows His love for us.

Do you love God with all your heart, and do you love your neighbors as yourself?

All the stories during the past week have something to do with loving God or loving our neighbors.

1. Michael thought it was funny that Jord was afraid of high places, and it's easy to think that others are being silly when they do things we don't understand. Think of something someone else does that you think is stupid. Now pretend you're that person, and give every good reason that he or she may have for doing that thing.

2. An old saying says "Many hands make light work." Last Sabbath's text says "Carry each other's burdens." Think of at least one thing you could do to help carry the burden of someone else at home or at school. Become a "burden bearer" by doing this task for at least one week.

3. Wednesday's text has four parts of a word picture that David wrote to tell how he felt. Have you ever cried out to God like David did? How did you feel? Using ideas from Psalm 69:1-3 as a pattern, either write or tell how you felt. If you prefer, draw or paint a picture of what you felt. Then show how God answered your cries to Him.

4. Look back at all last week's texts, starting with Sabbath, and tell which hang under love to God and which hang under love to our neighbors. What does each one teach you about love?

On these two commandments hang all the Law and the Prophets. Matthew 22:40, NKJV.

MARCH

19

Charlie's Exam

Therefore keep watch, because you do not know the day or the hour. Matthew 25:13.

Charlie dreamed of having a good job and earning lots of money. To do this, he needed an education, but with so few schools in his country, he first needed to make one of the top scores on the entrance examination. He studied hard and was sure he would do well.

The exam was set for a Wednesday. All candidates were to be at their assigned school, in the examination room, and ready to write by 10:00 a.m. At that precise moment the door would be shut, and no other student allowed to enter.

Charlie lived a two-day walk from his examination center.

"Go a few days early," his parents advised.

"No," he argued. "I'll make it easily in two days."

Early Monday morning he started out and marked a steady pace on the paths that wound up and around and over the steep mountains. He was sure he would arrive on Tuesday afternoon, but he had not counted on the storm that gathered higher in the mountains. Rain began to pour down. He kept going. The next day, when he reached the river at the usual crossing, water swirled by dangerously swift and deep. It was impossible to cross. The only thing he could do was to detour miles downstream to the bridge. Darkness fell. He hurried on until he could no longer tell which direction to take. Finally he took shelter. At daybreak he saw that he was still a long way from the school. He ran. Up and over and around. Scrambling through brush, taking shortcuts. The sun slanted toward midmorning by the time he finally saw the school. He forced himself to run faster. Then he was dashing across the campus toward the examination room. He was eager to slide into a desk and actually have an examination paper in his hand. Then he stopped short.

"No!" he exclaimed. "It can't be!"

But it was. The door was closed. Frantically he pounded on it. "I've come to write the examination," he gasped to the teacher who opened the door.

"Sorry!" The teacher shook his head and pointed to his watch. "You're too late. It's five minutes past 10:00."

MARCH

The Ten Virgins

This is a dramatic reading from Matthew 25:1-13. (Instructions are on page 28.)

NARRATOR: At that time the kingdom of heaven will be like ten virgins who took their lamps and went out to meet the bridegroom. Five of them were foolish and five were wise. The foolish ones took their lamps but did not take any oil with them. The wise, however, took oil jars along with their lamps. The bridegroom was a long time in coming, and they all became drowsy and fell asleep. At midnight the cry rang out:

CRIER: Here's the bridegroom! Come out to meet him!

NARRATOR: Then all the virgins woke up and trimmed their lamps. The foolish ones said to the wise,

FOOLISH VIRGINS: Give us some of your oil; our lamps are going out.

WISE VIRGINS: No, there may not be enough for both us and you. Instead, go to those who sell oil and buy some for yourselves.

NARRATOR: But while they were on their way to buy the oil, the bridegroom arrived. The virgins who were ready went in with him to the wedding banquet. And the door was shut. Later the others also came.

FOOLISH VIRGINS: Sir! Sir! Open the door for us.

NARRATOR: But he replied,

SIR: I tell you the truth, I don't know you.

NARRATOR: Therefore keep watch, because you do not know the day or the hour.

✦ ✦ ✦

Something to think about:

1. This parable refers particularly to Jesus' second coming, and the oil represents the Holy Spirit. We also need this "oil" in everyday situations. Give at least three situations, and explain why you would need the oil.

A. ______________________________

B. ______________________________

C. ______________________________

2. In what ways did Charlie in yesterday's story have an experience like that of the ten virgins? ____________

____

____

At that time the kingdom of heaven will be like ten virgins who took their lamps and went out to meet the bridegroom. Matthew 25:1.

MARCH

21

Is Determination Enough?

There is a way that seems right to a man, but in the end it leads to death. Proverbs 14:12.

Captain Robert F. Scott, the British explorer, wanted to be the first person to reach the South Pole. His efforts to do that made his name famous—but he never lived to enjoy that fame.

In 1911 he and four companions set out, and for more than two and a half months they battled their way across hundreds of miles of one of the coldest and most desolate landscapes in the world so that they could have the honor of being the first people to reach the South Pole.

Professional polar explorers of the time recommended methods and equipment that they had found most suitable. But Scott had his own ideas. He decided to use ponies rather than sled dogs, and he chose food, clothing, tents, and other supplies that the men with more experience questioned. Nevertheless, he knew what he wanted.

Despite the hard going and the serious problems they had with their equipment, Scott and his men pushed themselves onward because they knew others also wanted to be first. On January 17, 1912, battling against a headwind in temperatures of 22° F, they reached their goal.

"The Pole. Yes," Scott wrote in his diary, "but under very different circumstances than those expected." They found flags snapping in the wind, flags left 34 days earlier by a party of Norwegian explorers led by Roald Amundsen.

Extremely disappointed, Scott and his men turned back northward. By now they had to pull their sleds by hand—their ponies couldn't take the extreme conditions. The deadly cold penetrated their clothing, which lacked the extra protection of furs. They hadn't cached enough food for their return. Finally, in mid-March, frostbitten and starving, they couldn't go any farther. Seven months later a search party found their bodies and the diaries they had kept of their struggles. They were only 11 miles from a large cache of food and supplies.

Scott's bravery in his death has made his name legendary, but had he listened to the advice of those with more experience, he and his four companions need not have died when they did.

As Amundsen, the explorer who reached the pole first, said, "Bravery, determination, strength they did not lack. A little more experience would have crowned their work with success."

MARCH

22

Al and the Puff Adder

If we confess our sins, he is faithful and just and will forgive us our sins and purify us from all unrighteousness. 1 John 1:9.

Al was definitely old enough—and certainly smart enough—to understand the dangers of handling poisonous snakes without using the proper equipment. But he liked snakes and enjoyed the excitement of catching them.

"Snakes are helpful," he would say to the workers on his farm, and then tell them how some snakes help control the rats and mice, which damage farm crops. "People don't need to kill them; they should just leave them alone."

If he'd only followed his own advice, all may have gone well.

Several kinds of poisonous snakes lived in the area where he worked. He enjoyed playing with them and had caught several. One day he saw a puff adder basking on a path. On impulse he caught it. Carrying it home, he held it as one must hold a venomous snake. He put his forefinger on top of its head and slipped his thumb and middle finger into the spaces between the rear angle of its jaw and its spine. Held that way, it couldn't strike. He draped the mottled yellowish-brown body along his forearm and stopped to show his neighbor.

"Isn't it beautiful!" he exclaimed, holding his arm toward her and passing his free hand along the rather stout body.

His neighbor took a step backward. "I suppose you could say that," she said, trying to keep her voice steady.

"I'm going to keep it safe in my house!" Al continued.

The snake, though, didn't understand. When Al tried to put it down, it flicked its head around and bit his finger.

Puff adder venom attacks body tissue and blood cells and can cause death. Al knew this and became very frightened, so he rushed to the hospital for help. Fortunately he didn't get a killing dose of the snake's poison, but his arm became swollen and turned black all the way to his shoulder, and his finger will probably always be stiff.

Al knew about puff adders. Still he risked handling one without proper equipment, and now he'll have to live with the consequences for the rest of his life.

Can you think of ways that sin is like the puff adder?

Thank God that He is always ready to forgive even when we make foolish choices, but sometimes He has to let us live with the consequences of those choices.

MARCH

23

Talk to God Often

Why do you call me, "Lord, Lord," and do not do what I say? Luke 6:46.

Kurt and Rob and a gang of their friends had piled into Kurt's dad's old pickup and headed toward the foothills for an afternoon of hiking. As they bounced along the dirt road, the tire caught the end of a broken branch, flinging it upward. Its knobbed end crashed against the door just at the edge of the open window.

"Whoa!" exclaimed Kurt. "That was close!" A worried expression crossed his face. "I knew we should've prayed before we left. Someone could've gotten hurt."

"What?" Rob demanded. "It sounds like you think prayer's a good luck charm—so you won't get hurt."

"Of course not!" Kurt's answer was definite. "But the Bible promises that God'll send His angels."

Rob was silent for a moment.

"The angels must have been here anyhow," he finally said. "No one was hurt."

It was Kurt's turn to be puzzled by his friend's idea. "Don't you think it's good to ask God's protection before you go somewhere?" he asked.

"Sure. But I'd rather talk to God enough so that I know His angels are with me all the time. Besides, haven't you ever heard about good Christians, praying people, who've been killed in accidents even when they've prayed for God to send His angels?"

"Yeah . . ."

"So, what happened?"

"Maybe God thought it was best for them to die then."

"But they prayed and believed that He'd send his angels to keep them safe on the road. And bang! That was it. Wouldn't that make a person mad?"

Kurt began to chuckle. He was beginning to see Rob's point. "How could they be? The next thing they'll know, they'll be seeing Jesus coming in the clouds. Instead of getting to wherever they'd planned to go, they'll be on their way to heaven."

Rob nodded. "That's why I like to talk to God often, not just call for protection when I expect trouble or ask for things. If we're going to be like Him, then we've got to know what He's like. I always want His angels and His Spirit to be with me so that I'll be ready to go to heaven at any time."

MARCH

24

The Appearance of the Likeness, Part 1

This was the appearance and structure of the wheels: They sparkled like chrysolite, and all four looked alike. Each appeared to be made like a wheel intersecting a wheel.
Ezekiel 1:16.

Ezekiel saw things—a whirlwind with fire and lightning, creatures with four wings and four faces, and wheels with rims full of eyes—and he heard powerful noises. Now he had a big problem. As far as he knew, no other person had ever seen such sights, yet God expected him to tell the people about them.

God's people, the children of Israel, were captives in Babylon. To help them understand why, God chose Ezekiel as His messenger. Ezekiel was overwhelmed with the task God gave him. What words could he use to describe the strange yet fantastic things he had seen? How could he describe them so that the people would understand? Even though the task was difficult, Ezekiel obeyed, and not only did he tell the people the messages God gave him, he also described the visions in a book.

In the first chapter of his book, Ezekiel tells about seeing creatures and wheels and an "expanse, sparkling like ice, and awesome" and hearing sounds "like the roar of rushing waters, like the voice of the Almighty, like the tumult of an army." Over and over in his efforts to describe the scene, he used expressions such as "was like" or "looked like" or "like." Since no one had ever seen such wonders, the best Ezekiel could do was to compare them to things they did know.

Ellen White had the same problem trying to describe what she saw in her visions of heaven. She had no choice but to use words and references to everyday things that we know.

People still puzzle over Ezekiel's descriptions of the wheels within the wheels, and they wonder what exactly he did see. Ezekiel himself, though, gives an explanation of that vision. He says, "This was the appearance of the likeness of the glory of the Lord" (Ezekiel 1:28).

SOMETHING TO DO: Using the index to the writings of Ellen G. White, find the reference for and look up a vision that she had of heaven. What words and techniques did she use to describe what she saw?

MARCH

25

The Appearance of the Likeness, Part 2

I saw that from what appeared to be his waist up he looked like glowing metal, as if full of fire, and that from there down he looked like fire; and brilliant light surrounded him. Like the appearance of a rainbow in the clouds on a rainy day, so was the radiance around him. This was the appearance of the likeness of the glory of the Lord. Ezekiel 1:27, 28.

Yesterday we talked about the difficulties Ezekiel had in describing what he saw in the visions God gave him. In order to get an idea of the problem Ezekiel had, pretend that you know someone who has never seen or heard of an airplane. This person doesn't even know what a car or a motor is. How would you describe a jet airliner to the person? What comparisons could you make so that he or she could picture its size and shape and sound? Here are some idea starters.

A jetliner is shaped like ____________________.
It looks like ______________________________.
It is as big as/bigger than __________________.
Inside it is like ___________________________.
It flies like ______________________________.
It sounds like ____________________________.

You can also experiment with having another person draw an object as you describe it. Keep the object out of sight. (A good thing is a baby's small busy box with simple, moving parts.) Without using the names of the object or its parts, tell what it looks like. Use place words such as "on," "under," "behind" to tell where the different parts are located. How does the picture compare with the original item?

Now have someone with a expressive voice read Ezekiel 1 aloud from a modern language version such as the *Good News Bible*. While you listen, close your eyes and try to picture what Ezekiel saw. Describe the picture you would paint to match Ezekiel's description of his vision.

MARCH

26

Why Do Bad Things Feel So Good?

Love the Lord your God with all your heart and with all your soul and with all your strength. Deuteronomy 6:5.

"How can anything that feels so good be so wrong?" Jeremy was crying. He and his girlfriend were in trouble—big trouble. They were young, way too young to get married, yet they faced a very big decision. What should they do about the baby?

Love is one of the best and strongest feelings in the world. There's nothing that can be compared to being in love with someone who loves you back. But love out of control is also one of the most dangerous feelings in the world. That is why God has given so many commandments about love. We could list them in this order:

1. Love the Lord with all your heart (Deuteronomy 6:5; Luke 10:27).

2. Love your neighbor as yourself (Leviticus 9:18; Luke 10:27).

3. Thou shalt not commit adultery (Exodus 20:14; Deuteronomy 5:18).

If things that lead us into trouble didn't feel (or look or taste) good, we would never have any problem with sin. Satan knows this very well. That's why he catches our attention with things that seem good, then uses them as a trap. That's why God begs us to love Him more than anyone else and to trust Him enough to follow His commandments. He gave the "thou shalt nots" to help us stay out of trouble.

The seventh commandment is about impurity of any kind. It's against doing or saying or even thinking anything impure. Love itself is pure and good, yet the good feelings of love can be dangerous. They feel so good that, like Jeremy, you can wonder why anything bad could ever possibly happen because of them.

If you have chosen God as your best friend, and if you talk to Him about everything, He will help you know when your feelings are starting to lead you into trouble. He wants you to choose to do things His way. When you make that choice, He will help you be strong. He also provides help in the form of Christian counselors and books and other information. Remember, keep God first. Talk to Him about everything. Don't be fooled into doing dangerous things just because they feel good.

MARCH

27

Rob's Bible

Come near to God and he will come near to you. Wash your hands, you sinners, and purify your hearts, you double-minded. James 4:8.

"You can't follow God unless you refuse to do what *you* want and choose to obey *Him*."

Pastor Brown's words zinged into Rob's thoughts. He dropped his eyes and studied his Bible. It was leather-bound and had lots of illustrations and notes. "It's made to last for years," Gramps said when Rob had opened it on his birthday. "Make it your special study Bible."

Rob had intended to do just that. He loved to read in the evening, and he put the Bible on the stand beside his bed. *That's just the problem,* he told himself as he turned the Bible over in his hands. *If only . . .*

The Bible stayed on the stand, close at hand, but inside the stand Rob had a stash of adventure stories. *Just a couple of chapters,* he always promised himself when he crawled into bed. But once he'd started a book, Rob couldn't seem to make himself put it down until he had finished the last page. Then, eyes heavy with sleep, he'd stuff the book back into his nightstand, too tired even to look at his Bible.

Sometime past Saturday midnight, Rob started awake. The curtains flapped, and wild drops of rain pelted his face. He jumped up and slammed the window shut. The next Friday, during his usual one-two touch of room cleaning, he picked up his Bible. It felt puffy. He opened it, and most of Genesis turned in one lump. He tried to pull the pages apart, but they were as stuck as if someone had poured glue over them. Then he remembered the storm and his open window.

If I'd looked at my Bible even the next day, he scolded himself. *Maybe I could have dried it properly.*

"Come near to God, and He'll come near to you," Pastor Brown continued.

Rob still stared at his Bible. The cover looked good, but he'd had to take out most of Genesis. *I do want to come near to God,* he told himself, *but I couldn't keep this Bible nice for even one year—not because I used it too much, but because I didn't use it enough.*

MARCH

28

Be Still!

Be still, and know that I am God; I will be exalted among the nations, I will be exalted in the earth! *Psalm 46:10, NKJV.*

"Would you please *be still!*"

Have you ever heard that said by a parent, a teacher, a brother, or a sister?

What words best describe the tone of voice that is usually used when you hear those words?

______________________________.

Why do you think that tone of voice is used?

______________________________.

Is it possible to be noisy and not make a sound?

______________________________.

Think about Rob and his Bible in yesterday's story.

Rob wanted to get to know God better, and he intended to study his Bible. But . . . Even though he wasn't boisterous and rowdy, Rob was "noisy" in his relationship with God. His mind was so occupied with adventure stories that he didn't make time to read his Bible.

We need to spend time being still in order to know God, but often, even when we are very quiet on the outside, our thoughts can be very noisy. They rush off into exciting adventures, and we imagine ourselves heroes of dangerous missions, or involved in a thrilling romance, or the star of our favorite team, or . . . There are as many daydreams as there are people. Daydreaming keeps our mind too busy to think God thoughts, and sometimes it takes something very loud—maybe even harsh—before He can get our attention.

For Rob, it took having his good Bible ruined before he realized the importance of spending a quiet time with God. God's number one way of speaking to us is through the Bible, but He also speaks to us by the Holy Spirit's impressions on our minds. In order to recognize the Holy Spirit, though, we have to learn to listen. We need to "be still" to know God.

What are some of the "noisy" things that could get in the way of your taking time to know God better?

____

____

Make a three-step plan for cutting down the "noise" so you can spend more time being still and getting to know God.

1. ______________________________
2. ______________________________
3. ______________________________

MARCH

29

Lawrence

Do not be overcome by evil, but overcome evil with good.
Romans 12:21.

Lawrence stuffed his hands in his pockets and scrunched up his shoulders. It was as if by looking down he could sort of disappear and not be noticed by the others. It was not fun to be fat and to have the biggest—and flattest—feet in the class. The others thought his size was a big joke, and they never tired of reminding him. Their teasing hurt. Lawrence could not deny that he was fat and had big, flat feet. He hunched down even farther in an attempt to blend into the grayness of the chair he'd chosen in a far corner of the gym.

"Each of us has a special talent."

Fat chance! Lawrence slouched down even more.

"We need to be honest with ourselves," the speaker continued, "and accept our handicaps, then focus on what we can do well. I can't walk anymore, but that doesn't mean I can't live a useful life. I just have to live differently than you."

For the first time Lawrence focused on the man.

"Most of us try to hide our problems. One of my friends is going deaf, and for years she wore a hairstyle that hid her hearing aid. The strange looks she received when her replies didn't fit the conversation started her to thinking. She began wearing her hair so people could see her hearing aid—that helped others realize she couldn't hear well, and they began speaking more directly and clearly to her.

"For me, it's pretty hard to hide my wheelchair."

Lawrence laughed along with the others.

"At first I felt angry about being crippled. Then I learned the secret of focusing on what I can do. That's not only helped me; it also helps others to be more accepting of my handicap. Life becomes happier when we find the good things about ourselves and put our energies into developing them. It's the old principle of overcoming evil with good."

That idea started Lawrence to thinking.

Do you waste your energy by worrying about your problems and handicaps? Or do you invest your energy by developing your talents?

MARCH

30

The World's Largest Easter Egg

Then I saw another angel flying in midair, and he had the eternal gospel to proclaim to those who live on the earth—to every nation, tribe, language and people. Revelation 14:6.

"Wow!" Travis pointed at the huge bronze-and-silver-and-gold egg that was more than 25 feet long. It stood on a slim stand in the Vegerville park and turned gently in the wind like a giant weather vane. "That looks just like the egg Grandma has—why's it there?"

"The people of the town had it made as a special gift in honor of the one hundredth birthday of the Royal Canadian Mounted Police," his mother replied.

"Huh? An egg for the police?"

"Well, you see, a lot of people who live here in the Vegerville area, like us, are descendants of settlers who came from the Ukraine to farm on the Canadian prairies. And you're right, this egg is similar to the keepsake egg Grandma has."

Travis wrinkled his face. "So . . . ?"

"So," his mother repeated, "the Ukrainian people have a special art of decorating Easter eggs—*pysanky*, they call them, which comes from their word meaning 'to write.' Each design has a special meaning, and the people used to make eggs for each other and exchange them on Easter morning. For example, giving farmers eggs that had the symbol for wheat would be a way of wishing them to have a good harvest.

"But why'd they put an egg here for the police?"

His mother laughed. "The people appreciated the bravery of the Mounties in protecting the early settlers. Since many of them were Ukrainians, they decided to make the world's largest *pysanka* to carry their special one hundredth birthday wishes."

She pointed to the silver band going around the huge metal egg. "That band and those three pointed stars represent the pioneers' strong faith, and the silver triangles pointing to the band are the wolves' teeth design, which stands for the main message of the egg—that the RCMP protected the pioneers and made them feel secure on their farms."

"You mean an egg can say all that?" Travis asked.

"And more." His mother pointed to some of the other designs. "Ask Grandma. She can tell you all about *pysanky* and their meanings."

Does your family follow any tradition for giving good wishes such as sending flowers or cards or treats? Do those good wishes include the best news of all—that Jesus Christ died and rose and has gone to heaven to prepare a place for us?

MARCH

31

Most Beautiful of All

Because of our sins he was given over to die, and he was raised to life in order to put us right with God.
Romans 4:25, TEV.

So you want I should tell you all about *pysanky*."

Travis nodded. He sat on a stool close to the fireplace. He enjoyed listening to his grandmother's accent and the interesting way she put her words together.

"To tell everything would take many days talking," she said, "but I tell you when I was little girl on farm, my own grandmother she showed me about *pysanky*, how you take eggs without cooking and use dyes and beeswax and *kitska*—that pen special for making *pysanky*—and after many, many days' working you have beautiful *pysanky*."

As he listened to the rhythm of his grandmother's voice, he looked again at the *pysanka* standing in a special box on a shelf of her bookcase, and he thought of the huge *pysanka* in the park. His grandmother talked on about how making these special eggs goes back to the time when the people in the Ukraine still worshiped pagan gods. About the year 1000 missionaries came with the story of Jesus, and then the people gave Christian meanings to the symbols of this egg-decorating art.

The sun became the Son of God. The three-pointed star that once meant air, fire, and water now represented the Father, Son, and Holy Spirit. People even started telling a story about a peddler named Simon, who long, long ago was taking his basket of eggs to market one Friday when he met an angry crowd hollering insults at a man carrying a heavy cross. The man looked so weak that Simon felt sorry for him. Setting his basket of eggs at the roadside, he put the cross on his own shoulder and carried it for the man. When he came back to where he left his basket, all his eggs had been changed into beautiful *pysanky*, and ever after that, he always had those beautifully colored eggs to sell.

"Is that true?" Travis asked.

His grandmother shook her head. "That's just story someone made up, not at all like story in Bible," she said.

"Traditions are interesting," his mother added. "People in the Ukraine used to believe that *pysanky* could protect them against fire and other dangers, and they kept baskets of them sitting in the house for good luck. From these and other stories of the *pysanky* we can learn many things about our forefathers' beliefs—and the art itself is also very beautiful."

"Yes, beautiful," agreed his grandmother. "But most beautiful of all is truth about Jesus in Bible and how He died for us so we can be made right with God."

APRIL

1

Only Joking

Like a madman shooting firebrands or deadly arrows is a man who deceives his neighbor and says, "I was only joking!"
Proverbs 26:18, 19.

"Come quick! Kalim's hurt himself!"

The shrill of Laura's voice sent a stab of fright through Mrs. McNab. She jumped up from her chair and hurried to the office door.

Laura stood in the hall, motioning her to hurry. "He's fallen!" she exclaimed. "He can't move."

Mrs. McNab dashed toward the end of the hall where Kalim's body lay in a grotesque huddle. "What happened?" she asked Laura as she dropped to her knees and reached out to feel his forehead. Just then both Laura and Kalim burst into peals of laughter.

"April fool!" they both shouted.

Mrs. McNab straightened slowly, head down, shoulders starting to shake. Laura and Kalim stopped midlaugh and stared. Mrs. McNab was not laughing as they had expected. She was crying.

"But . . . but it's just a joke!" Laura explained, not knowing what else to say.

Mrs. McNab said nothing.

"It's April Fools' Day." Laura's words sounded stupid in her own ears.

Mrs. McNab looked up. Her face looked sort of chalky, and she didn't smile. "Some jokes are not funny." Her voice sounded flat. "I've been called before when someone was"—she paused a moment—"worse than hurt." She shook her head. "It's terrible." She started to say something else, but instead turned and headed toward her office, leaving the two young people with their thoughts.

Medical science tells us that a merry heart really is good like a medicine and that a good laugh is excellent for your health. April Fools' Day is a good time to have healthful laughs—if you have good jokes.

Make five rules that could help everyone have a happy, healthful April Fools' Day.

1. ______________________________
2. ______________________________
3. ______________________________
4. ______________________________
5. ______________________________

APRIL

2

According to His Will

If we ask anything according to his will, he hears us.
1 John 5:14.

One Thursday night 11 men followed their Leader along a quiet path that led away from the city. It had been a long and busy week, and they were tired—very tired—and worried. Their Leader seemed to have a lot on His mind.

"Wait here," He told eight of them.

He motioned for the other three to keep following Him. By now He seemed extremely upset and worried, and after a bit He told them He felt so sad that it was like being crushed to death. He begged the three to watch with Him—and pray.

That was Jesus' last night on this earth with His disciples. He knew it was their last night together, but they didn't. He also knew that soon a crowd would come to arrest Him and that before the sun would go down the next day He would be tortured and crucified.

The thought was terrifying. How He wished He didn't have to die like that. He knew He really didn't have to, but eons earlier He and His father had made a plan. The future of the entire universe depended on what He did that very night.

In terrible agony Jesus threw Himself down on the ground and pleaded with God. "Father, all things are possible with You. Take this cup of suffering away from Me. Yet, not what I want, but what You want."

Jesus knew it was God's will that He die, but He still asked to be excused—if possible. Earlier, He'd also shared an idea like this with His disciples.

IF . . . we ask according to God's will,
and
IF . . . we know that He listens,
THEN . . . we know we'll get what we've asked for.

Jesus followed His own advice and asked according to God's will. God heard and answered—He sent an angel to give Jesus strength.

Are you willing, like Jesus, to do God's will? God will send His angels to give you the strength you need.

APRIL

3

Pastor Phillipe's Cross

If anyone would come after me, he must deny himself and take up his cross daily and follow me. Luke 9:23.

Pastor Phillipe stirred in his sleep. He seemed to hear voices, many of them. Then in a dream he saw people filing by, among them the members of his congregation, and each one carried a cross—some crosses were big, some were little. Deacon Ezekiel paused as he passed. "Hurry!" he called to the pastor. "Get your cross and join us before it's too late."

"My cross? Where?"

Deacon Ezekiel pointed behind the church. "Over there," he called. "Hurry!"

Pastor Phillipe found his cross, and it looked very, very big. He knelt with one knee on the ground, hoisted the cross onto his shoulder, then struggled to his feet, and took a few steps. The cross was so heavy that he could hardly walk. He stopped and watched the line of people going by. All the other crosses seemed smaller than his.

How can I possibly be expected to carry such a big cross? Pastor Phillipe wondered. He looked thoughtful. *I know what I can do,* he thought. He carried the cross around to his shop, found a saw, and cut a chunk from the bottom of it. *No one will ever notice the difference,* he told himself. He lifted the cross to his shoulder and found it much easier to carry. Then he took his saw and hooked it onto his belt under his coat.

Before long, the cross began to feel heavy again. When he thought no one was looking, Pastor Phillipe carried it to the side of the path, took out the saw, and cut off some more. He did this several more times.

Finally, after they'd been walking for a very long time, he could see a big beautiful white church in the distance. People seemed to put their crosses down, then go into the church. When Pastor Phillipe got closer, he saw that a deep chasm cut across the path between them and the church. As each person reached the edge, the canyon's steep walls moved either farther apart or closer together until they exactly matched the length of the cross the person carried. He saw Deacon Ezekiel stop at the edge. The walls moved. He set his cross down—it exactly bridged the gap, and he walked safely across.

When Pastor Phillipe's turn came, he watched the walls move farther and farther apart. As he looked down, down over the steep walls into the darkness below, the saw fell from his belt. He could never get to the other side—his cross was too short!

APRIL

4

The Missing Stop Sign

These things happened to them as examples and were written down as warnings for us, on whom the fulfillment of the ages has come. 1 Corinthians 10:11.

It was a just-right spring day for the family to go exploring in their new car. They crisscrossed farmland, then followed roads into the gently wooded hills, and then turned again toward another valley.

"Oh, look!" Shana said as she pointed toward another farm. Flower beds flanked the house, but her attention went to the white-fenced paddock beside the barn. "See all the horses! Aren't they beautiful?"

Her father slowed so that they could have a better look.

"Are horses all you can think about?" her brother teased.

The road led uphill toward another intersection. A pickup truck swooped along the sloping crossroad. Her father gave it a quick glance, but maintained his speed.

"Daddy!" The word shrilled into a scrream that blended into a loud smash. The car was dragged around into a skid, and slid to a halt against the dirt bank, while the blue truck careened on down the hill.

"Are you all right?" Her father's question took in the entire family. They climbed out, shaky but unhurt, and gathered to stare at the car's crumpled front. In a few moments the truck drove back to where they stood. The door on the passenger's side was caved in. The farmer hurried toward them. He shook his head and pointed to a broken post beside the road. "That's where the stop sign stood last night," he said. "Some young folks think it's a big joke to steal stop signs."

"Joke?" Shana looked at their bashed-in car and at the pickup. *If the stop sign had been in its place, Daddy wouldn't have hit that truck,* she thought.

The police came, noted the evidence, and declared it a "no-fault" accident. Insurance would fix both the car and the truck, but that couldn't bring back the carefree happiness of the afternoon. Shana was glad they were not hurt, but she wondered how those who had taken the stop sign would feel if it were their new car that had been wrecked.

Satan tried to break down the "stop signs" that God has given us in the Bible. What are some of them? Why are they there?

APRIL

5

Hard as a Diamond

It will be like living among scorpions. Still, don't be afraid of those rebels or of anything they say. Ezekiel 2:6, TEV.

Get that thing!" Sherry screamed and pointed toward the corner. The "thing" steadied its flat, red-brown body on a series of legs as it groped about with two large-jointed arms that ended in heavy pincers. The pincers opened and closed methodically. A barbed stinger was poised at the end of the whiplike tail that arched over its back. "Get it!" she screamed again.

Bill dashed into the room. With a deftly aimed shoe, he took care of the invader. "All that noise for such a little thing!" he exclaimed. "Why, it's hardly more than two inches long!"

"There'd have been even more noise if someone had stepped on it in the dark!" his wife replied.

The mission house hadn't been lived in for several months, except by the assortment of small creatures that awaited Bill and Sherry's arrival. "Always use a light at night," their neighbors warned. "You never know what might be out and about. One of the earlier missionaries didn't, and he sat on a scorpion."

Some scorpions in the mission area carried a dangerous poison. Others caused a painful, though harmless, sting. Sherry had waged a housecleaning war, but hadn't yet cleared out all the invaders.

"I now have much more sympathy for what Ezekiel had to put up with when God called him to be a prophet to the captives in Babylon," she said to Bill one day. "God warned him that carrying His message to them would be like living among scorpions! Those people must have been terrible! How could he ever have had the courage to do it?"

"God promised to make him as tough as they were," Bill replied. "He said He'd make Ezekiel as firm as a rock and as hard as a diamond." Bill smiled. "That gives me the courage to know that no matter where God calls us—whether to our misison here or elsewhere—He'll give us the strength we need if we trust Him. He'll even give us the courage to cope with real scorpions!"

Sherry laughed and nodded. "Courage, yes," she agreed. "He has given me the power to cope, but I still don't like looking at those ugly little brown creepy-crawlies!"

Have you ever had to do anything that was like "living among scorpions"? In what ways did God make you "hard as a diamond" so that you could cope with the situation?

APRIL

6

Abbey Kalenga's Story

Don't let anyone deceive you in any way. 2 Thessalonians 2:3.

"I always miss your husband when I'm in town," the young man apologized when Mrs. Cowlings answered the door. "I'm Abbey Kalenga. My mission isn't far from his ADRA projects—and I need his help."

Mrs. Cowlings listened sympathetically as Abbey told his story. He seemed like such a nice young man.

"I have friends in Europe who want to send school and medical supplies for a project I've started in another village," he explained. "Since I'm from out of town, I'm wondering if your husband would let me use his address. If he will, I'll share the supplies with you."

"I'll ask my husband when he gets back," Mrs. Cowlings promised.

Not many days later Abbey Kalenga came to see her again. They chatted, sharing experiences and talking of Bible promises. "A terrible thing happened this morning," he confided after a while. "You know the place they call thieves' corner. I'd just come from cashing a check at the bank. Some fellows bumped into me, grabbed my briefcase, and disappeared. All my money for my trip home is gone!"

Such things happened frequently.

"I was wondering—could you lend me enough to get home? I hate to ask. I can pay it back my next trip into town."

"It was a lot of money," Mrs. Cowlings admitted to her husband later, "but he was such a pleasant young man, and he talked about the Bible as though he knew it very well. His story seemed so believable."

As it turned out, Abbey Kalenga didn't work for any mission. Rather, he was a very talented con artist who specialized in telling lies in order to get money and things from missionaries. He and one of his buddies had been staying at another Protestant denomination. Mrs. Cowlings didn't find this out, though, until after he'd disappeared with her money.

She learned the hard way that it's not wise to trust strangers—not even those who are nice and pleasant and who can quote the Bible—without first checking the truth of what they say.

APRIL

7

The Young Man of God

But even if we or an angel from heaven should preach a gospel other than the one we preached to you, let him be eternally condemned! Galatians 1:8.

A young man received a message from God to take to the king. "Deliver this message, but don't stay to eat or drink anything afterward," God told him. "Don't even go back the same way you came."

The young man of God delivered his message, climbed onto his donkey, and started home by another route. Soon he heard someone riding up behind him. It was an old man. "Come home with me and have something to eat," the old man invited.

"I can't," replied the young man of God. "The word of the Lord said that I wasn't to eat bread or drink water or to return by the way I came."

"I'm also a prophet," said the old man. "An angel told me by the word of the Lord to bring you back to my house so you can eat bread and drink water."

This man's a prophet, and he's older, thought the young man of God. *And God's told him to take me to his house and feed me.* Even though God had warned him not to eat or drink anything, he turned his donkey around and followed the old prophet to his house. While they were sitting at the table, the word of the Lord came to the old prophet.

"The Lord says you disobeyed Him," he told the young man. "Because of this you'll be killed."

After they finished eating, he helped the young man saddle his donkey, and sent him on his way. As the young man was riding along the road, a lion attacked him and killed him.

This strange story, told in 1 Kings 13, shows the importance of trusting God's Word, no matter who may say it's been changed. When the old prophet invited the young man, the Bible adds this sentence—"But the old prophet was lying" (verse 18, TEV).

People, like Abbey Kalenga in yesterday's story, can sound so truthful. "I thought about checking with the mission where he said he worked," Mrs. Cowlings said later. "But he was so polite and nice, and everything he told me sounded so believable. I just took him at his word."

"Don't let anyone—not even someone who seems like an angel from heaven—tell you anything different than the gospel of Jesus," warns Paul in the New Testament.

APRIL

8

The Most Important of All

The stone which the builders rejected as worthless turned out to be the most important of all.
Mark 12:10, TEV.

"You can't," God told King David, "but your son can."

David was very disappointed. He wanted to be the one to build a temple for God—the most beautiful temple in all the world.

"But you can make the plans and get everything ready."

David sent people to different countries to search for the finest building materials. He ordered gold and silver, bronze and iron, wood and stone. He had detailed plans drawn so that everything could be made to measure. Lumber was trimmed to the exact size in the forest. Stones were cut to precise dimensions in the quarries. Each piece taken to the building site in Jerusalem would be ready-made to fit exactly into its place without having to be cut or trimmed.

When the huge stones for the foundations and the walls were ready, workmen hauled them to the city. One large stone lay across the path. It was big and awkward and didn't seem to fit anywhere, so it stayed where the haulers had dumped it.

"Can't anyone take this big thing out of the way?" several of the workmen complained as they struggled to drag other stones around it. So they pushed it to the side.

Finally the builders were ready to lay the cornerstone. They looked and looked for the right stone. It must be big and strong and have the right shape, because the safety of the entire building depended on it. They tested several. Some cracked during weather changes; others crumbled under heavy weight. Finally someone suggested the big, awkward stone. The builders examined it. Neither summer sun nor winter storms had damaged it. They gave it the pressure test, and it stood firm. They brought it to the corner, and it fit exactly. It had been made for that position, but even the trained builders had not recognized it.

In a vision the prophet Isaiah saw that this stone represented Christ. When Jesus came to this world, many Jewish leaders who studied the Scriptures didn't recognize Him as the Messiah. Others did, though, and they accepted Him as their Saviour.

Is Jesus the chief cornerstone of your life? Does He fit into your heart and mind? Is He the most important one to you?

APRIL

The Crippled Woman

This is a dramatic reading from Luke 13:10-17, TEV. (See page 28 for instructions.)

NARRATOR: One Sabbath Jesus was teaching in a synagogue. A woman there had an evil spirit that had made her sick for eighteen years; she was bent over and could not straighten up at all. When Jesus saw her, he called out to her,

JESUS: "Woman, you are free from your sickness!"

NARRATOR: He placed his hands on her, and at once she straightened herself up and praised God.

The official of the synagogue was angry that Jesus had healed on the Sabbath, so he spoke up and said to the people,

OFFICIAL: "There are six days in which we should work; so come during those days and be healed, but not on the Sabbath!"

NARRATOR: The Lord answered him,

JESUS: "You hypocrites! Any one of you would untie his ox or his donkey from the stall and take it out to give it water on the Sabbath. Now here is this descendant of Abraham whom Satan has kept in bonds for eighteen years; should she not be released on the Sabbath?"

NARRATOR: His answer made his enemies ashamed of themselves, while the people rejoiced over all the wonderful things that he did.

1. In this story, what two things did Jesus do to heal the woman?

____

2. Why might this make the leader of the synagogue angry?

____

3. Why did His answer make His enemies ashamed of themselves?

____

Using the ideas in this story as thought-starters, make a list of at least five things to do on the Sabbath that would be pleasing to God. (Suggested answers are on page 380.)

1. __________________________________
2. __________________________________
3. __________________________________
4. __________________________________
5. __________________________________

I, the Lord your God, rescued you by my great power and strength. That is why I command you to observe the Sabbath. Deuteronomy 5:15, TEV.

APRIL

10

Simba's Measure

With the measure you use, it will be measured to you. *Matthew 7:2.*

Excited voices passed the message from house to house. "An elephant has been shot; the chief wants all the men to come."

"Take baskets and knives," the chief instructed the men when they gathered, "and prepare the meat. When you have finished, bring everything to my house."

The men hurried off to do as the chief had said. Several sang as they worked, but Simba did not. His name meant lion, and he was known in the village for being one of the strongest hunters. He was also known for his bad attitude. He went from person to person. "What does the chief expect by telling us to bring all the meat to his house?" he asked.

"The chief has spoken, and we must do as he says," the others said.

"You go ahead," Simba retorted. "He makes us do all the work, and then he takes everything for his own family. He'll see what he gets from me!" He found a place in the shade of a tree and sat and watched while the others worked. When at last everyone was ready to leave, he jumped up and started scooping things into his basket. "Just see how the chief likes this!" he muttered to himself as he hoisted his heavy load to his shoulder and started down the trail after the others. When they reached the village, the men carried their baskets to the chief 's courtyard.

"This is indeed a day of happiness!" the chief exclaimed when he saw the many full baskets.

"Happiness!" Simba grumbled to himself. "For him, of course, because he takes everything."

"You have done well," the chief countinued. "I want each of you to pick up your basket and take it to your house and give it to your wife. There will be feasting for you and your families."

Sounds of happiness echoed through the village when the women saw all the food their husbands had brought home. That is, there were sounds of happiness from every house but one. Simba's wife turned from him in disgust. "Look what this miserable husband has brought for his family to eat!" she shouted to her neighbors.

Curious, they came to look. Simba's basket was heaped with nothing but dirt and garbage.

"In the same way you judge others, you will be judged, and with the measure you use, it will be measured to you."

APRIL

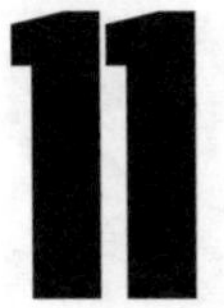

A Pattern Prayer

This, then, is how you should pray. Matthew 6:9.

When Namib prayed, his thoughts skipped around so that sometimes he'd even forget that he was talking to God.

"Try writing out your prayers," his grandfather suggested.

Namib did. One day he used the Lord's Prayer as a model. This is what he wrote:

"**Our Father in heaven, hallowed be your name.** God, do You mind if I call You 'Dad'? That makes it easier for me to talk to You.

"**Your kingdom come, your will be done on earth as it is in heaven.** I wish You'd send Jesus to take us to heaven so we could get away from all the bad things here. But I guess it isn't time yet, so, like Grandpa says, I need help learning how to do things Your way.

"**Give us today our daily bread.** Mom has lots of stuff in the cupboards, so we've got plenty to eat. But, I know, I eat too many sweets. I need help not to overdo so my mind'll be clear and my body strong.

"**Forgive us our debts, as we also have forgiven our debtors.** I still don't even want to talk to Loren because of the eggs that he and his gang smeared on my dad's office windows—just because they don't like where we come from. You know, too, how much fun I have teasing Yves and calling him 'Frog' 'cause it makes him mad. I want You to forgive me—so I guess You want me to forgive Loren and apologize to Yves, and . . . I never thought about it before, but it seems as though forgiveness has a lot to do with treating others the way we'd like them to treat us.

"**And lead us not into temptation, but deliver us from the evil one.** Back to the last point for this one. I guess kids like Yves don't find my teasing so funny. I want to be like You, so that means I have to learn how to hold my tongue. But I need Your help. Oh, how I need Your help!"

Experiment with rewriting the Lord's Prayer as Namib did. Think about one section at a time. What everyday things—good and bad—in your life fit each section? Use specific words to tell God about them.

APRIL

12

Names Make News

Our Father in heaven, hallowed be your name. Matthew 6:9.

"Hey, did you see the paper this morning?" Jason held up a copy of the local daily, and then without waiting for an answer he opened to page 7 and spread it on the desk. "See!" He pointed to a story in the bottom right corner. "There's my mom's name. It's all about the cooking school she's helping with at the church."

News people know that most folks are like Jason—they like to see their own names or names of people they know in the paper, and they'll even buy extra copies of a paper with their story in it to share with friends. That's one reason that in the newspaper business they say, "Names make news."

Seeing our own name in print or having someone we don't know all that well call us by name makes us feel good. In some cultures, though, calling an older or respected person by a personal name is very impolite and shows a lack of respect. Instead, one would use expressions such as Father, Mother, Pastor, Older Brother, or Older Sister. You would never even think of speaking the name of your own older brother or sister.

In Bible times parents gave babies names that stood for the kind of person they hoped their children would become. God also uses names—names that stand for the kind of person He is. One time when He talked to Moses, this is what He called Himself.

"The Lord, the Lord, the compassionate and gracious God, slow to anger, abounding in love and faithfulness, maintaining love to thousands, and forgiving wickedness, rebellion and sin. Yet he does not leave the guilty unpunished" (Ex. 34:6, 7).

That's a very long but a very good name, a name that tells us what God is like. Some people say He is so holy, though, that He should be called only by the special name YAHWEH. Others say that since He wants to have a special, close friendship with us, we could call Him Daddy.

The Bible uses many different names for God, but the way we can give His name the most honor is to become like Him.

Which of God's names is most special to you?

Remember, the important thing is not which of His many names you use when speaking to Him or about Him, but that you give honor to His name by being His kind of person.

Do you make His name hallowed by what you do?

APRIL

13

You's Prayer

YOU is an average Christian kid. He's a bit absent-minded, but he wants to be good, and sometimes he reads his Bible and says his prayers. One day as YOU was praying, something happened. Since prayer is like having a conversation with God, this thought ladder gives an idea of what happened during the prayer YOU offered. (If possible, use two readers—one for GOD, one for YOU.)

GOD *(thinking to Himself)*: "I want everyone to be saved."

YOU *(praying)*: "Your will be done."

GOD: "This is a great opportunity, but YOU doesn't understand what he's just asked. Holy Spirit, help him."

YOU *(to himself, as the Holy Spirit stirs his thoughts)*: "Oh, I just remembered. My Sabbath school teacher said that it's important to ask God into our hearts. *(praying)* So, God, I'm asking You now to come into my heart."

GOD: "Fantastic! But YOU's thoughts are so full of school and sports and videos and music—some good, some pretty bad—that he doesn't have space for Me. The Spirit needs to do something about that for YOU."

YOU *(to himself again, not realizing that the Spirit was impressing his thoughts)*: "Oh! I just now remembered. The teacher said that the best way to get to know God is to read the Bible. *(praying)* God, I don't know You very well, but I want to know You, so I'm going to start reading my Bible every day."

GOD: "This is tremendous, but YOU is so busy that it will be easy for him to forget. The Spirit needs to find a good way to remind him."

YOU: "I'm going to put my Bible on the stand beside my bed so that I'll remember. I want to know You, God, so I can be like You."

Your will be done on earth as it is in heaven. Matthew 6:10.

APRIL

14

Our Daily Bread

Give us today our daily bread. Matthew 6:11.

Many stories tell of God's miracles that answer the "Give us today our daily bread" prayer.

Joseph Bates, the Advent preacher of long ago, one time ran out of food and money, and the very day when he had nothing more in the house a letter with money came for him.

Elijah the prophet hid during a famine, and God sent ravens to feed him.

When the cupboards are stocked, though, and the freezer is full, and jars of canning stand in pretty rows on the shelves, do you still need to pray, "Give us today our daily bread"?

"Share your food with the hungry," says Isaiah.

Then if you have enough to eat and more, another way to pray that part of the Lord's Prayer goes something like this: "Thank You for all the food that we have. Today, help us share our blessing of 'daily bread.' "

To answer that prayer God might even send you a classmate who doesn't have enough lunch.

The "daily bread" prayer includes even more yet. It also has to do with taking good care of your body, not only for God but for yourself. Eating good foods at the right time and in the right amount helps you be healthier, happier, and more alert so that the Holy Spirit can speak to your mind.

Some common bad habits include eating between meals, eating too many sweets, and just plain eating too much. Do you have a "food" problem? If so, talk to God about it in your "daily bread" prayers.

Some families use "daily bread strategies." Here are two:

1. If your family has a common "food" problem—eating between meals, for example—make a family pact that for one week anyone caught nibbling between meals has to go to the "penalty box." Decide appropriate fines—such as doing certain tasks or losing certain privileges or even paying money. (The money could go to a soup kitchen or for Christmas baskets.) Write the "fines" on a slip of paper and put them in a "penalty box."

2. Arrange kids' kitchen times. Plan a set of healthful menus that you can make. Follow the food chart. (If you don't have one, look for one at school or at a library.) Include foods that are both fun to make and fun to eat. Make your meals happy as well as healthful.

APRIL

15

The Unforgiving Servant

This is a dramatic reading from Matthew 18:21-35, TEV. (See page 28 for instructions.)

PETER: Lord, if my brother keeps on sinning against me, how many times do I have to forgive him? Seven times?

JESUS: No, not seven times, but seventy times seven, because the Kingdom of heaven is like this. Once there was a king who decided to check on his servants' accounts. He had just begun to do so when one of them was brought in who owed him millions of dollars. The servant did not have enough to pay his debt, so the king ordered him to be sold as a slave, with his wife and his children and all that he had, in order to pay the debt. The servant fell on his knees before the king.

SERVANT: Be patient with me, [he begged] and I will pay you everything!

JESUS: The king felt sorry for him, so he forgave him the debt and let him go. Then the man went out and found one of his fellow servants who owed him a few dollars. He grabbed him and started choking him.

SERVANT: Pay back what you owe me [he said]!

JESUS: His fellow servant fell down and begged him

FELLOW SERVANT: Be patient with me, and I will pay you back!

JESUS: But he refused; instead, he had him thrown into jail until he should pay the debt. When the other servants saw what had happened, they were very upset and went to the king and told him everything. So he called the servant in.

KING: You worthless slave! I forgave you the whole amount you owed me, just because you asked me to. You should have had mercy on your fellow servant, just as I had mercy on you.

JESUS: The king was very angry, and he sent the servant to jail to be punished until he should pay back the whole amount. That is how my Father in heaven will treat every one of you unless you forgive your brother from your heart.

Forgive us our debts, as we also have forgiven our debtors. Matthew 6:12.

APRIL

16

What Color Is Forgiveness?

This is how my heavenly Father will treat each of you unless you forgive your brother from your heart. Matthew 18:35.

When you read yesterday's parable about the unforgiving servant, how did you feel about that man? What best described your feelings? ____________________

____

Do you feel the same way when someone does something unkind and unjust to you? ____________________

____

What sort of picture would you paint, and what colors would you use to show how you feel? ____________________

____

Mean, angry, pounding, and hard words best describe the usual feelings toward someone who is mean and unfair. The pictures often look dark and angry, or they might be in bright and harsh colors.

Now, how would you describe and show the feelings of forgiveness? ____________________

____

____

This time did you use soft, warm, comfortable words and name colors that make you feel good?

To forgive means to stop being angry with someone. That includes giving up bad feelings and not wanting to get even for what happened. That's not easy to do. Yet God says that before He can forgive us, we need to be able to forgive others.

Keep that in mind as you prepare one of the following:

A. Choose one or more of the following lines from Jesus' parable of the unforgiving servant. Take three to five minutes for your worship group to plan a short skit based on everyday life in which one of the characters will say those exact words. Then act out your skit.

1. How many times do I have to forgive him?
2. Be patient with me!
3. Pay back what you owe me!
4. I will pay you back!

B. Write a modern-day parable in which the characters use one or more of the lines from activity A. As you write, keep in mind Jesus' parable. You may want to follow the pattern He used. Choose an everyday situation with real-life people, and write the words they might have said. Read your parable for worship.

APRIL

17

Protection From the Evil One

And lead us not into temptation, but deliver us from the evil one. Matthew 6:13.

Aaron can quote several entire books of the Bible. He doesn't have any special gift for memorizing, nor did he decide one day that he was going to learn long passages of Scripture. It's almost "by accident" that he can quote so much of the Bible.

Aaron's parents were missionaries, and when he was still in elementary school they had to send him to a special boarding school for missionary children. One of the school requirements was that each morning in private devotions each student had to memorize at least one Bible verse. So every morning Aaron, along with the other children, had to be able to repeat a new text before he was allowed to have breakfast.

By the time he graduated from high school, he could repeat thousands of texts.

Just think how many texts you would know by heart in one year if, besides learning your Sabbath school and Bible class memory verses, you would memorize one text each day in your private devotions. For fun, let's work that out. If each week you learn one text for Sabbath school and say an average of two for Bible class at school, and then seven for your private devotions, that would make _____ verses each week. There are 52 weeks in a year, but school's in session for only about 36 weeks. Using this information, if you faithfully learned all your texts, how many would you know at the end of one year?

36 school weeks x _____ texts = _____ texts
16 vacation weeks x _____ texts = _____ texts
total for one year = _____ texts
(Answers are on page 380.)

The Bible contains 31,173 verses. If you continued to memorize Scripture at this rate, it would take nearly 65 years for you to memorize the entire Bible. Most people who, like Aaron, memorize books of the Bible, usually learn longer passages rather than just one text at a time.

Jesus answered Satan's temptations in the wilderness by quoting scriptures He had learned when He was growing up.

By memorizing passages from the Bible, you make it easier for the Holy Spirit to bring answers to your mind when you need them.

APRIL

18

When God Says "No!"

How much more will your Father in heaven give good gifts to those who ask him! Matthew 7:11.

Justin lived in a huge apartment complex, and after school he had to stay alone until his parents came from work. More than anything else, he wanted a puppy to keep him company. "I'm going to pray for a puppy for my birthday," he told Ronny, his best friend.

"But your mom and dad won't let you get one," Ronny reminded him. "They say you can't keep one in your apartment."

"I'm still going to pray."

Every night Justin asked God to find some way to make it possible for him to get a puppy. On the morning of his birthday, he got up hoping against hope that his prayer had been answered. But there was no puppy. Instead, he found a new bicycle. He phoned Ronny and asked him to meet him when he took if for a trial ride.

"I told you that you wouldn't get a puppy," Ronny said, running his hand over the shiny green frame with the luminescent sparkles. "See, God didn't listen to your prayer. He didn't give you what you asked for."

Justin looked thoughtful for a moment. "He listened all right," he finally said, "and He answered—but He knew it's against the rules to keep a puppy in our apartment, so he had to say 'No.' "

God promises to answer our prayers if we ask in faith. Justin asked in faith, but God still said "No." The first part of Matthew 7:11 says: "If [parents], then, though [they] are evil, know how to give good gifts to [their] children, how much more will your Father in heaven give good gifts to those who ask him!" Think about this text when you answer these questions.

Have you ever asked God for something that was really important to you, only to have Him say "No"?

____

When? __________________________________

Why do you suppose He said "No"? ____________

____

Give two reasons that you think God said "No" to Justin's prayer? __________________________

What are some other reasons God might have for saying "No" to prayers? _______________________

Sometimes the reasons for God's no's are easy to see. Many times they're not. Even though He says "No," He still has good gifts for you—the best is the gift of eternal life.

APRIL

19

A Matter of Peace and Joy

They were proud of their beautiful jewelry and used it to make their detestable idols and vile images. Ezekiel 7:20.

Jerilyn draped the gold chain across her hand and imagined the lovely accent it would make against her dark sweater.

I just don't understand, she argued with herself, letting the chain drop back into the box on the counter. *This chain doesn't cost half as much as the silk scarf Ms. Johnston wears. It's delicate and pretty, yet at school they say it's a sin to wear 'cause it's jewelry.* She sighed and turned her back on the counter so she wouldn't tempt herself any further.

At home she and her mother discussed the subject again. "I just don't understand," she said for at least the hundredth time. "Ladies in the Bible wore jewelry, and men had their rings."

"It was different then."

Her mother's standard answer about family wealth and signet rings didn't make sense to her. Jerilyn didn't want to be stubborn—she honestly didn't understand.

"I know that Paul says our beauty should come from the inside, but do you honestly think he meant that we shouldn't wear any jewelry at all?" She faced her mother. "I heard Mrs. Jones criticizing Mrs. Vogel for wearing a wedding ring. Yet you said that the church says it's OK for people to wear wedding rings if they believe it's right.

"Mom, what's the right thing to do?"

"Jerilyn, I personally and truly believe that this is a matter that must be handled with Paul's principle of peace and joy—where he says it's better not to do anything that will offend or upset others (Romans 14 and 15). Our church in North America has taken a strong stand against jewelry, but times are changing. People from other cultures have brought new ideas. Folks like me, though, have grown up believing that wearing jewelry is a big sin, and that idea's still strong. Remember, there's a difference between looking good and using beauty to attract attention. Jewelry easily becomes an idol—you can look good without it."

"I know, Mom. It's just that—well, I guess you're right—and Paul too. A little gold chain isn't worth the big fuss I know it would cause if I wore it."

What Bible texts would you use to help Jerilyn understand how you feel about wearing jewelry?

APRIL

20

Getting the Picture Right

The Lord is good, a refuge in times of trouble. He cares for those who trust in him. Nahum 1:7.

Daddy . . ."

Dad looked up from his magazine. He wanted to read, but . . .

"Daddy, what's this man's name?" Sissy was looking at an old family album and had a continual series of questions.

"Julius LeDuc," he replied absentmindedly, wondering how he could get her interested in something else so he could read. Then he noticed an old magazine with a map of the world. "I'm going to make you a puzzle," he said, knowing that Sissy loved puzzles.

"I want you to show me how quickly and quietly you can put it together." He cut the map into a stack of big, jagged pieces. "OK," he said, scattering the pieces on the carpet. "See if you can put the world together before I finish reading."

Sissy studied the pieces as she tried to decide how to make them fit together, and Dad settled down with his magazine, sure that he had time to read it all. Before he had finished the first article, though, he felt Sissy patting him on the arm. "Look, Daddy!" She pointed to where she had been working on the puzzle. "I'm finished."

Dad looked. To his surprise, the pieces were all in their proper places, and the world was back together. "However did you do that so quickly?" he asked in surprise.

"It was easy!" Sissy exclaimed. "There was a picture of Jesus on the other side. When I got the picture of Jesus right, that took care of the world."

When we get the picture of Jesus right, that does take care of our world. When bad things happen, though, how can you be sure that "the Lord cares for those who trust in him" when you or someone you know—

is hurt in an accident?

is hurting inside because Mom and Dad are getting a divorce?

has a friend or family member dying from AIDS?

doesn't have enough food to eat?

is handicapped?

never has enough money for nice clothes?

God was listening when Jesus was in the Garden of Gethsemane—and He was sad. He didn't want Jesus to be tortured. And killed. He couldn't grant Jesus' wish, though, so He sent angels to give Him the strength to do what He had to do.

When you get the picture of Jesus right, that does take care of the world!

APRIL

21

A Good Name

A good name is better than fine perfume. Ecclesiastes 7:1.

Listen!" Julie motioned for her brother to be quiet.

Jason paused. "Sounds just like a clock!" he said. He continued to listen. "A clock that's stuck," he added.

It was April, and the twins were spending their spring break in France with their parents. "When the cuckoos start to sing, you know spring's here for sure," their father had told them.

"That has to be a cuckoo," Julie agreed. "What else could it be?"

European cuckoos are famous around the world because of the clocks that imitate their call, yet they are very unpopular with their bird neighbors because they're like their American cousins, the cowbirds. They never bother to build their own nests.

When spring comes and the cuckoos return from their winter holiday in Africa, the female chooses certain bird families in the area that she and her mate have claimed and watches until they have their nests ready. When the other mothers begin laying eggs, so does Mrs. Cuckoo. One day she goes to one nest, another day to another, and pushes out one of the other bird's eggs and lays one of her own in its place.

She does this until she has laid about 12 eggs.

When a baby cuckoo hatches, it is completely naked and has a very sensitive spot on its back. If anything touches that spot during the baby's first few days, it arches upward and squirms. By the time the tiny bird is over its touchiness, its squirming has pushed all the other babies out of the nest.

Even though it's now the only chick in the nest, it never seems to get enough to eat and keeps both foster parents busy feeding it.

This huge appetite is possibly the reason the real parents never bother to build a nest. They're still big eaters, and while the other birds are busy feeding the babies the adult cuckoos are busy eating. To their credit, they eat mostly insect pests. In fact, they eat one pest, a bristly caterpillar, that no other bird can eat.

Cuckoos are famous for their call. Some say that when they sing, it is a sure sign of rain, but it's certainly never a compliment to say someone is cuckoo.

A good name must be earned by good actions.

APRIL

22

Do You Know What These Things Mean?

Son of man, pose a riddle, and speak a parable to the house of Israel. Ezekiel 17:2, NKJV.

God gave Ezekiel a riddle about two eagles and a vine. He said that a big, powerful eagle broke off the top of a cedar and planted it in a city of traders. Then He told Ezekiel about another powerful eagle, and how the branch grew into a fine vine. Then God asked the question "Will the vine survive?"

Faith in God needs to be based on good logic, and riddles sharpen our ability to think things through. Test your reasoning with this riddle Greg likes to ask his science students. See if you can get the right answer by tomorrow. (The answer is on page 380.) Here's the riddle:

As a certain man was walking home from work one day, a woman gave him a bag of apples. On his way he met a friend. Being generous, he gave his friend half his apples plus half an apple. Farther along he met another friend. Again he shared his apples by giving this friend half of his remaining apples plus half an apple. When he reached home, he still had one apple to give to his wife. Now the man had given away all the apples that had been given to him. He did not cut any of the apples, nor did he eat any himself. How many apples did the woman give him? How many did he share with each person?

When God sent Ezekiel with the riddle about the eagles—some translations call it an allegory or a parable—for the captives in Babylon, He said to ask the people, "Do you not know what these things mean?" Then He went on to explain that the riddle symbolized the punishment of their king because he broke his covenant with God.

God also promised that He would again make the land a wonderful place to live. The chapter ends with these words: "I the Lord have spoken, and I will do it."

Do you know what these things mean?

If you enjoy doing puzzles, read Ezekiel 17 and see if you can find the meaning for each of these symbols in the riddle God gave Ezekiel:

the first great eagle ____________________
the top of the cedar ____________________
the plant that sprouted ____________________
the other giant eagle ____________________
the plant where the birds live ____________________

APRIL

23

The Lucifer Box

For false Christs and false prophets will appear and perform great signs and miracles to deceive even the elect—if that were possible. Matthew 24:24.

Did you get the answer to yesterday's riddle? How many apples did the lady give the man?

There are several other interesting ways to stretch your reasoning ability. Playing with words by imagining pictures for their meanings is another.

"Where is the *lucifer* box?"

The question was in Dutch—a language I was learning. But one word stood out. "Lucifer"? A lucifer box? Crazy pictures formed in my mind. I struggled for the meaning in English. "Oh, yes. Match! She wants the matchbox."

Learning other languages is fun. It's interesting to see how certain words in our language can have entirely different meanings in another language.

I'd always thought of Lucifer as simply another name for Satan, but I've learned that Lucifer is the Latin form of the name Satan had in heaven back when he was the head of all the angels and next to Christ in power. It means "light bearer." Knowing that meaning makes it easier to understand why it's a good word for "match." In fact, one meaning for "lucifer" in the English dictionary is "an early kind of friction match."

Satan still wants to be Lucifer, the light bearer. Since Jesus died on the cross, though, Satan knows there is no way for him to ever go back to the wonderful life he had in heaven.

The day I first heard the expression "lucifer box," I pictured a box for a little red devil with hooves, ready to spear someone with his pitchfork.

By always picturing Satan, the devil, as ugly—with hooves and horns and a tail—and mean-acting, we might be caught off guard if he did appear as someone handsome and kind. By coming as an angel of light—as Lucifer—and performing wonderful miracles, Satan could easily fool lots of people into thinking that he is Jesus.

That makes it doubly important to stay close to Jesus and to study everything He has told us about Himself in the Bible. If we know the truth and use the reasoning ability He has given us to get the picture of Him right, we can know the difference.

Jesus Himself is our very best protection, though. He wants you to know what He's like, and He wants to be your good friend—your very best friend—so no one can fool you, not even an angel of light.

APRIL

24

A Poor Reflection

Now we see but a poor reflection as in a mirror; then we shall see face to face.
1 Corinthians 13:12.

"What's that?" Linda pointed to a picture in my album of favorite photos from our summer's travels. Among shots of the English seacoast, Dutch windmills, Pacific beaches, Alberta lakes, mountain streams, and peaceful sunsets, it stood out as different—very different.

"That's one of your famous sights right here in Washington, D.C.," I replied. "At night."

She studied the multicolored squiggles that traced across a black background. Some were tightly packed into the copper glow of an electronic circuit, some dropped into an evenly matched series of loops and scrolls, others faded into the distance. But they all moved attention toward a phantom of white light that repeated itself slightly left of center in a series of candle-shaped smudges.

As she was puzzling over the picture, I remembered out loud about that midnight when our flight settled into its final approach for landing at Washington's National Airport. City lights spread in every direction, and I tried to pick out landmarks. Then I saw it, standing like a pillar of light. I quickly braced my camera against the window and pressed the shutter release. In fully automatic mode, the camera chose an extremely slow speed. Just then the plane bounced into a layer of turbulence, and I pressed the camera against the window to hold it steady. At last I heard the shutter close. By then we were zooming low over the Potomac River and banking back toward the runway.

"Oh, I see!" she exclaimed. "The Washington Monument! That's really good!"

As seen through a camera lens at night from a plane bumping its way down through turbulent air, the Washington Monument's sharp-lined grandeur fades into a blur of smudges. Though it is a beautiful picture, without an explanation no one can guess what it is.

Our knowledge about heaven is as inexact as a night picture taken from a bouncing plane. Paul says it's like seeing a poor reflection in a mirror. Mirrors those days were made from pieces of polished metal and gave only hazy reflections, something like you get when looking at the side of a tin can. Whether like a dim reflection or a blurry picture, our ideas of heaven and the new earth are nothing compared to the real thing. Even so, with what we do know, we can say, "That's really good!"

APRIL

25

The Happiness Texts

The man who makes no allowances for others will find none made for him.
James 2:13, Phillips.

That's one of my happiness texts," Grandpa said, closing his Bible.

"Happiness texts?" Shandra asked, raising an eyebrow. "What's happy about that?"

"The man who makes no allowances for others will find none made for him," Grandpa repeated, then chuckled. "Don't do what it says!" he exclaimed. "Do what it doesn't say, then you'll be happy. In other words, if I give folks the benefit of the doubt, they'll be apt to treat me the same way."

"You mean like the golden rule?"

Grandpa nodded. " 'Do to others what you would have them do to you'! (Matthew 7:12). That's the basic rule for getting along well with others, and getting along makes us happy—so it's a happiness text. Can you think of any texts with good advice?"

" 'Give, and it will be given to you'? (Luke 6:38)."

"Excellent," Grandpa said. "Now, can you think of others?"

"There must be some in the Proverbs."

"They certainly have lots of good advice about how to live a happy life," Grandpa agreed. "One of my favorites is 'Without wood a fire goes out; without gossip a quarrel dies down' (Proverbs 26:20)."

"How about this memory verse that we learned in school last week?" Shandra asked. " 'He who is kind to the poor lends to the Lord, and he will reward him for what he has done' (Proverbs 19:17)."

"Another excellent happiness text!" Grandpa exclaimed. "The important thing to remember, though, is not just to store them in your memory, but to put them into practice."

At least six other of Shandra's grandfather's happiness texts have been used for April devotionals. Look back to find them. State the reference for each, and then tell in what ways the advice it gives can help you be happy.

1. ______________________________
2. ______________________________
3. ______________________________
4. ______________________________
5. ______________________________
6. ______________________________

If you're not sure which of the April texts Shandra's grandfather chose for his list, look on page 380.

APRIL

26

The Price of a Mistake

For none of us lives to himself alone and none of us dies to himself alone.
Romans 14:7.

It was late. Nearly all the workers at the Chernobyl nuclear plant in the Ukraine were home and asleep. Suddenly an explosion ripped through the graphite core of reactor number 4, and flames boiled into the night.

Fire fighters scrambled to the rescue, but they couldn't stop the radioactive cloud that spilled into the sky. Silent, invisible, deadly, it ballooned upward for three miles. Thousands of workers were rushed from their apartments to safer areas, but many were already dying from deadly doses of radioactivity. Their homes became unsafe for anyone ever to live in again. The buildings will one day fall to the ground and have to be buried the same as any other nuclear waste.

Soldiers ordered in to clean up after the accident wore lead suits as protection against radiation, but even then each one was allowed to work only one minute and then was evacuated. They covered the faulty reactor with a metal and steel building to block further contamination, but they couldn't work quickly enough. Radioactive hot spots developed hundreds of miles away as the invisible cloud of radioactivity hopscotched across the continent, its contents falling with the rains. This danger that could be neither seen nor smelled forced hundreds of thousands of people to leave everything and begin new lives in other places.

Nuclear power is easy and inexpensive to produce, but it must be handled with extreme care.

Under the direction of Italian physicist Enrico Fermi, the first nuclear chain reaction was produced about 50 years ago at the University of Chicago. In 1956 the British became the first to produce electricity in a large-scale nuclear power plant. The United States alone now has about 50 plants that each produce more than 1 million kilowatts of electricity.

Those who work in nuclear plants have a great responsibility. The lives of people around the world depend on their strict following of safety rules.

Somebody's mistake caused the Chernobyl disaster—a deadly mistake. Scientists predict that it will take 20,000 years for the effects of that mistake to disappear.

The effects of Eve's and Adam's mistake will never disappear. Even after God completely destroys sin, the nail prints on Jesus' hands and feet will stay as a reminder of the costly price of sin.

APRIL

27

More Than Magic

Don't listen to mediums—what they tell you will do you no good. Isaiah 8:20, TEV.

Spencer says his mom's throwing a party," Tonya told her mother when she came in from work. "It sounds like fun. He says there'll be magic and tricks and games. Can we go?"

"What kind of magic?"

Tonya shrugged. "The usual stuff, I suppose. One of his mom's friends is a magician."

"I'm not so sure it's the usual stuff you think it is," her mother responded. "Other neighbors have told me . . ."

"Oh, Mom, you know what you say about gossip."

"It's not idle gossip," her mother replied. "It's, well . . . This isn't the kind of magic you want to get involved in."

"But Mom, Spencer says . . ."

"How well do you know Spencer?"

Tonya shrugged. "I talk to him sometimes. He's usually on his way from his school when our bus drops me off, and we walk home together. He seems really nice."

"Does he ever say anything about the meetings his mother attends?"

Tonya wrinkled her nose. "Of course not! Guys only talk about who beat who in hockey. Sometimes he says something about his magic tricks. He says he wants to be a magician."

"Did he say what kind of magician?"

Tonya gave her mother a strange look. "Why all these questions just because his mom's giving a party?"

"I've already heard about the party. I've also learned that Spencer's mother belongs to a satanist group. This is more than a party—it's intended as . . . well . . . you could say it's evangelism with magic that goes beyond the usual tricks. The walls talk, and sofa cushions and other small objects float."

Tonya listened in surprise.

"This is not a party for us."

"But Mom, Spencer says it'll be good fun, and you know what you say about being neighborly. Anyway, we're Christians, what could hurt us?"

"Before we talk more about this, read Isaiah 8:19, 20 in your *Good News Bible,* then read about Jesus' temptation in Matthew 4:1-11. Pay special attention to verse 7."

Read the passages. What message do they have for Tonya about the party?

APRIL

28

The Strongest Power

Worship the Lord your God, and serve him only. Matthew 4:10.

"Hey, I missed you at the party." Spencer was waiting for Tonya at the bus stop a few days later.

Tonya shrugged. "I wasn't able to come," she said vaguely, then on impulse she added, "Do you really go to a satanist church?"

"Sure," he replied matter-of-factly. "Why?"

"Oh—I—" Tonya shrugged again. "I just wondered what it's like."

"We just sit around and stuff."

"Do you really offer sacrifices and all that?" The next question just popped out.

Spencer seemed to stiffen. "My mom says reporters give us bad press," he said. "People just don't understand the power that can be theirs."

"Power?"

"Yeah. When you connect, you can do all sorts of exciting things." He seemed to relax a bit as he talked. "My mom can even fly. Sometimes she goes at night with her friend, and she talks about places all over where they've been."

Tonya couldn't believe her ears. "She can fly? You mean like on a magic carpet?"

"I said you can do exciting things when you connect. I'm getting ready for my initiation. I wish I could ask you to come to it, but everyone there has gotta believe before it'll work. And I know you're a Christian and stuff. So . . ." He shrugged.

"Yeah," Tonya said. "I'm getting ready to be baptized into our church. That's a special day for me, and I wish you'd come. Anyone can come—whether they believe or not. We don't do any of the exciting things like fly on a carpet." She didn't say so out loud, but she found that idea very spooky. Instead she heard herself saying, "But being a Christian's very special, and when you're in touch with God, you have access to the strongest power in the universe."

Tonya surprised herself with what she was saying. "You know, Spencer, I think you'd enjoy being a Christian. When you get to know God, something very special happens inside of you—it's almost like you can be happy no matter what."

Spencer seemed really interested.

APRIL

29

Don't Be Deceived

Satan himself masquerades as an angel of light. 2 Corinthians 11:14.

To hear Spencer so easily admit that he was planning to be initiated into a satanist cult alarmed Tonya more than she realized at first. She didn't want to say it out loud to anyone, not even to herself, but she knew inside that she was beginning to like him in a special way. And from the way he waited for her at her bus stop after school, and walked her home, and talked, she suspected that he liked her too—a lot. She needed help.

"What should I do, Mom?" she asked after she had decided she needed advice. "I like him. I'm sure he likes me, and from the way he's talking I think he'd probably come to church with me. He might even ask me home, but so far he hasn't because he knows I have chores and practice and can't go anywhere after school. But what if he *does* invite me over to his place? I know you'd never let me go unless his mom's home, and that's just the problem. Because what if I'd go, and what if they'd start doing some of that satanist stuff he's talked about? What if I let myself get involved?"

"You're asking the right questions at the right time," her mother assured her. "Now you need to find the right answers." She reminded Tonya of Isaiah 8:19, 20 and Matthew 4:7, 10 and 2 Corinthians 11:14—the texts we've used for these stories. With these texts in mind, if you were Tonya, what would you do?

1. Continue being friendly with Spencer and go over to meet his mom when he asked, because that would be one way of being able to witness to them about God.
2. Invite Spencer to come to Sabbath school and church with you the next Sabbath—before he could get you involved in satanism.
3. Pretend to be in a terrible hurry when you get off the bus so that you couldn't take time to talk with him on the way home.
4. Arrange with a friend to go to her place after school so you wouldn't have to see Spencer.
5. Tell him to "get lost!"

Which of the above would be best? Or do you have another solution?

Nice people do become involved in Satanism and the occult. Are you reading your Bible and taking time with God so that you'll know to say No to things that seem harmless but could be dangerous?

APRIL

30

You Are What You Eat

The god of this age has blinded the minds of unbelievers.
2 Corinthians 4:4.

I've decided I'm not going to run away from the Spencer problem," Tonya told her mother the next morning. "I've talked to God very seriously about it, and I'm asking Him to continue to put wise answers in my mouth, as He did when Spencer told me about his initiation. Besides, there's really no after-school problem. Believe it or not, Spencer's not allowed to have anyone in till after his mom's home, so we're both OK there. If anything else comes up, well, I'm counting on God—and on you—to be here." Tonya gave her mother a big smile.

The test came after school that day. "Would you go to the movies with me this weekend?" Spencer asked suddenly when they were walking home.

Tonya flushed. "What movie did you have in mind?" she asked.

"The new one—you know, that one about . . ."

It was the newest, biggest movie out, and no one could escape knowing about it. It was also heavy with the supernatural.

Tonya took a deep breath. "I'd really like to go with you," she said, "but, Spencer, there's something you need to know. I'm a Christian, and that's really important to me."

"So?" he stopped walking and faced her. "I know lots of Christian kids. They're normal."

Tonya laughed. "Being a Christian and knowing God is all about being a normal person. That's why . . . Well, we've been studying about our brains—whatever we put into them stays. What we feed our minds determines the kind of person we'll be, so I'm careful about what I read or watch."

Spencer looked puzzled.

"This is going to sound terrible," Tonya continued, "but I'm a Christian; you're into satanism. The two just can't mix, and I don't want to feed my mind ideas about the supernatural."

"But it's a great film. You'd like it."

"I'm sure I would," Tonya agreed. "That's just the problem. Oh, Spencer, I know this must sound all mixed up to you, but there's something special about being a Christian and knowing God that . . . Well, you have to know about it to . . . I wish you'd come to our church, then maybe you'd understand."

"Hey, Mom, you'll never guess what!" Tonya exclaimed when her mother came home from work. "Spencer's coming to our youth discussion group at church this weekend."

MAY

1

Gifts From the Heart

Each man should give what he has decided in his heart to give.
2 Corinthians 9:7.

Travis folded the paper, trying to crease it just so along the edge of the box. A big bow and fancy ribbon lay on the table. This present had to look good because he wanted everyone to know that he cared enough for Shelley to put special effort into making her gift look extra nice.

It's easy to spend time, money, and effort in order to give good gifts to those we really like, and the happy look on Shelley's face when she saw her gift repaid Travis many times over for the extra time he'd taken.

You've probably heard a hundred times, though, that it's not the gift but the thought that counts. That's what today's text is about, and it goes on to say, "God loves a cheerful giver."

Love notes and gift coupons have been popular for years—coupons to Mother for chores she can request, a love note complimenting your sister on her good-looking hairdo, a coupon redeemable for one hour of after-school help for your teacher. Those are only a few examples.

Have you ever thought of giving God a set of gifts from your heart—a set of coupons for doing special kindnesses in His name? This is how it works. Make a set of coupons, put them in a box, then each morning take out a card, and what it says will be your special gift to God for that day. Your coupons could include gifts such as these:

I'll memorize one Bible promise today.

I'll offer one hour of free baby-sitting (or other specific chore) to a neighbor who needs my help.

I promise to say something kind and encouraging to ________ (an unpopular classmate).

I promise to smile at at least three different people, ones I usually ignore.

I promise to compliment ________ (someone I don't like) and say something good about ________ (that person) to someone else.

I'll make a list of Your blessings today.

If your family is not in the habit of having worship together, offer to read the day's devotion (at a meal you eat together is a good time) and pray.

You can probably add hundreds of ideas to this list. Remember, being kind to others is a way of giving to God. Give Him a gift from your heart.

MAY

2

Believe

Believe in the Lord Jesus, and you will be saved. Acts 16:31.

Believe . . . and you will be saved."

Torrey let the words slide by his ears. He'd heard the same thing so many times, that . . .

I could preach the sermon myself, he told himself.

"If you want to give your heart to Jesus, then stand right where you are."

Of course, I want to, Torrey answered in his thoughts. And he stood, just as he'd stood what seemed to him a hundred times already.

As his dad drove the car home after church, Torrey stared out the window, but he really wasn't seeing anything. *Believe,* he said to himself. *If you want to give your heart . . .*

Torrey believed. He believed in God and Jesus and the Holy Spirit, and he believed that Jesus is coming back to this earth to get all who believe in Him and take them to heaven. He'd always gone to church with his folks—and to the local church school—and he took for granted that he'd be going to heaven when Jesus came. But he'd been waiting for . . .

He wasn't sure what exactly he had been waiting for, but he expected some extra-special something to happen that would let him know that Jesus had come into his heart—some magic change like if he'd say "I want to give my heart to Jesus" enough times, then suddenly, wow, there he'd be, this wonderful, terrific, happy Christian.

"Dad . . ." Torrey spoke, then let his voice drift away.

"Yes?"

"Dad, how can you know for sure that you have Jesus in your heart?"

"Good question, son," his father replied. "The answer is as easy as breathing, and yet it's one of the most difficult ideas of all time to understand if you haven't come to the point of knowing that you indeed do have Jesus in your heart. The easiest way to explain it is to say that I just know."

"But how?"

"I know because . . ." Torrey's father slowed and eased to a stop at the Five Corners' light. "Well, I've chosen to have God as my friend—that's probably the most important part. And then I make a point to keep in touch with Him at all times. And . . . actually it's quite a long story. Let's talk about it after lunch."

MAY

3

Not Wanting but Doing

"Yet not as I will, but as you will." *Matthew 26:39.*

After the dishes had been cleared away, Torrey and his father went into the den to talk.

"When Pastor Samuelson was preaching this morning, I suddenly realized that I could probably stand up and preach his sermon for him," Torrey said. "I've heard all that about believing in God and wanting to give your heart to Him so many times. And then suddenly I realized that even though I've heard it over and over, I don't know what it means."

"I think I know what you're talking about," his father said. "Only I was much older by the time I made that discovery. I kept waiting and waiting for something to assure me that I was a real Christian and that God had changed my life. But it never came."

Torrey nodded his head and waited for his father to go on.

This is what his father said.

"I believed that God loved me and that He had sent Jesus to die for my sins. I also believed that I should love God and that I should keep His commandments in order to prove that I really did love Him. So I went to church on the right day, and I tried not to swear . . . or steal . . . or lie, because those are things that Christians don't do. Then I'd hear someone say, 'I'm so happy being a Christian.'

"But I don't feel all that happy, I'd tell myself. And I wondered what was wrong.

"The summer you were a baby, Mom and I decided to drive across America. Mom was driving and I was reading a book when suddenly the words on the page hit me with a *wow*. It said that the secret of the Christian life is to live it in the will.

"I'd always heard about the will, but until I read that book I never understood that the will is my power of choice, that when Jesus knocks on the door of my heart I must choose to open the door and invite Him in.

"Right then and there I opened the door of my heart and told God that no matter what I might feel like doing in the future, I had decided to choose to do His will, not mine.

"Since that time I know that I have Jesus in my heart, that I belong to God. Some days, though, I'm stubborn and do what I feel like doing. I sin. When I realize what I've done, I feel bad. God always forgives—if we ask. I know that as long as I choose to have Him, He'll stay in my heart."

MAY

4

The Airport Window

We take every thought captive and make it obey Christ.
2 Corinthians 10:5, TEV.

What happened to that? I asked myself as I sat in the airport restaurant, taking my time.

There was absolutely no need to rush. We had hours of waiting until our next plane and not much to do to help the time pass more quickly. There were no shops; taxi service into town was very expensive; and, besides, there was no place to leave our luggage in safekeeping if we did want to go into town. We were doomed to a long day at the airport. Date, my husband, volunteered to stay with our luggage while I went upstairs for lunch.

Windows along the length of the restaurant overlooked the runways, and I chose a table facing one—but there really wasn't much to see. No planes came; no planes were getting ready to go; the only thing of interest was the window itself. The section in front of me looked like any normal window—clear, but smudged. The next section, though, resembled a magnified microscope slide, a crosscut of some smear that varied from light egg-yellow to a deep yellow-orange with a spattering of clear dots and bubbles embedded in it. The unevenness of the color and the strange dots and circles gave the window a blistered, warped effect.

Maybe it was from lack of sleep and from the long days we'd been traveling, but, whatever the cause, a story began to grow in my mind. I pictured one of those big, bumbling jumbo jets on the tarmac, tail toward the airport, ready to taxi out, when suddenly, through some technical quirk, an engine surged into power, directing the full blast of its engine in such a way that it targeted the one window, scorching the glass, causing it to bubble and change color.

That's a wild, impossible idea, I scolded myself. But I liked it. Such a window had to have a good story.

"What happened to that window?" I finally asked when the waiter came by again.

He shrugged. "Nothing special," he said. "It's just been tinted for visibility."

"Tinted!" My catapulting ideas fell flat. I'd asked for the facts, and got them.

Paul warns against simply looking at outward appearances and believing false ideas. Make sure your ideas about God and the gospel are based on the facts of the Bible.

MAY

5

Freed

The broad red, white, and blue stripes of the Dutch flag snapped in the wind, flying for the first time from the village flagpole after years of having been hidden away. Laughing and talking, crowds gathered along the road. Pieter squeezed through to a spot right on the roadside and shaded his eyes so he could see better.

"Here they come!" someone shouted, and Pieter joined the cheering as the Canadian soldiers marched into their village. For the first time in his life, he was not afraid of soldiers. Behind them, though, a muffled rumbling marked the approach of several dull green tanks. The ground began to tremble as they neared. Pieter didn't like their noise or the big guns that poked out of them or the shaking of the ground. He slipped back through the crowd and onto a quiet path that led along the canal.

A noise from the bushes startled him. Cautiously he crept up and peered in. "Enemy soldier!" he gasped to himself and started to run. Then he stopped. Crying? Just then he saw Meindert, his oldest brother, and waved for him to hurry. "Look in there!" He pointed to the bushes.

"Wow!" he exclaimed. "Whatever are you doing here?"

The soldier cowered on the ground in front of them. "I hurt my ankle," he said, choking back his sobs. "We were retreating and I couldn't keep up, so I crawled in here." He looked so pathetic that Pieter felt sorry for him.

"I hate war!" he exclaimed. "But they forced me into the army, and now they've left me." He started to pull himself up by the bushes, but his face twisted with pain, and he crumpled back to the ground.

Pieter stayed while Meindert went for help. "What are they going to do with him?" he asked when his brother returned with two men, who put the soldier on a stretcher and carried him away. "Will they shoot him?"

"Why, no!" Meindert exclaimed. "They'll put him in a hospital until his leg is better. After that he'll be kept in a prisoner-of-war camp until the war is completely over. Then he'll be free to go home."

In the war between good and evil, Satan doesn't care if we're hurt serving him, but God offers help and freedom to all.

Everyone who believes in him may have eternal life.
John 3:15.

MAY

6

The Giant Space Kite

"You live in the midst of deception . . . ," declares the Lord. Jeremiah 9:6.

Look at the kite I'm getting!" Aric pointed to an ad in his magazine.

"Wow!" exclaimed Kyle. "When?"

"Probably next week. I mailed the order this morning."

" 'Giant! High-flying! Get this authentic space kite!' " Kyle read the ad aloud.

"Dad said that I should get one in town, but this one looks bigger and better, doesn't it? I'll let you fly it with me when it comes," Aric promised. "It'll be fun!"

One week passed and then another. A whole month went by. Aric waited impatiently until finally, at the end of the second month, his package came. He ripped off the packing and pulled out a roll of red and blue plastic. He flipped it open, then stood and stared. It was shaped like the kite in the ad and had the fancy lettering along its flank. But it wasn't as big or as colorful as he thought it would be. Aric sorted through the pieces for the string and the reel and the tail shown in the ad picture. All he found was a little piece of white paper that said "Assembly Instructions." He needed to buy the rest himself.

Sadly, Aric thought about things his father had pointed out when he first wanted to order the kite. The ad didn't give the exact size, nor did it tell the quality of the material, nor even mention if the string and reel shown in the picture were included. If he had listened, he could have bought a better kite for the same money, and he wouldn't have had to wait.

Aric isn't the first person to be fooled by an advertisement or a commercial that was created to make us believe more than it actually says. These ads use words such as "giant," but they don't say "giant" as compared to what. And big, impressive-sounding words such as "authentic," but that simply means that something is what it is.

"You live in the midst of deception," wrote Jeremiah, and he didn't have our kind of media back then.

Nowadays the average kid sees 20,000 TV commercials a year plus magazine ads and other advertising. If ads can trick you into believing things they don't actually say, think how easy it must be for the devil to trick you into believing his lies.

MAY

7

The Pot Makers

If anyone makes himself clean from all those evil things, he will be used for special purposes, because he is dedicated and useful to his Master, ready to be used for every good deed.
2 Timothy 2:21, TEV.

John-James sat in the shade of the house, his chemistry notebook on his knee. It was hot and he was tired of trying to put all the formulas into his head. Across the yard his mother worked in the shade of a clump of banana plants. Her pounding stick made a soft *splough-splough-splough* as she brought it down on the clay with movements as even as a drummer's. He felt a pleasant tightness circle his chest as he watched. The women of the village made good pottery, but when visitors came to buy they always asked first to see his mother's work.

"Everything is important," she said when asked the secret for making such nice pottery. "The clay, the work, the polishing, the hardening."

Sometimes John-James helped her gather wood and husks and leaves for the fire. "It takes a careful fire to make a strong vase," she always said.

After the raw pots had dried in the sun and she had polished them with special polishing stones, she arranged them over the fire. When they had hardened into the beautiful red that made the pottery of their village famous, she examined each piece and tapped it.

"Good pots have a pure voice," she explained. "They will not crumble when water is placed in them, nor will they crack on the cooking fires.

"Put the best clay and the best work into your life, too, my son," she often added. "Learn each thing at the proper time. Don't be afraid of difficult work. Do it carefully, and it will harden your character and give your life a pure voice. You can become a man who can stand with honor before God and before our people."

John-James watched his mother a moment longer, admiring the firm strength of her dark arms, and then he looked back at his notebook.

Now was the time to learn.

Are you putting the best clay into your life? What are some of the things you are learning that will give your character "a pure voice"?

MAY

8

Pick a Proverb for Mother's Day

Many women do noble things, but you surpass them all.
Proverbs 31:29.

This is a round-robin reading of "The Capable Wife" from Proverbs 31:10-31, TEV.

Read these verses in turn, then choose the one you think most fits the person you'd like to honor today. Girls used to claim the verse that matched their birthday as their special text. Those born before the tenth would use verses 11-19.

10. "How hard it is to find a capable wife! She is worth far more than jewels!"

11. "Her husband puts his confidence in her, and he will never be poor."

12. "As long as she lives, she does him good and never harm."

13. "She keeps herself busy making wool and linen cloth."

14. "She brings home food from out-of-the-way places, as merchant ships do."

15. "She gets up before daylight to prepare food for her family and to tell her servant girls what to do."

16. "She looks at land and buys it, and with money she has earned she plants a vineyard."

17. "She is a hard worker, strong and industrious."

18. "She knows the value of everything she makes, and works late into the night."

19. "She spins her own thread and weaves her own cloth."

20. "She is generous to the poor and needy."

21. "She doesn't worry when it snows, because her family has warm clothing."

22. "She makes bedspreads and wears clothes of fine purple linen."

23. "Her husband is well known, one of the leading citizens."

24. "She makes clothes and belts, and sells them to merchants."

25. "She is strong and respected and not afraid of the future."

26. "She speaks with a gentle wisdom."

27. "She is always busy and looks after her family's needs."

28. "Her children show their appreciation, and her husband praises her."

29. "He says, 'Many women are good wives, but you are the best of them all.' "

30. "Charm is deceptive and beauty disappears, but a woman who honors the Lord should be praised."

31. "Give her credit for all she does. She deserves the respect of everyone."

MAY

9

Borrowed Seed

A farmer went out to sow his seed. Luke 8:5.

Sean ran outside with an open package of cookies. "Here," he told his friends. "Have one."

"Sean! Please come here for a moment."

He ran to where his mother stood on the porch.

"Are those your cookies?"

Sean shook his head.

"Did you have permission to take them?"

He looked down at the almost empty bag and shook his head. "No, but my friends are hungry and they wanted some cookies."

"Even if your friends are hungry, you aren't to give them things that don't belong to you."

"I just wanted to share."

Young Sean had not yet learned that sharing happens only when we give away things that belong to us.

In the parable of the sower that Jesus told, the farmer didn't plant borrowed seed, nor did he use seed that belonged to someone else. He planted *his* seed—the seed that belonged to him. Jesus was talking about Himself and the good news about God that He brought to this world.

We also are to "plant" the gospel, to share God's love with others, but, like Sean, we can't share something that's not ours. If we don't know God, we can't share His love. The following are examples of what someone might say to witness about God. Which are like "borrowed" seed? Which are real "shared" seed that belong to the person who is talking?

________ 1. The Bible says you should go to church on Saturday, so you should come to church with me next week.

________ 2. I really enjoy my Sabbath school. Wouldn't you like to come with me next week?

________ 3. The Bible is so interesting to read. I really enjoy the stories of Jesus. Have you ever read about the time He walked on water?

________4. If you want to know about God, you should read the Bible.

________ 5. When you're in trouble, pray. The Bible says that God answers prayers.

________ 6. Every morning when I wake up, I pray first thing. I tell God all sorts of things. Even though I can't see Him when I pray, I know He hears me.

(Answers are on page 380.)

MAY

10

Like a Busy Highway

The seeds that fell along the path stand for those who hear; but the Devil comes and takes the message away from their hearts in order to keep them from believing and being saved. Luke 8:12, TEV.

Have you ever thought of your mind as being like a busy highway with many, many thoughts traveling through it each day? Take a few minutes right now to do a traffic check of what's been through your mind already today. What thoughts have you had that remind you of any of the following?

a racecar ______________________

a tractor-trailer ______________________

a bulldozer ______________________

a tour bus ______________________

a Lamborghini ______________________

a motorcycle ______________________

a Rolls-Royce ______________________

a trailer ______________________

a bicycle ______________________

a police car ______________________

Even if your thoughts are all good and you do only good things, the traffic in your mind might still be too heavy. In *Christ's Object Lessons*, page 44, Ellen White suggests that the seed sown by the path represents "the word of God as it falls upon the heart of an inattentive hearer"—the heart of someone whose mind is so full that he or she does not realize a need for Jesus.

As you read the following, put a star (*) by the things you do and enjoy, an (X) by the things you do only because you have to or that you wouldn't want to do, and a zero (0) by the things you never do even though you think you should.

___ read storybooks
___ have morning worship
___ read Bible each day
___ care for younger child
___ play computer games
___ pray
___ practice music/art
___ go shopping
___ play with friends
___ clean room
___ help cook dinner
___ do homework
___ play minor sports
___ attend choir/Pathfinders
___ watch video/TV
___ go to Sabbath school
___ listen to Bible lessons or tapes
___ go swimming
___ write letters
___ mow the lawn

Does the traffic in your mind give you time for the Word of God? Do the stars show that you are spending time with Jesus?

MAY

Rocky Ground Christians

Some fell on rock, and when it came up, the plants withered because they had no moisture. Luke 8:6.

An unused strip lay along the edge of the school grounds, and Ms. LeMar asked if her class could make a garden there.

"The soil is too hard and too poor," Mr. Blake, the caretaker, warned. "Nothing'll grow well."

"The children understand that," Ms. LeMar replied. "They still want to try. They want to get advice and to bring fertilizers and things."

Mr. Blake shook his head. "It'll be lots of hard work, and they won't be able to accomplish much this year. Don't you think they'll become too discouraged with gardening?"

"It's our experiment." Ms. LeMar smiled and continued, "We're acting out the parable of the sower."

The children dug and planted and watered, and all their seeds sprouted and grew quickly. One group of children came back after school and carried in extra soil and added fertilizers to their plots. Their plants grew green and healthy, but the plants in the rest of the garden seemed to stop growing. Soon they looked yellow and droopy because they didn't get the proper food, nor did they have enough water.

Many people, like those plants, grow quickly, becoming enthusiastic Christians when they first hear the good news about Jesus—but after a while they become careless about "feeding" on the Bible, and soon their experience begins to die.

One of Canada's most famous gardens, the Butchart Gardens in Victoria, British Columbia, was once a quarry for the Butcharts' cement plant. The old quarry made a large, ugly gash on the countryside, and nothing would grow there. Mr. and Mrs. Butchart decided to change that by carrying in good soil and planting a few roses and sweet peas. That first small garden made such an astounding change that the Butcharts decided to expand their gardens. They began to collect flowers and plants from around the world, and they created such an interesting group of gardens that people now come from many nations to visit and take pictures of them.

Rocky ground hearers of God's Word don't have to remain that way. Rock gives stability; it can hold the soil. By feeding on God's Word and spending time with Jesus, their lives can be changed. They can become beautiful, loving Christians.

MAY

12

A Place for God

The seed that fell among thorns stands for those who hear, but as they go on their way they are choked by life's worries, riches and pleasures, and they do not mature. Luke 8:14.

A spread of sturdy plants with pretty lavender blooms stretched across the field.

"Fwowers!" exclaimed little Patty. "Pwetty fwowers. Want to pick fwowers."

Grandpa chuckled and put a hand on her shoulder. "Those are pretty flowers," he agreed. "But those plants are mean—all stickery and prickly. They're thistles, and they hurt if you touch them."

Many thorns and thistles do have colorful flowers, but their coarse, prickly stems grow quickly, and if not controlled, they spread out in tight-ranked patches that choke the good plants.

The thorns of sin also grow anywhere quickly and easily, needing no special attention—except to be weeded out. Even doing too many good things can crowd out time for God—at least that's what Jason found out.

He'd decided to have a quiet time with God each day. In the mornings, though, he was always too rushed getting ready for school, and in the evenings it seemed that before he knew it, his mother was sending him off to bed. Someone suggested that he write down a list of everything he did in a day—the time he got up, ate, the hours he was away at school, his after-school activities—and estimate how much time each thing took.

"Wow!" he exclaimed when he saw what he'd written. "I do lots of just fooling around after school." He discovered that by setting specific times for things—practicing music, doing homework, working with his hobbies—he had plenty of time for himself and for God, too.

This is the after-school schedule he made:

3:45-4:30	Change clothes, tidy room, relax
4:30-5:00	Practice
5:00-6:00	Homework
6:00-6:30	Dinner and family worship
6:30-7:00	After-dinner chores
7:00-8:30	Hobbies, recreation, special projects
8:30-9:00	Personal Bible study and Sabbath school lesson
9:00	Bed!

If you find "thorns" choking out your time for God, try making a schedule. It can be like a garden plan that has a special place for Him.

MAY

13

A Good Garden

But the seed on good soil stands for those with a noble and good heart, who hear the word, retain it, and by persevering produce a crop. Luke 8:15.

I love gardens—pretty gardens, and clean, with tidy rows of lush, green healthy plants, but I'm really not fond of gardening.

I can think of a hundred things I'd rather do than go out and pull weeds. To me the ideal garden would be one in which you'd go out, prepare the soil, plant the seeds, and then sit back on the patio to watch everything grow. If I were to do that, though, I would see everything—both good plants and bad—grow. That's the way of gardens. So if I want a nice garden, whether I like to or not, I must be willing to work in it. Fortunately, though, I have a husband who loves to garden.

No matter how hard he works, and no matter how well the soil is prepared, and no matter how good the seeds are and how carefully they're planted, weeds still manage to get in and grow. A good gardener has to be constantly on the lookout so that the weeds will not crowd the good plants and take their food. A good garden is not a garden in which weeds cannot grow. It is one from which they are weeded out.

In the same way, a good heart is not a heart without sin. Sin can grow in a good heart just as easily as weeds can grow in a good garden, but a good heart is one that belongs to a person who believes in God and puts into practice what the Bible says, which includes weeding out the bad plants of sin.

Once upon a time a man decided he was going to have the best garden in his neighborhood. He prepared the ground. He went to the biggest garden shop, bought the best fertilizers, the best pesticides, the most expensive tools, and packages and packages of seeds. Then he took everything home and put it in his garden shed.

"When are you going to start your garden?" his wife asked.

The man shrugged. "Maybe next week."

The next week came and went. The weeds began to grow. They grew taller and taller. The garden things stayed in the shed. All the man's good intentions and all his good equipment didn't do his garden any good because he didn't use them.

Wanting to be a good Christian is not enough. Having a good heart is not enough. We must use the tools of Bible study and prayer.

MAY

14

A Rose or a Sunflower?

I will be like the dew to Israel; he will blossom like a lily. Hosea 14:5.

"Which would you rather be—a rose or a sunflower?" Ami read the topic that Mr. Janzen had written on the board for "write-now" time. *That's simple,* she told herself, picking up her pencil. *Roses are pretty and smell nice. Who'd want to be a big, bulky sunflower?*

She thought for a moment. Mr. Janzen always said to make the first sentence as interesting as possible. Then she began to write.

"Have you ever heard of a florist advertising a dozen yellow sunflowers as the perfect gift for someone you love?"

The room became quiet except for an occasional cough and the sound of pencils hurriedly forming words on paper. Mr. Janzen preferred that his students use pencils and good erasers when they wrote. "That way you don't get so uptight about mistakes," he always said.

Ami was just ready to start her last sentence when Mr. Janzen said they had only 60 seconds left. "And that's why I'd like to be a rose!" she finished in neat letters, feeling sure that everyone else in the room had made the same choice.

"Who would like to share your thoughts this morning?" Mr. Janzen asked.

Rik's hand shot up. Mr Janzen nodded.

"A field of sunflowers with their yellow faces held high in the sunshine—that is the meaning of the word 'beautiful,' " Rik began. "Sunflowers are big and bright yellow. They grow fast and take little care, and they produce valuable seeds. Roses, on the other hand, need lots of attention. I know. My grandma grows prize roses, and she's always fussing over them, making sure they have the proper food and enough water. She mulches them and prunes them and sprays them and fertilizes them—and she gets prizes for them every year in the rose show. Her roses are beautiful, but only because she takes such good care of them.

"Because of their delicate beauty, I suppose most people would choose to be a rose, but I'd rather be a sunflower and stand tall in the sun and send out my roots to feed on the good things in the soil so that I can produce hundreds and hundreds of nutritious seeds. Sunflowers are valuable—even for art! A very famous and valuable painting by the Dutch painter Van Gogh is of a field of sunflowers."

Do you agree with Ami or with Rik? Would you rather be a rose or a sunflower?

MAY

15

Which?

After Rik read his essay about wanting to be a sunflower, Mr. Janzen took a vote. "No matter what you've written," he said, "I want you to vote for which you'd rather be—a rose or a sunflower." Ami was surprised to see that the class was almost evenly split. Almost half wanted to be sunflowers. The rest, like her, preferred to be roses.

"Roses and sunflowers are very different, to be sure," Mr. Janzen continued, "but each has a very special beauty in its own way. Some of you really are more like roses, with a quiet, delicate beauty. Others of you are more like sunflowers—big, bold, and sunny. The important thing is that you grow into the best person you can be, that you feed on the truth of God so you'll have the beauty of real love."

The class listened. Mr. Janzen had a way of using his assignments to make them think about God.

"Real love grows in a pure heart," he continued, "a heart that belongs to God. A pure heart is like a good garden—whether a rose garden or a sunflower field, or a backyard vegetable garden, it'll never be totally free from the weeds of sin, but its purpose is to grow only the good and to weed out all the bad." He smiled. "We need God's help each day to keep at those weeds of sin."

Pretend that you're choosing seeds for your garden and that everything you plant is going to represent something about real love. Which of the following would you plant? What makes that plant like real love? Which would you not plant? Why not?

___ broccoli	___ beets
___ asters	___ peas
___ cabbage	___ thistles
___ marigolds	___ dandelions
___ wild oats	___ strawberries
___ lettuce	___ squash
___ radishes	___ carrots
___ zinnias	___ wild flowers
___ sweet peas	___ spinach
___ lilies	___ cauliflower
___ okra	___ morning glories
___ beans	___ collards
___ baby's breath	___ pumpkins
___ tomatoes	___ Brussels sprouts

The ultimate aim . . . is . . . love which springs from a pure heart, a good conscience and a genuine faith. 1 Timothy 1:5, Phillips.

MAY

16

The Baobab

The great dragon was hurled down—that ancient serpent called the devil, or Satan, who leads the whole world astray. He was hurled to the earth, and his angels with him. Revelation 12:9.

Look at that funny tree." Kimberly pointed toward a dry hillside. "Looks like its roots are kicking in the air!"

Her father laughed. "That's a baobab," he said. "One of Africa's special trees that, according to a legend, was thrown out of heaven by the Creator because it looked so bad. It landed upside down, and all baobabs have grown that way ever since."

"Then it really does grow upside down." Kimberly was serious.

"That's just a story," her father assured her. "Its huge, misshapen trunk and stubby, rootlike branches make it look that way. Now every time I see a baobab, I think of the story in Revelation about how God threw the devil out of heaven and down to our earth. Then, because of Adam's and Eve's choice at another tree, sin took root and is growing everywhere in this world."

"Then it's a wicked tree?"

Kimberly's father shook his head. "Not at all!" he exclaimed. "Really, it's more of a savior, and its looks are what makes it so good. The woody bark covers great thicknesses of spongy tissue that soak up water to keep it alive through long periods of drought. Its fruit makes a good drink that has lots of vitamin C. It can be dried into a powder from which cream of tartar is made. That gives it its other name—the cream of tartar tree. The young leaves cook up like spinach, its wood makes excellent fishing floats, and the inner bark beats into a strong fiber for making rope and nets.

"Pioneers traveling across these dry lands by foot or by oxcart often sheltered under a baobab. It's even possible to sleep inside some bigger ones, and their water has saved more than one traveler from dying of thirst. A large baobab near Victoria Falls in Zimbabwe became the favorite camping spot for travelers on their way to the other side of the Zambezi River. They called it 'Big Tree.' We'll see it tomorrow."

Several miles had passed while they were talking. "Look, there's another baobab." Kimberly pointed across a flat field. "And it looks as upside down as the other."

"But it's a very useful and important tree," her father reminded her. "In one place they even used one for a jail. I like to think of it as a symbol of the help God gives in this world of sin."

MAY

17

Where Were You?

The earth and the sky will tremble. But the Lord will be a refuge for his people. Joel 3:16.

I certainly haven't forgotten where we were."

As the adults talked, Christopher pictured the flat-topped mountain they'd seen as they landed at the Portland, Oregon, airport.

"Me neither," added Uncle Mark. "My buddies and I were camping up on Salt Spring Island when there was this big boom, but we couldn't see a thing."

"We lived toward the coast and didn't hear it," said Aunt Judith. "With the winds carrying everything inland, we had no inkling about the eruption until Dad turned on the news that evening—and then we worried."

"We didn't hear it, either, but I'll never forget the ash," Nadia said.

"What was it like?" Christopher wanted to know.

"It looked like snow, but it was scary. It was dark already, and my two brothers and I crouched by the window as we watched these tiny flakes rain straight down. They were kinda pretty, silvery-gray in the streetlights, but we looked like creatures from space. We'd been listening to advice on the radio and had tied coffee filters over our faces so we wouldn't breathe in any of the fine dust."

Christopher had read about Mount St. Helens, the volcano in Washington State, that blew up in May 1980, two years before he was born. Molten rock poured down the mountainside, and hot ash spewed into the air, killing 57 people. The eruption blasted away more than 1,000 feet from the peak.

"It certainly doesn't look like the same mountain anymore," said Aunt Judith. "It was so beautiful, like a big peppermint pink ice-cream cone in the sunset, its rounded dome snow-clad and peaceful. We never in our wildest dreams thought this would happen during our lifetime, even though Indians' stories told of many eruptions. But the last was more than 100 years earlier."

"The sleeping lady," Uncle Mark mused. "No one expected her to wake up so soon—but when she did, what a mess! She started forest fires and melted snow and created mud slides that washed away buildings, roads, and bridges. She knocked down millions of trees and spread thick layers of volcanic ash over a wide area.

"But look how quickly trees have grown back and wildlife returned. The scars are healing."

People can usually tell you where they were and what they were doing the moment a sudden, dramatic event happened. Are you ready so that when Jesus comes He won't catch you off guard?

MAY

18

The Rainbow Chaser

Kind words bring life, but cruel words crush your spirit. Proverbs 15:4, TEV.

Colorful oblongs were splashed about the room—on the walls, on the furniture, and on the carpet—rainbows, many of them. Little Craig laughed when he saw them and hurried to pick one off the carpet. As he bent to get it, it disappeared. He looked up at his mother, a question on his face. She called him to her.

"Look now," she told him, pointing. There the rainbow was, just where it had been before. He reached for it again, and it disappeared. He backed away, and there it was.

"Look," his mother told him again. She pointed toward the window. See the little crystal heart hanging there? That's called a prism. When the sun shines through it, it scatters rainbows about the room. But when you get between the prism and the rainbow, the rainbow disappears. It shines on your back, and you can't see it. Look again." And she showed him.

Hanging in the window to catch the sunlight, the "Rainbow Chasers" cast cheery splashes of rainbow color about the room. The Sun of God—Jesus—shining through our hearts casts rainbows of happiness about us because of the kinds of things we say and do. When something gets in the way, though, the rainbows disappear, and kind words often become cruel.

The following five sentences are the sort that crush spirits—both of the person that says them and of the person they're said to. Try saying them just the way you imagine they might really be said.

1. "Yuck! That's an ugly shirt."
2. "Get out of here!"
3. "You always make such a mess!"
4. "Don't be so stupid!"
5. "Can't you do anything right?"

What tone of voice did you use? ______________

How did you feel as you were talking? __________

Now change each sentence into a compliment, and practice saying them just as you'd like to hear someone say them to you.

1. ____________________________________
2. ____________________________________
3. ____________________________________
4. ____________________________________
5. ____________________________________

What tone of voice did you use this time? _______

How did you feel when you said these sentences?

____

Let Jesus shine through your heart.

MAY

19

The Tallest Tower

Therefore do not be foolish, but understand what the Lord's will is. Ephesians 5:17.

According to a story that a friend told me, the people of a certain Dutch village were very, very proud. Their new church was finished and stood solid and firm with its tower pointing toward heaven.

"A fine church, isn't it, Farmer Jansma?" said Greengrocer Zijlstra when the two of them met on their way to the service the next Sunday morning.

"Very fine, indeed," replied Farmer Jansma.

"What a very fine tower," added Milkman Bosma as he joined his two friends. "You'll not see a finer steeple in all our province."

"Nor a taller one," Farmer Jansma commented with pride. "Our church has the tallest tower of all the churches in Friesland."

The three men stopped to admire their church with its slate-gray steeple silhouetted against the rich, blue sky. The steady sea breeze scudded big puffs of cloud across the sky, twisted at leafy green branches, and scooped at the men's loose-fitting trousers, but it could do nothing to the solid church other than whistle around the towering steeple and along the edges of the tiled roof.

"The tallest tower in all Friesland," repeated Greengrocer Zijlstra.

Many years went by. The children and the grandchildren of the three men, and then their children, had grown up and carried on the family businesses. In all that time no other village built a church with a taller tower. Then word began to circulate that folks in a distant town intended to build a new church with an even taller tower. During the night some of their men sneaked into the village churchyard. One, carrying a long rope to measure the tower's exact height, climbed to the very top of the church tower. They would build theirs a half meter higher.

Somehow the village men learned what had happened. A few nights later they sneaked into the new town church and cut one meter from the rope that was being used as a measure, but no one said a thing—not until after the new church tower was finished.

Until this day, Tjim still has the church with the tallest tower—by one half meter—in all the province. But does having the church with the tallest steeple bring anyone nearer to God?

As Paul says, "Do not be foolish, but understand what the Lord's will is."

MAY

20

Build Something

You are all sons of God through faith in Christ Jesus. Galatians 3:26.

Mrs. Schmidt sat on a bamboo stool in the shade of the mango tree, studying the reports she'd received during her visit to the mission school that morning. Leon, one of the younger boys of the family with whom she was staying, slipped up beside her. "I tried and tried," he said. "But it didn't work." His eyes brimmed with tears.

"What didn't work?" asked Mrs. Schmidt.

"I washed and washed with soap, but my skin didn't get white."

Mrs. Schmidt slipped her arm around Leon. "Washing won't change the color of our skin," she said.

"But *he* said . . ." Leon pointed toward a bigger boy. "He said if I scrubbed and scrubbed, I could be white. I want to be white like you."

"Oh, Leon," Mrs. Schmidt exclaimed, "you're just the right color the way you are."

"But if I were like you . . ."

Mrs. Schmidt shook her head. "God wouldn't love you any more, and neither would I or anyone else. We're all God's children, and the important thing is to show your love for Him by becoming the best person you can be and by using the talents He has given you in the best possible way."

Giuseppe Verdi, the great Italian composer, may have wished he had been born with better opportunities. From the time he was small, he showed remarkable musical abilities, and when he was old enough, he applied to enter the Milan Conservatory, one of Italy's great music schools. Since his father was an innkeeper, he hadn't been able to send Giuseppe to the right preparatory schools, and the conservatory wouldn't accept him because he lacked the proper schooling.

Instead of giving up, Giuseppe kept on with his music, continuing to develop his talents. His work became well-known, and he became so famous that the same school that had refused to accept him as a student was later renamed "Verdi Conservatory of Music."

"Man can shape circumstances," Ellen White once wrote, "but circumstances should not be allowed to shape the man. We should seize upon circumstances as instruments by which to work. We are to master them and not permit them to master us" (*The Ministry of Healing*, p. 500).

An old saying puts it this way: "No matter what your lot in life, build something on it."

MAY

21

Better Than Silver or Gold

A good name is to be chosen rather than great riches, loving favor rather than silver and gold.
Proverbs 22:1, NKJV.

"Date. That's an unusual name."

My husband's name often draws comments.

"It's a good name," he replies.

Appropriate pauses usually invite the rest of the story.

"It's Dutch. I'm named after my uncle Date."

Being different makes a name distinctive and special, but a name gains its real worth from the person to whom it belongs. Date enjoys punning with his name, but he'd learned its serious value back when he was a boy during the war in Holland.

"Don't expect me to go to church if that's what Christians are like." He remembers hearing the disgust in his father's voice. "Just because there's a war, everyone runs to church. Now, if they actually followed what the church teaches, then I might think it'd do some good."

"Koop, you know better," his aunt argued.

"I know what happens when my boys work for your church deacon," his father retorted. "In the morning when they get to his farm, his clock has the exact time, but every evening it's a half hour slow. Since they're paid according to his clock, tell me how it can be right every morning and slow every evening?"

There was a pause, then he heard his father's voice again. "What good is church if it doesn't teach a man to be honest? We don't go to church, but we teach our children to be honest. We want them to have a good name."

As he listened, Date slid his hand into his pocket and felt the silky smoothness of three marbles. With the war going on and being one of the younger brothers in a big family, he had few treasures that he could call his own. Until that morning, the marbles in his pocket were part of a collection the baker's boy kept in a tin under the counter in the bakery.

He'll never miss three, Date had told himself when he went to the bakery. While the baker was getting the bread, he reached around the counter and helped himself to the marbles.

"To be honest. To have a good name."

His father's words needled his conscience. After a serious struggle in his thoughts, Date returned the marbles.

Is your name better than silver or gold?

MAY

22

Soldiers Are Coming

Now it is required that those who have been given a trust must prove faithful. 1 Corinthians 4:2.

"Quick! Soldiers are coming."

The warning sent Date's heart grabbing at his throat.

"They're taking bikes!"

Cinders crunched under his wooden shoes as he spun around and sped toward home. "Jan!" he yelled to his older brother. "Your bike! Soldiers."

Jan needed no explanation. As the war had dragged on, supplies ran short for the occupying troops. If they needed bicycles, they went through a village and took what they found. Jan's bike was the only one the family had, and they depended on it. "Give me a hand." Jan grunted as he hoisted his bike against the house. "Let's lift it onto the roof."

"Hey, fellows, what're you doing?" their father demanded, coming out of the carpentry shop.

"Soldiers are after bikes!"

"They'll see it there. Bring it to me, and then go tell your mother to show you the loose boards in the living room." Their father got a wrench and started taking the bicycle apart.

Throughout the village, people hurried to hide bicycles. Farmers buried bikes in manure piles. Some pushed theirs into hollows in their haymows. Others threw theirs into canals. But Jan and Date carried the bicycle parts into the house and shoved them under the loose floorboards of their living room.

Heavy steps thudded onto the porch, and someone banged on the door. Date ran into the kitchen and dived under the table. Soldiers stomped into the living room. If they found the loose boards under the carpet and learned that he'd helped hide the bike, why, even if he was only 8, he could be shot. He crouched in the far corner.

In the living room the soldiers tried to make themselves understood. Mother only shook her head. She couldn't understand their language. They couldn't understand hers. At last they left, mumbling among themselves.

Date waited a long time, until he could be sure that it was absolutely safe, and then scrambled from under the table. He and the bike were safe.

Have you ever had to protect anything that was as important to you as the bicycle was to Date's family? God has entrusted you with something very important to you and your family—the good news of salvation. How do you protect it?

MAY

23

To Be Hungry

Two shots echoed through the night. Date shuddered. Soldiers shot at anyone out after 8:00 p.m. Steps clattered across the porch. The door burst open, then slammed shut, and Jan leaned back against it, pale and shaking.

"They almost got me," he gasped. "But, here, I got this." He held out a bag to their mother.

Date looked at it hungrily, then across at the big woman sitting in their mother's favorite chair. *If that woman doesn't get it first,* he thought angrily.

The woman sat there solidly, her hands clasped, her face expressionless, but behind her big, black eyes, he imagined millions of wheels turning, wheels full of plans for her own self. Fury welled up inside him. He wanted to pick her up and throw her out of the house. He wondered how his mother could be so patient when this woman was so lazy and so selfish. He was hungry, and he was angry.

"Good for you, son." Mother took the bag from Jan. "Tomorrow we can feast."

Hunger pains gnawed at Date's stomach that night. "It seemed he'd always been hungry. For weeks they'd eaten nothing but potatoes and turnips—and he couldn't stand turnips. Every day the others tried to trick him, telling him that they were carrots so he'd eat them. But he would rather starve than eat one more bite of yucky turnips.

His mouth watered as he thought ahead to dinner the next day. Jan had brought fresh meat. Date stirred restlessly, trying to escape the empty knotting of his stomach, but he was squeezed between his two younger brothers in a narrow cot. Refugees had their beds. These days there were always extra people in the house. They came from that secret called "The Underground." The word was always whispered. Date didn't know exactly what it meant, except that people were frightened and that his family shared their food—even the little they had—with these strangers, including the fat woman, and gave them beds, and kept them safe.

At last he drifted to sleep, dreaming of food, mountains of good, delicious food, more than he could possibly ever eat. He knew what it was like to be hungry, terribly hungry.

Blessed are those who hunger and thirst for righteousness, for they will be filled. Matthew 5:6.

MAY

24

Cast Your Bread

Cast your bread upon the waters, for after many days you will find it again. Ecclesiastes 11:1.

Dinnertime finally arrived. Date watched as the food started around, hungrily awaiting his turn. He was the last to be served, and there was getting to be less and less food on the platter. But in his family they always shared, and his mother always made sure that each person had a fair share.

The platter came to the big woman. She picked the meat over, looking carefully at each piece. Date waited. She seemed to take forever. At last she speared the biggest piece, then another. That left two pieces—one for Jan and one for Pieter. Date wanted to cry, but he bravely took the empty platter when it came to him and handed it to his father. He did not bother to take potatoes, and he would rather starve than eat turnips. He would just sit—and watch.

Mother saw his empty plate. "What is it?" she asked.

Date tried to answer, but no words came. He just looked toward the woman's plate.

Mother looked at her son's thin body, then at the huge woman. She started to speak, but before she could say a thing, his father broke in.

"Why, you . . ." His voice rose sharply. "You come in the name of God and plead for mercy. And now you steal our children's food—from their very plates!"

Even Date cringed at the anger he heard in his father's voice.

"Go! Now! Go!"

"But where?" the woman whimpered. "They'd send me to a camp."

"You can't send her away like that." Mother tried to soothe the situation.

"Let her at least give the boy his food!"

That evening the woman was gone.

"Where?" Date asked.

"The Underground made arrangements," his mother explained. "We mustn't blame her for acting the way she does," she continued. "She's suffered so from this war, even more than we have. Her family is all dead; her home, gone. We're fortunate to live in the country, and it's only fair that we share what we have with those who have nothing. Always remember, share, and others will share with you."

MAY

25

The Camel He Loved Best

Date clenched his teeth, trying not to cry out. Maybe his mother hadn't been so right after all about sharing. The nurse continued to bend over him, steadying his head with one hand. In the other she held a pair of tweezers and one by one pulled the hairs from an infected area of his scalp.

The war was over, and for the first time that he could remember, he could eat all he wanted to eat. But his lanky body was thin from having had too little for too long, and he, along with many of the other children, was sick from not having the proper food.

"You'll be better soon," the nurse told him as she yanked out yet another hair. "We've just got to get rid of all this bad hair so your scalp can heal. We have food and medicines and vitamins now, and soon you'll have a beautiful head of new hair and be strong and healthy and handsome."

He could hear a wink in her voice, and that helped, but he still didn't like having to have his hair pulled out. "Maybe if we hadn't shared our food with all those others, if we'd have just fed our own family . . ."

His mother shook her head firmly when he suggested the idea. "If we hadn't shared, others wouldn't have shared with us. The only reason we ever got extra food was that we kept refugees. Besides, other folks hid your brothers when the soldiers wanted to send them out of the country to the work camps. No. You never can give too much."

An old Arabian proverb says, "If you give away that which you love, it will come back to you." They use a puzzle to show how this can work. Here is the puzzle:

An old man had 18 camels. He decided that it was time to divide them among his three sons, but he wanted to keep the camel he loved best for himself. That left 17 camels for his three sons. According to custom, he must divide his herd like this—

one half to his oldest son =
one third to his second son =
one ninth to his third son =
How was he able to do this?

Use the clue from the proverb to work out the answer. (The answer is on page 380.)

Remember this: Whoever sows sparingly will also reap sparingly, and whoever sows generously will also reap generously. 2 Corinthians 9:6.

MAY

26

The Test

Test everything. Hold on to the good. *1 Thessalonians 5:21.*

Date's head healed, and his body began to fill out, but times remained hard—a bit too hard for his liking. It seemed as though all the boys had fishing poles—all except him. "Mom," he begged, "can't you get me a fishing pole?"

"Sorry. We just can't."

"But, Mom . . ."

"Maybe later."

He understood, but right then there was nothing he wanted more than a fishing pole. He tried to think of a way to get one for himself, but there was no way he could earn money to buy one, and no one he knew had an extra one. About that time he started going to Sunday school with some of the neighbor boys. He was about to give up the idea of ever getting a fishing pole when his Sunday school teacher taught them a lesson about prayer.

"God will answer our prayers," he assured the children. "If there's something you need, ask God."

There's something I need, all right, Date told himself. That night he prayed his first real prayer—for a fishing pole.

After school the next day he tried to convince Andre to play soccer with him.

"Can't," Andre said. "This afternoon I've got to help my dad put up poles for the beans."

"Too bad," Date sighed.

"Ja. And do you know what we have to use for sticks? Fishing poles."

"Fishing poles!" Date could hardly believe what Andre was saying. "I need a pole for fishing."

"Why don't you come by? I'm sure Dad would let you have one."

That afternoon Date went home with a fishing pole. He'd tested prayer and found that it worked.

MAY

27

Under His Pillow

"Date's such a good boy," Jan overheard their grandmother telling their mother. "He always sleeps with his Bible under his pillow. He'll be a fine man."

Jan told the others, and then how they teased him, but Date just shrugged. He knew as well as the others that keeping a Bible under his pillow wouldn't make him good. He'd gotten the Bible at Sunday school and just wanted to keep it nice.

"Date is different from the other boys," he often heard his parents say. And he knew what they meant by that, too. He had to wear glasses; the others didn't. They all did well at school; he didn't. In fact, at school he was dumb, just plain dumb. Everyone knew that he would never learn well, but he was strong—so strong that the others called him Samson—and he could work hard.

"He's going to be a good man," his grandmother had said, and he intended to make her words come true. He wanted to be a farmer, to someday own his own farm and be rich. In the meantime, he had an after-school job on a farm, then when he turned 15 he could drop out of school and work full-time. His grandmother owned a small farm, and she had promised that he could buy it from her as soon as he was ready. He'd work and learn everything he could about farming and save his money. Then in a few years he'd be ready to take over her farm.

For the time being, though, he continued to sleep with his Bible under his pillow, never dreaming of the changes it would one day make in his life's plans.

I have hidden your word in my heart that I might not sin against you.
Psalm 119:11.

WTG-6

MAY

28

A Quiz About the Bible

We know that what the scripture says is true forever.
John 10:35, TEV.

Try to answer these questions about the Bible. They're based on the King James Version. The answers are on page 380.

1. What is the longest verse in the Bible?
2. What is the shortest verse?
3. How many chapters does the Bible have?
4. Which is the middle chapter?
5. What is the longest word in the Bible and what does it mean?
6. Which was the first Bible to be printed in North America?
7. In what languages was the Bible first written?
8. When and why was the Bible divided into chapters and verses?
9. Where did we get the word "Bible"?
10. Which are considered the most beautiful passages in the Bible?

While it's interesting to know things about the Bible, the most important thing is to know the truth about God that the Bible contains.

Which is your favorite
verse? ____________________
passage? ____________________
chapter? ____________________
book? ____________________

MAY

29

The Race

Everyone who competes in the games goes into strict training. They do it to get a crown that will not last; but we do it to get a crown that will last forever. 1 Corinthians 9:25.

"Ready . . . Set . . ." The starter's pistol cracked.

Date pushed off, pedaling with all his might in order to catch the lead group. His dad had told him that he didn't stand a chance of winning with his old bike, but he was strong, and intended to prove that he could do it.

He passed one racer, then the next and the next. Another biker edged toward him. Date strained harder to stay ahead. The other cyclist brushed against him. Date heard a crunch as he thudded against a parked car, then felt a grinding pain as he skidded on his side in the loose gravel. Not minding his bleeding face and arm, he grabbed up his bicycle and jumped back on, eager to regain the lost time. He'd trained hard for this race and was determined to win.

The pedals spun, but the bike didn't move. Date slid off to check the damage. Broken chain, broken spokes, bent frame. The last racers whizzed past. He watched as they rounded the corner and disappeared. Date turned his crippled bike and limped toward home. Disappointment masked the pain of his own injuries.

"Forget about racing," his father advised when he saw the mess. "You'll never get that bike fixed, and you haven't money for another."

Date wasn't to be discouraged that easily, though. He patched up the old bike and three months later entered another race. This time he was on guard against interference from other racers. He worked his way into the lead group and won the prize money for making the fastest round.

"I placed fourth, even on that old bike," he announced proudly at home.

He entered more races and won more medals, but he soon realized that the rewards didn't equal the work they required. His father was right—he had neither the time nor the money to become a professional racer.

God calls us into a race for Him—a race that demands time and endurance—and the reward is more than worth the effort. The best part is that each one who enters His race is guaranteed of becoming a champion if he or she chooses and of receiving the best prize of all—eternal life.

MAY

30

Changes

Work with your hands . . . so that your daily life may win the respect of outsiders and so that you will not be dependent on anybody.
1 Thessalonians 4:11, 12.

During his last week in the army, Date received a letter from his father. "Your grandmother has sold her farm," he wrote.

"Sold the farm!" Date could not believe his eyes. That one simple sentence blacked out all the plans he had made.

What was he to do now? The Dutch peacetime army was being cut back, so he couldn't reenlist. Farm jobs were almost impossible to find. He had no education for a city job.

He went home, not knowing what to do.

Unemployment was causing many others to look for their fortunes in the New World. He thought of the Canadian soldiers who had liberated their village at the end of the war. He thought of former neighbors who had gone to Canada and who now owned their own farms. Then one day he received another letter—this time from Jan, who used to live next door to them.

"Come to Canada," Jan wrote. "I need someone to work on my dairy."

Within six months Date was at work on that dairy snuggled in a small valley among the mountains of British Columbia.

He settled into the routine. Maybe it was good, after all, that his grandmother had sold her farm to someone else. Canada was a land of opportunity. He would work hard for Jan, save his money, and someday have his own farm in Canada instead of in Holland.

Date had grown up with what is called the "work ethic." When he was young, he learned to work with his hands, and he no longer had to be dependent on anyone. He intended to use his abilities to create a good future for himself. He'd also learned lessons of honesty and sharing. He knew that God answers prayer and that the Bible is a good book.

He expected to be a good neighbor and a good citizen in his new country. He could take care of himself, and this, he assumed, was all that he needed in order to have a good life. He was happy with the way his life was going.

Although his life fulfilled the advice of today's text, what else did Date need in order to have an even better life? ____

____.

MAY

31

When Bad Things Are Good

And we know that in all things God works for the good of those who love him, who have been called according to his purpose. Romans 8:28.

Bill, another young Dutchman, owned the farm across from Jan's dairy, where Date worked. The two became good friends. In town Bill was Date's interpreter; at home he was his pal.

"Be careful of Bill," Jan's wife warned Date. "He has some strange beliefs, and he'll try to get you to believe the way he does."

Date didn't foresee any problems, except for one. Bill's farm was for sale. "I hope your farm doesn't sell," he told his new friend. "Not now, anyway. I don't want you to move."

"But I don't like farming," Bill replied. "The sooner this place sells, the happier I'll be. I've prayed for a buyer, and I don't know why God hasn't already sent one."

Hearing Bill talk about prayer reminded Date of how his prayer for a fishing pole had been answered. He wanted to make religion part of his new life so he went to church with Jan each Sunday. But the English just floated past him. "God," he prayed, "help me understand the sermons."

He bought an English Bible, and by comparing it with his Dutch Bible, the one he used to keep under his pillow, he began to understand English. Then a question started to bother him. "Bill," he finally asked, "why do you go to church on Saturday?"

The answer to that question marked the start of big changes for Date. He began going to church with Bill, then he was baptized, then he decided to go back to school.

"School!" exclaimed Jan when he heard Date's plans. "But you're already past 20, and you didn't even finish grade school in Holland. Stay on the farm. I'll raise your wages."

Date shook his head. "God's calling me to a new way of life," he said, and he left the farm.

Going back to school took lots of hard work, but somehow learning had become easier for him, and he found himself among the top students. In a few years he became a teacher himself, then a principal, then a missionary ADRA director, and, among other things, he teaches others how to be good farmers.

"Because of two farms—" he sometimes says, "because my grandmother sold hers and because Bill couldn't sell his. God certainly can work for good in situations that we don't understand." By the way, Bill's farm sold later.

JUNE

1

On Things Above

Set your hearts on things above. Colossians 3:1.

"Oh, look!" Holly pointed toward the beach.

A long parade of kites in a brilliant rainbow of colors strained at their tethers in the steady sea breeze. Some trailed long tails. Some soared like giant birds with wings widespread. Some billowed into jointed fiery-colored dragons. Others danced and looped above the waves.

"There must be a hundred of them!"

She watched, fascinated, as folks have been since kites were first flown in China more than 2,000 years ago.

I can remember wishing for a big, beautiful store-bought kite when I was a girl, but I had to settle for making my own.

"Like this," Dad said as he showed me how to slice thin sticks from a long piece of cedar to make the ribs, then lash them into a cross, notch the ends, and stretch the string frame. Mom helped me staple on the newspaper cover and tie a series of crushed newspaper bows together for the tail. With careful balancing and by bowing the cross rib just enough, we could make these newspaper creations fly surprisingly well.

A tall fir tree marked the border of our farm. It stood alone, a remnant of the forest that used to cover the land, seeming to reach as high as the clouds as it towered over the alder brush that crowded beside it. My goal was to make a kite fly higher than that tree, and one did fly better than the others. It rose easily on the breeze, lifting high above the meadow, responding gracefully to my tugs on the string, flying higher and higher. I urged it on until it was flying above that tree.

I watched, elated to have reached my goal, when suddenly the string went slack in my hand. The kite whooshed backward, giving a quick jump as if delighted to be free, then looped into a big circle. At the top of the loop it faltered, tipped, then dropped into a swinging zigzag that carried it lower and lower and farther and farther from where I stood. I held the broken string and looked on helplessly as the kite settled from sight in a rambling of brush and brambles, where it was ripped and tangled beyond repair.

The brush and brambles of sin wait to snare those who break their connection with Jesus. Keep your connection. Keep your hearts on things above.

JUNE

A Good Connection

Such confidence as this is ours through Christ before God.
2 Corinthians 3:4.

Kite flying is popular and fun, but to be safe, kite flyers need to obey a few commonsense don'ts:

1. Don't fly a kite near electric power lines or transmission towers or antennas.
2. Don't fly a kite in wet or stormy weather.
3. Don't use wire or anything metallic in a kite line.
4. Don't fly a kite over public streets, highways, or above bystanders.

Those are the rules. Follow them, and you can fly a kite anytime, anywhere, right?

Well, that depends. You could keep those four rules perfectly and still not have the right conditions to fly your kite. For example, to fly well, kites need a steady wind of about 5 to 15 miles per hour, and of course, an open area. Beaches are great, and so are schoolyards, parks, farmlands, empty parking lots, and even rooftops. But your kite can have problems if it gets too close to trees and buildings, because they can create turbulence up to three times their height.

Following all the rules and taking a kite to a wide open field on a sunny day when the wind is just right still will not do any good unless you have a strong kite string that you hold securely. Kites will never get off the ground or stay aloft unless they have a good holding connection that creates the resistance they need in order to ride on the wind.

It's the same in our everyday lives. Here's a checklist of good things. Mark those that you do.

___ Go to church on Sabbath.
___ Give offerings.
___ Pay tithe.
___ Be kind to neighbors.
___ Do chores without complaining.
___ Use only "clean" language.
___ Avoid unclean foods.

Many people do all these and many other good things, but, like the kite, they never get their Christian life off the ground because no one is holding the kite line.

You need to keep the rules, but you also need to keep in touch with Jesus in order to be a Christian.

JUNE

3

God Cares

When I look at the sky, which you have made, at the moon and the stars, which you set in their places—what is man, that you think of him; mere man, that you care for him? Psalm 8:3, 4, TEV.

Tony rolled over onto his back and looked up. The moon spread a silver-gray wash over the campsite, and the stars hung like embedded points of light in a laser photo. Some were large and pulsing, seeming just beyond the treetops. Others were tiny and still—dots set deep into the distant reaches of the sky.

He held up his hands, squinted through the rectangular frame he formed with thumb and forefingers, and started counting.

Have you, like Tony, ever tried to count the stars on a clear night? Difficult, isn't it? Actually, there are so many stars that no astronomer can count them. Millions and millions of galaxies spread through the universe, and each contains millions of stars.

Scientists think that the most distant stars they've seen are billions of light years away. The nearest star to the earth is, of course, our sun, and as far as stars go it's just average. At that, it's almost as big as a million earths. If the trip were possible, a jumbo jet would need about 19 years to get there. Just think how old you'd be by the time you'd made the round trip! Of course, the sun's so hot—about 10,000° F on the surface—you wouldn't consider the trip anyway.

Light from the next closest star, Proxima Centauri, takes more than four years to reach us. Since light travels 5.88 trillion miles a year, that makes it about 25 trillion miles away. Light takes about 100,000 years to travel from one side to the other of our Milky Way Galaxy, so how far is it across? __________ . Notice how many zeros it takes to just write the number. (The answer is on page 381.)

Now let's come back to earth. It measures 24,900 miles (39,940 kilometers) around at the equator. Suppose it were possible for us to form a human chain around it. A person's reach is about the same as his or her height. If everyone were six feet tall (1.8288 meters) and just touched fingertips, how many people would it take to reach around the earth? __________________

That's several times the world membership of our church—and that's just to reach one time around our earth, a very small planet in God's universe.

Lying in his sleeping bag, looking up at the stars, Tony knew that he was just a tiny speck on tiny Planet Earth in a galaxy that's only one of millions and millions. Even so, he also knew that God cares for him.

JUNE

The Praying Mantis

The Pharisee stood up and prayed about himself: "God, I thank you that I am not like other men—robbers, evildoers, adulterers—or even like this tax collector." Luke 18:11.

"Mantis?" little Craig asked, pointing at a slender green insect balanced on the rose stem. The insect rocked slightly and turned its triangular head toward him.

"Yes, that's a praying mantis," his mother agreed. "See how it holds its front claws up and folded as if it's praying."

Even though it looks pious, the praying mantis should have its name spelled p-r-*e*-y-i-n-g, because it's born hungry and spends its life hunting and eating other insects. When it hatches it's tan, wingless, and about the size of a mosquito, but it's easy to recognize because of the way it holds its front claws. As soon as it dries, it begins eating—preying on any edible tidbit it can find. At first it feeds on aphids, but it will eat its brothers and sisters, too, if they don't scamper out of reach.

Soon the mantis changes from tan to a lively green to match the shrubbery where it waits, claws poised, ready to grab anything tasty that happens by.

The bigger the mantis grows, the more it eats. When it reaches adulthood—in about two months—it needs grasshopper-sized meals. Then it's about three and a half inches long, has full-sized wings, and is ready to mate. After mating, the female often eats her husband. Because they do eat so many insects, praying mantises are beneficial, although their actions do not match their name.

When Jesus told the story of the Pharisee who was praying "I thank You that I am not like others," He gave a good example of "preying mantis behavior"—of those who, with folded hands, are just waiting for another victim.

Praying people usually don't go around eating their families. Their prayers may even be full of all the right words, but sometimes they prey on others by gossiping and criticizing. Which of the following are *praying* and which are *preying* words?

__________ "I'm sorry . . ."
__________ "Do you know what she did?"
__________ "She wears such dumb clothes."
__________ "Let me help you."
__________ "They went swimming on Sabbath."
__________ "He got a D in math."
__________ "Their cousin has AIDS."

Some of these can be either "praying" or "preying." Suggest ways to make all of them "praying" words.

JUNE

5

Why Big Ben Was Slow

Catch for us the foxes, the little foxes that ruin the vineyards, our vineyards that are in bloom. Song of Solomon 2:15.

Big Ben, that famous clock in the tower of the parliament buildings in London, was slow—it was losing 15 seconds each day!

The keeper cleaned it thoroughly and oiled all the mechanisms, but still the huge clock continued to lose time.

This would never do, because Big Ben had a reputation to keep. It was known for being exact. Its long hands always pointed out the precise time, and its gigantic bell always boomed out the exact hour.

The keeper did not know what to do. He had gone through all the inside works and could find nothing wrong. He decided to check the outside again.

Big Ben had earned its name honestly twice over. When it was installed in 1859, the bell was named for Sir Benjamin Hall, the tall, stout commissioner of works at that time. It is big, too—nine feet in diameter, seven and a half feet high, and weighs 13½ tons. The name later was used for the clock as well—its minute hand is more than six feet long.

The keeper looked at the clock from the outside. He wasn't sure, but maybe there was something on the minute hand. He climbed up to check, and he did find something. A mother bird had built her nest on the minute hand, and there she sat with her six babies, riding around Big Ben's face every hour, unaware that their weight was causing one of the world's biggest and most famous clocks to go too slow.

Little things *do* make a difference. Our text mentions the little foxes—playful little foxes, just the right age to be tumbling about in fun—that damage the vines when they're in bloom.

Pierre, a businessman, spends 23 seconds in the elevator for each trip to or from his apartment. Twenty-three seconds isn't much, but he doesn't like to waste time. He calculated that in three years he would spend 42 hours riding that elevator—42 hours of standing and doing nothing. Since he couldn't remove these seconds, like the keeper could take away the bird's nest or chase them off like baby foxes, he decided to use them. During those few seconds alone in the elevator, he began saying short prayers, talking to God about anything that happened to be on his mind.

What are some of the little things that could make a difference in your life?

JUNE

The Parable of the Ten Minas

To everyone who has, more will be given, but as for the one who has nothing, even what he has will be taken away. Luke 19:26.

This is a dramatic reading from Luke 19:12-25. (See instructions on page 28.)

JESUS: A man of noble birth went to a distant country to have himself appointed king and then to return. So he called ten of his servants and gave them ten minas.*

MAN: Put this money to work, until I come back.

JESUS: But his subjects hated him and sent a delegation after him to say,

SUBJECTS: We don't want this man to be our king.

JESUS: He was made king, however, and returned home. Then he sent for the servants to whom he had given the money, in order to find out what they had gained with it. The first one came and said,

FIRST SERVANT: Sir, your mina has earned ten more.

KING: Well done, my good servant! Because you have been trustworthy in a very small matter, take charge of ten cities.

SECOND SERVANT: Sir, your mina has earned five more.

KING: You take charge of five cities.

THIRD SERVANT: Sir, here is your mina; I have kept it laid away in a piece of cloth. I was afraid of you, because you are a hard man. You take out what you did not put in and reap what you did not sow.

KING: I will judge you by your own words, you wicked servant! You knew, did you, that I am a hard man, taking out what I did not put in, and reaping what I did not sow? Why then didn't you put my money on deposit, so that when I came back, I could have collected it with interest? . . .

Take his mina away and give it to the one who has ten minas.

---

* A mina was about three months' wages.

JUNE

7

Little Things

Read this paragraph from *Messages to Young People*, then answer the questions.

"Never underrate the importance of little things. Little things supply the actual discipline of life. It is by them that the soul is trained that it may grow into the likeness of Christ, or bear the likeness of evil. God helps us to cultivate habits of thought, word, look, and action that will testify to all about us that we have been with Jesus and learned of Him!" (p. 202).

In what ways could doing—or not doing—each of the items in the following pairs help you grow into the likeness of Christ? What might they have to do with discipline?

1. Tossing a candy wrapper onto the sidewalk *or* walking the few extra steps to throw the candy wrapper into a trash bin.

2. Smiling at the classmate who gets on your nerves *or* saying mean things behind the back of the classmate who gets on your nerves.

3. Learning your memory verse for Sabbath school *or* giving a quick look at your Sabbath school lesson but not bothering to learn the memory verse.

4. Helping clear the supper table and do the dishes even though it is not your turn *or* saying that you have lots of homework to do and excusing yourself quickly from the supper table.

5. Inviting the visitor who has walked into your Sabbath school to come sit by you *or* ignoring the visitor who has come into your Sabbath school because you do not know who he or she is.

6. Hiding your new science lab kit when your cousins visit because you think they'll want to do some experiments and you don't want to use up the chemicals so soon *or* inviting them to do some experiments with you.

"The most successful toilers are those who will cheerfully work to serve God in small things. Every human being is to work with his own individual thread, weave it into the fabric that composes the web, and complete the pattern" (*Messages to Young People*, p. 203).

"Well done, my good servant!" his master replied. "Because you have been trustworthy in a very small matter, take charge of ten cities." Luke 19:17.

JUNE

A Bunch of Crickets

Dear friend, do not imitate what is evil but what is good. Anyone who does what is good is from God. Anyone who does what is evil has not seen God. 3 John 11.

"You and your friends remind me of a bunch of crickets," Uncle Bob said with a twinkle in his eye.

Shane stopped mid-step and pivoted to face his uncle. "Crickets?"

His uncle laughed.

"Crickets sing; we don't!"

"That's just the point. I doubt that a one of your friends would sing unless you decided they should."

"Me?"

"Well, maybe someone else in your group. You all have lots of influence on each other—peer pressure, they call it. The whole lot of you create a social environment, and each of you reflects that environment with your fads."

Shane threw his hand up in mock disgust. "OK, I give up. What do all your big words have to do with us and crickets?"

"Well, for one thing, look at the jeans you're wearing."

"Yeah. Pretty nice, huh? Got them at Fadi's. They're the best . . ."

"And your shoes."

"What's wrong with my shoes?"

"Not a thing. But I never tie mine like that."

"Everybody does—I mean, that's just the way you tie shoes."

"So . . . all crickets make their music by using one wing as a fiddle, the other as a bow—that's just the way they do it. And the warmer the night, the more syllables in their song. The 'temperature' cricket even tells the exact temperature by his song. Count the number of chirps it makes in 15 seconds, add 40, and you'll have the exact temperature in degrees Fahrenheit. All crickets react in a way predictable to their environment."

"So?"

"Well, you pretty much wear the same kind of jeans, tie your shoes the same way, and in general do things the same as other kids. Friends have influence—you know the old saying 'Show me your friends, and I'll tell you what kind of person you are.' No self-respecting cricket would sing a different rhythm than his friends, and that's the way it should be. As long as you and your friends make a good environment for each other, there's nothing wrong in doing things the same."

Does your group have special trademarks—words? clothes? music? pastimes? Do you create a good spiritual environment for each other?

JUNE

9

The Bat

Do not spread false reports. Exodus 23:1.

Janis shrieked. A dark, haunty-winged creature was whipping soundlessly around and around her room. She screamed again, then scrunched into a huddle under her comforter. She heard her door open and her mother's startled "Oh! a bat!" Then, "It won't hurt you. I'll get Josh's butterfly net."

"Won't hurt?" Janis felt a shiver go down her spine. She'd heard enough spooky stories. Bats stalked their prey at night as they look for blood. They preferred girls with curly hair, and she had natural curls. They carried rabies. She heard the door open again, then something whisking about. She sneaked her head above the covers just in time to see her mother give the butterfly net a quick twist. Something struggled in the sack. "What're you going to do with it?" she demanded.

"Let it go outside," her mother said.

"You're not going to kill it?"

"These little fellows do more good than harm."

Janis heard her mother's voice going into classroom mode. "This is a little brown bat. It can catch and eat 900 insects an hour. A colony will eat 110 pounds (50 kilograms) of insects during a summer . . ."

"But they carry rabies."

"Some do," her mother admitted. "That's why I used the net—a bat's a wild animal. Bats with rabies usually aren't aggressive, but their only self-defense is biting. This one just happened to fly into the wrong place."

"Oh, Mom!" Janis exclaimed. "You're just too practical. Bats are spooky and weird, and I can't stand looking at them."

"They are different," her mother chuckled. "They're mammals, but they fly. They have wings, but they're not birds, though many fly better than birds. They're active at night and sleep upside down during the day. In fact, they spend most of their lives hanging upside down."

"Mom! OK! You're a biology teacher. You like your creepy things." A laugh touched Janis' voice.

"I'll have to admit, I don't care for bats in the house. With their love for warm, poorly ventilated places, a colony can create quite a smell," her mom said. "But they're victims of too many false reports."

"Mom!"

"OK. I'm taking it out. Have a good sleep!"

JUNE

10

Strange Things Happen

My prayer is not that you take them out of the world but that you protect them from the evil one. John 17:15.

Janis felt relieved when her mother carried the bat outside and let it fly off into the night. Usually bats are quiet, and they almost never attack humans. They're too busy catching insects at night and too sleepy during the day.

Because they eat so many night-flying insects, they really are very helpful little animals. Even so, there are many untrue stories about bats being linked with evil and witchcraft and sorcery and disease, and bat silhouettes make a favorite spooky decoration for Halloween. Why do you think this happens? Why are bats so scary? Give three reasons.

1. ______________________________
2. ______________________________
3. ______________________________

Bats are blamed for things they don't do. But strange things do happen to people who believe in spirits and let themselves come under the power of the evil one.

Papa Mulungu, one of our African friends, tells a story that he insists is true. An old man went to the market to buy fish. Ready to return home from the market, he set his basket of fish down and turned to get his bicycle. In that instant a thief grabbed the basket of fish and ran away with it.

When the old man saw that his fish were gone, he mumbled something to the effect that the thief would be back, then he set his bicycle against the wall, took out his bicycle pump, and started to pump up the bicycle tire. While he pumped, he continued to mutter under his breath. In a few minutes a man with a very fat stomach came with the basket of fish.

"Here," he said, "take your fish."

The old man shook his head. "You wanted the fish," he said. He continued to pump, and with each stroke of the pump, the man's stomach grew bigger.

"Please. Take your fish!" The man set the basket down.

"You're sure?" the old man asked.

"Yes, yes, I'm sure."

"Very well," said the old man, and he began to let the air out of his bicycle tire. In that instant the man's stomach also began to go back to its usual size.

Neither the devil nor any haunting tales of evil can have any power over you if you choose to have the protection God offers against the evil one.

JUNE

11

To Do Good

Then Jesus asked them, "Which is lawful on the Sabbath: to do good or to do evil?" Mark 3:4.

Mr. and Mrs. Downs decided to give Bible studies on Sabbath afternoons, and the Clarks agreed to study with them. One late spring Sabbath afternoon the Downses arrived with their Bibles, ready to study. Mr. Clark, dressed to work in the garden, met them in the yard.

"I was sick last week," he explained, "and I'm late planting my garden. My children promised to help this afternoon. We still have some potatoes to plant. If you'd like to help, we'll finish soon enough to have some time to study the Bible, too."

Not wanting to work on the Sabbath, Mr. and Mrs. Downs excused themselves and went home.

What would you have done? ____________________

____

Why? ____

Mrs. Vincent had a reputation for speaking plainly. She seemed to consider it her duty to point out to the "young ladies of the church"—as she called them—the inappropriateness of the clothes they had chosen to wear to the Lord's house.

Jill had a new dress that she had bought especially for church. It was pretty and stylish, and wearing it made her feel good about herself. Her friends warned her that she looked too good and should be on the lookout for Mrs. Vincent. Jill devised a plan. As she walked across the vestibule, she saw Mrs. Vincent start toward her. Jill turned to meet her.

"Why, good morning, Mrs. Vincent!" she exclaimed before the older lady had a chance to say anything. "Isn't it so good to have the Sabbath so we can come to worship God?" She patted Mrs. Vincent's arm and smiled. "Now, have a happy day!"

"Uh, thank you," Mrs. Vincent managed to reply as Jill hurried away.

What words would best describe the way you think Jill felt? ____________________________________

____

What words do you think would best describe how Mrs. Vincent felt? ______________________________

____

What connection do you see between what Jill did and Mark 3:4? ______________________________

JUNE

12

The Father's Day Gift

Honor your father and your mother, as the Lord your God has commanded you. Deuteronomy 5:16.

Shelley wondered what to give Uncle Wally for Father's Day. He and Aunt Edna had made her feel very much at home since her parents' divorce. She had a comfortable room to herself. She could bring friends over to swim in their large pool. She had lots of nice clothes that they'd given her. Now she wanted to do something special for Uncle Wally to show how much she appreciated everything he did for her.

She thought of the usual gifts—a tie, socks, a shirt—and shook her head. Uncle Wally didn't need any of those.

A book . . . maybe, she told herself.

Uncle Wally loved books and had shared several of his for her to keep in her own library in her room. She'd just been reading one, *Messages to Young People*, and on pages 211 and 212 had found this:

"Children and youth should take pleasure in making lighter the cares of father and mother, showing an unselfish interest in the home. As they cheerfully lift the burdens that fall to their share, they are receiving a training which will fit them for positions of trust and usefulness. Each year they are to make steady advancement, gradually but surely laying aside the inexperience of boyhood and girlhood for the experience of manhood and womanhood. In the faithful performance of the simple duties of the home, boys and girls lay the foundation for mental, moral, and spiritual excellence."

"I know what I can do," she suddenly exclaimed.

Uncle Wally loved gardening and often talked of the garden he wanted to make with the big rocks that had been dug out of the ground when they had put in the pool.

"I'll get him a book about rock gardens, but that's not enough."

She thought some more. "I'd really like to learn more about gardening myself." She looked thoughtful. "If Uncle Wally'll let me, I'll help him make the rock garden. There's lots I could do to make it easier for him." She pulled out a sheet of writing paper. "Dear Uncle Wally, You choose the plan you want, and I'll help you."

What special gift could you give your father or the person you wish to honor on Father's Day?

JUNE

13

Visiting Great-Aunt Abigail

The Lord your God is gracious and compassionate.
2 Chronicles 30:9.

Great-Aunt Abigail lived with her husband in a brown-shingled cottage in one of the last of the old Columbia River fishing villages. Boardwalks strung the houses together and reached out to the weathered-gray docks. No cars or telephones or electricity had ever come to this village, and between fishing seasons the biggest event was the riverboat's twice-weekly mail stops. Every now and then for a special treat Dad would pack us into his boat, and we'd travel the two hours downriver to spend the day at Aunt Abigail's.

Aunt Abigail had a friendly collie dog and a lazy, old marmalade-colored, striped cat. She kept a comfortable house with an interesting collection of souvenirs from what she called the "olden days." Her living room window framed a thickly forested hillside dropping down onto the rocky beach and a piece of river reaching widely into the distance.

Other than a few fishermen who came and went with the seasons and a spinster who seldom left the house she had inherited from her father, her only neighbors were the Lawrences, who lived across from them in a prim white frame house. When we visited, Mother always took me there for a polite call.

Mrs. Lawrence used to teach school back in the early days. Tall and sturdy, she wore her hair in rigid braids around her head and always dressed in crisply starched, perfectly pressed, long-sleeved dresses. A certificate in an impressive frame hung on her living room wall—a long-ago award for her beautiful penmanship. She also kept a huge bearskin draped just so over a chair. She said her husband had killed the bear a few years before—just up the path a ways. "There are still bears in the woods," she informed me each time we visited, which I understood to mean "Don't you dare go wandering off." Everything in her house had its exact place, and when I was there I did too—sitting on a chair, very quietly, across from the bearskin. The fur looked soft and smooth, and I wanted to pat it, but I didn't dare. Mrs. Lawrence was too particular, so I just sat with my hands folded in my lap.

Back then, until one particular visit, I thought God was a lot like Mrs. Lawrence—strict and stern and watching for me to do something wrong.

Did you ever think that God is like someone you know? What was it about that person that made you think that? Have your ideas about God changed? As I grew older, mine did.

JUNE

14

Aunt Abigail's Black Cats

The eternal God is your refuge. Deuteronomy 33:27.

Even though Aunt Abigail had few neighbors, she had lots of friends—the deer that came during late summer to eat the windfalls from her apple trees, the coons that nested in the bank that dropped away to the river, and the crows. On one visit she talked about her seven black kitties.

"Where are they?" I asked.

"They live under the walk at the side of the house and only come in the evening when I feed them," she explained. "They don't take much to strangers."

"But I want to see them."

"They're black kitties with white stripes!" Aunt Abigail said, emphasizing white stripes.

"Stripes? Oh. O-o-o-h, they're . . ."

Aunt Abigail nodded.

"Mrs. Lawrence hasn't spoken to us for weeks because of them," Uncle Hugo added.

"Why?"

"Well, we warned her, but you know Mrs. Lawrence—she expects everyone to do things her way."

I nodded.

"Sure enough," Uncle Hugo continued, "wouldn't you know that the mama and the little ones were out for a stroll on the walkway, and here came Mrs. Lawrence, marching right along toward them, never slackening her stride. I suppose she expected the skunks to do the same.

"Evidently Mama Skunk misunderstood, because she suddenly spun around—and, whew! We could smell the results of their meeting from here."

Images of the dignified Mrs. Lawrence shrouded in skunk spray hung in my horrified thoughts.

Somehow after that, Mrs. Lawrence never seemed as awesome as she had. When we visited her, she still expected me to sit quietly, and she still warned me about there being bears in the woods, but just knowing that a skunk had dared to spray her made Mrs. Lawrence seem more human and less frightening.

As I got to know God better, He also seemed less frightening. One of my school roommates claimed that He was just like her grandfather—bearded and kindly, only bigger. I laughed about that until I realized that she had a nicer God than I did. As I studied my Bible I began to understand that He isn't out to catch me for breaking His rules, but that He is my friend.

JUNE

15

Hannah's Discovery

The Lord God is my strength. Habakkuk 3:19, KJV.

Hannah hid in her room and listened.

"Shame, isn't it?" said one voice.

Hannah stared at the floor. She wouldn't go out—those ladies might speak to her, ask her questions, try to make her talk. And then . . . The thought made her feel faint.

God, help me! She formed a silent prayer about her fears—of people, of the dark, of high places, of being closed in, of falling sick, of dying, of having to talk, especially of having to talk.

"Yes," agreed another voice, "she could be such a lovely girl, if she weren't so afraid and if she could just learn to talk properly."

Why won't You help me? she cried out in her thoughts. She'd grown up praying, believing that God answers prayer, but He never seemed to pay any attention to hers. Here she was a teenager, and she couldn't say a proper sentence to anyone. Her words always caught in her throat, then tumbled out in jumbled bits and pieces—and she'd given her life to Jesus when she was 11.

Hannah continued to pray about her stammering, and God seemed to continue to ignore her. When she was 19, her father took her to a religious convention. Even though the crowds frightened her, she agreed to go to some meetings. At the last one those who felt called to mission service were asked to stand. Hannah sat glued to her seat. *With my handicap, God could never use me for a missionary,* she told herself.

Then the speaker asked which parents were willing to offer their children to mission service. Hannah saw her father stand. That was too much. She rushed out of the meeting and back to her room, where she fell on her knees. For the first time she realized that for God to be real in her life she would have to yield to Him her total life—all of it, including her stammering tongue and her fears.

That was the turning point. Instead of begging for help, she gave herself totally to God, and the healing began. Gradually her stammering improved and her fears faded. She did become a missionary to the Jews in Palestine, and she also became a writer.

One of Hannah Hunnard's best-known books is *Hinds' Feet on High Places,* an allegory of overcoming fears and becoming a new person in Christ, the Chief Shepherd.

JUNE

16

Are You Willing?

He will make my feet like hinds' feet, and he will make me to walk upon mine high places. Habakkuk 3:19, KJV.

I've prayed!" Rad exclaimed. "Every day for all of my life I've prayed. And look at me—what has God done to answer my prayers?"

"I've given God a chance." Heide looked serious. "I used to think we had a pretty good relationship, but He's just not there anymore."

"I want to be a Christian," Juan said, "but if God doesn't listen . . ." He shrugged.

Have you ever felt like Rad or Juan or like Hannah in yesterday's story—confused because God seems not to listen to your prayers? Have you, like Heide, even thought that God maybe isn't even there?

If so, you're not the first Christian to question God or to be disappointed because you see no answers to your prayers.

"Lord, I want to be a Christian," says the old spiritual, and wanting to be a Christian is a good starting place. That's all it is, though, a starting place. Wanting is just the first W of the two W's that it takes to be a Christian. The second is "willing."

I "want" to travel around the world, so I've planned my route, ordered my tickets, and made hotel reservations. I'll never get anywhere, though, unless I'm willing to take those first steps to the airport and actually get on the plane. Hannah wanted help with her stammering—it made her so embarrassed. God seemed to ignore her prayers, though, until she became willing to give Him her stammering tongue and let Him use it as He could. At that point her life began to change.

Are you *willing* to give God every part of your life? Your shyness, your difficulty in making friends, your awkwardness, your handicap—any problem that makes you feel unloved? When you decide to give Him all of that and you become willing to accept His will for you, He will give you strength and, as Habakkuk says, He will make your feet like hinds' feet.

The hind, the female red deer, one of the swiftest and most graceful of the mountain animals, is known for its surefootedness. Its back feet step in exactly the same spot the front feet have just been as it leaps up the dangerous mountainsides.

Add willingness to your wanting. God will make your feet like hinds' feet.

JUNE

17

A Sabbath Story

The Lord has commanded that tomorrow is a holy day of rest, dedicated to him. Exodus 16:23, TEV.

This is a dramatic reading from Exodus 16:12-31, 35, TEV. (Directions are given on page 28.)

LORD: I have heard the complaints of the Israelites. Tell them that . . . in the morning they will have all the bread they want. . . .

NARRATOR: In . . . the morning there was dew all round the camp. When the dew evaporated, there was something thin and flaky on the surface of the desert. It was as delicate as frost. When the Israelites saw it, they didn't know what it was and asked each other,

ISRAELITES: What is it?

MOSES: This is the food the Lord has given you to eat. The Lord has commanded that each of you is to gather as much of it as he needs. . . .

NARRATOR: The Israelites did this, some gathering more, others less. When they measured it, those who had gathered more did not have too much, and those who had gathered less did not have too little. Each had gathered just what he needed.

MOSES: No one is to keep any of it for tomorrow.

NARRATOR: But some of them did not listen to Moses and saved part of it. The next morning it was full of worms and smelt rotten. . . . Every morning each one gathered as much as he needed; and when the sun grew hot, what was left on the ground melted. On the sixth day they gathered twice as much food, four quarts for each person. All the leaders of the community came and told Moses about it, and he said to them,

MOSES: The Lord has commanded that tomorrow is a holy day of rest, dedicated to him. Bake today what you want to bake and boil what you want to boil. Whatever is left should be put aside and kept for tomorrow.

NARRATOR: As Moses had commanded, they kept what was left until the next day; it did not spoil. . . .

MOSES: Eat this today, because today is the Sabbath, a day of rest dedicated to the Lord, and you will not find any food outside the camp. . . .

NARRATOR: On the seventh day some of the people went out to gather food, but they did not find any. Then the Lord said to Moses,

LORD: How much longer will you people refuse to obey my commands? . . .

NARRATOR: So the people did no work on the seventh day. The people of Israel called the food manna.

It was like a small white seed, and tasted like biscuits made with honey. . . . The Israelites ate manna for the next forty years, until they reached the land of Canaan.

JUNE

18

The Lesson of the Manna

Today is the Sabbath, a day of rest dedicated to the Lord. Exodus 16:25, TEV.

It's morning. Your stomach feels empty, too empty, and you don't feel like doing anything. You overhear your father talking with the men who are camped beside you. "I really thought Moses knew what he was doing," your father says. "And now . . ."

"We'll starve," adds your neighbor. "Where can we ever find enough food in this forsaken place?"

As you listen you know they're serious. *Is God going to let us die, after everything that's happened?* you ask yourself. At that point, how would you most likely feel about God? ______________________________

____

The next day there's this strange white stuff on the ground, and Moses explains how to collect and prepare it. How do you feel about God now? ________________

____

The white stuff—manna—continues to come. What lessons do you learn about both God and the Sabbath as you help collect and prepare it for your family? Reread yesterday's reading for ideas. ____________________

____

JUNE

19

The Captain's Lesson, Part 1

A mocker resents correction; he will not consult the wise. Proverbs 15:12.

Noel leaned against the rail and stared into the distance. "Impossible chap," he said to himself. "Rude and tactless, not a proper English gentleman in the least."

The ship plowed along, riding the slow rhythm of the open sea, being lifted and then gently lowered with the long, smooth swells. Noel pondered the problem. *Someone has to do something,* he thought. *Those poor passengers!*

A silvery shape arched from the water and glided over the ship's bow. Noel followed its flight with his eyes. He'd seen hundreds before, maybe thousands. He watched somewhat absentmindedly as more flying fish broke the water's surface, throwing themselves into the air with a great sweep of their strong tails, then stretching their large, winglike fins and gliding. They sailed 500, maybe 1,000, feet before splashing down, body muscles and tail fin guiding their flight.

A sudden splat followed by a frantic flapping on the deck caused Noel to turn. A steward hurried up with a deck scoop and tossed the fish back where it belonged—whenever they passed through a school, several usually landed on board. Another fish misjudged its bearings and plopped onto the deck. Suddenly Noel had an idea. He called to the steward.

As a planning consultant Noel traveled to many countries. He liked going by freighters—they had comfortable quarters, only a dozen or so passengers, and followed interesting routes. Besides, airlines didn't yet fly everywhere he needed to go. A group of American missionaries filled the other cabins, and they were having a good trip except for one problem—the captain.

Always the last person to enter the dinning room in the morning, the captain said a gruff hello, seated himself, and rang for the steward. The rest was routine. The steward came with a large covered silver tray, placed it before the captain with a flourish, and removed the cover to reveal his breakfast—one boiled egg. The menu never varied, neither did the captain's behavior. He singled out a missionary and for the rest of the meal harassed her with rude and embarrassing remarks.

"He's no gentleman!" Noel was indignant as he spoke to his wife that evening. "Insulting his passengers. Someone needs to help him see what he's doing, and I have a plan that should at least get his attention." A smile crinkled the creases around his eye as he laughed. "Then . . . if he'll only listen."

JUNE

20

The Captain's Lesson, Part 2

If you are a mocker, you alone will suffer. Proverbs 9:12.

That evening the deck steward delivered a package to Noel's cabin, and a bit later Noel went to visit the cook. The next morning when they gathered for breakfast, none of the others seemed very happy.

"I don't even like to come for my meals," one of the ladies confessed. "The captain's comments are so, so . . ."

". . . rude and embarrassing," Noel finished for her.

She nodded. "I'd heard from others how pleasant and relaxing a trip this usually is, and I was looking forward to it. But I'm sorry now that we booked with this company."

"Is there anything we can do to help him see how unpleasant he's making this trip for us?" her husband asked.

The smile creased Noel's eyes again, and he tilted his head in that way of his that said, "I've got a plan."

"Do you have any ideas?" He looked at Noel.

"I think we'll get his attention this morning," he replied.

At that moment the captain entered, late as usual, gave his usual gruff good morning, and seated himself in his chair. He rang the bell, and the steward entered, carrying the large silver tray on one hand, shoulder level, set it on the table as always, and removed the cover with a flourish.

An absolute hush fell as the captain and all 12 passengers stared at the platter.

Even Noel stared. Flying fish were quite tasty, he'd heard, but he saw no beauty in those two fins standing at attention, crisply fried, just as he'd ordered.

"Take them away," the captain ordered. His voice sounded flat and cold. "And bring me my egg!"

Noel cleared his throat, hoping for a chance to make the witty remarks he'd planned so they could have a good laugh all around and then get on to happier mealtime conversation.

The captain refused to acknowledge Noel's presence.

His egg came. He ate it in complete silence, not saying another word during the meal. In fact, he didn't say another word—rude or otherwise—to his passengers, for never again during the rest of the trip did he return to the dining room to eat.

"If you are wise, your wisdom will reward you," says Proverbs 9:12. "If you are a mocker, you alone will suffer."

Because of his mocking rudeness, the captain, in the end, suffered alone.

JUNE

21

The Secret Annex

You are my hiding place and my shield; I hope in Your word. Psalm 119:114, NKJV.

Anne Frank, a Jewish girl growing up in Amsterdam during World War II, received a diary for her thirteenth birthday. Two days later she began writing. Soldiers were taking Jews away, and three weeks later the family went into hiding in the Secret Annex, a narrow apartment above and behind the warehouse where Anne's father ran a spice business. For the next two years Anne, her sister, their parents, and four others tried to carry on a normal life in that apartment. But they could never go outside, and during the day they didn't dare make any noise for fear of being heard by the workers down below in the warehouse.

Four people, though, knew where they were and brought food and news. The news was bad—many of their friends had been taken away.

During that time Anne continued to write in her diary, telling about life in their hiding place. She and Margot, her sister, and Peter, the son of the other family staying with them, studied during the day so they could keep up with the schoolmates they never saw.

June 1944 brought good news. American and British soldiers had landed in Europe. Anne hoped they'd be freed soon.

The troops couldn't get to Amsterdam quickly enough, though, and on August 1, 1944, Anne wrote in her diary for the last time. Three days later a truck stopped in front of the warehouse, and police went directly to a bookcase on the third floor, which hid the stairway leading into their hiding place. Everyone in the Secret Annex was forced into the truck. They were in the last group of Jews taken to the concentration camps of World War II. No one ever found out who told the police.

Miep, one of the workers who'd helped them, found Anne's diary scattered on the floor and gave it to Anne's father when he returned to Amsterdam after the war (he was the only one of the little group still alive). At the urging of his friends, he had the diary made into a book.

That book, *The Diary of Anne Frank*, is sold around the world in 50 languages, and the Secret Annex is now a museum.

Anne and the others hid safely for more than two years before they were found and taken away. On this earth there is no safe hiding place. Our only real safety is in Jesus.

Do you have His safety?

JUNE

22

Now Is the Time, Part 1

And the Lord made the shadow go back the ten steps it had gone down on the stairway of Ahaz. 2 Kings 20:11.

Eduardo marked a heavy line in the dirt with the point of his stick. "We have to leave as soon as the shadow from the roof reaches this line," he told his two younger brothers. He glanced at the colorful watch strapped around his wrist. "That'll be at 1600 hours," he said, using the 24-hour time system. "If we stay any later, night'll fall before we can cross through the forest." From the look on Juan's and Pedro's faces, he knew they understood.

The fringed shadow of the thatch roof crept closer and closer to the line.

This introduction is intended to catch your interest and cause you to wonder "What's going to happen?" From the story so far, tell:

1. Who is the main character of the story?

____

2. About how old is he? ____________________

3. Where might he live? ____________________

4. What clues tell you that? ________________

5. What is the most important thing that will determine what will happen in the rest of the story?

A. Where they go.
B. How they go.
C. When they go.
D. Why they go.

Eduardo is, of course, the main character, and he's probably 11 going on 12. Because he and his brothers have Spanish names, we suppose they're living in a Spanish-speaking area where thatch is used on buildings. These details are not so important, though, as the time. Because of its emphasis and reemphasis, our attention focuses on the time. Time is so important to Eduardo that he can make a mark on the ground showing where the shadow will be at 4:00 in the afternoon.

Time is important. For thousands of years people have told time by the shadows on sundials. When Hezekiah was king, a specially made stairway was used to tell time, and God made the shadow go backward as a sign to King Hezekiah that he would be healed. We now have atomic clocks, which scientists say will neither gain nor lose more than one second in 30,000 years. They also say we may soon have clocks based on lasers and mercury atoms, which will be 100,000 times more accurate.

Eduardo wore a digital watch. Still, he marked the ground in the traditional way of their village so that his brothers could see when it'd be time to leave. Tomorrow we'll continue the story.

JUNE

23

Now Is the Time, Part 2

The Good News was promised long ago by God through his prophets, as written in the Holy Scriptures. Romans 1:2, TEV.

"We have to leave now!" Shadow fingers already touched the line Eduardo had drawn on the ground. "We'd better run."

The three boys grabbed their woven pouches from where they'd tossed them against the house and slipped the straps onto their shoulders, then the quick slapping of their bare feet against the beaten earth marked their hurried way along the path that cut through the towering grasses. They ran across the clearing, down the hill, across the pole bridge, up the other hill, and through the corner of the forest.

"The younger brother of the chief saw the phantoms last night." Juan's words jarred in time to his steps.

The boys all slowed. "And he came to no harm?" Pedro asked.

"He was already beyond the tree that marks the edge of the village territory. I overheard the cousin of the son of his other brother talking. He said the chief's brother stood behind the tree and saw their shadows walking down the hill toward the enchanted hollow."

Eduardo looked over his shoulder. "We must hurry!" he exclaimed. "We can't be even a minute late tonight."

The boys knew that they must pass the boundary tree on the village side of the forest before the going down of the sun—only then would they be safe from the phantoms that came to the place-of-the-warm-water-rising-from-the-ground. For as many years as their grandfathers could remember, the spot where the spring bubbled out of the ground had been sacred to the phantoms of the spirit world, and no one could safely go into that section of forest at night except for the medicine man.

The three boys passed the spring each morning to set bird snares at the edge of their parents' cornfield. Each afternoon they returned by the same path to collect their day's catch. They believed that they would come to no harm as long as they reached the village side of the marking tree before the sun set.

They worked quickly, clearing their snares. As they worked, Juan began to hum a catchy tune. Then the words began to come.

"The B-i-b-l-e . . ."

"What's the B-i-b-l-e?" interrupted Pedro.

"The Bible—the book about the missionaries' God," Eduardo answered quickly. "We've got to hurry."

"Is their God really stronger than the phantoms?"

If you'd been there, what answer would you have given?

JUNE

24

Now Is the Time, Part 3

I sought the Lord, and he answered me; he delivered me from all my fears.
Psalm 34:4.

Eduardo pulled up the last stake they used to anchor the snares and stuffed it into his hunting bag.

"Is it?" repeated Pedro. "Is the missionaries' God really stronger than the phantoms?"

Eduardo shrugged. "They say so," he said, "but how would I know? I've never tested them."

"I believe He is." Juan had stopped singing and spoke for the first time. "I believe the stories of the Bible that the missionaries have been telling us, and I believe their God is stronger than any phantom."

"Even stronger than those that come to the place-of-the-warm-water-rising-from-the-ground?"

Juan nodded, but Eduardo gave his younger brothers a disgusted look. "We've got to hurry!" He spoke sharply. "I don't want to test any spirits or any god tonight."

The boys shouldered their catch and their snares, and turned down the path toward home. They hurried, but the edge of the sun had already slipped behind the distant hills by the time they reached the slope by the warm spring.

"Run!" Eduardo barked the command, and three sets of bare feet pounded the path in long, pumping strides. Pedro led, and just as they passed the hollow of the spring, he looked over his shoulder—and screamed.

The sun had disappeared, leaving only the evening gray. And something shadowy was moving through the trees toward the spring. Ahead, the boundary marking tree stood lone and tall. The boys' footsteps pounded even harder and faster. They must reach the tree before . . .

An echoing scream split the evening just as the boys reached the tree. Then all was silent. They pounded on past the tree, toward their home. At the edge of the village they stopped. "I—I saw a shadow phantom!" Pedro said shakily.

"And I heard it scream," Eduardo added.

"The God of the missionaries *is* stronger." There was excitement in Juan's voice as he spoke. "As we ran, I prayed to that God. I asked Him to stop the phantoms from hurting us, to not let them touch us, to keep us safe until we reached home. And here we are! God has saved us!"

Are you safe in God's care—now?

JUNE

25

Rebecca's Problem

Do not be afraid of what you have heard. Isaiah 37:6.

"Mom!" Anger added sharpness to Rebecca's voice. "Did you hear what Eb said? He called me a bad name."

"Just ignore him."

Rebecca was tired of hearing her mom say that. "*Do* something to him!" she screamed. "He's always saying mean things." She rushed at her brother, her hands clawed to scratch and pinch.

Like Rebecca, have you ever felt so angry because someone kept jabbing mean words at you that you wanted to hurt that person until he or she would never dare insult you again?

King Hezekiah could have felt that way when the Assyrian king sent an officer to insult him. The Assyrians were strong, they were on the attack, and they had captured some of his cities.

"You are no match for even the lowest Assyrian official," the officer hollered. He yelled even worse insults.

All the people around could hear, but everyone kept quiet. Not a person said a word because Hezekiah had told them not to say anything. Instead, he sent messengers to the prophet Isaiah, and the prophet sent a message back that the Lord said not to be afraid of what he'd heard, that the Lord would take care of the Assyrians. And He did. Second Kings 18 and 19 tell the story.

Eduardo and his brothers knew that they couldn't save themselves from the phantoms they feared, but Juan prayed and they arrived home safely. Rebecca, though, wants to save herself by hurting Eb so he'll stop calling her bad names.

God can save us from any danger—even the danger of wanting to hurt back when someone says mean things—just as He can save the boys from evil phantoms.

Think about these questions.

1. In what way is wanting to hurt someone back dangerous—even if you don't touch or even say mean words back to that person?

2. How might God be able to save Rebecca from wanting to hurt Eb?

If you need help finding good answers to these questions, look back at the story "The Battle of the Hairbrush," on January 18.

What is the best advice you could give Rebecca or someone who has a problem like hers—that of wanting to hurt back when someone says something mean? ____

____

JUNE

26

Tiny but Powerful

They did God's mighty acts and performed miracles in Egypt. Psalm 105:27, TEV.

God sent plagues of lice and flies on the land of Egypt. One of those insect plagues may have actually been mosquitoes. Read the following statements about mosquitoes, decide which are true and which are false, and then answer the questions.

1. Mosquitoes eat mostly fruit juice and the nectar of flowers.

2. Only female mosquitoes bite people.

Mosquitoes are one of the most disliked insects, but they feed mainly on fruit juice and flower nectar because the energy from plant sugar helps them fly and stay alive. Only females bite when they need our blood, because it has proteins that help them produce eggs. Males eat nectar during their entire lives because their mouthparts aren't strong enough to pierce skin.

So number 1 is __________, and number 2 is __________.

3. Mosquitoes cause more human deaths than any other insect.

4. Insect sprays are the best means of controlling mosquitoes.

Malaria, which is carried by the female anopheles mosquito, has killed hundreds of millions of people. In her short life, Mrs. Anopheles takes only one or two blood meals. If her first is from someone with malaria, then she may take the sickness to the second person. Mosquito species carry 100 diseases.

They develop resistance to many sprays, but the mosquito fish eats their larvae and is our number one mosquito weapon.

Number 3 is __________, and number 4 is __________.

5. Mosquitoes bite all people and some animals.

6. Which has more mosquitoes—the Arctic or the tropics?

Mosquitoes prefer some people and won't bite others, and no one knows why.

Many different kinds of mosquitoes live in the tropics, but they aren't as thick as in the Arctic, which has only a few kinds. Tundra pools produce hordes of mosquitoes that literally blacken the sky, and Canadian scientists report that one person can be bitten as many as 9,000 times in one minute.

Number 5 is __________, and number 6 is __________. (Answers are on page 381.)

Imagine how powerful a plague of mosquitoes might be.

JUNE

27

The Book of Life Club

You will seek me and find me when you seek me with all your heart. Jeremiah 29:13.

Do you mean I could get crossed off?" Jeremey said as he pointed to his name on the list of those who qualified for the Super Scrambler Good-Time Afternoon.

"That's right!" Stefan said and nodded his head. "Anyone can join our club and qualify for the Super Scrambler, but the leader takes only those who can be trusted with keeping the club rules."

"Then how can you ever be sure you'll be allowed to go?"

"Oh, that's easy," Stefan said. "We like our leader and want to protect the club's good name."

"But how does the leader know I can be trusted?"

"By your actions. I can see that you like our leader a lot—that's the first step. If you like the leader, you'll be able to be trusted. Besides, you chose to belong to our club, and you're enthusiastic about our activities."

Having your name in the book of life is like belonging to a special club. If you didn't like the leader, God, you probably wouldn't want to join in the first place, because it's all about liking Him and doing things His way.

The following are some normal activities for members of the Book of Life Club. Using a scale of 0-10 (0 = never; 10 = always), rate yourself as to how likely you would be to do each.

_____ Memorize a section of your Guidebook (Bible) each day.

_____ Study your Guidebook each day.

_____ Spend your afternoon off playing with your 4-year-old neighbor so his mother, who's had the flu, can rest.

_____ Talk to your Leader (pray) several times each day.

_____ Give up your seat on a crowded city bus to someone who looks tired—even if your feet hurt.

_____ Invite others to join your club.

_____ Include the gangly can't-catch-a-thing kid from down the street on your softball-in-the-park team.

_____ Give your free afternoon-at-the-pool ticket to your cousin who's visiting from out of town.

_____ Go to weekly meetings at the clubhouse (church).

_____ Volunteer to do a special chore each week on behalf of your Leader.

It doesn't matter whether your score is high or low—what counts is whether or not God can trust you. Remember, all God wants is for you to become like Him.

JUNE

28

Doing What Is Right and Just and Fair

Without wood a fire goes out; without gossip a quarrel dies down.
Proverbs 26:20.

What pictures would you draw if you were told to illustrate these expressions?

"He's always flying off the handle!"

"She's gone from the frying pan into the fire!"

"That doesn't amount to a hill of beans!"

"Our class is having a white elephant sale."

Your pictures probably wouldn't have a thing to do with what the person meant who said the words. These expressions and others like them give our language colorful shortcuts for explaining things. They come from everyday happenings that, as time passed, were used to mean something else.

The early settlers cleared their land by hand, cleaning away underbrush, cutting down trees, digging out roots. It was slow, tiring work. As they chopped away, their ax blades frequently loosened and would "fly off the handle." To have a sharp, double-edged ax blade suddenly flying off, out of control, in some unexpected direction was not only annoying; it was downright dangerous. As time went on, anyone who "lost his or her head" in anger was said to "fly off the handle."

What do the other three expressions mean? (Answers are on page 381.)

1. ______________________
2. ______________________
3. ______________________

People in Bible times used many colorful expressions in their everyday language. The most famous collection is in the book of Proverbs. According to Solomon, the author of many of them, these sayings are useful "for acquiring a disciplined and prudent life" and "doing what is right and just and fair" (Proverbs 1:3).

Today's text, for example, states something very obvious. Without wood the fire goes out. But its meaning, as explained in the last half of the verse, has good counsel for those who tend to talk too much. "Without gossip a quarrel dies down."

Give at least four more wise sayings you often hear, and tell what they mean.

1. ______________________
2. ______________________
3. ______________________
4. ______________________

If you can't think of any just now, look in the book of Proverbs. Some good ones are in Proverbs 25:11-14, 19, 20; and 26:1, 2, 7, 8, 18-21.

JUNE

29

The Time of the Singing of the Birds

The time of the singing of birds is come, and the voice of the turtle is heard in our land. Song of Solomon 2:12, KJV.

A rasping noise funneled through the bedroom window, but I rolled over and tried to ignore it.

Hgwaar-hgwaar, hgwaar-hgwaar, hgwaar.

The noise kept on—*loud!* I wanted to go back to sleep, but I couldn't. I looked at the clock. Only 5:30, and the noise kept going. It sounded like two big birds with very bad throats, and they kept repeating themselves . . . and repeating . . . and repeating.

Before we had arrived in Africa, we'd been warned to watch out for snakes and bugs and bad water. But noisy birds? I got up, stumbled to the window, and looked toward the tall eucalyptus tree across the road, where the noise seemed to be coming from, but I couldn't see a thing.

"There are some terribly noisy birds that wake me up too early every morning," I complained to Bernice, my mission neighbor from down the road.

"You must have a pair of ibises close by," she said. "They're nice birds. You'll get used to them."

"Nice?" I didn't see how anything so noisy could be nice, and I was certain I'd never get used to them. Then one day I saw them. Their plump, dark, heavy bodies, and their heads set on too-thin necks did not make them beautiful. But a pretty, metallic green glinted from their neatly folded wings. They plodded across the field and carefully picked at the earth with long, curved, scythelike beaks. All day long they worked, walking the fields, picking here, reaching there, collecting insects that could harm the crops.

"Ibises," I said to myself. "Hmmmmm."

The word sounded gentle and kind, but their daybreak duet remained loud and harsh—never quite on pitch. One always spoke a fraction after the other. Their two-beat rhythm never varied. Now that I knew what they were, though, I began to hear them differently. There was something special in their call. Every morning without fail they used their voices, no matter how raspy, to call out enthusiastically to the world, to let everyone know that another day had come, that the fields were still there, and that they were ready for their work of insect-picking.

That's when I began to hear the words of their song, "It's all right, all right, all right . . ."

When we moved to another mission, I missed the singing of those birds.

JUNE

30

To Walk Like an Indian

But be very careful to keep the commandment and the law that Moses the servant of the Lord gave you: to love the Lord your God, to walk in all his ways. Joshua 22:5.

The three men slipped silently along the heavily wooded mountainside. Not a twig snapped to betray their passing. Not a branch swayed to mark their path. Not a stone gave way beneath their feet. With quick and sure steps, they hurried on, and when they were gone, they'd left no sign to trace the way they'd taken.

The early Indians of North America were famous for their way of walking. They could move swiftly and silently. In addition, they had such a keen sense of balance that if one were turned to stone while he was taking a step, the statue would probably stand balanced on one foot!

Indians learned to walk with ease and sureness when they were small because they were molded to walk that way. Right after birth, the babies were laid flat on their cradleboard, and their little legs were stretched as straight as possible with their feet making right angles. Then they were wrapped to the board. The mothers often took the wrappings off and gently worked their babies' legs and spine to make them straight, and then they always made sure to rewrap the babies so their toes pointed straight forward.

As the babies grew older, they learned to walk with toes pointed straight ahead. With each step they placed their body weight on their whole foot. This gave them a steady balance that allowed them to put their moving feet down gently. As they grew toward adulthood, they developed a walk with a rolling motion, their hips swaying, their paces long, and their steps nearly flat-footed. Because of the way they walked, they seldom tripped and could move noiselessly through the forests.

Nowadays most people walk with up-and-down knee action, their hips rather rigid, their toes pointing outward, and their heel hitting first. This walk works well as long as the ground is firm and level, but when the stride is lengthened even a little it becomes tiring. Because the weight falls first on the heel, the moment the walker steps down he or she has little control of balance. And if the foot comes down on something slippery—whoops!

If you would practice carefully for a long time, you could possibly learn the Indian way of walking, but it will never be quite as natural for you as it was for Indian babies who, from the day they were born, were formed to walk that way.

Are you letting yourself be molded by God's love? Are you learning to walk in His way?

JULY

1

Madeline's Good Fight

Fight the good fight of faith, lay hold on eternal life. 1 Timothy 6:12, NKJV.

Today is Canada's 127th birthday.

When it's getting late into the long northern evening but not yet dark enough for fireworks and everyone's kind of lazy from the big picnic dinner, Uncle Werner may make himself comfortable in his lawn chair and share a story from the early days of Canada. One of his favorites comes from Quebec.

Madeline and her younger brother went to Quebec from France when their father, Captain Devercheres, was sent to take charge of a fort down from Montreal. The captain had to go to Quebec City with all his soldiers and leave his two children alone in the fort with an old, wounded soldier who couldn't travel.

"I don't expect any trouble with the Indians," he told the soldiers' wives, "but if for any reason you need to come to the fort, Madeline's in charge."

Although only 12, she was a spunky, mature girl, and her father had confidence in her. "If there's a problem," he told her when he left, "just use your good sense."

The days passed. Bent under the hot sun, the women worked their fields. One of the women straightened to rest her back. Just then she noticed a movement at the edge of the forest. "Indians!" she hissed to the others.

They all grabbed up their things and rushed to the fort.

Madeline and her brother ran to the basement where the wounded soldier lay. "Blow up the powder keg," he advised.

"No!" said Madeline. "I have a plan. We have plenty of guns and powder. You help my brother load the guns, and I'll shoot."

By the time the Indians attacked, loaded guns stood by every firing post. Madeline ran from gun to gun, shooting, as her brother reloaded the empty guns. The Indians never guessed that they were fighting against the guns of just one 12-year-old girl. Finally after two days they disappeared into the forest and did not come back.

Exhausted, Madeline tumbled into her bed and fell into a deep sleep. She roused when someone shook her.

"Indians!" she gasped and tried to force herself out of bed. Then she heard the hearty laugh of her father. "The Indians are gone," he said. "You fought a good fight. You saved our fort, and I'm proud of what you did." And he gathered her up in a big hug.

Are you fighting a good fight against temptation?

JULY

A Happy Day

If you call the Sabbath a delight . . . , then you will find your joy in the Lord. *Isaiah 58:13, 14.*

Sabbath is a happy day . . ." Little Alexander clapped his hands as he sang. "Sabbath is . . ."

Lyssa wanted to clap her hands—over her ears—and tell her little brother to stop. But she didn't. She kept her thoughts to herself. *Happy?* she asked herself. *How can Sabbath be happy?*

Other confusing questions bothered her. Questions like these:

What's so special about Saturday?

Why are there so many things I can't do on that day?

Is the Sabbath *really* that important?

What can I do on Sabbath to make it a good day?

Lyssa's family were new Adventists, and their joining the denomination had made many changes in her life—changes such as going to church instead of going shopping on Saturday mornings, and preparing Saturday dinner on Friday afternoons instead of just planning to go out to eat after worship services.

At church she found herself with other problems—like having to try to fit in with a bunch of young people who seemed to expect her to take for granted that things were supposed to be done the way they did them.

Her parents tried to explain why they had changed churches. Their reasons made sense, but she wished for someone her own age who enjoyed the Sabbath to put all the reasons into words. Maybe then she could learn to feel good about it.

"If you call the Sabbath a delight and the Lord's holy day honorable," wrote Isaiah, "and if you honor it by not going your own way and not doing as you please or speaking idle words, then you will find your joy in the Lord."

God intended for His Sabbath to be a delight, a happy day, a day of joy. Perhaps it hasn't always been happy for you. Perhaps you had to ask yourself some of the same questions that Lyssa asked. If so, what answers did you find that you could share with someone like Lyssa? ______________________________

____

____

What about the Sabbath makes it a happy day for you? ______________________________

____

JULY

3

A Pleasant Sleep

At this I awoke and looked around. My sleep had been pleasant to me.
Jeremiah 31:26.

"Do you really think I have to take this along?" Lawry kicked at a tight blue roll. "I mean, real woodsmen just scoop out a few hollows in the ground and use spruce boughs, don't they?"

Uncle Les laughed. "If you want to enjoy your trip, take that mattress along," he said. "It'll be the best piece of gear you have with you."

"But we're going hiking!" Lawry exclaimed.

"That's why you need it. If you sleep well, you can stand all sorts of tough going."

In the mountains Lawry learned the truth of what his uncle had said. Even though his mattress was only a thin pad, it was made just for camping and was surprisingly comfortable, with excellent insulation that kept his body heat from being sapped away into the ground.

The first night he'd put some spruce boughs under it because he wanted to feel like a real woodsman.

"Making a good bed of branches takes lots of time and lots of springy branch tips," his uncle said.

Lawry tried anyway, but when he crawled into his sleeping bag he soon began scrunching around and tossing out branches because they felt hard and full of pokes. Then he fell into a good sleep. Even when the night got its coldest just before sunup, he slept on.

Before the days of warm, lightweight sleeping bags and mats, campers had fewer choices for good bedding, but the basic ideas are still the same. Warmth depends on insulation, and since the ground carries away body heat, it is important to have good protection under as well as over. Dry air trapped inside covers makes good insulation, so loosely woven, fluffy material is warmer than something tightly woven and heavy. Of natural fibers, cotton is the coldest, wool warmer, and feathers warmer yet, but the warmest natural cover is made from caribou—or reindeer—skin. Not only is the hair very close and thick, but each hair is hollow and contains air.

By the end of the third day, Lawry already understood that having a good rest did make the hiking easier. He had become expert at choosing a good sleeping spot, and each night he slept warm and snug because of his good equipment.

"My sleep had been pleasant to me," said the prophet Jeremiah, because God had given him a dream full of good promises.

Do you keep your mind "insulated" with the good equipment of faith in God's promises so that your sleep is pleasant?

JULY

4

Pulling Up the River

Does not the ear test words as the tongue tastes food?
Job 12:11.

The Fourth of July brings back memories of family picnics featuring potato salad and baked beans, scrumptious cobbler made with fruit from Granny's early apple tree, and lots and lots of cold lemonade. After we'd eaten, the big folks would sit under the trees on the grassy bank, and the little kids would play down among the stones and sand along the riverbank. I was kind of in the middle—neither big nor little—so I'd stretch out in the grass in the shade and watch the little kids and listen to the big folks.

"I'd pull up da river," Granny was saying, "to wisit . . ."

But I missed the rest of what she was telling about visiting some long-ago friend back before my dad could remember. She was born in the Old Country, and my mind did tricks with her funny way of saying things. *Pull up the river,* I was thinking.

I knew very well what she meant, but I imagined my little granny reaching around our fat green-brown river and pulling it up like you'd pull up a weed. Or I'd suppose that she'd tie a rope around it and pull it like you'd pull a stubborn calf into the barn.

"We'd pull back and fordt . . ."

At that next little snatch, I could just see her and one of her friends each holding an end of the river, pulling it back and forth between them.

Our road wasn't built until long after she and Gramps settled on their farm, so in those early days the only way to go anywhere was by boat. Whenever she wanted to visit her friends, she had to "pull" her boat—that is, she rowed—and the easiest way to row is to sit with your back to the front of the boat and "pull" the oars.

Sometimes we get so comfortable with words we use all the time that we don't stop to "test" them, to listen to what we're actually saying—even in our prayers. Even in church prayers words get put together in interesting ways, such as "We've gathered together to come apart." Everyone knows what is meant, but . . .

I haven't been back on the Fourth of July since I went away to college, but sometimes I wonder if families still have picnics on the grassy bank under the trees, and if anyone still "pulls" up the old river like Granny did.

JULY

5

The Stump in the Field

I press on toward the goal to win the prize for which God has called me heavenward in Christ Jesus. Philippians 3:14.

I liked July and haying time. The men worked long days cutting the hay, raking it into long rows, and turning it, always keeping an eye on the sky and praying that the rains wouldn't come until they had it safely in the barns. When at last it stood in big, golden mounds ready to be loaded onto the hay wagon, they often needed an extra hand to drive the tractor. I always volunteered for that job.

Then came the summer of the big Ford truck. I was big for my age, strong, and sure I could handle it, so, as usual, I volunteered to drive.

The afternoon they decided to use my help, they were loading hay from a long flat field that stretched between my grandparents' house and our farm. It was a beautiful, clear stretch of land, empty except for one huge stump centered near the far end. My uncle drove with me for a while, until I had the feel for clutching and shifting. "And don't forget where the brake is," he teased when he left me on my own.

I laughed.

We worked our way down the field. I carefully stopped the truck beside one haystack and then another, while keeping my eye on the big stump so that I would be sure to steer clear of it. We moved nearer and nearer. Suddenly the stump seemed too near. I just stared at it—and kept my foot on the gas.

"Whoa!" someone yelled.

I slammed on the brake just in time.

"What you look at is where you go," my uncle explained later. "Keep your eyes on your target and not on what you want to miss."

In what ways might the following be like the stump in the field? Complaining about homework. __________

____

Criticizing another family for what they do on Sabbath. ______________________________________

____

Playing computer games instead of practicing music. ____

____

Reading a storybook during private devotions. ____

____

Remember, keep your eyes on your goal, not on what you want to miss.

JULY

6

Catch a Rat and Paint It

Then the Lord said to Abraham, "Why did Sarah laugh and say, 'Will I really have a child, now that I am old?' " Genesis 18:13.

Jerry laughed. "Catch a live rat!" he exclaimed. "And paint it!" He laughed again.

"That's what the book says." Angela stood with her hands on her hips. "It says catch one rat alive, paint it with oil of phosphorus, then set it free. Because phosphorus glows in the dark, it'll scare all the other rats away."

"I've never heard of anything so ridiculous!" He forced another laugh.

"The book says it's been tried with great success." Angela was very serious. "We've got a problem with rats. So . . . Well, I hate rats, so anything's worth a try."

Jerry realized that his sister really meant what she was saying. Living on a mission in the bush gave them a chance to try things they never could have done back home. "It'd be fun to try," he agreed. "But we have at least two problems. Number one, we'd have to catch a rat. Number two, we don't have any phosphorous stuff to put on it if we did catch one."

"Well, it sounds like a good idea. Do you suppose we could get Dad to buy some?"

"Where?" Jerry demanded.

"Yeah, you've got a point there. I'll put it on my list of things to get during furlough."

This time Jerry's laugh was real.

Perhaps you laugh when you hear about things being done in a way that's not only different but that seems, well, just plain stupid—even impossible. Sarah did. She laughed when God said that she'd have a baby. Women her age didn't have babies. Didn't God know that it was impossible?

But God said she would see. And she did.

Clarissa laughed when her roommate said she'd make a good teacher.

"Me teach!" Clarissa exclaimed. "Never! No way will anyone get me in front of a roomful of kids. Why, I'd rather herd pigs 367 days a year than be a teacher!"

God had other plans for Clarissa, though. One year she found herself substituting when the regular teacher fell ill. To her surprise, she loved working with the children—so she went back to college to get her teaching degree.

"Catch a rat and paint it?" Who knows? The idea just might work.

JULY

7

Thann's Super Frosty Shakes

Like cold water to a weary soul is good news from a distant land. Proverbs 25:25.

Thann thought the day would never end. The old clock on the mission schoolroom wall finally creaked to 11:30, then noon, and his supervised study was over for the day.

"When do you think Dad'll be home?" he asked his mom, dropping his Home Study International books on the table. "This afternoon?"

"Maybe," his mother replied.

"Hope so."

"We all do." His mother looked at Thann and smiled. "We're all *very* eager to get the mail, aren't we?"

Thann grinned and nodded. "I haven't had a letter from Garry in ages. And maybe my test results will come."

"I'm hoping for letters from Grandma and Dianne."

Living on a mission station and getting mail only when someone went on a business trip, Thann and his mother always waited with keen anticipation for the return of the person who would be carrying their letters. Thann especially. Since he did his schoolwork by correspondence, all his lessons and all his grades came by mail.

"It's hot!" Thann exclaimed, changing the subject.

"Why don't you whiz up some of your super shakes for lunch?" his mother suggested.

"Sure!" Thann loved doing "specialty cooking," as he called it. One of his specialties was banana shakes. Since they bought bananas by the stalk, they usually had some in the freezer—they peeled the ripe bananas and froze them in bags. Here's his recipe.

1 frozen banana	4 ice cubes
1 cup milk	1 teaspoon vanilla

Put everything into the blender, and whiz at top speed until smooth and creamy.

Thann usually adds raspberry or orange punch syrup for flavor, and sometimes he drops in a crispy cookie last thing and pulses it an instant to chop it and swirl the chunks through the shake.

Just as he set two raspberry shakes on the table, the door burst open. "Dad!" he exclaimed. "You're back early!"

"And am I'm thirsty!" His dad held out the bag he carried. "Whew! It's a hot and dusty drive."

"I've got just the thing for you," Thann said as he reached for the bag. "Have one of my super frosty shakes while I check the mail."

Are you as eager for God's good news as Thann was for the mail?

JULY

8

Actions Speak

Do not merely listen to the word, and so deceive yourselves. Do what it says. James 1:22.

"Actions speak!"

Those two words contain a complete sermon, because it is not what you say that truly counts.

Body language—gestures, expressions, posture, tone of voice—tells us more about what a person really feels and thinks than do his or her actual words. This is also true in the animal kingdom. Elephants are a good example of this.

If you happen to be in Africa or Asia or driving through a safari park and you meet an elephant that curls its trunk up and out and trumpets loudly, you'll probably feel like running for your life. The animal looks and sounds ferocious, but its body language says it's only bluffing. If, on the other hand, it curls its trunk under and starts toward you without a sound, *run!* The elephant means business.

Should you be out for a walk in one of the mountain parks of North America and stray close to an elk, pay attention. It may send some definite messages. If it raises its head toward you, curls its lips, grinds its teeth, snorts, and shows the white of its eyes, it is saying that you're too close. Don't stay around and ask it to repeat what it said.

If you come too close to the young of some ground-nesting birds such as the killdeer, the parents will pretend to be injured and try to get you to follow them away from their babies.

Among themselves, animals also use body language to communicate. When a Virginia white-tailed deer raises its flaglike tail, it warns the others that possible danger is near. If you happen to be that "danger," the upright tail also means, "I see you, so why bother to attack, because we can get away."

Bees use dances with complicated steps that describe where they can find food. Beavers smack the water with their broad, flat tails to warn their families of danger.

Other animals use elaborate language to find a mate. The male orb-weaver spider picks the outer threads of his ladylove's web in a special rhythm. If she likes the beat, she lets him come to see her. If she doesn't, she'll catch him and eat him.

You can say that you are a Christian, but your actions will show whether or not you mean what you say.

Remember—actions speak!

JULY

9

A Good Picture

Let us fix our eyes on Jesus, the author and perfecter of our faith. Hebrews 12:2.

Cassandra wants to be a professional photographer. In order to learn more about photography now, she reads photo magazines and books and has made five rules for taking good pictures.

1. Plan carefully. Good photographers "compose" their pictures much in the same way that a "composer" writes a song. They arrange light and color and subject so that the picture will tell a story.

2. Use the rule of thirds. Look through the viewfinder and imagine that what you see is divided into thirds—up and down and side to side. Any of these imaginary lines make good place lines, such as trees or the horizon. A good place to put the main subject—or focal point—is at one of the four places where these lines intersect.

3. Pay attention to the light. Light is about the most important thing in picture taking. Besides using the proper setting for the amount of light, you must determine if the subject should be in full sun or full shadow or in some of each in order to give the picture the best effect.

4. Choose the focal point. The direction that people face makes a difference. Looking out, they give the idea that something not in the picture is more interesting than the contents of the picture itself. Looking in, they draw attention to the focal point of the picture.

5. Decide on the angle. The angle from which a picture is taken can make a big difference.

Cassandra wanted to take a picture of a lake, but the beach was strewn with litter. In order to blot out the messy trash lying on the beach, she found a grassy spot and held the camera close to the ground. The grassy foreground hid the trash and gave a clean view of the lake.

What you say and what you do today will compose a picture for others that tells a story of your faith.

—In what light will it be?

—Will parts of it be strewn with litter?

—Will it give the impression that things "on the outside" are more important and more interesting?

—Or will it draw attention to Jesus as its center of interest?

Using Cassandra's rules along with these last four questions, plan a picture that will represent a happy Christian life. If you have a camera, take that picture.

JULY

10

Elder Berry's Secret

Whatever is covered up will be uncovered, and every secret will be made known. Luke 12:2, TEV.

Elder Berry walked into the committee room for his first meeting with the mission staff. As a leader he knew the importance of making a good first impression and of earning the respect of those he worked with. So he carefully prepared what he wanted to say and made sure his clothes were just so. Behind his natural friendliness, though, lurked a problem—he had a bubble of mischief running through his personality.

"No silliness this evening," he'd warned himself in the mirror as he'd arranged his thick hair. "Tonight you behave with the dignity that befits a mission director." His quick grin argued with the seriousness of his words. "Please," he said, glancing upward in a reminder of his earlier long talk with God, "a hefty helping of Your Spirit." Then, with a "See you later" to his wife, he slapped on his cap and hurried out into the evening.

As Elder Berry started to sit in the chairman's chair, Dr. Fast's grin put him on instant guard. Suddenly Dr. Fast half-stood, leaned across the table, and reached toward him. "We don't wear our hats inside," Dr. Fast asserted.

"Oh, I'm . . ." Elder Berry's own hand wasn't quick enough, and his "sorry" was never spoken.

The room froze into total silence. Dr. Fast's mouth dropped open. Elder Berry stared at Dr. Fast's hand and let his own hand drop onto the smoothness of the top of his head. Dr. Fast held not only his hat—but also his hair! And then Elder Berry did just what he'd been afraid that he'd do—he broke into his silly, uncontrollable laugh.

"Well," Elder Berry managed at last, again smoothing his hand over his very bald head, "now that this secret has been made known, I guess we can get down to business."

A comfortable laugh filled the room as Dr. Fast bowed with mock dignity and handed the hairpiece back, and Elder Berry slipped it onto his head.

A ready sense of humor can save awkward situations, but there will be no smoothing away the facts when God is forced to reveal secret sins on the day of judgment.

We can't hide a thing from Him, but He has promised to hide every sin—secret or not—in the blood of Jesus so that it will never have to be remembered again. That's His offer. It's up to you to accept it.

JULY

11

A Bird on the Wing May Report

Do not revile the king even in your thoughts, or curse the rich in your bedroom, because a bird of the air may carry your words, and a bird on the wing may report what you say.
Ecclesiastes 10:20.

Mallory and Reena climbed into the touring van, eager for their first visit to the Nairobi game park. An older lady already sat on the very front seat next to the driver, talking to him in a very knowing way. Her words, etched in artificial tones, carried toward the back, where the two young tourists sat.

Mallory wrinkled her nose and pointed toward the front. Reena ignored her and focused on the brochure about the park tour.

During the afternoon they saw giraffes and more giraffes—some tall, others very tall—and ostriches off in the distance like so many squat haystacks on stilts, and vast herds of impala flowing with tawny grace across the brushy uplands. Their guide pointed out these and other animals, explaining their habits and habitats, and the lady at the front of the bus continued to add comments of her own as if to impress everyone with her knowledge.

"She certainly is weird," whispered Mallory.

Reena shook her head and put her finger to her lips.

At that warning, Mallory switched from English to French, which they both spoke and which she assumed no one else on the bus would understand. "Listen to the way she talks," she said sarcastically. "Do you think she's all right?" She tapped her head.

"Shhhh." Reena's warning was almost silent.

But Mallory paid no attention and added another uncomplimentary remark in French.

At the end of the tour, just as they were about to return to the hotel, Mallory again spoke to her friend in French. "How much do you think we should tip the driver?" she asked.

"I'm not sure," Reena replied.

Just then the older lady at the front of the bus turned to them and said in flawless French, "It isn't necessary to tip him, but if you wish to show your appreciation you could give him a small amount."

A strange look passed over Mallory's face. "*Merci* [thank you]," she managed to reply.

Reena made no comment. The kindest thing, no matter how safe the situation may seem, is to leave certain thoughts unspoken.

JULY

12

Millions and Millions

Make up your mind not to put any stumbling block or obstacle in your brother's way.
Romans 14:13.

The guide beamed his powerful light upward, fixing it on a series of uneven stump-sized bumps on the roof. "Giant stalactites once hung there," he explained.

As he talked, Corty imagined how the cave must have once looked with dozens of the giant icicle-shaped mineral deposits stabbing downward.

"Stalactites form much as icicles do on the eaves of houses, only much more slowly," the guide continued. "Icicles form when snow melts, trickles over the roof edges, and then refreezes in the cold air. Stalactites grow when water containing lime seeps through the ground, forms droplets on a cave roof, and then evaporates, leaving a tiny dab of carbonate of lime.

"Vandals robbed this cavern," he explained. "A rich man wanted our stalactites to give the decor of his house a unique touch, so he hired marksmen to shoot them down. Of course, that was long before the caves became protected property." He went on to explain the evolution of the series of caves that Corty and his family were visiting in England with their British friends.

"Shame," said Gavin. "And after all those millions and millions of years!"

"What?" Corty cut back. "Do you believe that evolutionary stuff?"

"That's what the scientists teach." Gavin's voice was calm, but Corty could see a surprise of hurt in his new friend's face.

"I guess I've always listened to others who see the evidence differently." The sharpness had drained from Corty's voice. He'd been wrong in speaking so quickly, but since Gavin was a Christian who believed in God as his friend, he'd just assumed that he believed in a short chronology for the age of the earth.

"Oh, I believe that God's the real Creator," Gavin said with a grin.

Corty nodded. The guide started to move their group on. This wasn't the time to discuss differences. They had lots more to see in the caves.

Here's something to think about: Is it possible for good Christians, people who know God as a friend and practice His commandment of love, to have beliefs on topics such as the Creation story that differ from ours? What in Corty and Gavin's story indicates that this might be possible? Why is it good to find points upon which you agree when talking about your beliefs with others?

JULY

13

Corty and the Catacombs

His master replied, "Well done, good and faithful servant! You have been faithful with a few things; I will put you in charge of many things." Matthew 25:21.

A stairway angled down, carrying Corty and his family from daylight toward the darkness of an underground passage. Their vacation travels had taken them from England to Italy, and they were entering the catacombs—the ancient burial grounds honeycombing the earth under the outskirts of Rome. Corty let his imagination carry him back through the centuries, but all his thoughts ended in questions.

Was this one of the tunnels used by those long-ago Christians? Did they actually hide from their persecutors down here? And hold meetings among the graves?

"Don't wander away from me!" the guide called. "It's easy to get lost."

Corty realized that he was the last in line and lagging. He took several hurried steps to catch up and started to open his camera pouch, eager to take pictures to prove that he'd actually been down in the catacombs.

"Did the long-ago Christians actually hide down here?" he asked as he pulled his camera from its pouch.

The guide shrugged. "The catacombs have been here a long time, and there are many stories, but we don't know for sure." He glanced at Corty's camera and pointed to a sign.

"No photography," it warned.

Corty's shoulders slumped. They'd seen potential terrorist targets where photography was forbidden. Usually the reasons were obvious. This time he saw no reason. "Why?" he asked.

"See that mosaic," the guard said as he gathered their entire group to listen. "There are many artifacts like this in the chapels and alcoves down here," he explained. "We used to allow visitors to take pictures, but, of course, flash is necessary. Burst after burst of light that bright began to fade the colors. If people continue to take pictures, the many flashes will literally eat the pictures off the wall. One person taking one picture makes no visible difference. Many people taking many pictures will make the design completely disappear."

Wow, thought Corty. *By keeping one little rule, I can help protect the catacombs.*

Do you have any rules about "little things" at home, school, or church? What are they? Why are they important? How can obeying them help you become a faithful steward?

JULY

14

Mr. Grimble's Glass Eye

"We will do everything you have told us and will go anywhere you send us. We will obey you, just as we always obeyed Moses." Joshua 1:16, 17, TEV.

"We will do everything you have told us." The people's promise must have sounded good to Joshua. Then they added, "We will obey you, just as we always obeyed Moses."

Sudden thoughts of a golden calf and of complaining crowds no doubt crossed his mind. He may have chuckled and said wisely to himself, *We'll see. We'll see.*

Promises are easy. Keeping them, though . . .

Mr. Grimble, so the story says, had come to build a mission clinic. He hired several men—strong, capable fellows—to work for him. They learned quickly, and as long as Mr. Grimble worked with them, they worked well. When at times he was called away, he always left them with precise instructions.

"Oh, yes, sir, we'll do exactly as you say," they always promised.

But each time he returned, the work was never completed.

"Why didn't you finish?" he'd ask.

Always he received a long story of explanation.

Now it so happened that Mr. Grimble had one good eye and one glass eye. He decided that he would use some of the superstitions of the area to encourage the men to work better. The next time he prepared to go into town, he took out his glass eye and set it on a table in the room where the men were working.

"While I'm gone I expect you to continue working as quickly as you have been working with me this morning," he said.

"Yes. Yes," said the men, looking at the eye.

"And begin the other side wall when you finish that one."

The men all nodded in agreement.

"My eye will be watching you," he told them as he went out the door.

When he returned, Mr. Grimble found that the one wall had been finished and that the men were busily working on the other. He was very pleased with himself for having found such an easy solution to keep his men working as they should.

Some days later, Mr. Grimble had to leave again. And once more he left his eye on the table. When he returned, he expected to find that the men had faithfully continued their work, but he found it unfinished. He started to say something when he looked at the table. Someone had put a hat over his eye!

Do you faithfully keep your promises?

JULY

15

Baby Swallow's Adventure

Even the sparrow has found a home, and the swallow a nest for herself, where she may have her young. Psalm 84:3.

Dad docked his boat and gathered his things. Fishing was heavy work, but he felt good about the catch. The money would make a good start toward paying the children's church school tuition, and for him that was very important. At the moment, though, all he wanted was to get to the house, shower, and tumble into bed.

Just then a fluttering of swallows swooping at the end of the dock and the sound of splashing attracted his attention. He went to investigate.

A young swallow wallowed in the water. It was probably one from the nest in the piling that secured the upper end of the floating dock—a hole near the top of the piling made a favorite nesting spot for swallow families, and it was time for the current nestlings to start flying.

Dad watched as the young bird struggled. It thrashed the water with its wings and kicked wildly with its spindly legs, which were so totally unsuited for swimming. Dad was about to go for a dip net to rescue the little thing when suddenly one of the adult birds zoomed in. It made a series of passes, swooping down at the unfortunate tiny bird. It first poked the juvenile from one side, then coming in from the other direction, it used its beak to tug at the nestling's feathers. With each pass, it become more and more obvious that the adult swallow had a certain goal in mind—a nearby log.

Other birds joined in. They locked their streamlined wings into glider position and swooped low, skimming the water toward the baby, prodding or pulling as they passed at slow speed. Closer, closer, inch by inch, they nudged the fledgling until it was against the log. With more tugging, they had it out of the water. At last the waterlogged bird lay, tiny and exhausted, on the log. Rivulets of water drained from its feathers, tracing spidery patterns on the log's weathered surface.

Dad continued to watch, amazed at the birds' efforts. It was as if they cared for this little bird as much as he cared for his children.

Once rested and dried, the young bird was able to stretch its wings again.

This time it flew.

JULY

16

In the Light of the Sun

The Lord is my light and my salvation—whom shall I fear? Psalm 27:1.

The setting sun glinted through the reeds and spread a coppery glow across the water as evening settled onto the marshlands of the nature preserve.

A teal surfaced, sending a silent circle of ripples wrinkling outward on the copper-toned surface. The bird passed a freshly-snagged minnow to a lone baby teal. In the distance, a scattering of coots paddled at their ease. Closer by, a muskrat cut the reflection. Its coarse, brown back was hunched, and its tail guided its direction. Dragonflies, high-speed wings crackling in the late summer reeds, exploded into the open and swooshed off on who-knows-what business.

The city seemed far away from this spread of nature, yet a few minutes' drive would put us back on its doorstep.

Enjoying the evening, I crouched on the observation platform and angled my camera for a sunset shot of lake, reeds, and ducks. Something blurred across the view-finder, close and out of focus. I lowered the camera to check for the problem.

A spider web hung from the rail of the platform. I bent lower and was about to sweep it away with my hand when I noticed that from this angle it caught the evening rays, becoming a golden outline against the low-hanging sun.

"Beautiful," I whispered.

Immediately other thoughts entered my mind, and I switched the lens to macro in order to move in for a special effects close-up. Now the viewfinder framed a delicate silk and spun-gold weaving. "And to think I was about to destroy this wonderful picture!" I told myself.

I was about to press the shutter when I became aware of something else. A smattering of ugly, dark splotches blurred across the sun-gold beauty. I focused more sharply.

"Gnats!" I spat the word out in disappointment.

The web had done its job. Dozens of the tiny insects stuck to the slender threads, and their dead bodies spoiled the web's beauty with the reality of why it hung there.

Like the web of sin, I thought. *It hangs ready to trap us where we don't expect it, and it's difficult to see until we look carefully against the light of God's Son.*

JULY

17

Fashions for Cows

Command those who are rich in this present world . . . to put their hope in God, who richly provides us with everything for our enjoyment. 1 Timothy 6:17.

Did you know that the latest fashions for cows include summer jackets with matching hats?

A Japanese university professor developed these unique garments to protect cows from sun, insects, and disease and to help them produce more milk. The outfit consists of three straw pieces that cover the cow's head, back, and abdomen.

When cows are exposed to the sun during the summer, the professor explained, they lose their appetites and produce less milk. After being in the sun for only about 20 minutes, the back of a black-haired cow can get as hot as 140° F. If she wears a jacket, though, she'll stay cooler and can spend more time eating grass, and, therefore, will produce more milk.

These jackets may not yet be available in dairy supply stores, but farmers do take care of their cows to keep them happy and healthy. They know that well-cared-for cows produce the most milk.

Parents also do their best to give their children the food, clothes, and things they need. They also like to give them special gifts that they know will make them happy. Sometimes these gifts are things. Sometimes they are gifts of time or of going places together.

Write down one gift that you received lately.

____

What about getting it made you happy?

____

(If you haven't received something, that's OK. Mention something you know your mother or father or other relative would like to give if he or she could, and why it would make you happy.)

Now write down something you have given or would like to give to someone special. ________________

Why would you give that particular gift? ________

____

God also gives us gifts. Write down three that He has given you already today.

1. ________________
2. ________________
3. ________________

Why are these gifts good? ________________

Prayer suggestion: Thank God for these three gifts. Tell Him why you're happy to have them. Also thank Him for being able to give and receive the other gifts you mentioned above.

JULY

18

God Is Fair

God will bring to judgment both the righteous and the wicked. Ecclesiastes 3:17.

The tall monument spired upward from the center of the common grave. "To think that those were people who once lived and worked and played here—people just like us."

Hearing his mom's words gave Justin that tight, scary feeling again. "U'm-hum," he grunted and looked up the path that wound around the hill, not wanting her to know how he felt.

It was very warm, verging on the hot—the too hot, actually—and the eastern Washington countryside stretched away in a brittle gray-brown. Even the chirping insects grated on his nerves. They sounded dry and raspy. Everything about the day was too dry and too hot and . . . They'd just been through the visitor's center at Whitman Mission and had seen the displays about Marcus and Narcissa Whitman and their mission and how the Indians had massacred them and the children they'd taken in.

It's not fair, Justin told himself. *If they were teaching the Indians about God, why did they have to get killed? Especially for something they didn't do?*

His thoughts churned, mixing everything together. When they had been driving down to Walla Walla the day before, there had been this horrible wreck. A guy who had been drinking lost control, and his car veered across the median and plowed into oncoming traffic. Just as they had crested a hill, they saw cars swerving this way and that, crashing and running off the road. His dad had jammed on the brakes. Luckily they were far enough back.

The morning paper had pictures—six people killed, several hurt, five cars totaled—and the drunk guy had lived through it.

And here on this spot, more than 100 years ago, the Indians had killed the missionaries because they blamed them for a measles epidemic that was killing their people. And the missionaries had been trying to help!

"I don't get it," he said aloud, his feelings pushing him to the point where he had to talk.

"What don't you get?" asked his mother.

"Why do good people have to die—especially for things that aren't their fault? Like those people in that grave there. And in the wreck yesterday."

His mother nodded. "That's a question many people ask."

"If God's fair, why doesn't He protect the good folks and let the bad ones die?"

His mother drew a deep breath. "God's fair," she said at last. "But sin isn't."

JULY

19

Don't Feed the Bears

No discipline seems pleasant at the time, but painful. Later on, however, it produces a harvest of righteousness and peace for those who have been trained by it. Hebrews 12:11.

What bears eat depends on the time of year. In the spring they eat mostly grasses, dandelions, and horsetail ferns; in early summer, mostly ants and ant larvae; then from midsummer on they eat mainly berries.

At least, that's what bears *should* eat.

Long ago, though, park bears learned that people had good food, and if the people didn't share, the bears would just take it. They started hanging around campsites and garbage dumps, waiting for handouts and leftovers. Bear life became easier, and they grew fatter.

Being almost always hungry and very strong, they left a definite mark when they took food—flattened and torn tents, damaged cars, even injured people.

Signs were posted. "Don't feed the bears!" they warned.

But those bulky, black animals looked so cute that many people still couldn't resist giving them "just a little bit."

One family threw some popcorn from their car window to a bear in a parking lot. The bear wanted more. The people rolled up their windows quickly. Not to be outwitted, the bear scrambled onto the car, thoroughly scratching the paint and denting the roof before a ranger could shoo it away.

A man had a chocolate bar. He threw half of it to a bear and stuffed the rest into his hip pocket. The bear wanted the other half, too, and with one swipe of its huge paw took it. The man had to be rushed to the hospital.

A lady forgot to roll up her window, and when she returned to her car, there sat a bear in the driver's seat, telltale cookie crumbs on its snout.

For the protection of people and property, and for the bears' own good, park authorities in many places have enforced strict laws. Problem bears are taken to remote areas, where they can no longer find their way back to places of easy food. Some bears have even had to be destroyed. Campers and visitors are required to keep all food in safe places away from the bears, and garbage must be dumped in special bear-proof containers. This has forced the animals to go back to eating a more natural—and healthful—diet, and makes camping safer.

Anyone caught breaking a "Don't Feed the Bears" warning may have to pay a very big fine—but this severe discipline is needed to protect both the people and the bears.

JULY

20

The Power, Part 1

They overcame him [Satan] by the blood of the Lamb. Revelation 12:11.

The red-brown dirt of the mission road was hard under our feet, and the sun filtered in splotches through the leaves of the mango trees that arched overhead, as we headed up the hill toward the guest house. The governor and his wife and Elder Krause from ADRA International were visiting ADRA projects. Bob, our pilot, had gone ahead.

Two men dressed in skin skirts came down the road toward us. Bands of beads crisscrossed their bare chests, and strings of bells jangled around their ankles. Thinking they were dancers on their way to entertain at some distant village feast, Date held out his hand in greeting.

"Welcome to our mission," he said.

Both men stopped abruptly. They clapped their hands tight against their bodies.

"Welcome," Date repeated, still holding out his hand—local etiquette expected a handshake on greeting.

The men shook their heads and stepped back. "We can't shake hands with you," one explained.

Date let his hand drop. "Well, welcome anyway," he managed to say.

"Those were witch doctors," the governor said after the men had gone on down the road. "They've completed their rituals of preparation. Now they're dressed and ready and are on their way to perform some ceremonial mission—probably to cast a spell on someone."

"But I only wanted to greet them," Date replied.

"You're a Christian. If you'd touched them, they'd have lost power."

The governor had grown up with all the traditions of village life and knew firsthand about the power of the spirits. He'd also been a high priest in a mystery cult.

"Power is very important to those who practice the magical arts and deal with the spirit world. They're always looking for a stronger power, yet they're afraid to give up their magic to become Christians. I know the power of the spirits."

For a moment there was nothing but the sound of our feet on the hard-dirt road.

"I know now that God is stronger than any spirit," he said.

JULY

The Power, Part 2

[Simon] offered money to Peter and John, and said, "Give this power to me too."
Acts 8:18, 19, TEV.

After dinner we sat in the shade of the front porch and shared stories about how we'd seen God's power at work.

"Pastor Thaddeus, one of my friends, had a very unusual experience with the power of prayer," the governor said, and he told this story.

Pastor Thaddeus and his wife had moved to the capital city. They found a house in a good neighborhood, but they soon learned that several of their neighbors were involved in witchcraft. This did not worry Pastor Thaddeus, though, because he believed strongly in the power of prayer. Besides, he had come to share the gospel with and pray for those who were under the power of Satan.

One afternoon as he was studying his Bible and praying, he was startled to his feet by a loud boom.

"A bomb?" The heavy object slammed against the roof on the back of their house. Then it clattered across the metal roofing. His wife ran into the room.

"What was that?" she asked.

Pastor Thaddeus shook his head.

The two of them rushed to the back door, but saw nothing in the yard. They looked up on the roof, but they could see no damage or anything that could have made such an explosive noise.

"You and your prayers!" his wife finally exclaimed. "That must have been something to do with your praying."

Pastor Thaddeus only shrugged his shoulders. His wife's faith was good, but she didn't like him being so involved in working against the evil forces with his prayers. Since they couldn't find what had crashed into their house, he went back to his room and his wife went back to her work.

The next day they heard a determined pounding on their door. A delegation had come to see Pastor Thaddeus. "We want to buy the power you have," the spokesman said after they had visited awhile.

"But I don't have any power to sell," Pastor Thaddeus explained, not knowing why they were asking.

"Oh, yes you do," said the spokesman. "We know you have a very strong power, but you just don't want to share it."

"I don't know what you're talking about."

"What about yesterday?" the spokesman asked.

And then Pastor Thaddeus remembered the noise on the roof.

JULY

22

The Power, Part 3

God's free gift is eternal life in union with Christ Jesus our Lord. Romans 6:23, TEV.

"We know you have a very strong power," the spokesman said again to Pastor Thaddeus.

He shook his head. "I have no power to sell," he repeated.

"Oh, yes you do. Yesterday your next-door neighbor tested it. She is the one among us with the strongest powers." The spokesman looked at the other three men with him, and they all nodded in agreement.

"She was flying above your house, and such a strong force was rising that it knocked her from the sky and onto your roof. She fell with such force that her arm was broken."

At this point the governor interrupted his story. "I know about these flying witches," he said. "Maybe you don't hear about them in America."

"Not as much," we agreed.

"One night one fell from the sky—that sometimes happens, you know—and this one fell into our courtyard," he continued. "The guard came to waken us and asked what he should do with her.

"We got up and went out. The poor woman was naked and confused and groping about as if she couldn't see, as they usually do when they fall, and mumbling about running out of fuel and not being able to find her cord. My wife got some clothes for her, and we had the guards open the gate and send her on her way. She was still groping about as she went down the street.

"Anyway, Pastor Thaddeus saw his neighbor the next day, and she did have her arm in a plaster cast," the governor said, getting back to his first story. He told how the visitors began to get upset with the pastor.

"You just don't want to share your power," the spokesman said. "You want to keep it all for yourself."

"I have no power to sell, but I'll show you what I have." He excused himself and a few moments later returned carrying his Bible.

"This is my power," he said holding it up.

"But that's just a book," complained the spokesman. "You're just trying to trick us. You don't want to share your power."

"This is it," insisted the pastor. "This is my power—the Word of God. You can have it too."

"How do you expect us to believe that?" the spokesman asked.

Pastor Thaddeus knew they weren't ready to listen, but he said, "To have it, you must believe."

JULY

23

The Mustard Seed

Then Jesus asked, "What is the kingdom of God like? What shall I compare it to? It is like a mustard seed." Luke 13:18, 19.

The ruler of the synagogue ground his teeth to hold back his anger. *What's this young upstart after, anyway?* he asked himself.

He'd just watched Him heal a crippled woman—right there in the synagogue in front of everyone. On the Sabbath day! Everybody knew that such work was strictly forbidden on the Sabbath, and when he, the ruler, had spoken up, this smart young Fellow started talking about donkeys and oxen and untying them and watering them, and people had started sniggering.

And now He's asking them leading questions—about the kingdom of God. And talking about mustard plants!

The ruler wished for a way to get even, to make the people see that they were wasting their time in chasing after and listening to this—this radical who wouldn't even keep the law. But the Fellow had an answer for everything, and now here He was talking about nothing more important than mustard seeds.

In those days mustard grew everywhere, and everyone used the seeds for seasoning. Even though it was far from the smallest seed they planted, it was so common that they often used it in their sayings to stand for something very, very small. And compared to other herbs, it did grow into a giant bush, often standing higher than a person's head.

Birds—especially the small linnets and finches—found the seeds very tasty, and as the seeds began to ripen, the birds would perch on the branches and feast.

"The kingdom of God," said Jesus, "is like a mustard seed, which a man took and planted in his garden. It grew and became a tree, and the birds of the air perched in its branches."

While the ruler of the synagogue grumbled to himself, the other people listened. This young Teacher talked about everyday things they knew about, and He made God sound kind and understanding.

The kingdom of God a mustard seed? mused one old man to himself. *That's good.*

As he listened, the lesson became clearer. *It starts small, it grows fast, and it grows big. It makes things taste good, and once you put it in the food, the taste spreads all through it. Hmmmm. And the kingdom of God is like that.*

And as Jesus talked, that seed took root in another heart.

JULY

24

Object Lessons for Today

The crowd that gathered around him was so large that he got into a boat and sat in it out on the lake. Mark 4:1.

We lived in a valley beside a river—a slow, thoughtful, deep-green river that rose and fell with the ocean tides. Downriver just a ways was the log dump. I loved to watch logs being hoisted from the trucks, then dumped down the ramp. They hit the water with a gigantic splash, spraying water far into the air. Then as the water settled they bobbed to the surface to float with the tide into the rafting area.

Sometimes the dump operator trimmed the ramp logs with his double-bladed ax. From my faraway side I could see him lift the ax and bring it down with strong, cutting blows, but I never heard the chop when the ax hit wood. I always heard the sound as he lifted the ax for the next blow. That puzzled me until I learned that sound travels much more slowly than light, even though it carries clearly for long distances across smooth water.

One day as Jesus was teaching by a lake, the crowd became so big that He got into a boat and pushed out from shore to talk to them. From the boat, His voice no doubt carried very well. From the boat, He could also see the farmers planting on the fertile hillside that sweeps up from the lake. Watching the farmers, He told His famous parable about the sower.

Many of His parables were about common everyday things that the people could see as He was talking. If Jesus had talked to the people by my river when I was a girl, He would no doubt have made lessons about logs and axes and sounds and tides.

What parables and object lessons do you think Jesus might use if He would come today and speak in a large convention center and have His talk carried live via satellite around the world with simultaneous translation into other languages? Can you think of a spiritual lesson He might make from the following?

1. The microphone and amplifiers ______________
2. The translators ______________
3. The TV satellite system ______________
4. An artificial potted plant ______________
5. A computer ______________
6. Traveling in a jumbo jet ______________
7. The convention center ______________

What other things might He use as object lessons for modern parables? ______________

______________________________.

JULY

25

Let Not Your Heart Be Troubled

Do not let your hearts be troubled. Trust in God; trust also in me. John 14:1.

Sara had no close friends, and she wondered if there might be something wrong with her. Then one day as she walked down the hall on her way to class, she turned, and there was Mace. From that moment they were friends, very good friends.

"You know, you're really a nice person," Mace told her many times. "It's so easy for me to like you."

Sara felt better about herself with Mace's friendship. With Mace beside her, saying nice things to her, she began to gain self-confidence.

When school was out, Mace went north for a summer job. Sara waited for his letters. As she picked up his letter one day, she immediately knew it wasn't like the others. The envelope was thin—too thin. She opened it and forced herself to read.

"And so it's better that we don't see each other anymore."

At first Sara's mind refused to accept the words that her eyes were reading. Then she began to feel numb. What would she do without Mace?

Feeling lonelier than she'd ever felt before, Sara dragged about the house for the next several days. As she sat in her room one morning a fragment of a text began to repeat through her mind.

"Let not your heart be troubled. Let not your heart . . ."

She'd known those words since she could remember, but she thought they were only about Jesus' second coming.

"Let not your heart be troubled. Trust in God."

Suddenly she began to understand. Trusting in God was more than going to church and believing that Jesus would come again. It included everything, even friendships.

She stood up and went to the window and stared out, but she wasn't seeing the big maple tree or the hedge of roses. Instead, her mind focused on a day by the lake, strolling hand in hand with Mace, happy, wishing she could always be with Mace because he made her feel so good about herself. She let her head drop against the window. "And now that's over."

A new feeling began to work itself around the ache of missing Mace. "Let not your heart be troubled. Trust in Me."

"OK, God," she said. "I trust You, but I never realized before that it included this, too." And she knew that she was going to be all right.

JULY

26

Sins in a Basket

I think drugs are the worst sin." Lana almost spat her words out.

"The worst?" Kelcie didn't sound so sure. "All sins are bad."

"But drug addicts get hooked bad. And look at the drug runners and pushers and all the terrible things they do—like in the news about everyone who's gotten killed in South America because of the drug business. Those people are terrible."

"God loves the addicts and the drug lords just as much as He loves you and me," Kelcie countered.

"But they're so gruesome—and cruel." Lana made a face.

"Anyone who's mean, even with words . . . Well, little things can be evil, too. And God's ready to forgive everyone."

"But there are big sins and little sins," Lana argued.

"And sins in a basket, my grandpa says," Kelcie added.

"In a basket?"

"Yeah. Sins hidden away, like in the story Grandpa tells about the church in his grandfather's village in the old country. The people there got to worrying about all the secret sins in their congregation, 'cause they thought God couldn't bless their church if they let sinners sit in their pews. Then someone got a 'revelation' about a basket—how they should rig it up and weigh folks for their sins. If anyone fell through, it'd be a sure sign of secret sin, and that person would be banned from the congregation."

"But that's . . ."

Kelcie nodded. "And it just so happened that the deacon's wife was what Grandpa calls 'on the larger side of life.' She was really fat. When it came her turn to be weighed, she stepped into the basket, thinking she was no more sinful than anyone else. The men pulled hard, and the ropes strained through the pulley as they lifted her. Suddenly the bottom gave way, and there she hung, gasping, legs dangling just above the floor, stuck in the broken basket.

"As Grandpa says, some sins are just more obvious than others. The important thing is to have God in our lives and leave the judging of others to Him."

Do not judge, or you too will be judged. For in the same way you judge others, you will be judged, and with the measure you use, it will be measured to you. Matthew 7:1, 2.

JULY

27

Because She Did Not Remember

Because you did not remember . . . Ezekiel 16:43.

Jeremy, please. The door!"

At the sound of his mother's voice, Jeremy felt an angry flush rising round his neck. He stomped his left foot down and turned hard. Grabbing the edge of the door, he gave it a quick swing. It banged shut.

"Jeremy!"

Fists clenched, head down, Jeremy scuffed into the den.

"What's wrong, Jeremy?" His mother sat at her desk, chin braced on her hand, looking at him.

Jeremy didn't look up.

"Problems again?"

Jeremy rubbed his knuckles against his thighs, still not talking.

"You forgot . . . ?" His mother let her voice trail into a question.

Jeremy nodded.

"Sit down, son."

Jeremy sat down. His shoulders drooped and his fists were still knotted, but now he worked them against the sofa cushions. He stared at the floor.

"Once upon a time," his mother began, "a very handsome Prince was walking through the fields of His kingdom. Beside the path He saw something terrible. There was a newborn baby crying and squirming in the dirt. 'Take the baby,' He told His servants. 'Clean it and care for it.'

"Years later the Prince was in the area again, and He saw that baby, only now she had grown into a very beautiful young woman. The Prince fell in love with her. They were married, and the Prince made sure that she had the best of everything. That baby who had been left to die by her mother became a very honored queen, and fame of her beauty spread through the whole world. That made her very proud. She no longer loved her Husband as she should. She forgot what He had done for her and began to run around with other men and waste the Prince's riches. She became a very disgusting person because she did not remember who she was."

Jeremy listened, but he didn't get the point.

"That's the story of God and the children of Israel—God told it to Ezekiel." His mother looked down at the accounts she'd been working on, then back at Jeremy. "Their pride in their riches caused them to forget who'd blessed them—the worst kind of forgetting. But everyday forgetting has other causes."

JULY

28

A Junior Astronaut

The Lord your God has chosen you. Deuteronomy 7:6.

While his mother told her story, Jeremy's thoughts churned. He knew that if he really cared, he'd not forget things like shutting the door. His shoulders sagged even more. It had been a bad day.

At computer camp it seemed he'd done nothing but forget. He forgot to make the backup disk that was due before he left. The tutor had docked him for some dumb mistakes when he checked his handwritten reports. Then to top everything, just before he got off at his bus stop he discovered he'd forgotten to bring the permission slip for his mother to sign. Without her signature he couldn't go with the group that had been chosen to take part in a special mission at the Alpha 7 Challenger Center the next day.

"Not everyone has the chance to be a junior astronaut—and I forget my permission slip!"

His patience with himself was stretched to its limit. The city's space and science center was doing a simulated rendezvous with Halley's comet, and his computer camp had free tickets for the 10 kids with the best overall projects. Jeremy had been chosen as one of those junior astronauts. They'd be taking a space station on a mock-up mission to rendezvous with the comet's tail and launch a probe into the heart of the comet.

"Isn't that fantastic!" he was grumbling to himself as he banged into the house. "I'm chosen—and I forget my permission slip! Just how do I get it signed in time!"

At that moment his mother hollered at him about the door—and then had to tell him this story about a Prince and a bawling baby! Jeremy's hands were still knotted when she finished talking. He stared at the floor, not wanting to say a decent word.

"What's that got to do with anything?" he finally asked.

"Suppose you tell me about your day, and then we'll try for an answer," his mother suggested. With a few good questions, she managed to prod the story from him.

"Permission slip!" she exclaimed when Jeremy got to that part. "That's no problem!" She picked up her pen and pulled out a sheet of stationery. "Am I proud of you for being chosen!" She smiled. "I'll just write a note to your camp director and ask her to clip it to an official permission slip. That should take care of tomorrow.

"Then we'll talk about some strategies for remembering."

JULY

29

Cupbearer's Cure

"But when all goes well with you, remember me and show me kindness; mention me to Pharaoh and get me out of this prison." Genesis 40:14.

You and I do the same kind of forgetting. It's more of the cupbearer kind."

Jeremy wrinkled his nose. "Cupbearer?"

"From the story of Joseph—you know, the one whose dream Joseph interpreted. When the cupbearer got back to work for the king, he got so busy that he forgot all about his promise to tell Pharaoh about Joseph—until Pharaoh had a dream.

"That's the most common kind of forgetting, and it happens to everyone—young and old. We've got our minds so stressed with so many projects that it doesn't always give us all the right information at the right times. That's why folks have invented so many *mnemonic devices*.

"So many what?"

"Mnemonic (nee-MON-ick) devices—which simply means something to aid or help the memory.

"Remember when you started taking piano you used the sentence 'Every Good Boy Does Fine' to learn the names of the notes on the lines of the treble staff? And F-A-C-E to remember the names of the notes in the spaces? Those are mnemonic devices. Many use the first letter of a list of items to make a word or sentence. Here are more." Jeremy's mother wrote these.

HOMES = the Great Lakes—Huron, Ontario, Michigan, Erie, Superior.

Roy G Biv = the colors of the visible spectrum or rainbow—red, orange, yellow, green, blue, indigo, violet.

Mary's Violet Eyes Make John Stay Up Nights Pacing = the order of the planets in the solar system from the sun—Mercury, Venus, Earth, Mars, Jupiter, Saturn, Uranus, Neptune, Pluto.

Did Mary Ever Visit Brighton Beach? = the order of British hereditary titles from most to least important—duke, marquis, earl, viscount, baron, baronet.

"Then there's the 'spring forward, fall back' saying as a memory aid for setting clocks for daylight saving time—an hour forward in the spring, an hour back in the fall.

"Since ours is a 'cupbearer problem,' maybe the old string-around-the-finger would best help us remember."

Jeremy gave his mother a disgusted look.

"Of course, you'd probably prefer to set the alarm on your watch. I use my computer's alarm. When it rings, I remember!"

Remember

I will remember.
Psalm 77:11.

This is a collection of thoughts to read aloud—and to be *remembered*.

You can do these as a round-robin reading with each person reading one in turn, or one person could read them all.

1. Remember your Creator in the days of your youth,
   before the days of trouble come
   and the years approach when you will say,
   "I find no pleasure in them."[1]

2. A certain ruler asked him, "Good teacher, what must I do to inherit eternal life?"[2]

3. My son, if you accept my words
   and store up my commands within you,
   turning your ear to wisdom
   and applying your heart to understanding,
   and if you call out for insight
   and cry aloud for understanding,
   and if you look for it as for silver
   and search for it as for hidden treasure,
   then you will understand the fear of the Lord
   and find the knowledge of God.[3]

4. I will remember the deeds of the Lord;
   yes, I will remember your miracles of long ago.
   I will meditate on all your works
   and consider all your mighty deeds.[4]

5. Then those who feared the Lord talked with each other, and the Lord listened and heard. A scroll of remembrance was written in his presence concerning those who feared the Lord and honored his name. "They will be mine," says the Lord Almighty, "in the day when I make up my treasured possession. I will spare them, just as in compassion a man spares his son who serves him. And you will again see the distinction between the righteous and the wicked, between those who serve God and those who do not."[5]

6. So in everything, do to others what you would have them do to you.[6]

---

[1] Eccl. 12:1; [2] Luke 18:18; [3] Prov. 2:1-5; [4] Ps. 77:11, 12; [5] Mal. 3:16-18; [6] Matt. 7:12.

JULY

31

Problem Baggage

Listen, my son, and be wise, and keep your heart on the right path. *Proverbs 23:19.*

Forested hills rolled in every direction, and valleys with small streams cut this way and that. Everywhere looked the same with no special landmarks to break the monotony.

Jack checked the compass again. It hung as if frozen. "Useless!" He drew a deep breath. "How'll I find the airstrip?"

He looked down at the map on his knee, then out the side window. He needed the help of the compass to keep the plane on course across this huge upland wilderness.

Alone in the plane on this trip, he'd loaded it to the max with supplies for Riverbend Mission. As always, he'd balanced the weight by stashing heavy things to the center of the plane. The missionaries had ordered a supply of canned food, but it wasn't until after he was in the air that he discovered that with so much tin on board, the compass would not work.

Jack had flown the route before, and visibility was good. The river cut along the other side of the mountains. If he strayed off course, he could find his bearings once he reached that river. But it snaked around in such a way that without the help of the compass, it could be difficult to know which way to turn once he did find it.

God has given us the Bible as a compass for our travels toward heaven. Too often, though, in our everyday lives we take on baggage that "freezes" the compass, making it hang useless and causing us to stray off course.

When Jack reached the main river, he studied the twists of its valleys very carefully, comparing them to his map, and he was able to pinpoint his exact location. Riverbend Mission lay east-northeast. He landed safely, and after he unloaded the cases of canned foods his compass worked fine.

Is there any problem baggage that you sometimes take on board in your life? Something that causes you to lose your bearings on the way of God? Take a minute to tell God silently how you feel about that problem—talk to Him in your heart, tell Him you want to give that problem completely to Him.

Then, as the text says, listen. Give God some time to put good ideas in your mind. "Listen. . . . Keep your heart on the right path."

If you wish, take time to share with your worship group the ideas that God gives you.

AUGUST

1

Afraid of the Wrong Thing

The fear of the Lord—that is wisdom, and to shun evil is understanding. Job 28:28.

Sanna scooted under the covers of her bed and scrunched into a ball, her pillow stuffed against her ears. She wanted to escape the terrible noise of the storm, thinking that if she couldn't hear the booming and the rumbling of the thunder, she wouldn't be so afraid.

"When you hear the thunder," her mother said, trying to help her be brave, "then you know you're safe. It's the lightning that's dangerous."

Sanna believed what her mother told her, but she still didn't like the noise. On the other hand, she thought that lightning was pretty. Eager to see the next streak of lightning, as soon as the muffled roar had passed, she poked her head above the covers.

"Lightning is kind of like a snowflake," her mother had said. "Every bolt is different. It never flashes across the sky twice in the same pattern. But while a snowflake's soft and gentle, lightning's dangerous and unpredictable. I have to agree with you, though, that it's fun to watch."

The window of Sanna's room framed a large piece of sky, and in a few moments another flash seared across the clouds. Sanna saw it reach this way and that for a brief moment until it seemed to explode into a ball of light in the distance. Then she dived for her covers again, blocking her ears, knowing that at any instant there'd be another crashing and booming.

Have you, like Sanna, ever been afraid of the wrong thing?

She enjoyed watching the lightning write its amazing patterns in the sky. Seen from a distance lightning causes no harm, and caught on a photo its patterns are beautiful. But lightning is also one of nature's most dangerous forces. To enjoy its beauty safely, you must follow certain rules.

During a storm, always take shelter, but not under a tree—lightning often strikes the highest point. Immediately leave open, flat, or rolling areas—such as a golf course—that are far from a safe shelter and where lightning can strike anywhere. In the house, shut windows and doors.

One of the safest places to be is in an automobile—the large amount of metal absorbs the charge. If you are caught outside during a thunderstorm, make yourself as tiny as possible by squatting or curling up into a ball.

Sin, like lightning, can be very beautiful and dazzling, but it is even more dangerous and unpredictable. Our only safe shelter is the Lord Jesus.

AUGUST

2

A Rainbow in the Clouds

Like the appearance of a rainbow in the clouds on a rainy day, so was the radiance around him. This was the appearance of the likeness of the glory of the Lord.
Ezekiel 1:28.

Mark leaned against the rail fence and stared into the distance.

His father's fields stretched toward the horizon—hundreds of acres of golden wheat. The heads were plump and heavy, ready for harvest, but beyond them the sky hung like a big black slate. A sky that dark and heavy could mean only one thing—hail!

On the Canadian prairies, hail is one of the farmers' greatest enemies. Even tiny ice stones can shred plants, and heavier stones can beat an entire crop into the ground, destroying it. Already the wind from the edge of the storm slapped across the fields, and the grain moved as if it were being stirred by a big wave machine. Mark was too worried, though, to see the beauty of its billowing gold against the black background.

A jagged flash seared across the cloud.

Automatically Mark began to count. "One-and-one-thousand . . . two-and-one-thousand . . . three-and-one-thousand . . ." He had just started to say "Fifteen" when he heard the rumble of thunder. "Fifteen seconds. About three miles," he told himself. He drew a deep breath. "God," he pleaded, "keep the storm away from our farm." He thought of all their hard work. If the crop was good, they could pay the bills. If the hail hit, they had insurance. But it wouldn't be enough. "Make the wind blow it apart. Don't let the hail hurt us or any of our neighbors."

As Mark watched, a soft band of color began to appear on the cloud. Gradually it brightened into one of the most brilliant rainbows he had ever seen. Bits of the story of Noah flashed through his mind. The rainbow. God's promises. Even if hail did damage their crop, God wouldn't forget them.

The storm moved closer, and the distant black dulled into an angry gray. The rainbow faded, and ice pellets began to beat down as the storm edged overhead. Mark fled to the barn for shelter.

In a few minutes it was over, and the clouds broke, showing stretches of clear blue. Mark hurried out to look at the fields. A few patches of grain lay flat, but most still stood. He breathed a prayer of thankfulness.

AUGUST

Baby's Race

Happy slapped the harness in place, hooked the traces, and quickly jumped into the racing buggy. "Yahoo, Baby!" he yelled. "Let's go!"

Baby simply bounced on her legs and refused to take even one step forward, while all the others whooshed away from the starting line.

"Come on, Baby!" Happy pleaded. "Don't let those guys beat!"

But Baby wouldn't budge.

Happy raised his racing broom and fanned it beside Baby's head. With a sudden lurch, she sprang into action, her spindly neck stretching forward, her long legs reaching into giant strides. Like other ostriches, she can run faster than a horse, but even though she's tamed and trained, her lack of good sense makes her a poor racer. She has no idea that she and other ostriches are raced at fairs only because people enjoy watching the silly things they do.

The largest living bird, an ostrich stands seven to eight feet high and weighs 200 to 300 pounds when full grown. With its long neck and huge eyes, it can see for several miles. Its short wings are quite useless for flying, but they help lift it along when it runs. It can take strides up to 25 feet and can reach speeds up to 50 miles an hour.

Once, back when ostrich plumes on hats were in style, ostrich farming was good business. When the fashion changed, farmers could no longer afford to raise the big birds because they eat so much. They reach full growth in six months but can live to be 80 years old. Ostriches like grass, leaves, seeds, fruit, even smaller birds and insects, and they swallow stones, glass, bones, and other hard, gritty things to aid their digestion.

Some people call them the "camel bird" because they can go a long time without water and because their humping walk makes them look like a camel from a distance, and they, too, live mostly on dry plains and sandy deserts. Because ostriches keep their heads down so much hunting for food, people think that they hide their heads in the sand when they are afraid. That's not true—they run.

After that one burst of speed, Baby stopped again and never did finish her race. Happy had to bribe her back to her pen with food. As Job 39:17 says, God didn't give her "a share of good sense."

Are you running the race of life with the good sense that God has given you?

Let us run with determination the race that lies before us. Let us keep our eyes fixed on Jesus. Hebrews 12:1, 2, TEV.

AUGUST

4

Some Hot, Dry Facts

You have been . . . a shade from the heat. Isaiah 25:4.

"You have been
a refuge for the poor,
a refuge for the needy in his distress,
a shelter from the storm
and a shade from the heat.
For the breath of the ruthless
is like a storm driving against a wall
and like the heat of the desert" (Isaiah 25:4, 5).

Hot deserts cover about 20 percent of our earth.

The world's largest desert is the Sahara in Africa. It covers an area a little bigger than Brazil, but a little smaller than Canada. Only about one fifth of the Sahara is soft sand—the rest is stone and pebble. North America has more than 500,000 square miles of desert.

The driest place on earth is the Atacama Desert in Chile. It has gone without rain for more than 14 years. A desert may receive no rain for many years, then 10 inches might fall in a few hours.

The hottest temperature in the world was recorded at Azizia, Libya, on September 13, 1922. It was 136° F (58° C). On July 10, 1913, Death Valley, California, had 134° F (57° C). Deserts include the hottest places in the world because they absorb more heat from the sun than does land in humid climates.

Death Valley, which lies in California and Nevada, also has the lowest elevation in the Western Hemisphere—a spot near Badwater that is 282 feet (86 meters) below sea level. Along with other minerals, borax was discovered in this long, narrow valley. The mines closed long ago, but the 20-mule teams that hauled borax out of the valley are still famous.

Some desert animals have unique ways of putting up with the extreme conditions. Camels pack huge quantities of fat in their humps, and a camel can live for months on the water that's produced when its body breaks down this fat for use as energy.

Desert areas are growing bigger, stretching into the fertile lands that fringe them and causing, among other things, changes in weather patterns. People are responsible for this problem. Whether because they don't know any better or because they don't care, they use improper farming, grazing, logging, and mining methods, which destroy millions of acres of good land each year.

God is like an oasis, a refuge, in the desert and a shade from the burning sun. If we love Him, we'll also take good care of the earth that He created.

AUGUST

The Story of the Bricks

John looked up. Spatters of red-brown mud blotched his face and arms. More spatters covered his clothes. He smiled and held up the wooden form that he'd just emptied. Behind him a double line of solid red-brown blocks lay drying in the sun—hundreds and hundreds of bricks that he and his friends were making for their new school.

Making good bricks took lots of hard work digging clay, mixing it with just enough water, packing it into the wooden brick molds, and then carefully dumping the clay blocks from the molds so that they wouldn't twist out of shape. John was happy to help, though, because he wanted a bigger and better school.

As John looked at the sky, his smile faded. A mass of dark gray clouds gathered to the east. "Quick!" he called to the others.

They scurried to find something to cover their new bricks. But they weren't quick enough. Rain poured down, and the unprotected bricks washed into misshapen lumps. Rain even soaked into some of those they had managed to cover, crumbling their corners and warping the sides.

After the storm passed, the young men stared at the mess that had once been their neat double row of drying bricks. They could rework those that were soft enough, and they could chip the roughness off those with only a little damage, but many would have to be discarded. The boys had lots of work to redo.

This little story of the bricks contains many symbols of everyday Christian life. What could be meant by

John and his friends? ____________________
the sun? ____________________
the new school they're building? ____________________
the rain? ____________________
the ruined bricks? ____________________
the covering/protection? ____________________
the bricks soft enough to be reworked? __________
the bricks that had to be thrown away? __________

If we don't have God's protection, sin will force us into its mold and make us unfit for the place God has for us. Praise God! He can re-make us—if we let Him.

Don't let the world around you squeeze you into its own mould, but let God re-make you so that your whole attitude of mind is changed. Thus you will prove in practice that the will of God's good, acceptable to him and perfect. Romans 12:2, Phillips.

AUGUST

6

Questions God Asks

Stand up now like a man and answer the questions I ask you. Job 38:3, TEV.

Job was rich and strong and powerful. He was also kind and good and just—the sort of person who followed God with all his heart. Then everything went wrong, and Job didn't know why. He had no idea that Satan was trying to make him so miserable that he would curse God. Even his wife said, "Curse God and die!"

"You're talking foolishness," Job said, and he refused.

"What did you do to be punished like this?" his friends asked.

They thought bad things happened as punishment for a sin, but Job couldn't think of a thing he'd done wrong.

Finally God spoke, but He didn't say "It's not your fault, Job." He didn't even say why the bad things had happened. Instead, He tried to help Job and his friends understand about His goodness and power and wisdom by asking questions about creation and things of nature.

Here are some of the questions from Job 38, TEV. The number stands for the verse. Try to answer them. What do they tell you about God?

4. Were you there when I made the world? If you know so much, tell me about it.

18. Have you any idea how big the world is? Answer me if you know.

19. Do you know where the light comes from or what the source of darkness is?

22. Have you ever visited the storerooms, where I keep the snow and the hail?

24. Have you been to the place where the sun comes up, or the place from which the east wind blows?

31. Can you tie the Pleiades together or loosen the bonds of Orion?

32. Can you guide the stars season by season and direct the Big and the Little Dipper?

33. Do you know the laws that govern the skies, and can you make them apply to the earth?

35. And if you command the lightning to flash, will it come to you and say, "At your service"?

39. Do you find food for lions to eat, and satisfy hungry young lions when they hide in their caves, or lie in wait in their dens?

41. Who is it that feeds the ravens when they wander about hungry, when their young cry to me for food?

AUGUST

7

The Waves

Another big wave swept toward the rocks. "Hope you get all wet!" Trish spun toward her brother and stuck out her tongue.

"Pick-pick-pick-pick!" Nathan flapped his elbows in time to his chicken sounds, then took a bounding leap toward her.

Trish dodged with a quick sidestep toward the rail. "M-o-m . . . !" Whatever she planned to yell ended in a scream as the wave broke.

"Trish is a-l-l w-e-t! Trish is a-l-l w-e-t!"

A warning look from Mother put a quick period to Nathan's chant. "You'll dry." Her words in Trish's direction sounded tired, even fed up.

"I thought something would break," Aunt Susan remarked, lifting an eyebrow. "All the way here, I heard the waves building."

Trish plunked herself onto a bench well back from the edge of the lookout and pretended not to be listening. Nathan let her be and became busy gathering pebbles.

"To think! A wind on the other side of the ocean could have made these waves." Aunt Susan seemed to be talking to their mother, but both Trish and Nathan could easily hear what she was saying. "A breeze on smooth water makes pleasant little ripples, but if the wind continues, the ripples build into waves. The stronger the wind, the bigger and angrier the wave energy becomes until it grows into trains of waves that roll far beyond the reach of the wind that started them. The water itself doesn't move forward—it just churns up and down where it is—but the wave energy keeps traveling."

Aunt Susan talked on as if their mother were very interested in the science of waves. "They're like bad moods. Something starts them, then they're impossible to hold back."

"I doubt if moods are as hard to hold back as waves," Mom replied.

Here it comes. Trish felt herself tense all over. *Another sermon about how I should learn to control my feelings*, she said to herself.

"I don't know," said Aunt Susan. "Moods can get out of control. Jesus calmed a bad storm. He can calm bad moods, too."

Just then another giant wave hit the rock, and a cloud of spray caught Nathan.

But Trish didn't seem to notice. She was too busy wondering if Jesus could help calm the storm she felt inside herself.

Then [Jesus] got up and rebuked the winds and the waves, and it was completely calm. Matthew 8:26.

AUGUST

8

The Bishop's Swans

For everyone who asks receives; he who seeks finds; and to him who knocks, the door will be opened. Matthew 7:8.

Garby stood on the sloping lawn under the shade of the large tree. Behind him loomed the huge Wells Cathedral, and across from him stood the bishop's palace on a tiny island. Its stone-gray walls sheered down into the water of the moat that went all around it. He slid his backpack around on his shoulder and rummaged in it for the bag he'd brought. Several ducks started toward him.

"OK, OK!" he exclaimed as three heavy mallards opened and closed their beaks expectantly. He tossed a handful of bread toward them. Immediately another set of ducks that had been eyeing him from mid-moat turned toward the bank. Soon Garby was surrounded by ducks, and then as he'd hoped, a pair of large, white swans slipped up on his left. He flipped some larger pieces of bread in their direction, and they dipped their long necks and reached politely for the food.

Garby knew that the bishop's swans didn't need his bread. They're famous throughout England because they can "ring" for their dinner. When they're hungry, all they have to do is swim across the moat to the place where there's a little door in the palace wall. Beside the door, within beak's reach, hangs a bell. When it's mealtime, they reach up and tug at the bell with their beaks, and a warden will open the door and feed them.

In the Sermon on the Mount, Jesus told His followers not to worry about the things of this life—food and drink and clothes—but He also added, "Ask and it will be given to you; seek and you will find; knock and the door will be opened to you."

Too often, though, prayers become like the swans ringing their dinner bell. Even though they ring it at the right time and in the right way, the bell gives only one message—"We want food. We want food." Have your prayers ever become like that? Do they give only one message? "We want . . . We want . . ."

If all you did when you talked to your best friend was ask him or her to give you things, how long would you stay best friends?

Jesus said to seek *first* His kingdom and His righteousness, then all the other needs would be given. Make your prayers more than just ringing a bell to let God know what you want. Seek God's kingdom.

AUGUST

Recycling

So do not throw away your confidence; it will be richly rewarded. Hebrews 10:35.

Recycling is nothing new—birds and animals have been recycling since almost forever. Birds fashion nests using castoffs. Ravens line their nests with fur shed by bighorn sheep. Some smaller birds pick up bits of thread and string that people have dropped and weave them into their nests of twigs and grasses. Others even use their own extra feathers for nest lining.

Red squirrels make their homes in the pine cone scales that pile up when they peel them off to get the pine nuts. Mice nibble on the antlers that elk and deer have dropped. Raccoons make their homes in old, hollow logs. People, in the meantime, have been carelessly throwing away their junk.

Josh's grandmother gave him a model kit of the plane she'd flown in while she was on her recent trip to Europe. He loved planes and started putting it together, but it was a big, complicated kit, and halfway through he lost interest and left the pieces strewn on his desk.

"Clean up that mess," his mother ordered.

Not knowing what else to do, he gathered up the parts and threw them into the trash can.

SylviAnne and Trish were best friends. Trish jokingly said something one day that SylviAnne misunderstood. Feeling hurt, she stomped away. "I'm not going to be friends anymore with someone who says such mean things," she pouted. And, without giving Trish a chance to make things right, she threw the friendship away.

"If you don't like it, junk it" was a popular motto that many people still use. They don't like to be bothered with sorting their trash and putting one part into recycling bins and the other into throwaway bags. There are also other ways of recycling.

In what ways could Josh have recycled the airplane model? ________________________

Did SylviAnne need to throw away her friendship with Trish? ________________________

How might she have "recycled" it? ____________

____

Have you ever known anyone who's thrown away his or her faith in God? What idea from yesterday's story might help us keep our faith in God? ____________

____

______________________________ (The answer is on page 381.)

AUGUST

10

Hope in the Lord

The Lord is good to those whose hope is in him, to the one who seeks him. Lamentations 3:25.

Hang on!" Bob warned as he banked the plane and lined up with the airstrip. "This could be rough."

As we zoomed closer, my hands tightened around the edge of the seat. Clods of dry, gray dirt showed through the coarse stubble. Then, with a thump, the wheels caught the turf, and the mission Cessna shuddered and bounced, and with a final flounce it settled into an uneven taxi along the rough airstrip.

People pressed together at the far end of the strip—thousands of them—waiting for us. As we folded ourselves through the door and jumped to the ground, their cheers filled the morning.

"We've waited a long time for this moment," their chief said after he had welcomed us. "You can hear the happiness of the people."

Five years earlier he had returned to his village home, leaving a well-paid government job to become the great chief of his area. They lived away from the well-traveled roads, far from medical care and electricity and running water. There weren't even enough schools for the children.

"I told the people how they can have a better life," he told us, "and they agreed to build this airstrip—by hand."

A year later it stretched flat and clear. When it was finished, the chief convinced the people to make bricks for a clinic. "Then help will come," he promised.

The people worked hard. Four more years passed, and the airstrip still lay flat and empty. Not one airplane had ever landed on it. The clinic stood with bare, brick walls because they had no money to buy roofing for it. The people began to grumble. "What is the good of all our work?" they asked. "You promised us that a doctor would come, that the airplanes would come from the sky with medicines, but where are they?"

"And now you've come," the chief said. "People walked many, many miles from villages beyond those mountains to see your plane. They've never before seen one on the ground. You've brought us a miracle. You've brought us hope."

On that day less than five years ago we couldn't promise anything. We could only urge the chief to continue hoping and praying. And the Lord heard. Now there are schools, a clinic and hospital, and a church. In order to answer such prayers, though, He needs not only our hope but also our help.

AUGUST

Where the Moss Grows Thickest

Your statutes are forever right; give me understanding that I may live. Psalm 119:144.

Jason and Langley dashed from one tree to the other. "North side of this one!" Jason called.

"One on the east, two on the south," Langley called back.

"Then it's not true!" Jason exclaimed. "Moss doesn't always grow thickest on the north."

"So?" asked Uncle Lars when the boys reported their count.

"Why do folks say it does?"

"Because under the right conditions moss does tend to grow thickest on the north. What did you notice?"

"That moss grows thickest on any old side!"

Uncle Lars laughed. "True, but a good outdoorsman knows how to read the signs." He settled himself on a log and motioned the boys to sit beside him. "He wouldn't check a fallen tree like this or a leaning tree like that one over there, or in the forks of branches, or on projecting knots. He'd even ignore trees with rough bark."

"Why?" asked Langley.

"Moss prefers the part of a tree that holds the most moisture. Forks and knots and rough bark catch and hold rain, and the upper side of a leaning tree would be more damp than the lower. None of that has anything to do with the points of the compass, so a good woodsman would check the moss on straight-standing, smooth-barked older trees because they'd collect an even amount of moisture all around. Under normal conditions, they'd dry out less on the north-northeast and therefore should have the most moss on that side."

Uncle Lars pointed toward a clump of older, smooth-barked trees. "But he wouldn't pay much attention to those. Instead, he'd check the trees over there." He indicated the other side of the clearing.

"Hey! That's where I found the trees with moss growing thickest on the north!" exclaimed Jason.

Uncle Lars nodded. Those trees get sunlight throughout most of the day, but these stand in the afternoon shade of the cliff. Trees that are shaded like this aren't as reliable.

"The laws of nature are as true as God's other laws," he continued. "But in order to live by them, you need to be able to read the signs with understanding."

AUGUST

12

The Porpoise and the Boat, Part 1

The fear of the Lord is pure, enduring forever. The ordinances of the Lord are sure and altogether righteous. Psalm 19:9.

Elder Frank Johnson of Canada tells a story that happened while he was fishing with his father off the coast of British Columbia. Often when they traveled through a particular stretch of water off the Queen Charlotte Islands the porpoises would play near their boat.

The men enjoyed watching the porpoises hump along the surface of the sea, their shiny dark backs cutting a neat path. They'd angle toward the boat, some coming from one side, some from the other, building up speed as they neared. Then in a burst of speed, as if daring the boat to catch them, they'd surge ahead and crisscross just ahead of the bow, but always beyond danger of being hit.

Other porpoises would pace themselves with the slow chug of the heavy motor, keeping abreast of the wheelhouse, rollicking and clowning, seeming to have a good laugh at the boat's plodding speed.

"They didn't seem the least bit afraid of us," Pastor Johnson remembers. "We could walk around on the deck, and they'd stay right beside us as if daring us to catch them. They did get the joke on us sometimes when one would suddenly jump and blow and vent the full blast of its fishy breath at the person sitting at the wheel."

Pastor Johnson made a face. "Let me tell you," he exclaimed. "They have awful, fishy bad breath!

"If anyone on board raised his hand, though, holding anything that in the least resembled a pistol, every porpoise would immediately sound, disappearing deep into the water, and that would be the last we'd see of them during that trip. They must have been shot at before and through sad experience had learned the terrible dangers of staying within range of men with guns."

We think we're intelligent, and we've made many good laws to keep ourselves safe, but we're not always good at keeping them.

When porpoises and other animals have a rule, they keep it. The moment they see any sign of danger, they leave—as quickly as they can.

God knows the dangers of sin, and He's given us protective rules. When you see signs of danger, do you, like the porpoises, dive for safety?

AUGUST

13

The Porpoise and the Boat, Part 2

By them [the ordinances of the Lord] is your servant warned; in keeping them there is great reward.
Psalm 19:11.

One day when Pastor Johnson was at the wheel of their fishing boat, the porpoises came out again, and, as always, he enjoyed watching them frolic about and play their games. Suddenly there was a jolt—as if something had hit the boat—and a shuddering. He quickly cut the engines.

"A porpoise!" his father yelled from the back of the boat. "A porpoise hit the propeller!"

His father watched as the porpoise rolled away from the boat, leaving a wide trail of red. Immediately the other porpoises headed toward the injured one. Two flanked it, pressing their bodies against its sides to keep it afloat. The others swam in tight formation, ringing them, and the entire group headed toward the shelter of a nearby bay.

"That was the last we saw of those porpoises," Elder Johnson said. "We limped to the nearest port for repairs. That poor creature must have misjudged our speed," he explained. "Instead of swimming ahead of the boat, as they usually do in their games, it rammed into our propeller full speed, bending both the shaft and the propeller blade. The animal must have taken a nasty gash in its back, too.

"I don't know what became of it, because when we were back at sea the porpoises never again came to play alongside our boat. At first we thought little of it. Then, as time went by, we wondered if the porpoises had left the area.

" 'Have you seen the porpoises lately?' " we asked other fishermen.

" 'Sure,' " they told us. " 'They still come out to play by our boats when we go by the Queen Charlottes.' "

A few years later, the Johnsons sold their boat and bought another. Traveling in their new boat, they were happy to see the porpoises coming out to meet them. Sometime later they saw the owner of their old boat.

"Have you seen any porpoises off the Queen Charlottes?" they asked.

"Come to think of it, I haven't seen any for a long time," he replied. "At least not since I've had this boat."

The porpoises, it seemed, had established a new law, a rule to protect them from the boat that had so badly injured one of their friends.

In what ways are God's rules for our protection? Think of each of the Ten Commandments separately, and give at least one way it protects us from either physical or spiritual danger.

AUGUST

14

Like a Hog in a Wallow

For everyone born of God overcomes the world.
1 John 5:4.

Porky stretched full length in the shade under the old hay wagon, letting the coolness of the soft green grass temper the August heat.

"That's just not hog-natural," said Mrs. Perkins to Mrs. Jackson. "Any self-respecting porker would be down in the wallow on a day like this, letting the cool mud soak into his hide."

Porky wasn't just any hog, though, as Mrs. Jackson pointed out to Mrs. Perkins. He was Farmer Jackson's special orphan pig.

Porky had been hand-raised and hand-fed. From the time he'd learned to scamper about on his trotters, he'd never let Farmer Jackson get beyond his sight when he went about his farmyard chores. Porky always trailed close by. He lived more like a member of the family than one of the bunch who hung out down at the bottom of the farmyard.

Yes, Porky was different from your usual hog-growin', run-of-the-pen pig.

All the other pigs had waded into the wallow that afternoon, sloshing deeper into the gooey muck, enjoying the way it oozed its coolness around their bodies. They paid no mind to what its sliminess did to their looks, nor did they care about quiet shade and cool, green grass, or being clean. This was what they knew. It was comfortable, and as far as they were concerned, this was life at its best. They saw no reason to change and had no time for a strange pig like Porky or his doings.

As Mrs. Perkins said, "Porky just wasn't hog-normal."

So while Porky enjoyed his quiet shade and cool green grass and having a clean coat, the others grunted with contentment and dug deeper into their wallow.

They loved their mud.

Porky knew he was free to go down and wallow in the muck with the other pigs anytime he wanted. But he had gotten to know the farmer very well. He knew that he had found a better life.

Sin feels as normal and comfortable as mud to a hog in a wallow—until you get to know God. Then you'll want something better.

"For everyone born of God overcomes the world."

AUGUST

Believing Lies

Whoever does not believe God, has made a liar of him.
1 John 5:10, TEV.

Holly and Jamey were best friends. At school they were always together, and in the afternoons if the two of them weren't at one of their houses, they were sure to be at the other.

"Like two peas in a pod, those two," Grandma Fran always said. "They have the same taste in clothes and do their hair alike and listen to the same music and read the same books and talk about the same boys. They think so much alike that when one starts a sentence, the other can finish it."

"We'll be friends forever, no matter what," they both said.

Then one day the unthinkable happened.

"Jamey said you're a fake," NeldaSue said in a low voice to Holly. "She said she's sick and tired of hanging around with you and wishes you'd find someone else to tag along with."

Holly flushed. "I don't be . . ." she started to say.

"She said you wouldn't believe me if I told you," NeldaSue went on. "If I were you, I wouldn't have a thing to do with her for a minute more." NeldaSue gave a quick flick with her head that sent her long, auburn hair in a swish. "Eat lunch with me today, and don't even speak to her if she tries to sit with us."

Holly listened, her eyes wide with worry. She didn't want to believe what she was hearing, but NeldaSue spoke so convincingly. In shocked silence she trailed after her to the lunchroom.

Jamey came and tried to join them, but their icy stares and coldness left her completely baffled. She had no idea what had happened.

Several miserable days passed before Jamey learned the whole story and was able to convince Holly that everything NeldaSue had said was a lie.

Imagine that you are either Jamey or Holly. How would you have felt?

1. What color best describes that feeling?
2. What sound best captures that feeling?
3. What animal best represents that feeling?
4. What kind of weather best symbolizes that feeling?
5. What machine best represents that feeling?

The problem arose when Holly let herself be fooled into believing a lie about her friend.

Sin is believing a lie about God, a lie that spoils having a good friendship with Him. Have you ever been trapped by any of those lies?

AUGUST

16

The Salt of the Earth

You are the salt of the earth. Matthew 5:13.

Salt!" exclaimed the wise old man. "Throw it away. It's dangerous."

"But the White man gave it to us for the work we did." The workers looked troubled.

"That's just another of the White man's tricks so he can make you think that he's your friend. Can't you see? Salt this fine can come only from one thing—the ground-up skulls of dead men. He's trying to poison you with leprosy."

The men listened with alarm to the old man's warnings. They weren't sure about this White man who called himself a missionary. Maybe he was treating them the way they treated their own enemies—pretending to be friendly so that he could find an easy way to poison them. After all, he was building this thing called "school" so he could make their children live with him on the hill. Everyone knew that a long-ago king had cursed that hill. The story was one that their fathers and grandfathers told.

Because of a wild storm that had drenched him while his men were carrying him along the ridge of the hill in his traveling chair, the king had pronounced a curse on that hill and on anyone who would dare live there. The king was supposed to have power to call upon the spirits to do his wishes, so the people left the ridges a wasteland and cast the bodies of their dead into the marshes along its base, where the wild animals could get them.

To be safe now several of the men threw away the salt of the cursed hill. But they were curious and returned to work.

When the school stood ready, the people still feared the place. Maybe the White missionary had powerful medicine so that he could live there safely, but what about their children?

"Don't let them go there," the wise old man counseled. "They'll be poisoned with the missionary's ideas."

Many of the people sent their children to live with families beyond the other side of the mountain so that the missionary couldn't get them, but he convinced others to come.

As time went on, the people saw that the school was good. It became Gitwe College, the training place of the pastors and teachers who were the first to carry the good news of the gospel to many parts of central Africa. Instead of being afraid of the salt of the cursed hill, they were now the "salt of the earth."

AUGUST

The Saving Salt, Part 1

Salt is good, but if it loses its saltiness, there is no way to make it salty again. Luke 14:34, TEV.

Great-great-grandma used to tie her lumpy salt crystals into a seasoning bag and let the saltiness seep into her cooking, but after a few cookings the savor cooked out and she had to throw out the old salt and get new.

Most people think of salt mainly as a seasoning for food, but did you know that salt is used in more than 14,000 different ways—from preserving leather to melting ice?

In the ancient world it at times became so scarce that it was used as money. Caesar's soldiers received common salt as part of their pay—they called it *salarium,* from which we get the word "salary."

Jesus used salt to illustrate God's love and explain its effect in the lives of His followers. He didn't say, "Do My rules and you'll be like Me." Nor did He say, "Try hard enough and you'll become like salt." He simply said, "Have salt in yourselves."

"All who would present themselves 'a living sacrifice, holy, acceptable unto God' must receive the saving salt, the righteousness of our Saviour," wrote Ellen White. "But if the salt has lost its savor; if there is only a profession of godliness, without the love of Christ, there is no power for good" (*The Desire of Ages,* p. 439).

This chart shows the difference between having the saving salt and having salt that's lost its saltiness.

THE SAVING SALT OF JESUS

THE SAVING SALT— A POWER FOR GOOD	SALT WITHOUT SAVOR— NO POWER FOR GOOD
1. Choosing to have Jesus in your heart.	1. Doing what you feel like doing.
2. Reading the Bible and praying every day.	2. Saying "I'm a Christian" but spending *no* time with God.
3. Asking Jesus for the help of His Holy Spirit.	3. Trying to be good.
4. Believing that God loves you.	4. Working hard to be good enough so God will love you.
5. Keeping the commandments because you love Jesus.	5. Keeping the commandments because you have to.

AUGUST

18

The Saving Salt, Part 2

Have salt in yourselves, and be at peace with each other. Mark 9:50.

In Jesus' time, salt was used in two main ways—to flavor food and to keep food and other things from spoiling. It was also added to every sacrifice that the priests offered. Then it represented Jesus' way of life. Whether it's used to season food or to preserve things, the influence of the salt spreads through the whole thing.

It's the same with the Holy Spirit. When we choose to live like Jesus and have the Holy Spirit in our lives, it makes a difference in everything we do. Left on the outside, though, it can cause problems.

As you read the following, decide which in each pair best represents the saving salt of having Jesus in your life.

1. A. A Sabbath casserole with just enough salt to taste good.

or

B. An empty saltshaker.

2. A. A barnful of hay kept sweet-smelling and dry because salt's been sprinkled through it.

or

B. The hulk of an old boat that's all rusty and full of holes because it's been lying out in the salty sea air.

3. A. A long stretch of ice on a hilly highway that's melting because the road crews have sprinkled salt on it.

or

B. A car that drives through the slush made by the melted ice and salt—it looks OK, but the salty solution is eating holes through the bottom.

Salt is good when it's mixed into things, but it damages hard surfaces when it stays on the outside. A little salt mixed into water also makes a good gargle and helps kill some germs, but as you may have learned from sad experience, plain salt rubbed into a cut or scrape can be very painful.

The effects of salt depend on how it is used. As yesterday's chart showed, to be helpful, the saving salt of Jesus must be taken inside. If you don't have the saving salt in your life, ask Jesus to come into your heart right now.

AUGUST

19

Under the Bed

So do not fear, for I am with you; do not be dismayed, for I am your God. Isaiah 41:10.

Missionary Morrison and his family were trapped in their house between the rebels and the loyal troops. They didn't dare go outside. They didn't dare walk by any windows for fear of being hit by stray bullets. Shells and rockets shrieked overhead as well, and at any time one could fall short of its target and explode into their house. The safest place was in their center bedroom.

"Drag all the mattresses in here," father Morrison instructed. "And keep your heads down."

They stacked all the mattresses on and around the beds—as protection—then burrowed underneath.

"I'm scared," 5-year-old Alex began to whimper when a shell exploded just beyond their front gate.

Mother Morrison laid her arm around him. "We're going to be all right," she told him and his two older brothers. "God is going to keep us safe because I . . ." She let her voice trail away. ". . . I feel the presence of His angels," she said. She didn't know how else to explain it. "We'll be fine."

Alex snuggled against her, and there, crowded under the bed, the five of them began to sing. After a few songs and prayers, the boys drifted off to sleep. Mother and Father stayed awake awhile longer, discussing the possibilities of escaping to a safer place when the firing stopped. Then, feeling God's presence in their strange shelter, they too drifted off to sleep. In the morning the firing did stop, and they were able to be evacuated.

Two years later when they were on furlough in America, mother Morrison was telling a church group about their night under the bed and how they'd felt the presence of God's angels.

"Excuse me," the pastor said, standing up. "There's something you should know." He turned to his congregation. "Do you remember that day?"

Several heads nodded.

The pastor opened to the flyleaf of his Bible and read a date, a time, and then the words "Special prayer for the safety of the Morrison family." Then he explained. "As I was preaching that morning, I suddenly felt an urge to pray for your family. I stopped right then without having any idea that you were trapped in a war, and we prayed."

The date and the time were precise. They would just then have been taking shelter under the mattresses.

AUGUST

20

The Wrong Side of the Road

And the way of peace they do not know. Romans 3:17.

Rene stared ahead. The rolling grasslands looked the same as those they'd passed through hours before. The road ahead stretched toward the horizon, dirt-brown and uninteresting. Behind, everything disappeared into the billows of dust that whooshed up. Suddenly the car began to bounce like a jackhammer. Uncle Jim quickly slowed then veered toward the other side.

"You're driving on the wrong side!" Rene exclaimed.

Uncle Jim laughed. "Do you see any cars coming?" he asked.

"No. Haven't seen a one all day!"

"And you probably won't either. Anyway, you'd see the dust long before you'd see the vehicle."

"But why're you driving on the wrong side?"

"Because this is a washboard road, and the 'wrong side' is smoother," his uncle replied. "You see, when dirt roads are wet, ridges push up under the wheels of the passing traffic, building into a series of miniature waves. When they dry, they make driving horribly rough, but if you go in the opposite direction of the traffic that created them, it's smooth, like sliding over the top of the waves."

Rene shook his head in amazement. *What next?* he asked himself. Going on a mission safari with his uncle seemed more about understanding how to drive on rough roads than about preaching, although once they did get to the villages, there was plenty of opportunity to talk to the people. The distances between villages stretched into long days of monotonous driving with not many adventure tales to share with his Sabbath school, as he'd promised when he got back home.

"This washboard trick could illustrate the text 'the way of peace they do not know,' " Uncle Jim suggested. "Until I discovered it, I put in many long, rough hours of travel."

"Good idea," Rene said, thinking of the people in the previous village who didn't believe in God. Life could be much smoother for them if they learned to claim His peace. He pulled his pencil out of his pocket so that he could jot the idea on the pad he carried. Even though they were driving on the "smooth" side of the road, the words looked like he'd written them during an earthquake.

"You're right, Uncle Jim, about going on a mission safari with you. This could be a long and tiring trip, but when you're working for God, there's always something to learn."

AUGUST

21

Leaves of Healing

And the leaves of the tree are for the healing of the nations. Revelation 22:2.

Those are my trees of life." Grandpa pointed toward his garden.

The twins laughed. "There's nothing there but an old avocado tree, and a bunch of banana plants without any bananas, and a few papayas," said Jaslyn, proud of herself that she could already identify so many tropical plants. Grandpa was always teasing, and even though this was their first trip to visit him at his mission in Africa, she and Monroe had vowed that they weren't going to let him catch them with his jokes like he used to do when they were little and he was visiting them on furlough.

"That's true," he said, "but the Bible says that the leaves of the tree of life are for the healing of the nations. Even though that's talking about heaven, trees and their leaves do help heal us here on earth."

He pointed to the big avocado tree. "Fresh avocado leaves make a tea that helps cure the flu. Papaya leaf tea makes a good anti-worm medicine. And bananas . . ." Grandpa swept his hands toward the big tropical plants that look like trees, ". . . bananas are one of the best foods because of all the good things they contain, and the sap—"

"I've heard Grandma talking about banana sap and your clothes," said Monroe.

Grandpa laughed again. "Yeah. I've heard her mention that a few times myself. I can't help it, though, if when I'm experimenting in my garden a bit of banana juice drips on my clothes. It's clear, and you can't see it, but when it dries it makes a rusty-red stain that never washes out. But it's good stuff—it takes off warts."

"Are all plants good for medicine?" asked Jaslyn.

"Not all," replied Grandpa. "Some, like the seeds on that poinsettia bush over there, are poisonous, but many are good, and the 'root doctors' know some good cures. Tea made from the bark of one tree is good for snakebites. The Indians of Peru knew the bark of the cinchona tree cured malaria, and that's how we learned about quinine. The pioneers of North America boiled willow bark to make a tea for fevers—it contains something like aspirin. Trees give off carbon dioxide and moisture that we need. Some houseplants absorb harmful chemicals and make the air safer to breathe.

"Even though the real tree of life is in heaven, we can be healthier by using the leaves God has given us here."

AUGUST

22

Blackberry Memories

Remember the days of old; consider the generations long past. Ask your father and he will tell you, your elders, and they will explain to you. Deuteronomy 32:7.

The late summer sun made the morning warmer than usual, and drew the juicy-sweet, ready-ripe blackberry fragrance into invisible clouds that hung over the road. Well, over what used to be a road, but now was nothing more than two faint tracks tracing parallel ruts through the fuzzy-headed grasses and leading to Granny's old house.

Insects hummed. Odd patches of the green-brown river showed through breaks in the screening of vine maple and alder brush that lined the old dike road. I stopped, unable to resist sampling a handful of the juicy blackberries that hung in clusters on the haystack-high tangle of vines. Carefully bending aside a few heavily thorned vines that snagged out from the bushes, I reached for a clump of berries.

"Suckers," Granny called those long vines. Back in the long-ago summers when she and Gramps lived on their farm and we on ours, she and I spent happy afternoons picking berries from the wild brambles that bushed up along the pasturelands.

"You have to dress for it," Granny always reminded me. "Long sleeves and a hat."

Blackberry briars are mean—their long, whiplike suckers hang ready to hook any intruder with needle-tipped, inward-curving thorns, and the main vines are thickly armed with more jabbing thorns. So we dressed. I belonged to the daring new generation of girls who wore blue jeans and flannel shirts, but Granny came from a very long-ago time of long dresses and high-topped button shoes. She pulled on a pair of high shoes and a loose jacket; I pulled on a pair of rubber boots and another shirt. We both slapped on our straw hats and were ready for berrying.

Our tools included buckets and boards. Granny also carried a long-handled poker, an iron rod bent at the end for reaching into hot woodstove fires to reposition the wood, and her butcher knife. With them she pulled aside and cut off the suckers, then we laid our boards against the bushes and carefully walked them into position.

As I selected a few just-right berries, I remembered how then my goal was to one day be able to pick berries as fast as Granny could. She encouraged me—and in time I could.

Goals are important—especially the kind that will lead you closer to God.

AUGUST

To Shoo a Skunk

Resist the devil, and he will flee from you. James 4:7.

It was a lazy August afternoon just before blackberry time. Granny and I lingered on the back porch of her farmhouse. I leaned against the sink that Grandpa had built for washing up when he came in from chores. Granny sat on the little bench against the half wall that closed out the wind. Our conversation drifted into a pause. In the silence, I thought I could hear a snuffing in the grass below the walk. "Oh . . ."

"What is it?" Granny turned and looked down. "Oh dear! A skunk! What about my chickens?"

With the skunk so close and the chickens in their pens at the far side of the farmyard, I was not necessarily thinking of their danger.

"What shall we do? My chickens!"

Granny's chickens were her prize possessions, and skunks were their deadly enemies. I stared down at the plump little black body with the loud white stripes tracing its back. Its flag of a tail dragged behind as it rooted in a clump of grass. "Shoo it away," I supposed out loud. "But I'm not sure how to shoo a skunk," I added after a moment's reflection. "Especially if it doesn't want to be shooed."

But Granny had already gone into action. She had a standard method of moving creatures—cats, dogs, whatever—that didn't wish to move. That involved a pan of water. She opened the porch tap and started filling a basin.

"I don't think the skunk will like that," I cautioned.

"I want it to go away," she replied seriously, "and not come back."

"I wouldn't—"

A splash of water interrupted my protest.

The skunk spun around, dripping, tail up.

Granny and I jumped behind the porch wall.

A heavy odor filled the air.

Fortunately we were well above and to the side of direct attack. I looked at my little grandmother—her usual mildness transformed into a stance of determination, the empty pan still in her hand. "Is it gone?" she asked.

The skunk was gone, but the effects of its reaction to Granny's method of shooing lingered on our clothes. With the help of a good airing, we were able to wear them again, though.

"Resist the devil," says James. He'll flee, all right, but he delights in leaving us with the effects of sin. That's why we need the cleaning help of the Holy Spirit.

AUGUST

24

Never Forget

Remember what happened long ago; acknowledge that I alone am God. Isaiah 46:9, TEV.

"Never forget."

From through the years I seemed to hear the echoes of Granny's voice.

I haven't forgotten, I told myself as I stood in the old house. I had stood on that very same spot on my last afternoon before going away to college. Granny had sat on the third step, her usual place when we talked. I remember looking from the faded brown photo I held, to her, then back to the photo.

"And never let anyone take it away from you."

She sat there, a mite of a woman—she was only 4 feet 11 inches tall. Another of my earlier goals had been to be as tall as she, and I had long, long since passed that mark. She braided her long, dark hair and wound it neatly into a bun and wore her high-collared dress buttoned closely about her neck. Despite her seriousness, she had a kindly warmth.

As I held the little picture she had just given me, I sensed one of those moments of understanding that come when you're growing up. I held something very important that symbolized an inheritance that had been handed down to me through the generations of our family.

"Never forget," she repeated.

A solemn-faced little boy in a rich velvet suit stared out of that picture from the past century. He was family. When Granny's father had packed them up and sailed for the New World, she was only 2, and she didn't remember the world of elegance that they had left behind. Her father left the sea and the family shipbuilding firm in Norway and had finally settled on a homestead on the quiet coast of Washington state. By the time Granny was grown, the cousin in the picture, Roald Amundsen, was already a famous Arctic explorer—the first to sail the Northwest Passage and later the first to reach the South Pole.

"Never forget who you are."

Although her family had a tradition of seafaring and adventure, Granny was mild and cautious and never moved from the little valley where her father settled when she was a girl. Without actually saying the words, though, she urged me to set goals that reached beyond the little world of our valley. We talked about traveling to the Old Country when I finished school and visiting her old home and the cousins she'd never met.

Remembering stories from the past gave us worthwhile goals for the future.

The Bear

He said to them, *"Go into all the world and preach the good news to all creation." Mark 16:15.*

The northern sun slanted comfortably across the morning. Already miles and miles of dirt road lay between the Joneses' farm, where I'd stayed the night before, and where I pedaled as I headed steadily westward on my blue bicycle. A thick stand of trees bordered either side of the road, opening once in a while into a driveway that led toward a farmstead. I'd turn along it and tell the people about the books I carried.

Most were interested. How often did a college girl, alone, on a bicycle, selling religious books, venture into this area of farms scattered on the fringes of the Peace River country of northern Alberta? A few ordered something. I pedaled on, confident that I was helping spread the good news of the gospel. I aimed to reach the more thickly settled area to the west by noon.

"Mind you watch the road," Mrs. Jones warned before I left. "There's a bear been seen wandering the farms out that way."

I smiled and thanked her, assuring her that I'd watch.

Coasting down a hill in a long unpeopled stretch, I thought of Granny's reaction when she learned that I'd be staying in Canada for another year of college. "Next thing you know, she'll be off to Europe!"

If only I could! I wished, but that was before studying abroad had become popular and less costly. *It's a good thing, though, Granny doesn't know I'm on a bike in bear country.*

Just then a terrible noise erupted out of the bushes and closed in behind me. Fright pulsed through my body. I sprang from the seat into a crouch that threw my full weight onto the pedals. The bike surged forward. I pedaled frantically. When the noise began to drop behind, I at last dared to look around.

A grouse, wings flapping, neck outstretched, and beak working, chased after me. Then, apparently satisfied she'd shooed me far enough, she slowed and turned toward the scattering of chicks that trailed behind her.

I stopped and laughed shakily.

Before the week's end I did see the bear wandering across a distant pasture, and I sold more books.

Granny and I never did go to Europe together, but later I went with my husband and children. Now we're missionaries in Africa.

Goals are important. Travel and adventure can be part of preaching the good news. But the best goal is to know Jesus and be His friend. That's a goal you can reach right now.

AUGUST

26

Feathers of a Bird

Those who hope in the Lord will renew their strength. They will soar on wings like eagles. Isaiah 40:31.

A clattering on the glass roof of the adjoining sun room caught little Matthew's attention. He gave his fire engine a shove and held up his arms for Grandma to lift him to the window.

"Boo!" he said, pointing.

Two blue jays strutted past the glass. In the next instant they spread their wings and whisked away, banking a steep left to miss the big branch of the pear tree, and then they whooshed up and out of sight.

"Boo! Gone!" he said, still pointing, his learning-to-talk words missing sounds and syllables. The jays looped back over the yard again, tempting themselves to stop at the bird feeder, but, instead, flew toward the park.

Birds fly—most of them, at least—and the kind of flying they do depends on the kind of feathers they have. The golden eagle, for instance, can soar on updrafts without flapping its wings. That's because slots in its primary feathers, the main flight feathers of the wing, reduce the turbulence in the airflow.

The ruffed grouse, the bird that gave me such a fright when it chased my bike, also has slotted wings, but instead of being long and broad like the eagle's, they're short and rounded to help them fly through the trees. That's why it makes such an explosive sound on takeoff. Each of its primary feathers also twists to provide thrust, and this makes it able to change direction easily at slow speeds.

While grouse have a very noisy takeoff, owls can glide silently through the night because their fringed outer flight feathers on the wing act as silencers by breaking up the airflow.

Hummingbirds are famous for their ability to hover in midair. They can do this because the leading edge of their wings moves forward and backward in a figure 8. That gives lift on both the upstroke and the down-stroke, making it possible for it to "stand still" while it's flying. When they do move, hummingbirds appear to zing from place to place, their wings beating at such high speed that they make a whirring sound.

Tree swallows are also high-speed fliers, yet their wings beat slowly and quietly. They're long and narrow with a bend in the leading edge, which gives the precision maneuverability that they need to catch the flying insects that form the bulk of their diet.

Just as birds have different kinds of feathers and different flying styles, people are also different. But hope in the Lord will give each one the right kind of strength.

AUGUST

27

Don't Worry

The feathers of little Matthew's favorite birds, the blue jays, make it possible for them to stay through the long, cold winters at his home in Edmonton, Canada. During the winter these cold-climate birds have more down feathers than those who go to warmer regions. The fluffiness of the down keeps the birds warm by trapping a layer of still air around their bodies for insulation.

Another of the cold-climate birds, the willow ptarmigan not only grows extra down for the winter, but it also has thick feathers on its feet, toes, and beak to prevent heat loss. In addition, it exchanges its brown-and-white summer camouflage coat for a white winter coat to match the snow. On extremely cold nights it burrows completely into the snow, where it is well insulated and protected from the winds.

Feathers do more than keep a bird warm and help it fly—flight feathers have interlocking barbs, which, if they become separated, the bird can re-zip by preening. They're also for streamlining, waterproofing, camouflage, communication, flotation—and looks.

The great gray owl even has special feathers it uses for hunting. As well as having keen night vision and excellent hearing, it has focusing disks of feathers around its face, which aid in pinpointing mice under deep snow. The owl flies directly to the spot and plunges its feet and head into the snow to catch its prey.

Loons expel the air trapped in their feathers and air sacs so they'll ride lower in the water or sink slowly. This makes it easier for them to dive and chase fish underwater.

Dippers are different from most other songbirds. They feed underwater, and their stocky bodies and thick layers of feathers keep them warm in ice-cold streams. They use their wings for flying and for staying underwater in the swift currents.

The ostrich's small wings could never lift such a big bird from the ground, therefore it has no need for the streamlined feathers that long-distance fliers such as the stork have. Even so, ostriches have large, showy feathers that are valued for their beauty.

"Look at the birds," Jesus said, "and don't worry. Aren't you worth much more than birds?"

Look at the birds of the air; they do not sow or reap or store away in barns, and yet your heavenly Father feeds them. Matthew 6:26.

AUGUST

28

Late

And those who were ready went in with him to the wedding; and the door was shut. Matthew 25:10, NKJV.

A bright light beamed down on the parking lot of the immigration office, and I sat in the pickup cab, staring at the single metal pipe that barred our way. A heavy padlock locked it in place; it could not be moved.

"We'll have to pray our way through this one," Date had said a bit earlier. "I want to get home tonight, and I don't want to leave the pickup unguarded."

I stared past the light at the wall of darkness. Getting all the papers signed so we could pick up parcels from the post office had taken all morning and part of the afternoon. By that time it was getting late to start for home.

"The border office is open after 6:00," someone told us. "You can make it."

The sun hung just above the horizon, and the clock pointed to a few minutes past 6:00 p.m. when we finished filling in the forms and signing out of the country on one side, and the gate was opened for us to drive across that short stretch of no man's land to the border station of the adjoining country. Immigration officers cheerily checked us in.

This is easy, I thought.

"The customs officer is gone."

The words sounded cheerful enough, but I felt a sudden tightness of worry grab around my thoughts.

"If you have anything to declare, you'll have to leave it here and come back in the morning."

"In the morning?" Date and I looked at each other, and I saw that certain look on his face—the pickup was loaded with boxes, and we'd both heard about the local hotels.

"We'll spend the night in our vehicle," he told the guards.

I continued to stare out the pickup window, and I was praying—but it wasn't a happy prayer. I wanted to get home.

I'd just flown back from a visit to America, and Date had borrowed a pickup to meet me—ours was in for repairs—and to do some mission business that included picking up mail and parcels. Taking things from one country to another meant filling out lots of complicated forms and always took longer than necessary. Date didn't want to lose another day from work, so we rushed for the border. Our passports had all the necessary stamps—we could enter the country, but the road was barred.

We'd arrived eight minutes too late.

AUGUST

The Alarm

How then can we escape? Isaiah 20:6.

So close to home! I thought as I tried to make myself comfortable in the pickup cab. *If only we could persuade someone to open the gate, we could be there in a couple of hours.*

"The one with the keys is gone," said one official, "but I could show you to a hotel."

Date shook his head. He didn't want to leave the load of mission supplies and mail. "I'll put on the alarm," he told me. "Then if anyone tries anything . . ."

We settled back and I turned, bracing against the door to make myself more comfortable. Suddenly the alarm's loud shrieks pierced the night. Date poked at some buttons, and after what seemed like a very long minute, the alarm stopped.

"What happened?"

A guard pounding on the window interrupted my question. "Why did you do that?" he demanded.

Date shrugged. "Maybe someone touched the pickup."

"There's no one here!" the guard snapped.

"I'm sorry," Date said. "The alarm just went off."

"Well, don't do it again," he warned.

We tried to settle down. The voices of the soldiers on guard, and sounds from the little border town, and wishes that we hadn't been in such a hurry muddled into the prayers that I tried to form in my mind. I turned again, and the alarm exploded into a full scream. Date switched it off—quickly—but a giant of a soldier ran toward us swinging his rifle over his head.

"Why did you do that?" he demanded.

"I don't know!" By then Date had the window down.

"That's impossible! That's against the law! You're spies! Sending signals to our enemies! I can have you thrown into prison for being spies. You can't stay here; I'll put you in prison."

Two other soldiers ran toward him.

"Get out! Now!" He held the gun and was in no mood to discuss anything. We both opened our doors.

"Hurry up! You can't stay here!"

I grabbed for my purse and the pouch with our passports, slid to the ground, and turned to look for my carry-on bag.

"Go!" he screamed.

We went—toward the darkness.

One of the others slipped up behind us. "Just go to a hotel," he said quietly. "Come for your truck in the morning."

AUGUST

30

The Kangaroo Room

Live such good lives among the pagans that, though they accuse you of doing wrong, they may see your good deeds. 1 Peter 2:12.

We followed the footpath around the gate and toward the road that led into the darkness. The lights of a few fires dotted the night as people sat around their little charcoal braziers.

"I set off the alarm by bumping the door, didn't I?" I asked.

"Putting it on wasn't such a good idea," Date said.

"Now where shall we go?" I asked.

"I don't know." Neither of us nor anyone we knew had ever shopped for hotels in this village.

"Do you have any money?" I had lots of questions.

"No. No local currency. You know the problems it causes when you take it out of the country, so I brought just enough to use at the border."

"I still have a few U.S. traveler's checks," I said. "Do you suppose they'll take them here?"

"I don't know."

We trudged along the uneven roadside, tripping against rocks and clods, not knowing where to go. "Maybe we can find someone to help us find a good place to stay," I suggested.

Suddenly two shadows detached themselves from a tree and headed toward us. I tensed.

"Would you like us to take you to a hotel now?"

With relief I recognized the voice of the friendly border official.

"I know a place with good rooms."

We followed him and his aide, and soon we found ourselves in a dimly lit office. "These are missionaries," he said as if that were full explanation. "They need a room for the night."

He stayed until arrangements were made—and, yes, a traveler's check was fine. As he left he said, "Come when the border opens in the morning. You'll have no problems."

And so we spent the night in the sparse but clean Kangaroo Room. In the morning, our friend of the night before was at work in the border office. "These are missionaries," he said to the customs inspector in the same manner he had used at the hotel the night before. And before long, we were on our way with no further problems.

Even though the guard accused us of being spies, the fact that we were missionaries got us safely through the experience. The lives of other missionaries had made such a good impression on the one official that he was willing to help us.

AUGUST

A New Beginning, Part 1

Then Jesus told his disciples a parable to show them that they should always pray and not give up. Luke 18:1.

Justin sat by the table, tapping his knuckles against the edges of the notebooks and making the corner of the stack perfectly even. "Another year of school," he muttered flatly. He felt neither dismal nor excited; he was just there.

"Looks like you're ready for school," Grandpa said.

"Yeah. Guess so."

"You don't sound very excited." Grandpa pulled out a chair and sat down beside him.

Justin shrugged.

"Boy, when I went to school, the first day was one of the most exciting days of the year. We always had new clothes and new things and usually a new teacher, and we were anxious to know if there'd be any new kids in class." Grandpa fisted his hand and pounded the table to emphasize all the "news."

"Yeah," Justin said again, his voice still flat, "but by the time you get to sixth grade it gets to be just more of the same. Go to school, and you've got a bunch of boring schoolwork. Stay home, and you've got a bunch of boring chores."

"Whoa!" said Grandpa. "You make life sound dull."

"Well?" Justin looked up. "What's there to get excited about?"

From the look on Grandpa's face Justin expected to hear a long list of reasons. Instead, Grandpa pounded the table again and said, "Well!" And then he stopped and looked at Justin for a long moment. "Have you been saying your prayers lately?" he suddenly asked.

The question caught Justin off guard. "Well . . . Why?"

"Oh, just a question. You're usually a pretty energetic fellow, you look healthy enough, school's starting tomorrow, and you sit in Dullsville . . ."

"What's that got to do with my prayers?"

"Plenty!" That one word was bundled with enthusiasm. "Why . . ." Grandpa let his voice trail off, then he became quiet and serious. "When you talk to God following the pattern He's given, well, it kinda makes it hard to stay in Dullsville. I call it my 'ACT IS' prayer formula. That helps me remember."

"ACT IS!" Justin repeated. "Whatever does that say?"

"Depends," Grandpa said, "but for one thing, the *act* of prayer *is* what keeps me close to God. Is it OK if I write on a sheet of your notepaper?"

Justin shrugged. "Why not?"

SEPTEMBER

1

A New Beginning, Part 2

Praise be to God, who has not rejected my prayer or withheld his love from me! Psalm 66:20.

Grandpa stacked the letters A C T I S along the margin of the piece of notebook paper. "I got these from the Lord's Prayer," he said, "but I rearranged them a little. Here's what the letters mean, and how you can translate them into prayer. When I talk to God in my special prayertime, this is the order I follow."

The Word		**Meaning**
Adoration	—	I like you because . . .
Confession	—	I'm sorry that . . .
Thanksgiving	—	Thank You for . . .
Intercession	—	About (person's name) . . .
Supplication	—	Please, I'd like . . .

Justin looked over the list as his grandfather continued. "I begin talking to God by telling Him why I like Him. Then I go on with my 'sorry' prayers by confessing and getting off my chest some of the lousy things I've done. Then I thank Him for something special. It's amazing how many thank-Yous there are when you start talking to God. After that, I pray for someone else. You know, it does something to you when you pray for someone else. Then, last of all, I talk about myself and ask Him—well, for whatever help I think I might need."

Justin began to get a bit interested.

"I'll write my prayer pattern for you. It goes like this—

'Dear God,

I like You because ______________________________

____

I'm sorry about ______________________________

____

Thank You for ______________________________

____

About . . . ______________________________

____

Please, I'd like ______________________________

____.' "

Justin found that the ACT of prayer IS a help toward a better attitude and a more joyful day.

SEPTEMBER

The Open Door

For he will command his angels concerning you to guard you in all your ways. Psalm 91:11.

The last one in, Ilona had to wedge herself between the others and the door. The road wound up and around toward their farm in the hills, but Ilona let her thoughts race far ahead.

On my way! she exclaimed to herself. *On my way at last!*

The four passengers swayed in unison with the old pickup as it groaned around another hairpin curve.

Two more days, and we'll be there!

She wondered about dormitory life and about the stranger who would be her roommate and about living so far away in another state. She looked across at Sandy, glad that he, at least, would be going there with her.

Going away to a boarding school, a Christian school, had been her goal for a long time. She was eager for an education that would prepare her for God's service.

The truck looped into another curve. Ilona felt everyone shift in her direction, squeezing her even more tightly against the door. Then suddenly the door was no longer there. She found herself looking out over the embankment into the branches of the trees that grew on the hillside, keenly aware that everyone was pushing her toward that open space.

"The door!" someone screamed.

Even though details seemed to be processing through her mind in slow motion, she did not match her voice to the scream. She just heard it and felt the weight of everyone pushing against her.

This was in the days before seat-belt laws, even before seat belts had become standard equipment in vehicles. Ilona had no time to grab anything, not even time to be afraid. She just sat in her place, squeezed between the other passengers and the opening. She didn't budge an inch, but continued to sense being pressed against something solid as if the door were still where it belonged.

Sandy slowed the truck to a near stop, and amid the exclamations of the others she reached out to shut the door and lock it. Then it was that Ilona realized that all the laws of motion said that the instant the door popped open she should have gone hurtling toward the trees.

"Something was there!" she exclaimed. "Held me in!"

"It's a miracle." Sandy let out a breath of relief. "The angels of God!"

SEPTEMBER

3

On Their Way Home

And God said, . . . "let birds fly above the earth across the expanse of the sky." Genesis 1:20.

Look," Brenton said as he stood on the porch and pointed upward. "There goes another flock of our birds."

"Sure enough," his father said. "Now that they've enjoyed a summer with us, they're on their way home."

Eighty percent of the birds that nest in the United States and Canada spend the rest of their lives elsewhere, many of them tropical birds that come north only to nest.

Black swifts are one of these tropical birds. During northern winters they live in the dense forests of Central America. In spring they fly north to the Rocky Mountains and parts of British Columbia to nest in the cracks and crevices in the rocky walls of cliffs and canyons, often near waterfalls. The mother lays a single egg. After the baby hatches, it keeps both parents busy catching insects, but in about a month it's ready to fly and to catch its own food.

In September the family starts its long, dangerous flight south. They have to battle storms and fly around man-made obstacles. Even if they are fortunate and flying is clear, being on the wing day after day for such a long distance becomes very tiring.

When they do arrive at their winter quarters, the parents may be in for a dreadful surprise. Their old home may have disappeared. Each year more and more of the tropical forests are being cut down for industry and agriculture. The birds that winter in those forests find themselves forced into a smaller and smaller area, where they have to compete for the food supplies. While they are fortunate to have protected nesting areas in national parks, this is not true for all of their habitat.

People have a responsibility to make sure that there's food and shelter for their neighbors—including all the creatures of God's creation. Which of the following are responsible ways that can help us do just that? Why? (Answers are on page 381.)

_____ Keeping a bird feeding station
_____ Contributing to a wildlife fund
_____ Obeying the "Do Not Feed the Animals" signs in zoos and parks
_____ Studying biology
_____ Completing nature and Campcraft Honors in Pathfinders
_____ Visiting nature centers and natural history museums
_____ Being sure that pets are clean and well fed
_____ Reading the Bible

SEPTEMBER

Fishers of Men

"Come, follow me," Jesus said, "and I will make you fishers of men." Mark 1:17.

Another day on the river. Beautiful. Breakers to the Oregon side. A city-stretch of boats lined up at Buoy 10. Seals and sea lions popping up here and there. And the pelicans—so comical in their landing approach, feet spread at an angle before plopping into the water. Then up they come with a scoop of bait fish trapped in their long, baggy beaks."

Except for one comment, that was the entry in my journal about the day my brothers took me trolling down at the mouth of the Columbia River.

The Columbia is famous for its salmon, and we try to go fishing there at least once every year when I'm home. It's sort of important to us because that's where our dad fished—not with reel and line, but commercially with nets. Because of this, we grew up knowing the importance of tides and seasons and weather and the importance of keeping the boat and gear clean and in top shape. It also helps us understand certain parts of the story of Jesus and His disciples.

Jesus called James and John and Peter and Andrew to leave their fishing boats and follow Him. As fishermen the four of them knew the importance of fishing in the right place at the right time, and about keeping boats and gear clean and in good repair.

Jesus knew the importance of all that, too—that's why He told them that He would make them fishers of men. He knew that they would understand that you can't just go to any old place at any old time with just any kind of bait and expect to "catch" folks with the gospel. Fishermen must be prepared. They must know what they are doing.

Fishermen still need to know what they're doing, and we had a great time out on the water that day!

The comment I skipped, though, when I copied what I had written in my diary said, "We got skunked!" In other words, we caught exactly zero fish.

We were at the right place, using the right equipment and the right bait. According to the calendar, it was also the right time. What we didn't know was that the salmon were late that year. There were no fish to catch. In order to be a successful fisherman, you must not only be prepared, you must go where the fish are.

SEPTEMBER

5

The Pilot

Or take ships as an example. Although they are so large and are driven by strong winds, they are steered by a very small rudder wherever the pilot wants to go. James 3:4.

An iron hulk, barnacle-covered and rusted, juts from the sand. Pools of water are trapped against it where the waves have scooped out hollows in their daily comings and goings. The wreck of the *Peter Iredale* lies mostly buried where it was washed along a northern Oregon beach, a reminder of what can happen to ships trying to make it on their own in dangerous waters.

"The Graveyard of the Pacific" it's called, yet fine sandy beaches, including the longest unbroken sand beach in the world, stretch along this beautiful piece of ocean where the Columbia River sweeps into the sea. Despite its good looks, this is one of the most dangerous river entrances in the world and has been the scene of more than 200 major shipwrecks.

Ocean currents, storms, and heavy silting create ever-changing conditions, and all ships entering or leaving the river must take a specially trained Columbia River bar pilot on board. This pilot understands the deceitfulness of the bar—that bank which builds up naturally at the mouth of a river. Despite long jetties made of huge boulders to direct the tidal currents and to help keep the channel clear, the river entrance is treacherous. The bar pilot, though, knows the whims and changing conditions of the channels, and when he boards a ship he takes complete charge of guiding it through the dangerous stretch. Even the captain must follow his orders.

Throughout the centuries, sailors have developed many instruments, some with very impressive names—such as the sextant, octant, pelorus, compass, spyglass, and chronometer—to help them plot their courses and sail safely through the seas. Lighthouses and buoys were set up and maps charted. Modern electronic devices make navigation even more precise. Yet in areas such as the Columbia River bar, these aids are not enough.

James talks about the power of one very small part—the rudder—to determine the direction a ship goes. Without a pilot in control, though, the rudder would flop this way and that in the wash of the sea, and the ship would drift out of control.

Our tongues, though small, James adds, can also do great things and can get us into all sorts of trouble.

In what ways can you put a pilot in charge of your tongue? ____

____

SEPTEMBER

6

Sour Grapes

What do you people mean by quoting this proverb about the land of Israel: "The fathers eat sour grapes, and the children's teeth are set on edge"? Ezekiel 18:2.

Sam wanted a first-baseman's glove—a good trapper that would let him snag the ball. He felt like a natural when he played first base, but all he had was an old fielder's glove with a shallow pocket, which was hardly any better than no glove at all.

"If only I had a good glove," he said over and over to Bret, his best friend, "then I could stop any throw that came near the base. But it's taking me forever to save for a really good one."

"My neighbor's got a glove for sale," Bret told him one day. "See him. I don't think he's asking much for it."

Sam decided to go right after school. Somehow, though, he forgot, and when he went the next evening the glove had already been sold.

"It was probably cracked and not much good anyway," he told his mom.

"Are those sour grapes I'm hearing?" she asked.

"Sour what?"

"Grapes. When you don't get something you want and you know it was your own fault and you make excuses by saying it wasn't really any good anyway, it's like saying that a bunch of grapes you haven't tasted is sour."

In Ezekiel's day the people also used an expression about sour grapes: "The fathers eat sour grapes, and the children's teeth are set on edge." That was their way of saying that they were being punished for things they didn't do, that their ancestors had sinned, and now they had to take the blame. They didn't want to admit that they were responsible for their own sins.

In the next verses, though, God says, "You will no longer quote this proverb in Israel. . . . The soul who sins is the one who will die."

With God there are no "sour grape" excuses.

You can't blame anyone else or anything else for what you do or what you don't do. You are responsible for your own eternity. God wants us to live, though, and says, "Get a new heart and a new spirit. . . . For I take no pleasure in the death of anyone" (verses 31, 32).

Sour grapes or not, Sam continued to save his money, and by spring he was able to buy a new first-baseman's glove.

SEPTEMBER

7

All the Others

There are different kinds of service, but the same Lord.
1 Corinthians 12:5.

We sat in the hush of a huge cathedral. It was so big, so grand, so . . .

"Just think of all the people and all their hard work." Jean's voice blended into my own thoughts.

I nodded. I had been thinking. Architects and artists, engineers and craftsmen had worked for hundreds and hundreds of years building and rebuilding just that one building. *So much history,* I thought. *She's lucky to live here.* I imagined the historic pageants she'd told about with colorful costumes and famous choirs and orchestras, and how it sounded with music filling such a magnificent place.

"So many, many people doing so much."

"All that God-given talent," I agreed. The sun brushed across the stained-glass windows across from us.

"That window, for instance." She pointed toward the vivid colors that blended into a scene from the Bible. "Think of all the work it took to make just that one window."

"The designers, the artists, the craftsmen . . ." It was a work of art, and I wondered how many great minds had been involved in creating it.

"More than that," she said. "Think of all the others."

It seemed that she was trying to guide my thoughts in a different direction. "The others?" I asked.

"Yes. When they were little, someone had to wipe their noses . . . and make their meals . . . and wash their clothes . . . and mend. And take care of them when they were sick. Think of all the people who spent their lives doing all those jobs—those little tasks that we never remember. Without them this great cathedral never would have been built."

Paul says that each of us is part of the body of Christ, or in other words, His church, and that each person is necessary. He named several types of church workers in his time—apostles, prophets, teachers, and even included "helpers."

Think of your own church. Who are those who help others? Who besides the pastor and the Sabbath school leaders help keep it operating? ____________________

____.

How do you help? ______________________________

____.

SEPTEMBER

The Helper Quilt

How many people does it take to operate your school? Do you need just the principal and some teachers and a janitor and a few school bus drivers?

Notice the names in the blocks of this "Helper Quilt." In what way is each person below necessary to the operation of your school?

AUTO PARTS MAKER	COOK	FARMHAND	SECRETARY	ARTIST
CARPENTER	TEXTBOOK WRITER	JANITOR	ARCHITECT	HOMEMAKER
SCHOOL BUS DRIVER	SHEET METAL WORKER	TEACHER	ELECTRICIAN	EDUCATION DIRECTOR
PHOTO-GRAPHER	HIGHWAY FLAG PERSON		FACTORY WORKER	LETTER CARRIER
TELEPHONE REPAIR PERSON	FORKLIFT OPERATOR	PRINCIPAL	GROCERY STORE CLERK	FARMER
PRINTER	CEMENT MAN-UFACTURER	PAINTER	DOCTOR	PLUMBER'S ASSISTANT
ACCOUNTANT	FRUIT PICKER	SANITARY ENGINEER	BAKER	DECK HAND ON A SHIP

The center block is empty, making the pattern incomplete. Put your name on that block because your school is not complete without you. No school can operate without its students.

"The most successful toilers are those who will cheerfully work to serve God in small things. Every human being is to work with his own individual thread, weave it into the fabric that composes the web, and complete the pattern" *(Messages to Young People,* p. 203).

Now you are the body of Christ, and each one of you is a part of it. 1 Corinthians 12:27.

SEPTEMBER

9

Living the Sabbath

Dear children, let us not love with words or tongue but with actions and in truth. 1 John 3:18.

Jamie leaned back against the picnic table, his legs sprawled against a ridge of sand. The sun seemed poised above the rounded flow of the hills—a huge, red disk casting a crimson glow across the cloud trails and turning the lake's surface mirror to red-gold. As the edge of the sun slipped behind the hills, the colors of both sky and lake slowly softened until they faded into the soft gray of early evening.

"Happy Sabbath!" Jamie's father said softly.

Jamie didn't want to move, to break the spell of the quiet beginning of this new Sabbath.

His dad slapped him on his knee. "It's time for us naturalists to go home. Supper's waiting."

Jamie grinned. Fruit salad and cinnamon buns were on the table—they'd helped put them there before driving to the lake. His mom and his sister wanted to stay home and welcome the Sabbath with their music—both sang, and his mom played the organ, and his sister the piano. In their family Sabbath was special, and they often did special things to welcome it. "Keeping the rules of the Sabbath won't do you any good," his father often said, "unless you live the Sabbath the rest of the week."

"Huh?" Jamie had said the first time the sense of those words registered. "How?"

"Sabbath is a sign of having a special friendship with God, and friendship's not for just one day. It's all day, every day."

Jamie understood, but that week he was to face some decisions. In order to "live the Sabbath" what should he do?

Sunday afternoon Jamie needs some glue. He and his sister have an open-door policy, meaning they can go into each other's rooms to borrow certain school supplies and sports equipment with the other isn't around. His sister, though, has made him promise never to read her diary. Usually she keeps it hidden, but when he goes to borrow her glue, the diary is lying open on her bed, and he accidentally notices his name. Of course he wonders what she's written about him. Now what?

Tuesday's a scorcher, and by the time school is over, Jamie and his friends decide that the only way they'll survive is to cool off in the pool. He rushes home to get his things and then finds his mom's note reminding him that this is the afternoon he's to pick the tomatoes in their garden. He doesn't have time to pick them and still go to the pool. It's very hot. What should he do?

Do you live the Sabbath all week long?

SEPTEMBER

10

Trapped!

Be strong and courageous. Do not be terrified; do not be discouraged, for the Lord your God will be with you wherever you go. Joshua 1:9.

"Look, Mom! That's the set I was telling you about." Anders pointed toward two pictures at the end of the row of paintings that the artist had leaning against the wall in the shade of the roof overhang.

"Very good pictures," the artist said in broken English. "They tell old story of Rwandan people."

"What do you think, Mom?"

"That fellow's in some predicament!" his mother exclaimed.

"But not impossible," said the artist. "You missionaries?"

Anders and his mother both nodded.

"Then you know about God. You know nothing impossible." The artist pointed out the details of the first picture to them, but the story was clear even without his explanation.

A man had taken his machete and ax to cut down a lone tree by the river. He had nearly chopped through the tree when a lion came growling out of the forest.

The man looked around for a safe place to run, but just then a crocodile rose out of the river. It had its mouth open to swallow him. With the lion on one side and the crocodile on the other, the man had no place to go but up the tree, which was about ready to fall. He jumped up and grabbed the lowest limb and started to pull himself above his two pursuers. But he found himself face-to-face with a giant, black snake. The snake's tongue flicked a warning. He could not go up.

Below, on one side of the tree, the growling lion pranced menacingly toward him. On the other side, the crocodile leered up at him, its teeth huge in its open mouth. The man could not go down. He hung from the branch by one hand, seemingly with no possible way to escape.

But the second picture shows that even when everything seems completely impossible, salvation can come.

The tree fell, knocking the lion over the head, pinning the snake by the tail, and frightening the crocodile. The man ran to safety.

"Good story!" said the artist.

"A very good story," replied Anders' mother.

"And you're right," she said to Anders. "They're a good set of pictures to have."

SEPTEMBER

11

A Good Plan

Be strong and very courageous. Be careful to obey all the law my servant Moses gave you. Joshua 1:7.

Have you ever felt like the man who was trapped by the lion, the crocodile, and the snake? That you had no way of saving yourself?

Some people feel trapped by their own fears.

When God told Joshua to be courageous, He reminded him of the laws that Moses had given the people. These included the Ten Commandments, but there were also rules about everyday living.

Most people are afraid of what might happen—fire; theft; natural disasters such as floods, earthquakes, and tornadoes; sickness; and accidents. Most countries have laws against theft, but there are also many rules about everyday health and safety. For example, all children must be vaccinated against certain diseases, buildings must be made strong enough to withstand normal earthquakes, and public buildings must be constructed so that they can be evacuated easily in case of fire.

A variety of locks and security alarms can protect against thieves. Those who live where tornadoes are common are wise to have a basement shelter area. You could probably add lots more safety rules to these, but first, do this.

In the Fear column below, write the five things that frighten you most. Then in the What to Do column note the safety rules and practices that can protect you from the things that make you afraid.

FEAR	**WHAT TO DO**
______________	______________
______________	______________
______________	______________
______________	______________
______________	______________

Being prepared with a good safety plan helps people be less afraid, but the best safety plan always puts trust in Jesus at the head of the list. Then, no matter what happens, you know that He will be with you.

SEPTEMBER

12

The Fruit Salad

If a man remains in me and I in him, he will bear much fruit.
John 15:5.

Chrissie cradled two fuzzy, brown ovals in her hand.

"Fruit salad day—excellent idea!" her mother exclaimed after reading Ms. Bromwell's note. "Do you want to take those?"

Chrissie nodded. "They're my favorites, and Ms. Bromwell said to bring a piece or two of our favorite fruit."

"What can you tell about them for your report?"

"Well," said Chrissie, "they're called kiwi fruit. They come from New Zealand. They're green inside with tiny black seeds around the center. They taste real yummy and are good in fruit salads."

"Good start!" exclaimed her mother. "Most folks don't know much about them, though. Why, I'd never even seen one until after you were born—and now you can buy them in any supermarket. I've got a good article about them if you want to use it for your research."

After reading the article and looking in the encyclopedia, Chrissie wrote this report.

"The kiwi fruit gets its name from the kiwi bird because its fuzzy skin makes it look something like the bird. Both are from New Zealand, but the kiwi bird has been there longer. In 1904 a man brought some monkey peach seeds from China for a nurseryman. It was a small berry and it grew well, so they called it the Chinese gooseberry. They worked with it, and it grew into a bigger and tastier fruit.

"These became popular in Europe almost by accident. In 1952 someone in England ordered a shipload of lemons from New Zealand. The shippers put in 10 cases of kiwi fruit to fill extra space. There was a strike, making the ship late. The lemons rotted, but the kiwis were fine.

"Now they are grown in Europe and California and British Columbia and other places. People like them for their leaves and pretty white flowers, as well as the fruit. The plants grow fast, too, as much as eight inches a day.

"At cool temperatures they keep for a long time—six months even, and they're ready to eat when they're slightly soft to the touch. They're good for you, too, because they are high in vitamin C and iron and other good things. My dad says he eats them because they don't have any cholesterol—and not many calories, either."

Ms. Bromwell had the children put their fruit in a basket on her desk. Chrissie slipped her two kiwis among the other fruit.

SEPTEMBER

13

For the Good of All

The Spirit's presence is shown in some way in each person for the good of all. 1 Corinthians 12:7, TEV.

"Don't all these different kinds of fruit look good together?" Ms. Bromwell asked.

Chrissie thought the deep red apples beside the smooth yellow of the bananas with the purple grapes draped across the other fruit made the basket very pretty. In fact, all the fruit looked nice—except for the two dull green-brown kiwi fruits. And Ms. Bromwell had moved them to the top.

Why did I have to bring those? Chrissie asked herself, feeling a bit ashamed of the two small brown lumps sitting on top of all those other good-looking pieces of fruit. *I like pears about as much as I like kiwis.*

She took a deep breath, hoping that the other children hadn't noticed that she was the one who brought them.

"Not only do they look nice together—and we can enjoy having them on my desk like this until Mrs. Huston comes to prepare them—but their flavors will blend into a scrumptious fruit salad. Jesus said that if we keep His Spirit in our hearts, we'll bear lots of fruit. But, just like all these good favorites of yours, the fruit each person bears will be different, just as each person is different.

"When we play softball, we all want Trevor on our team because he can pitch so well. Shandra, though, often gets asked when someone's needed for special music because of her nice voice, and Jason's the one we can rely on when we need someone to play the piano." Ms. Bromwell went around the room, praising a talent for each of the children. "Later on this morning, I'm going to ask Chrissie to share her report with you."

Chrissie felt herself blushing.

"I've already glanced at the papers you handed in. Chrissie has a talent for being able to say things well on paper, and I think you'll enjoy what she's written about her fruit."

Chrissie was glad Ms. Bromwell didn't say which fruit just then.

"We all can't pitch or sing or play the piano or write equally well, so we need each other—just like these fruits will all blend together to make a tasty salad. As you each contribute your talent, they'll blend together to make ours a better and happier class."

SEPTEMBER

14

You Can Make a Difference

This is to my Father's glory, that you bear much fruit, showing yourselves to be my disciples. John 15:8.

When Geraldine Goertzen, a church member who lives in Kelowna, British Columbia, decided to take painting lessons, she never once thought that art lessons would have anything to do with her being a partner in overseas missions.

Geraldine enjoys painting for a hobby, and as her lessons progressed, she and her teacher, Samara Carrier, became good friends. Samara, who is a well-known Canadian artist, often donates prints of her paintings to raise money for "save the wildlife" and other projects.

Knowing Samara's interest in Third World projects, Geraldine got to thinking about some of her other friends. "How would you like to sell prints to build a school in Africa?" she asked Samara one day. "I know some missionaries. Thousands of kids where they work don't have schools to go to. If they could build even one school . . ."

As Geraldine explained, Samara became enthusiastic. "I'll do the painting if you'll do the selling," she promised. "I know we can build that school."

It was a great idea, but . . .

Geraldine has a knack for contacting people and had helped raise funds for local church and school projects, but she'd never before tried to do anything so big. Before long, she found herself with a huge stack of prints of eight of Samara's oil paintings.

Now what? she asked herself, looking at the boxes stacked in her hall. *Where do I start?*

The pastor arranged for her to sell prints at camp meeting. Another member helped with advertising, others helped with sales, and still others sold prints in other parts of Canada.

That was 1990, and before the year was over, they'd raised enough money to build an entire school for one village. ADRA-Canada arranged matching grants to build a health center as well.

Samara was elated. "This is just the beginning!" she exclaimed to Geraldine. "We're going to build a school every year for the next 10 years."

Because Geraldine was not afraid of the hard work her idea involved, there are schools where there never before have been schools—Christian schools filled with African kids, many of them learning about God for the first time.

You, too, can make a difference. If you give your talents to God He will bless them, and they will yield fruit for Him.

SEPTEMBER

15

And the Gift Goes On

Now he who supplies seed to the sower and bread for food will also supply and increase your store of seed and will enlarge the harvest of your righteousness. 2 Corinthians 9:10.

The story of Geraldine and Samara in Canada and the schools their project built reaches even further.

Kathleen grew up in a Christian family in the United States, and from her parents' example learned about giving and helping, but she decided against church. She and her husband worked for a television studio, and then her husband was struck down with cancer. Widowed and still young, Kathleen reexamined her life. She remembered hearing someone talk about "tithing time" and decided to give two years as a Peace Corps volunteer. Her assignment took her to Songa Adventist Hospital in Zaire.

There she served as a village water technician in cooperation with ADRA, but her television work had given her experience and a keen interest in photography.

"How'd you like to do some photography of the REACH-Italy child sponsorship program at our schools?" the ADRA director asked.

Peace Corps gave Kathleen permission to go, and her second stop was at the new Musamaria Mwema (Good Samaritan) School in Kamungu Village. This also happened to be the first school being built by Geraldine and Samara's art fund.

Kathleen took pictures of the children for the Italian families whose sponsorships give the children clothes and school supplies and even pay for the teachers' salaries. That made her, an American, a link connecting Canada and Italy in a partnership that provides schooling for children in Zaire.

The partnership network continues to grow. Paul, an older missionary kid from the Philippines, volunteered to drive supplies to the schools, and Dr. Teixeira, a missionary from Portugal, gave days off from Songa Hospital to treat the school kids and their families. The African kids themselves, along with their parents and other villagers, are the partners who volunteer to make bricks and carry supplies and do all the other little jobs that go along with building a school.

This is only one example of how one person's idea has made it possible for people around the world to work together in helping others. You, too, can become part of a worldwide network of helpers. Even though you're not old enough to become an overseas volunteer, and even if your family can't adopt a Third World child through one of the many sponsorship programs, you can pray that God will continue to increase the harvest of righteousness in Geraldine's and other projects.

SEPTEMBER

16

Is It Lawful?

Jesus asked the Pharisees and experts in the law, "Is it lawful to heal on the Sabbath or not?" Luke 14:3.

Several church families had gotten together for Sabbath potluck.

"Do you know what we saw last Sabbath afternoon?" Mrs. Marwich asked. "We were driving toward the park, and we saw Don Jones, the junior Sabbath school leader, over at his neighbor's. There he was, as big as life, helping put up one of those metal garden sheds."

"No!" exclaimed someone. "On *Sabbath*? Are you sure?"

"I wouldn't have believed it if I hadn't seen it with my own eyes."

"Yes, Brother Jones told me what he had done last Sabbath," a kindly voice added.

Everyone turned toward the speaker, the pastor. "He said that any passerby from the church would surely get the wrong idea, but he felt he was doing what Jesus would have done."

By now everyone was listening carefully.

"During Sabbath dinner, he saw his neighbor across the way struggling to put up a new garden shed. He'd set one wall in place, and then as he tried to position the next wall the first would fall down.

"It was quite funny to watch, Brother Jones said, but he couldn't imagine that sitting snug in his house and laughing at his neighbor's trouble was the best way to keep the Sabbath. He decided that if Jesus were there, He would go over and at least offer to hold the walls in place.

"I think you understand now why you saw him 'working' at his neighbor's last Sabbath."

How would you answer Jesus' question "Is it lawful to heal on the Sabbath?" or, as He asked another time, "Is it lawful to do good?"

If you had been Don Jones, what would you have done?

If you had been Mrs. Marwich, what would you have thought if you had seen him working on a garden shed on Sabbath?

If you had been the pastor, what would you have told Don Jones?

What do you think Jesus would have said to the people at the potluck who were talking about Don Jones?

SEPTEMBER

17

About the Sabbath . . .

For the Son of Man is Lord even of the Sabbath. Matthew 12:8, NKJV.

God gave the Sabbath to the world as a sign of His power to save us from our sins. Properly kept, it shows who worships the true God, because God intended it as a time for His people to learn to know Him better.

The children of Israel were slaves for the Egyptians for so long and were so used to being bossed around that by the time God delivered them they could no longer think for themselves.

After they had been freed, they were so ignorant about the Sabbath that God gave the miracle of the manna when they were on their way to Mount Sinai to teach them the pattern of Sabbathkeeping—prepare on Friday and rest from work on the seventh day.

They were still so stubborn and so careless that God made a law to get their attention. He ordered Moses to tell them that anyone caught working on the Sabbath would be put to death.

The threat of the death penalty helped them "remember" while they wandered around in the wilderness, but after they had settled in the Promised Land, they started forgetting. Soon they were copying the thrilling rites of their heathen neighbors.

Finally, after God punished their wickedness by sending them as captives to Babylon, the people decided that they had better become serious about Sabbathkeeping.

By the time Jesus was born, they were very serious Sabbathkeepers. They followed a long list of complicated rules. After all, by strictly keeping the Sabbath, they proved that they were God's special people, didn't they?

Then Jesus came. His mission was to save people from their sins. To do this, He had to die. First, though, He had to make His people understand God's love. After all, God had chosen the Jews to show the rest of the world that He is the true God.

Jesus showed that the Sabbath was not about rules, but about God's love. And as well as teaching in the synagogue, He healed people on the Sabbath day.

"Is it lawful to heal on the Sabbath?" the Jewish leaders asked Him.

His answer showed that their rules let them rescue a sheep on the Sabbath but not help another person. They became so angry that they wanted to kill Him.

And they did. On a Friday. Then they hurried home to keep the Sabbath.

Today is the Sabbath. Are you learning more of God's love?

SEPTEMBER

18

Corythosaurus Causarius

Cory towered above me, his knee level with my shoulder. He stood solidly, balanced on his tail, his small head staring forward, his skin bumpy with raised dots and ovals.

Could he have made a pet? I wondered. *Could I have ridden him like a horse? Or tied him like a watchdog?* Despite his monstrous size—he was 33 feet (10 meters) long, nearly 15 feet (4.5 meters) high at his shoulder, and weighed almost three tons—he was a grass eater and seemed to have been harmless enough.

Cory, short for *Corythosaurus causarius*, a duck-billed dinosaur otherwise known as a helmeted hadrosaur, is one of the mysteries of the past that puzzle scientists. When did he and the other dinosaurs live? Where did they come from, and why did they disappear?

Paleontologists, scientists who study plant and animal fossils, can tell us many facts about dinosaurs because, like detectives, they put together a picture of what the animals were like by clues they get from the fossils. Bones tell the animal's size and shape. Markings on the bones show how the muscles fit onto the bones and how big they were. Foot and body prints add more specific details.

By using casts of fossils, they made Cory's entire skeleton. They based his skin texture and foot shape on actual impressions. From the bone structure they learned that he could stand upright only when he was still. When walking or running he had to bend forward so that his spine was nearly horizontal with the ground and his tail up. He could use only his hind legs on land. The fossils are found in places that suggest he lived in wetlands and ate mostly soft plants.

I reached up and let my hand slide across Cory's bumpy gray skin. The scientists had learned enough to build this life-sized model for the museum, but they can't answer all the questions. They think that maybe he and the other big reptiles lived millions and millions of years ago. But that's just a guess. They just guessed, too, about his color when they painted him gray.

Someday I want to ask God about Cory and about the other dinosaurs. I also want to ask Him and Job about the leviathan and the behemoth that they talked about in the Bible story of Job. Some people think that they might be the crocodile and the hippopotamus or the elephant. Others think they were mythical animals—as is the unicorn. But are they really?

What questions do you want to ask God someday?

Can you pull in the leviathan with a fishhook? . . . Can you make a pet of him like a bird or put him on a leash for your girls? Job 41:1-5.

SEPTEMBER

19

The Old Chicken

When you bring a blind or sick or lame animal to sacrifice to me, do you think there's nothing wrong with that? Try giving an animal like that to the governor!
Malachi 1:8, TEV.

Today is Jeremy's birthday.

When he came down for breakfast, he found a big, crumpled, oil-stained paper bag by his breakfast plate. Inside was a pair of ice skates—scuffed, laces broken, and blades dull, nicked, and rusted—and stuffed into one was a piece of paper that read "Happy birthday with love from Mom and Dad."

Jeremy is a good skater and has been wanting a new pair of hockey skates. He knows that his parents can afford to get them for him. If you were Jeremy, how would you feel? ______________________________

____

God has feelings too.

In Old Testament times He asked the people to sacrifice their best animals. In the first place, He wanted them to understand that as the God of heaven He loved them and wanted them to show their love for Him by giving good gifts. In the second place, the meat from some of the sacrifices was for the priests and their families to eat—so the animals had to be healthy. Even today meat from sick or diseased animals is not to be marketed for food.

According to their traditions, the best gift the Luba people of Africa can give is a live animal. Whether it is to be eaten at a feast in honor of a guest or to be taken home, the animal is presented live so everyone can see that it is healthy and in good condition. According to custom, too, the person accepting the gift thanks the giver by saying how good it is.

On our visits to villages where ADRA has projects, we're often given chickens, sometimes even sheep and goats. This is the people's way of saying "Thank you for what ADRA has done for us."

One family brought us a rooster—a handsome fellow in rust-brown feathers tinted with blue and purple. I took him with both hands, as etiquette requires, and said the Swahili words that I thought meant "He is very nice."

The father looked shocked and repeated what I said.

When I heard him saying the words, I realized what they actually meant. "No! No!" I exclaimed, shaking my head, horrified at how I'd insulted them. "Not very, very old! But nice! Very nice!"

The story of Jeremy's skates was a "just suppose" situation, but what about the story of the gifts that you give to God? Is He able to receive them and say "Very, very nice"?

SEPTEMBER

The Bristle-backed Spider, Part 1

Therefore each of you must put off falsehood and speak truthfully to his neighbor, for we are all members of one body. Ephesians 4:25.

Samantha wore her hair pulled back into a long, dark ponytail; Karalynn kept hers short and curly. Samantha sang soprano in the school choir; Karalynn played saxophone in the band. Samantha came from a large inland farm; Karalynn lived in a small coastal town. Samantha's father was a colporteur; Karalynn's dad didn't even attend church. Samantha was short; Karalynn was tall. The two girls were different in just about every possible way, except that they both attended the same school and lived in the same dormitory. To be exact, the two were roommates.

"And we might as well make up our minds to get along," said the practical Samantha.

Karalynn, the creative one, nodded.

"And I expect to have the cleanest room with the shiniest floor," said Samantha.

Karalynn sighed. "And I expect to live in comfort."

"If we take off our shoes at the door, we can keep our floors looking shiny and polished."

Inwardly Karalynn bristled. *Her practicality goes too far,* she thought. Outwardly she simply shrugged. The girls did manage a peaceful coexistence, although Karalynn's casual housekeeping annoyed Samantha, and Samantha's complaining nettled Karalynn. Then Karalynn discovered Samantha's fear of "bugs."

"Have you ever seen a bristle-backed spider?" she asked innocently one evening.

"No," answered Samantha. "What're they?"

Karalynn spun a long, detailed explanation about an imaginary spider—huge and spiny and ugly with short, stubby, fuzzy legs.

Samantha's skin prickled as Karalynn's voice emphasized the disgusting details. She particularly despised spiders.

"They usually hide in woodpiles," Karalynn added, inventing more details as she went on. "Sometimes they get into houses, though, and then they'll crawl into dark places—like beds."

Samantha's shoulders scrunched up nervously. She believed the story, and she hated Karalynn's talking about bugs, but said nothing. Nor did she seem to notice that when she complained about Karalynn's housekeeping, Karalynn would somehow bring bristle-backed spiders back into the conversation.

Without realizing what they were doing, both roommates, by hiding their feelings, were setting the stage for a grand finale.

SEPTEMBER

21

The Bristle-backed Spider, Part 2

Let him who boasts boast about this: that he understands and knows me. Jeremiah 9:24.

Karalynn scuffed in from class, her head full of the essay she was planning. She was not aware that the soles of her shoes streaked a long smudge across Samantha's just-polished floor.

"Karalynn!" Samantha shrieked. "Look!"

Karalynn looked. She saw the long blotch from the door to her bed smudging an otherwise beautifully polished floor. "Floors are to be walked on," she snapped.

Samantha started to say something, but instead she picked up a book and sat at her desk, her back rigid and stiff.

The two girls didn't say much for the rest of the evening. Karalynn didn't even mention bristle-backed spiders. She climbed into bed first and turned to face the wall, and then she stifled a giggle as she heard Samantha preparing for bed. Suddenly there was a blood-curdling scream and a frantic scrambling.

Karalynn sat bolt upright just in time to see Samantha leap from her bed, jump up and over the bookcase they used as a room divider, and land, crouched, on the foot of Karalynn's bed.

"Whatever in the world?" Karalynn demanded.

"My foot touched something bristly." Samantha's voice trembled. "It . . . it felt like a bristle-backed spider."

"Should I go look?" Karalynn asked. Then, without waiting for an answer, she threw back the covers and with a quick snatch grabbed something. "The bristle-backed spider!"

Samantha screamed again, then looked at what Karalynn held—a hairbrush. "Why . . . Why . . ." Without finishing, she bolted from the room.

In about 15 minutes, the dean called Karalynn to her office. She talked to both girls—separately and together.

"Samantha likes rooming with you," she told Karalynn. "She likes your bouncy creativity, but people of her perfectionistic personality type need to have understanding and be given the privilege of living in an orderly room. I've explained to her that nagging doesn't help people with your personality to cooperate. But if you're willing to give it another try . . ."

Karalynn nodded. Being a Christian included being understanding. "Like you said before," she said to Samantha later, "we might as well make up our minds to get along. It's not such a big deal to take off my shoes at the door—and even be a little tidier. Then you won't have to nag. So who needs the bristle-backed spider!"

Both girls laughed.

SEPTEMBER

22

Good—No Problem!

Do your best to present yourself to God as one approved, a workman who does not need to be ashamed. 2 Timothy 2:15.

"Another storm blew through That! village last night." Mr. Smith, the ADRA director, looked grim. "A radio message says it ripped most of the roof off one of the school buildings."

Mrs. Smith waited to hear more. That! village had a reputation.

"Will they ever learn?" Mr. Smith sounded tired. "If I stand right there, they'll pound in enough nails to secure the roofing. But if I'm not there, they put in two or three, just enough to hold the roofing sheets in place so that they look good. The 'extra' nails and tie-downs go home in their pockets.

"If it were only the school roof . . ."

Mrs. Smith nodded. They'd worked with That! village enough years. They'd taught the teachers better ways of gardening, who in turn taught the same to the children. The children were excited about gardening, and they planted a huge field of pineapples. Not only did they learn while they were working, but a share of the fruit would be theirs to take home to their families. The plants grew quickly, and soon tiny rosettes appeared and began developing into healthy-looking pineapples—bigger than any that grew around the village. The morning that the harvest would begin, the children arrived at school ready for work, but all the ripe pineapples were gone—stolen by the villagers.

The older children had dug fishponds with a Peace Corps volunteer and stocked them. When the fish were almost ready to catch and the children were dreaming of what they could do with their share of the profits, the villagers came at night and stole all the fish. Now a school roof!

"I wasn't there when they put on this roof," Mr. Smith said, "but the chief assured me everything was 'good—no problem!' "

"Now the children can study good—no problem?" Mrs. Smith asked with a smile.

"That's just it." Mr. Smith sounded almost discouraged. "How will those kids learn about being good workmen and being true to God when they live with this tradition of cheating?"

"That's why we're here," his wife reminded him. "Habits won't change in the time it takes to build one school, but little by little we can point them to God's way. Will they be able to put roofing back on?" she asked.

"No problem," Mr. Smith replied, "if I send the nails they ordered."

Are you learning to be a good workman?

SEPTEMBER

23

Quick Words

Do not be quick with your mouth, do not be hasty in your heart to utter anything before God. Ecclesiastes 5:2.

Bored with life in general and dormitory Sundays in particular, Jacylyn pushed the iron absentmindedly over her dress. Mandy and Gabrielle came into the laundry room, and as Gabrielle disappeared around the corner to the washers a sudden inspiration for fun settled over Jacylyn.

"That Gabrielle!" she exclaimed, rolling her eyes upward. "I've never seen the likes."

Mandy looked startled.

"Thinks she's something!" Jacylyn forced her voice louder. "Stuck up thing."

"Sshh!" hissed Mandy. "She can hear you."

Jacylyn shrugged, but inside she was laughing. "Serves her right," she continued in fake sarcasm. She added more insults to make it sound like she meant every word she said.

"You shouldn't talk like that!" Mandy exclaimed.

Jacylyn forced a laugh, pleased that her joke was going so well.

"Stop!" Mandy's voice held a warning edge. She grabbed up her clothes and flounced out.

Jacylyn suddenly felt as if the breath had been knocked out of her. Her stomach knotted. Maybe her idea hadn't been so funny after all. She needed to explain, to tell Mandy—and especially Gabrielle—that she was only teasing. But her mind, so quick with all those unkind words that she didn't mean, now went totally blank. Worried, she hurried to her room. Before long, Mandy came to see her.

"Do you know that Gabrielle's in her room crying because of all those terrible things she heard you say? The dean may have to call the doctor."

Jacylyn felt her face stiffen. She shook her head. "I . . . I meant it all as a joke." She searched for the right words. "Gabrielle's so nice. I . . . I didn't think either of you would ever believe what I was saying. I was . . . Well, I wanted to be funny, to make you laugh by saying the opposite of what I really feel."

"What you said is no joke!" Mandy spoke firmly.

"I want to tell her that I'm sorry."

"I don't think she could handle seeing you now."

Jacylyn let her head drop. "Tell her for me," she said, wishing with all her might that her attempt to be funny had never happened.

Mandy nodded, but the quick words had already done their work.

SEPTEMBER

Pierre's Sabbath

Cast all your anxiety on him because he cares for you.
1 Peter 5:7.

Pierre worked for the government as an adviser in the department of education. He liked his work. He was able to travel and visit schools and share ideas with the teachers.

On his Saturdays off, Pierre often visited the Adventist church with his friend Dave. He liked the Adventist way of explaining the Bible. "In here I'm an Adventist, too," Pierre told Dave, and he tapped his chest over his heart.

Dave smiled. "I'm glad you feel that way," he said. "It's very special to be an Adventist." Dave didn't say anything more at the time. Pierre continued to come to church now and then. One Sabbath Dave saw that Pierre had something on his mind.

"That book you gave me—the one about the Sabbath—I read it last week." His face looked as though he were about to explode with happiness. "Wow!" he exclaimed. "The Sabbath is a very special day, very important. I had no idea until I read that book. God wants us to worship Him on the seventh day—His Sabbath day. He has a special blessing for those who worship on the Sabbath. It's fantastic. And it's all in the Bible." Pierre could hardly get the words out fast enough. "Do you know what? I saw the pastor. He's going to study with me, and from today on my family and I are going to keep the Sabbath."

"That's great," Dave exclaimed, but inside he was wondering how easy it would be for Pierre.

The next two Sabbaths Pierre attended church. The third week he arrived late, and the following Sabbath he stayed only for Sabbath school. Dave suspected problems, but the next Sabbath Pierre was at church, on time, nearly bursting with smiles.

"Keeping the Sabbath is not easy when you try to do it by yourself," he told Dave after the service. "The first week I told my boss that I was sick. The next week I again told him I was sick. But you can't get sick every Saturday, and in here it was bothering me." Again he tapped his heart. "I knew I couldn't keep telling lies. I prayed, how I prayed, then I went to my boss—and got right to the point about the Sabbath.

"He told me that he believed in religious freedom and that if I'd work an hour longer the other days, he'd give me my Saturdays free. Not only that, he called the others, told them what I'd be doing, and explained that Saturday is my Sabbath and that no one's to call me at home or bother me about work on that day.

"Thanks to God's miracle, here I am!"

SEPTEMBER

25

The Fence That Went All Around

For I have the desire to do what is good, but I cannot carry it out. Romans 7:18.

Smokey had a big backyard, plenty of good food, and a nice doghouse. He had a good life except that Jeff, his boss, and the big people he lived with left every morning—early—and stayed away most of the day.

Before he went, Jeff would give Smokey a big bowl of food and say some friendly-sounding words something like "Now, Smokey, be a good dog, and I'll be back to play with you this afternoon."

But, of course, all Smokey understood was "Smokey" and "good dog," and it seemed forever until Jeff came back and they could play and jump and wrestle, and Jeff would say "good dog" lots of times. Then Smokey felt so happy that he licked Jeff's face.

During the times called weekends, Jeff stayed home and played with Smokey more, and the big guy whom Jeff called "Dad" sometimes joined them in a game of throw and chase, and the lady whom Jeff called "Mom" gave him a special dog biscuit. Then the next day, early, they'd all go off again and leave him. That was the pits, because no matter what Smokey wanted to do, there was always the bothersome fence that got in his way.

One day Smokey discovered that if he pushed certain boards, they'd tip just enough so that he could jump clear over the fence. He wanted to be a "good dog" for Jeff, but he also wanted to have fun.

Smokey had a great day exploring the neighborhood, then, tail wagging, he hurried home and sat on the front porch to wait for Jeff. When Jeff came, he did not seem pleased. That evening he and the big guy called Dad braced the boards. The next day Smokey couldn't jump out of the boring backyard. And the next day it rained. The dirt under the gate got soft and mushy. Smokey tested it with his paws and then began to dig. Soon he had a hole just the right size, and he slipped out to enjoy a day around the neighborhood, but by the time Jeff came back home Smokey was waiting on the front porch, muddy and tail-wagging happy.

"Bad dog!" Jeff said very loudly.

Smokey knew that Jeff was not very pleased. He wished Jeff would say "good dog" and play with him, but he was too busy helping the big guy named Dad set cement blocks in the mud under the gate.

When Jeff came home the next day, Smokey sat waiting in the backyard. "Good dog!" Jeff said lots of times, and they romped and played, and Smokey was happy for the solid fence that kept him home.

What "fences" make you feel happy?

SEPTEMBER

26

Ralph's Train

For if the willingness is there, the gift is acceptable according to what one has, not according to what he does not have. 2 Corinthians 8:12.

Ralph is a model railroader. He has trains and tracks and tunnels and villages and stations and automatic gates and loaders—everything that a model railroader could want—stretched into a fantastic layout. Every detail fits to precise scale. With the controls Ralph can guide his trains anywhere the tracks lead. The automatic signals, the gates, the loaders, the switches, and all the other miniatures with moving parts work according to the signals he gives.

His collection represents a huge investment and years of carefully putting together all the tiny parts to make everything accurate and to scale.

"It's a fantastic showpiece—fun to watch," everyone who has seen it says.

"But for me it's a very lonely hobby," says Ralph. "I like others to share the fun of watching it, seeing everything it can do, but nobody can anymore."

And that disappointed him.

"I used to be able to share it," he says.

That was when he could still set it up in his room. You see, as his train collection grew, it became too big for his room. Then it grew too big to set up anywhere else in the house. Ralph had only one place to put it—the attic. There he could stretch out the track and work to his heart's content and not be in the way of anyone. He added pieces and continued building on it until the layout filled the entire attic. Then he had to stop building—there wasn't room for another extension, and there wasn't even room for anyone else to come and watch.

"I can lift one section of the track and invite one other person to come up here with me, but then that spoils the layout," he explains. "I literally have no way of running the train on its complete layout so others can see it."

Until Ralph can find space elsewhere, the train remains hidden in his attic, unable to be seen and enjoyed as it deserves. It has become a hidden treasure.

When we find God's love, it too needs to be shared. It's only by being shared that it will find room to grow.

SEPTEMBER

27

A Missionary Diary*, Part 1

For where your treasure is, there your heart will be also. Luke 12:34.

Mission headquarters
Lubumbashi, Zaire

Tuesday, September 24, 1991—It's a warm, summery day. And quiet. Too quiet. The mission office is closed. The workers have been sent home, and we're staying in our house—but we may have to leave too.

Trouble is spreading across the country with riots and looting, and soldiers fighting soldiers. Presidential troops are stationed all around town, patrolling, trying to maintain order. But we continue to hear rumors about war.

War, all-out, terrible war, could break out at any moment—here in our city.

There's rioting in Likasi, the next town. Two families from another mission are trapped there. When some of their missionary friends tried to get to them, they were turned back. Two African pastors were allowed in, though, and given permission to take them to a mission out in the country.

If we have to leave, we'll probably go by plane rather than try to drive. We can each take one suitcase weighing 66 pounds.

I look around the house.

What should we take? Passports, money, and clothes. Those things for sure. They say to take bedding. No one knows where we'll go—only that it'll be to some other country—or how long we'll have to stay. So . . . our sleeping bags. It's warm, but they'll make good mattresses. Of course I'll take my little notebook computer and the back-up disks for the books I'm writing—including the junior devotional. And my Bible—the one with all my notes—and my husband's.

There's still room in the suitcase. What else? Family pictures? Cameras? Keepsakes?

If you had been in our place, what would you have taken?

What treasures would you save if you suddenly had to flee from your home and had no idea if you'd ever be able to return? What are your most important treasures?

---

* The series "A Missionary Diary" is taken from actual notes in my personal journals about our experiences in the mission field.

SEPTEMBER

28

A Missionary Diary, Part 2

But the eyes of the Lord are on those who fear him, on those whose hope is in his unfailing love. Psalm 33:18.

Wednesday—We're still here. Dr. Delgado from Songa Mission Hospital is also with us. He came—before the trouble started—to buy medicines for the hospital, and now he's worried. He left his wife and children and two other missionary families at Songa. Kamina, their nearest town, is full of soldiers, and there's looting and shooting, and the field (conference) Adventist Book Center has been ransacked. Troops could easily storm Songa.

We were relieved to get a radio message this morning telling us that all the Songa missionaries are safe at an American AID project in another village. They got away during the night in a Land Rover along with the peace corps volunteers, whom the Americans are evacuating. They'll be airlifted out of the country.

This morning, though, shortwave radio reports from America and England say that people fleeing tell of riots and looting and general destruction in Lubumbashi. I hope none of our families in the United States or Canada or Holland hear that. They'll worry. Our telephones don't work. They'll not be able to contact us, and they'll think we're in the middle of a very dangerous situation. That's not true. We're fine and we're safe. Everything in town is calm. But they don't know that.

In other places the story is not so good. Praise the Lord that all the missionaries' families of all the different church groups are safe—including those from Likasi. Those who've fled tell of stores standing like naked skeletons, stripped bare, their windows and doors broken and shelves not only empty, but torn off the walls and carried away. As soldiers emptied one store, a woman stopped a soldier carrying a television set.

"I'm an officer's wife," she said. "You must give that to me." He refused. She tried to take the TV. In the scuffle she was shot—and killed—for a television set.

Just after the missionaries left another station, their houses were looted, the roofs stripped off, and fire set to the remains.

Many folks have their cars packed and ready to go. The main border crossing is a 1½-hour drive. All of us at the Adventist mission plan to stay for now.

5:00 p.m. Date, my husband, just received a letter from one of his friends. It warned us that we'll hear gunshots before the night's over, that we should accept any protection our embassies can offer, and that he should send me out of the country if at all possible.

SEPTEMBER

29

A Missionary Diary, Part 3

The salvation of the righteous comes from the Lord; he is their stronghold in time of trouble. The Lord helps them and delivers them; he delivers them from the wicked and saves them, because they take refuge in him.
Psalm 37:39, 40.

Thursday—We heard no shots last night. Someone said that when soldiers from a camp outside of town prepared to march they were given flour and oil and other food, and they agreed not to cause trouble.

This week's problems started because of food. Prices went high and wages stayed so low that a soldier could not even buy one sack of cornmeal with his month's pay. For others it's the same. Parents are going without so that their children can eat. The soldiers were promised a big pay raise this month. When their wages came and they had no raise, they revolted.

We're so relieved that no trouble has started here yet. Rumors say that the soldiers intend to keep the calm. But who knows what might happen! Many of the families from other missions left town this morning. We sent messages to be passed on to our families back home telling that we're safe.

The doctor, although he's happy to know that his family is safe, is anxious to know where they'll be taken.

Our next-door neighbors, the Nebreses, are on mission business somewhere in the central part of the country. Paul, their son, is here, but as of today no one can trace his parents' whereabouts.

The Hansons, our missionary family in Kinshasa, will be evacuated today. Their daughter was on the flight scheduled to land when the rioting soldiers took control of the airport. Their flight was diverted to another country. So much for her visit here with her parents!

A message from the Songa missionary group—there are seven adults plus seven children under 7 years—says that they spent a miserable night. They're part of a group of more than 30—the others mostly peace corps volunteers. They don't have enough food, water, or places to sleep. When one more peace corps volunteer arrives from an outlying village, they'll be airlifted out of the country. The doctor is here. His wife and three kids are there, and no one knows where they'll be taken.

Reports from Kinshasa say that calm has been restored but that the downtown business section is destroyed. Buildings are empty wrecks. Food. Medicines. Clothes. Everything. Gone. There is nothing to buy. No one knows where the people will be able to buy food.

Rioting continues in other areas.

SEPTEMBER

A Missionary Diary, Part 4

Pray that your flight will not take place in winter or on the Sabbath. Matthew 24:20.

Friday—It's work as usual—almost.

Instead of being flown out of the country, the Songa families may be brought directly here this afternoon, but probably not until Sabbath. We're waiting for confirmation of that plan.

Now to find beds for all—and food. There are seven adults and seven children under 7 years of age, and they may have to stay a long time because the road between here and Songa is not safe. We've heard reports of vehicles being shot at when driving that way and of others being stolen. They say bandits are everywhere.

Paul's parents have been located. They'll be airlifted with a group of foreigners fleeing the country, maybe to Brazzaville in the Congo, maybe elsewhere. Paul can't find out.

Belgian troops have arrived. They're staying in the school across from us, and their job is to protect the foreigners who are leaving the country. It's comforting to know that they're standing guard on our street, but the trouble's not over yet—not by a long ways.

With everything stolen from all the stores in most of the other cities, what will people have to eat? Prices here are already going up.

We and the other missionaries must decide what to do. Many of our friends from the other missions are leaving, and that makes our decision even more difficult.

Our choices are these:

1. Stay where we are and continue our missionary work no matter what.
2. Stay where we are but be ready to evacuate at a moment's notice.
3. Go to another country and stay until everything's calm, then come back and carry on our work.
4. Go directly home and stay.

We know that we can be witnesses (missionaries) for God anywhere. We also know that the safest place to be is where God wants us.

If we were your parents, what would you advise us to do?

"The salvation of the righteous comes from the Lord. . . . He delivers them from the wicked and saves them, because they take refuge in him" (Ps. 37:39, 40).

OCTOBER

1

The Riot in Ephesus

The following is a dramatic reading—Acts 19:24-20:1. (Instructions are on page 28.)

NARRATOR: A silversmith named Demetrius, who made silver shrines of Artemis, brought in no little business for the craftsmen. He called them together, along with the workmen in related trades, and said:

DEMETRIUS: Men, you know we receive a good income from this business. And you see and hear how this fellow Paul has convinced and led astray large numbers of people here in Ephesus and in practically the whole province of Asia. He says that man-made gods are no gods at all. There is danger not only that our trade will lose its good name, but also that the temple of the great goddess Artemis will be discredited. . . .

NARRATOR: When they heard this, they were furious and began shouting:

CROWD: Great is Artemis of the Ephesians!

NARRATOR: Soon the whole city was in an uproar. The people seized Gaius Aristarchus, Paul's traveling companion from Macedonia, and rushed as one man into the theater. Paul wanted to appear before the crowd, but the disciples would not let him. . . .

The assembly was in confusion: Some were shouting one thing, some another. Most of the people did not even know why they were there. The Jews pushed Alexander to the front, and some of the crowd shouted instructions to him. He motioned for silence in order to make a defense before the people. But when they realized he was a Jew, they all shouted in unison for about two hours:

CROWD: Great is Artemis of the Ephesians!

NARRATOR: The city clerk quieted the crowd and said:

CITY CLERK: Men of Ephesus, doesn't all the world know that the city of Ephesus is the guardian of the temple of the great Artemis and of her image, which fell from heaven? Therefore, since these facts are undeniable, you ought to be quiet and not do anything rash. You have brought these men here, though they have neither robbed temples nor blasphemed our goddess. If, then, Demetrius and his fellow craftsmen have a grievance against anybody, the courts are open and there are proconsuls. They can press charges. . . .

NARRATOR: After he had said this, he dismissed the assembly. When the uproar had ended, Paul sent for the disciples and, after encouraging them, said good-by and set out for Macedonia.

Paul has convinced and led astray large numbers of people here in Ephesus and in practically the whole province of Asia. He says that man-made gods are no gods at all.
Acts 19:26.

OCTOBER

Words That Laugh and Cry

The kingdom of heaven is like a net that was let down into the lake and caught all kinds of fish. Matthew 13:47.

Words are powerful. They can make us laugh or cry, or feel happy or sad, or pleased or angry.

Demetrius used words to turn the city of Ephesus into an uproar. The crowd grew bigger and bigger—everyone yelling—but most of the people didn't even know why they were there.

Jesus used words to make people think, and He made comparisons to help them understand. He said the kingdom of heaven is like many different things, including a man who sowed good seed, a mustard seed, treasure hidden in a field, a pearl, and a net.

If you were to describe the mob, what sound words would you use? ______________________________

____

What colors would you use for a picture of the scene? ____________________________________

____.

Using today's text about the net as a pattern, make a comparison that shows how the mob behaved. The mob was like a ___________________________________.

In those days what Paul and the others taught about Jesus was called the Way. What sound words would you use to help someone understand about the Way? _____

____

What picture would you draw to represent it? ____

What colors would it be? ____________________

Make a comparison to describe the Way. The Way is like ____

____.

Using these ideas, create a poem, a song, or a parable that shows the contrast between God's way and the world's. Or, if you prefer, draw or paint a picture.

OCTOBER

3

Animal Farm

His disciples asked him what this parable meant. He said, "The knowledge of the secrets of the kingdom of God has been given to you, but to others I speak in parables."
Luke 8:9, 10.

Another *Animal Farm,"* Aunt Judith declared, snapping off the news.

Jayne and Kirsten looked at each other. "Squawky chickens and poke-faced pigs." Jayne's attempts to talk dissolved into giggles.

"Yes, I said *Animal Farm*." Their aunt ignored their giggles. "That's the name of a book. A satire; an allegory." She waved her hand in her schoolteacherly way. "It's about a bunch of animals that got tired of being bossed around by their farmer. They chased him off and took charge of the farm themselves, but before long the pigs took the farmer's place, making the other animals do what they said. Finally the pigs became meaner and stingier than the old farmer."

The twins looked at each other again. Both wanted to laugh, but they listened.

"It was first sold as a children's fairy story."

"Huh?" Their parents and this very aunt always warned them against silly fairy tales.

"That was long, long ago near the end of the Second World War." Aunt Judith had the girls' attention. "The author saw the dangers of Communism and wrote the book, parable-like, using animal characters to show what could happen in a Communist—or dictator-run—government. Because of the world situation, publishers were afraid to print the book at first. Then they decided to make it a children's fairy story, knowing that thinking people would understand it as a warning about government systems that take freedom away from the people. Today the news told of another country that fits the *Animal Farm* story.

"Parables teach lessons," Aunt Judith continued. "Jesus used parables to help the people understand about God. They're easy-to-listen-to stories, but for thinking people they carry deep meanings.

"My students had to read *Animal Farm*, but I always had them use studyguides to help them find the hidden meanings."

"Do Bible parables have hidden meanings?" Jayne asked.

"Most of Jesus' parables have His explanations right with the story," her aunt replied. "But the amazing thing I find is that each time I read the Bible, even with those stories I've read a hundred times before, I see something new about God's love. God not only gives us the words in the Bible, but He sends the Holy Spirit to help us understand."

OCTOBER

4

She'll Never Like Me

If you obey my commands, you will remain in my love. John 15:10.

Scuffing through the scattering of leaves that the wind had ripped off the trees overnight, Darcy trudged down the street. He kicked at a stray stone. It tumbled through the leaves, hit the curb, then skittered to mid-street. He hunched his shoulders and took a deep breath.

What'll she say? he wondered. His leg showed white behind the denim blue where the large three-cornered rip flopped open, and his elbow smarted as it chaffed against his coat sleeve.

Where'll I go? He kicked at another stone and missed. It seemed like he was good at missing—at missing all the good intentions and all the wanting-to-be-good that he carried inside of himself. And after only eight days.

He wanted to please Mom Budgely. When she'd slipped her arm across his shoulders in a quick hug the day his social worker had dropped him off at her place, he'd felt for an instant that he'd come home. *If she likes me enough, maybe she'll keep me,* he'd thought.

Moving was the story of Darcy's life—one foster place after another. He wanted to have a real home, and he'd resolved to be good so Mom Budgely would let him stay. He'd done mostly OK that first week, and at school the other fellows pretty much ignored him. Then at recess they'd starting calling him "No-Home Foster."

"Bet none of you guys could beat me to the top of this," he had yelled on impulse and threw himself against the chain-link fence that circled the schoolyard.

Nobody challenged him as he hooked himself toward the top. He'd had plenty of practice climbing fences, and he also knew that it was against the strict rules of this school. Just as he had tossed his leg across the top strand of wire and started to balance himself, the supervisor blew the whistle. That had caught him off guard. He gave himself a quick hoist, and his jeans hooked on a fence barb and tore neatly as he tumbled, off-balance, toward the ground on the other side. Instead of running, he'd let himself be taken to the counselor's office. They had talked, and the vice principal offered suspended punishment if he'd take a note to Mrs. Budgely.

She'll probably call the caseworker when she reads this, he told himself. *I can't be good no matter how hard I try. She'll never like me.*

Have you ever felt toward God like Darcy feels about Mrs. Budgely—that He'll never like you because you aren't good enough?

OCTOBER

5

It Begins With Love

My command is this: Love each other as I have loved you. John 15:12.

Darcy trudged onto the porch and forced himself to open the front door. He wanted to get everything over in a hurry. "Here," he said, going into the kitchen and handing Mom Budgely the sealed envelope with the note. He didn't even try to hide the tear in his jeans. "I'll go pack my things."

"What!" exclaimed Mom Budgely. "I thought you liked living with us!"

Darcy just pointed at the envelope. "When you read that, you'll call my caseworker."

When Mrs. Budgely finished reading, she raised her eyebrow in a question. "You want to pack because of this?"

"Well, my social worker said this is my last chance to shape up and keep the rules. If I don't, I'll go straight to a detention home. And here, well it's so nice and I wanted to be good, and . . . well . . . I guess there's no use me trying." Darcy hadn't planned to say so much, and he certainly didn't plan to get that hot, stingy feeling behind his eyes. He swiped at them with his shirt sleeve.

"This says that you climbed over the schoolyard fence."

Darcy dropped his head. "Yeah."

"It also says that due to circumstances there'll be no punishment. Then the vice principal adds that I should be very proud of you because you didn't run away or try to get out of punishment by blaming someone else."

Darcy looked up. "What?" he asked.

"Well, I *am* proud of you. You broke the rules—why on earth you'd climb that fence I'll not ask—and you faced up to what you did. You also brought this home to me." She held up the letter. "I see you also brought home some mending." She smiled and pointed to his jeans.

"Aren't you going to be mad?" Darcy asked.

"I don't like mending jeans, if that's what you mean. But I have lots of respect for honesty. That's where love begins. And Darcy, that's where keeping rules begins. That's what Jesus told His disciples. He told them to stay in His love and that if they keep His commandments, they'd stay in His love. Then He went right on to say, 'My command is this: Love each other as I have love you.' You can't keep every rule by just trying to be good on your own. When you love someone, though, you want to please that person, and that makes a difference in how you behave."

Darcy felt that he was beginning to understand.

OCTOBER

A Missionary Diary, Part 5

He will call upon me, and I will answer him; I will be with him in trouble. Psalm 91:15.

Monday, September 30, 1991—The Songa families arrived yesterday, except for Jenny, who was flown down Sabbath afternoon with baby Eric, who has malaria. Doctor Delgado gave him medicine, and, thankfully, he's better today. Malaria's tough—high fever, then chills so bad the whole bed shakes. With medicine right away, though, you can usually knock it in a hurry.

Thirty-five people had potluck lunch with us yesterday, giving us all an opportunity to visit with the Songa families. After the first night, they were well cared for. Our peace corps friends were flown directly to the U.S. They took mail and promised to phone our families to let them know we are safe. In town business goes on more or less as usual.

Tuesday—Our local friends assure us that all will go well now. The government has promised changes that make the people think life will become better. They say we should stay here—even if our own governments tell us to leave the country.

Wednesday—The government promises weren't so good after all. There's been more rioting and looting in Kinshasa, and the students at the local government university threaten to start trouble here on Monday if they don't get their exams. The seniors have been waiting several months to take their final exams, but the teachers are on strike because they haven't been paid.

Missionaries from other missions plan to leave this weekend. They advise us to go too. This could be bad.

Thursday—The mission committee is meeting now to decide what we should do. Date and I want to wait out the problem—then if something erupts to evacuate with the Belgians. Or, if we're ordered to go, to take the next plane for Europe, where it will be easier to arrange to have ADRA send relief supplies of food and medicine.

I'm not sure whether or not to seriously fill a suitcase. Or for where. Europe means winter clothes. Africa means summer. There's so much to think about! I'm so nervous that I burned Willie's and Milliam's (our workers) breakfast to smithereens! It's difficult to concentrate.

OCTOBER

7

A Missionary Diary, Part 6

But see, I have made you hard and stubborn too—as tough as they are. I have made your forehead as hard as rock. So don't be afraid of them, or fear their sullen, angry looks, even though they are such rebels. Ezekiel 3:8, 9, TLB.

Friday—I packed yesterday. Winter clothes so we could go home to Canada today. University students were threatening to burn professors' houses if they didn't get their final exams. The exams were promised long ago, and the students have been waiting. The professors still refused.

If the students start trouble—the city is such a tinderbox of nerves—the whole place could erupt into violence. We don't want to be caught in the middle of things where we can't do anything.

But we're still here. The students and teachers met, and they've reached a solution. Now the students promise that they won't start any trouble.

I find God's promise to make Ezekiel tough very encouraging. It's so easy to imagine that things will go bad, very bad, and to feel afraid. I know worrying doesn't help, but it's easy to worry. I'm afraid that I'll be afraid.

"Don't worry," Jesus said.

When I look back, I see that I've never been helped by worrying. Instead, I see that whenever I've faced serious trouble, God has always given me the necessary strength at just the right time. Remembering that gives me courage to go on. But I still feel normal, and right now normal includes a little tinge of being afraid.

We do have other reasons to feel more secure today, though. The Belgians have sent lots of soldiers and weapons just to protect all the foreigners, including the missionaries who are living and working in this country.

They're camped in the Belgian School, which is just down the street from our mission. It's only about three city blocks from our gate to theirs, but the main road leading from the airport to the president's military camp cuts between us. We don't talk about what might happen if there's a sudden movement of government troops. In 1977 our mission was trapped under cross fire between United Nations' forces, who were bunkered about where the Belgian troops are now, and invading rebels. That was a few years before we came to Africa, but there are still bullet pocks in the walls of our houses.

Now our mission is marked with a large red circle on the Belgian military map. If anyone attacks, armed soldiers will be sent to rescue us. I'm praying that will never be necessary.

OCTOBER

Stones From Heaven

Again, I tell you that if two of you on earth agree about anything you ask for, it will be done for you by my Father in heaven. Matthew 18:19.

The village had no Adventist church building, so each Sabbath the members met in a home.

"How can we build a church?" they asked themselves. "Yet no one else wants to worship with us if we don't have a church building."

But they had no good answers. There seemed no way for only seven adults to build a church in their village in that little valley high in the mountains near the equator in Africa. Their valley had no trees, the rocks near the village were too small for building, and the soil was too poor for making bricks.

Several miles away near the top of one of the steep hills were good, big rocks that would make a beautiful church, but it would take years for the seven of them to quarry enough rocks and transport them down the hill.

"God will help us," they told each other. "Somehow God will help us get a good church." Each Sabbath they continued to pray for a church.

One night the wind began to howl, rain lashed down, lightning jagged this way and that across the sky, and before one rumble of thunder had echoed away, another exploded above the mountaintops. Other crashes and booms echoed through the valley. The people huddled in their houses, afraid. The wind threatened to rip the roofs from over their heads, and all the crashing and banging made them worry that an avalanche of rock might break loose and sweep over their village.

The storm raged throughout the night; then toward daybreak it began to calm. As soon as it was light the people, including the seven Adventists, peered out of their houses, wondering if their neighbors' houses were still standing. Then they all came outside and stood and stared in amazement.

There, beside the place the seven members had chosen for building their church, lay hundreds and hundreds of rocks—stones that had crashed down the mountainside during the storm, stones that were just right for building.

The members began to build almost immediately.

Today that church is filled with many, many members who gather to worship each Sabbath. For them it is a very special church, and they call it "The Church of the Stones From Heaven."

OCTOBER

9

Lies

Commit your way to the Lord; trust in him and he will do this: He will make your righteousness shine like the dawn, the justice of your cause like the noonday sun.
Psalm 37:5, 6.

What are you going to do?"

"Leave. Look for a job someplace else." Patrick didn't have a good answer because everything had happened too quickly. Because of someone's lies, and because others believed those lies, he had been fired from his teaching job and put out of the church. And that had all happened at a mission school.

"You must be very angry."

Patrick shook his head, but it was difficult to explain how he felt. He had to leave the mission, so he went to the city and found another job in another school. That school had classes six days a week—including Sabbath. Patrick went to see the principal.

"How is it that you still want to go to church on Saturday after what happened to you at the mission?" the principal asked.

"My problem's not with God," Patrick replied. "Someone lied. That doesn't change what I believe about God and His commandments."

"You're a good teacher, and we need you," his new principal said. "For this year, you have your Sabbaths free."

Patrick went to church each Sabbath in the city. To show his sincerity, he was rebaptized, and the church welcomed him back. Then he was called to be principal of a secondary school in another area. When he and his family arrived, they found only one other person who belonged to the Adventist Church.

The three adults started holding meetings every Sabbath morning at Patrick's house. Each Sabbath more people came, and soon they needed a bigger place to meet. Before long they needed to build a church.

By the time Patrick had been principal there for two years, many of his students and neighbors decided to be baptized. Then they decided to start a church school. Children flocked to their school, and the classes were filled to overflowing. More people came to church because they wanted to learn about the things in the Bible that their children were learning at school.

Each Sabbath the church in Patrick's village is filled wall-to-wall with people who have come to learn more about God. The church, its members, and the church school—all are there because Patrick chose to remain faithful to God even though he had been treated unfairly because of someone's lies.

OCTOBER

10

For This We Give Thanks

Be joyful always, pray at all times, be thankful in all circumstances.
1 Thessalonians 5:16-18, TEV.

And for this we give thanks . . ."

Kevin recognized the signal words and was glad that his turn came last. He wasn't sure about saying out loud what he was most thankful for. He listened while one by one each person at the table added a sentence of thanks to Grandfather's prayer.

Grandmother was first. " . . . that our children and grandchildren could be here to sit with us at this table today," she said.

". . . that Daddy was able to keep the car safely on the road when we hit that slippery patch coming over the hill this morning."

Several added soft amens to what cousin Arabell said.

". . . for Bossy, Grandpa's cow, who gives such fine cream to top off Grandma's super-scrumptious pumpkin pie."

There were a few cautious chuckles because everyone knew how oldest cousin Paul loved to eat.

". . . for the sunshine and the golden leaves."

". . . for the freedom we enjoy in our great country."

". . . for an A in arithmetic's last test."

". . . for my new job."

Everyone, young and old, added something to this special prayer. Kevin wanted to say what filled his heart. He hoped the words would come out right. Then it was his turn.

". . . for my new family," he said carefully, "and for my travel safely from orphanage in Vietnam to Canada to learn to be good Canadian and good Christian and have lovely new mother and father and brother and sister and grandfather and grandmother and aunts and uncles and cousins." It took awhile to say all those words, but he wanted God—and everyone—to know how he felt.

Grandpa reached over and laid his hand on Kevin's shoulder. "And on this Thanksgiving Day we give You special thanks for the love that Kevin has added to our family. Bless him. Bless us all. And bless this abundance of food."

A hearty chorus of amens echoed around the table.

Canadians celebrate Thanksgiving on the second Monday of October. Kevin's family has the tradition of everyone joining the prayer of thanks before their meal.

What traditions of thankfulness do you have? For what are you most thankful?

OCTOBER

11

On Strike

You ought to be quiet and not do anything rash.
Acts 19:36.

"No homework?" Gabriel's mother repeated with a big question in her voice. "I distinctly remember you saying that Elder Walson promised you a Bible assignment each day this week."

"Mom! That was revenge, not a promise, so we're on strike."

"Seventh grade? On strike?"

"Yup. We're not doing the assignment tonight 'cause Elder Walson always picks on us."

"Oh?"

"And he gave Kaarlo detention for the third day in a row."

"You're not doing your assignment because Kaarlo got detention?"

"Well, it wasn't fair, and Kaarlo got mad and told us that if everyone didn't do the assignment, then no one could get in trouble. So . . . we're on strike."

"Let me see if I have this straight. Kaarlo's punished for misbehaving. He gets angry, talks up a storm, and convinces the rest of you to skip your learning opportunity this evening just to prove that he has more control of the class than the teacher."

"M-o-m!" Gabriel exclaimed.

"Well?"

"OK. It's Kaarlo's idea, but everyone clapped and cheered and promised not to do the assignment."

"I wish you had taken time to think this over and weren't just following the crowd. But . . ."

1. In what ways is Gabriel's class strike like what happened in the story of the riot in Ephesus? ________

____

2. If you were Gabriel, what would you do?

A. Go along with the strike and not do the assignment.

B. Do the assignment, but not turn it in until you saw if anyone else had done it.

C. Phone the teacher; tell him about the strike and that you were doing your homework, hoping he'd give you extra credit.

D. Phone a few of your classmates, including Kaarlo; tell them that you had decided the strike wasn't such a good idea after all and that you were going to do your homework and hand it in. Have them phone the others in the class.

Gabriel chose solution D. Everyone, including Kaarlo, did the assignment.

OCTOBER

12

The Scoffers

They were longing for a better country—a heavenly one. Hebrews 11:16.

"Fish that can fly!" The man tapped his head. "Whoever heard of such a thing!"

"He's a liar!"

"For sure!" added another. "Fish with fins they use like bat's wings—flying fish that even landed on their boat." He forced another laugh. "A great imagination—and the queen believes him! Ha!"

"He brought her 40 parrots!"

"And where's the gold?"

"He claims that will come later—that the parrots are just a promise of what's there."

In those days everyone in Europe believed that any land with parrots was a land of gold. When Christopher Columbus brought back parrots from his trip to find a shortcut to Asia, a number of people believed his claim that he had landed on the islands below China and Japan. Others accused him of coming back from that 1492 trip full of lies and tall tales.

Enough people did believe, though, and in 1493 Columbus again sailed westward to what he thought was Asia, only this time he commanded 17 ships and had about 1,000 passengers, who took along their cows and horses and pigs and sheep and intended to make their fortunes on the rich, romantic islands.

This trip took him south of the Bahamas, where he had landed the year before, to Dominica, Jamaica, and Puerto Rico. It began what is called the Columbian Exchange.

Before the travels of Columbus, Europeans had never heard of potatoes, corn, tomatoes, or tobacco. Neither had there been animals such as horses, cows, sheep, chickens, or pigs in the New World, nor did bananas, peaches, oranges, or cabbages grow there. But Columbus changed all that.

Before Columbus' time, sugar was a luxury—most of the people used it only when they were sick to help the medicine taste better. Columbus carried a few pieces of sugar cane in his ships and found that it grew easily on the tropical islands where he landed. By the mid-1700s African slaves were taken there to cultivate vast cane plantations—and Europe was hooked on sugar!

Christopher Columbus looked for a shorter route to the riches of Asia. He made four trips, carrying settlers to the islands he reached, but he died never knowing for sure that he had discovered the "New World" of the Americas.

Are you looking for a better country—a new world?

OCTOBER

13

Love Yourself

Doesn't she love herself?"

"Stupid question! She's so stuck on herself that she doesn't even see anyone else."

"That's 'cause she doesn't love herself."

Pieces of the pointed conversation intended just for her jabbed at Mayline's thoughts. *They don't understand!* A heavy weight seemed to be pressing against her chest. *I can't stand the way everyone picks on me.*

"He's weird. Can't see past his own nose. Weird and dumb! His face'd crack if he'd ever smile."

Reg tossed in his bed. The remarks he'd overheard were throbbing in his thoughts. He hurt. *If I could find someone. Just someone who'd be my friend.*

✦ ✦ ✦

Both Mayline and Reg are angry and hurt because of the way they've been treated. Both want to have friends and to be kind, friendly people, but neither seems to know how.

"If you want to have friends, be friendly" is good advice. But no one has ever shown them how. There's an easy starting place, though, for anyone with a friendship problem.

God is love, and He cares about our problems. He also wants us to love our neighbors. To do this, Mayline and Reg need to get to know God better, because knowing God is learning about love. They also need to learn to love themselves as God's children and to tell Him exactly how they feel, giving specific problems instead of just praying "Please send me a friend."

God won't fail to help, but the help He sends may be a guidance counselor or a book about personalities. The suggestions they get may not be easy to follow, and changes may take a long time, but their lives can be happier—if they are willing to choose God's way.

Sometimes God sends another person who is willing to take the chance of being friends with someone who seems unfriendly and even weird. If you were to help either Reg or Mayline, where would you begin? ______

____

What five friendship "rules" would you give them to follow?

1. ______________________________
2. ______________________________
3. ______________________________
4. ______________________________
5. ______________________________

The entire law is summed up in a single command: "Love your neighbor as yourself." Galatians 5:14.

OCTOBER

14

A Sabbath Problem

I will bless those who always observe the Sabbath and do not misuse it. I will bless those who do nothing evil.
Isaiah 56:2, TEV.

It's Friday afternoon. Your dad's an Adventist pastor, and he and your older sister have gone to a weekend conference, leaving you at home with your mother and baby brother. Twenty minutes before sundown your mother is sliding the Sabbath dessert into the refrigerator when your baby brother pads up behind her on all fours, pulls himself up, and grabs at his carton of milk. Your mother tries to stop the action, but with a crazy topple, the carton sloshes milk down her skirt, over the baby, and lands on its top, quickly glubbing the rest onto the floor.

Your mother scoops up the dripping baby, calls for you to bring the mop, and heads for the bathroom.

Mopping up a half gallon of milk is no half-minute job. As the hands of the clock move toward that magic minute of sundown, you're sponging up what you know is all the baby's milk—leaving him none for the Sabbath. Your parents have taught you well about guarding the edges of the Sabbath. What do you do?

1. Mop up the milk quickly, then take your bike to the nearest store and buy another carton of milk—even though you know you'll never make it by sundown and even though you have to go past Mrs. Clutcheon's place. She's your nearest Adventist neighbor and has the reputation for seeing—and commenting on—everything.

2. Leave the milk, even though it's starting to seep under the edges of the fridge and the cupboard, try to make it to the store before sundown, then come home and finish cleaning up the milk.

3. Tell your mother that it's the baby's own fault that he dumped the milk, and even though he's only 13 months old, he may as well start learning now to live with his mistakes and just do without milk until the Sabbath is over.

4. Clean up the milk, get your mom's permission to go to Mrs. Clutcheon to see if by any chance she has milk you can borrow for the baby for over Sabbath. You're positive that she doesn't. Then if she doesn't, go buy some.

5. Clean up the milk, then as soon as your mom's changed, offer to watch the baby and suggest that she drive around by the back way to a store on the other side of town, where no one knows her, and buy some more milk there.

6. ____

____

OCTOBER

15

Little Black Cloud

Therefore keep watch, because you do not know on what day your Lord will come. Matthew 24:42.

One Wednesday evening during the prayer meeting that used to meet at our house when I was in first grade, I listened as the adults talked about the end of the world.

"We'll see a little black cloud in the sky," Mrs. Heldt commented. "It'll be small, just half the size of a person's hand," she said, holding up her fist. "That will be Jesus coming with His angels."

I made a fist with my hand. *Just this size and black,* I told myself. I understood that as it got closer it would look bigger and bigger.

The older folks talked about the other things that would happen as the cloud came closer—thunder and lightning and earthquakes—and about how the wicked people would run to hide from Jesus.

"Keep watch," they said, quoting the Bible.

I took the advice quite literally. Many afternoons after school I'd stand behind my grandfather's woodshed, where there was a clear view of the sky, and scan the clouds for one that would be tiny and black. If I'd see one in even a suspicious gray, I'd get scared and watch it closely to see whether or not it would come closer and get bigger. And I'd hope that when the thunder and lightning and earthquakes started, I wouldn't get so frightened that I'd run and hide with the wicked people.

Other folks admit having watched the clouds for the same reason when they were younger. Have you ever watched—and been afraid that Jesus might be coming? What makes you feel afraid? ______________________

____

As the years slipped by, I learned that "keeping watch" doesn't mean to look for a little black cloud. Rather, it means to choose to have a friendship with Jesus and to get to know Him really well. That takes the scariness out of ideas about His second coming.

Why would having Jesus as a friend make the idea of His coming less scary? ______________________

____

Jesus has promised to return to take us back with Him to heaven, and He says that the time of His coming will be a surprise.

I'm looking forward to the surprise of seeing that little black cloud. Aren't you?

OCTOBER

16

A Missionary Diary, Part 7

So keep up your courage. Acts 27:25.

On Friday Date visits the Belgian colonel in charge. The soldiers are getting homesick, they have to be in uniform at all times, and they can't leave their camp. "It's a vicious circle," the colonel explains.

They're here to protect the expats—short for expatriates, or foreigners. Because they're here, the expats won't leave. Since the expats won't leave, the soldiers have to stay. They stay, and the expats won't leave.

They probably wish something would happen so . . .

"Madam." Milliam, my helper, has slipped in by my desk. "The vegetable ladies are here."

The three ladies, with their bundles of fresh fruit and vegetables, stop at our mission each morning. Times are hard now—for everyone. I try to buy something from each of them. If we don't need all the food, our African neighbors do. All the beds in the hospitals are full, and the halls are lined with sick people lying on mats. Too many people are too hungry and have no strength to fight all the sicknesses that are going around.

The weather is just changing from the long, dry season, when the temperatures are comfortable, to the hot, rainy season. Many people always get sick—especially with malaria—when the rains start. This year it's worse, much worse. Prices have gone way up and wages haven't. Most families no longer earn enough to buy the food they need. They can't even think of buying medicine.

We're missionaries, and our job is to help. But the problem is too big for us to solve. We can give food and medicine and clothes to only a few in comparison with the many who suffer.

We live in a comfortable house in a land that's always like spring or summer. The window across from my desk frames palm trees and flowers; the mangoes will soon be ripe; a dozen different kinds of birds are singing; our cat is curled up on a patio chair, snoozing; the sky is a beautiful, clean blue; it's warm and comfortable. Everything seems so peaceful that I find it hard to believe that within two blocks of where I'm writing this soldiers are on the alert because trouble is brewing, and we may have to run for our lives.

There's a suitcase in the closet—packed—and I have other things organized so we can grab them in a moment's notice. But I don't want to leave our African friends and neighbors, who have to stay and face whatever happens.

OCTOBER

17

A Missionary Diary, Part 8

Like a scarecrow in a melon patch, their idols cannot speak; they must be carried because they cannot walk. Jeremiah 10:5.

We've just learned that soldiers have forced or shot their way into every store, business, and big house in the main part of the town where Pastor Mande lives. Since his house is next to a large store, the soldiers might have thought he owned the store. They shot the lock off the door, burst into the house, and pointed their guns at the pastor and his wife.

"Do you have any arms [guns]?" one of the soldier's demanded.

"Yes," replied the pastor.

"Get them for us!"

A soldier with a gun followed the pastor. The pastor went to his table and picked up his Bible. "This is my protection," he said, holding it up.

The soldiers laughed roughly. "We won't find much here," they said. "This is just a poor pastor."

They grabbed two suitcases in which the pastor and his wife stored some of their things, fired shots into the ceiling, and left.

Pastor Mande's faith is in Someone much stronger than soldiers or idols or anything or anyone else, for that matter.

Jeremiah says that idols are like scarecrows—they can't talk or walk, and they have to be fastened in place with hammer and nails so that they won't fall.

Our church doesn't have idols, but does that always keep you from worshiping things that can't walk or talk?

Mark any of the following things that you think could become an idol. How could that happen?

___ books	___ money	___ videos	___ work
___ music	___ clothes	___ food	___ computers
___ school	___ people	___ Bible games	___ jewelry
___ furniture	___ shoes	___ pictures	___ sports

If you faced a soldier with a gun, could you hold up your Bible, as Pastor Mande did, and say "This is my protection"? Or are there scarecrows that come between you and God?

OCTOBER

18

The Amber Sunglasses

They will call on my name and I will answer them. Zechariah 13:9.

A solid mass of angry gray barred the horizon in front of the mission plane.

"I wish I knew what happened to my amber sunglasses!" Bob squinted as he scanned the cloud bank for an opening. "I've looked everywhere. In the guest room. In my flight case. In the plane."

Everyone on the mission knew that he had lost his glasses. "They help me see much more clearly when it's cloudy," he'd explained. Folks prayed that he would find them before he needed them.

I stared at the solid wall of clouds and wondered if we'd make it to the REACH International school project we planned to visit. As if reading my thoughts, Bob said, "Looks like there may be an opening there to the left. If I had my glasses I could tell . . . Wonder if they might have got in with my tools in the back?" As if by force of habit, he reached down to his flight case standing between our seats, where he usually kept them, flipped up the double flaps, and reached in.

"My glasses!" he exclaimed, quickly putting them on. "There—on top of everything. And I'd looked! Several times! Took everything out, turned it upside down, shook it . . . The angels are with us."

With the glasses he easily found his way through the clouds, and we landed safely at the school.

Sometimes God does help us in remarkable ways. At other times He seems to ignore our prayers. Accidents. War. Crime. These and other bad things happen even when good people pray. Does that mean God doesn't care? Think of John the Baptist. Crowds flocked to hear him preach and to be baptized by him. God's Spirit was with him. Then, not long after he baptized Jesus, Herod threw him in prison. Questions played in John's mind, and he sent two of his men to ask Jesus if He was really the Messiah.

Instead of answering directly, Jesus told them to tell John what they saw and heard. Jesus didn't perform any miracle to free John. He didn't even send him a special message. A few months later John was beheaded. Had God forgotten him?

John's story is sad, but it gives a good answer to the question about God's care. After John's disciples left, Jesus told the people, "There is no one greater than John."

God *does* care, even when He doesn't perform a special miracle.

OCTOBER

19

When God Turns His Back

The angel of the Lord encamps around those who fear him, and he delivers them. Psalm 34:7.

Angels do help—several Bible stories prove that.

Angels rushed Lot, his wife, and his daughters out the gates of Sodom and away from the blazing inferno that came down on their city.

An angel awakened Peter and took him out of the heavily guarded prison in which he was being held.

An angel visited Cornelius with a message from God.

Even today we hear stories of people being miraculously rescued.

War raged through the country. It was dangerous to be out, but Pastor Samuel wanted to visit his members and encourage them. While he was at one house, raiding soldiers stormed through the door.

"You. You're working with the enemy," they yelled at him. "Come with us."

Two soldiers grabbed him, pulled him outside, and forced him to stand against the garden wall. "This is what we do to the enemies of our people," one said. Another raised his gun.

Pastor Samuel saw him start to squeeze his finger on the trigger. It happened fast, yet every detail seemed to stamp itself on his mind. *This is the end,* he thought, trying to form a prayer for the safety of his family as he watched that trigger finger tensing.

Just then the pastor felt himself jerked upward. An instant later he landed on his feet at the edge of the cornfield on the other side of the wall. "Run!" he heard a voice urging. "Run!"

He ran, zigzagging through the tall plants.

Pastor Samuel is one of several who relate stories about how their lives were miraculously spared.

But what about yesterday's question? What about the horrible accidents and murders when God didn't send His angels, and so good people died even though they prayed and trusted God to send His angels? Does that mean that God didn't hear? Or that He doesn't care? Or that He isn't fair?

Suppose someone dies in an earthquake. What is the next thing that person will know? Jesus' second coming, isn't it? Can you imagine him or her being annoyed and saying, "But I prayed for Your angels. Why didn't You send them to save me? Let me go back and get on with my life on earth!"

Such a conversation on the way to heaven is unthinkable, isn't it? Because of sin, God had to stand back and watch Jesus die on the cross. Even now God sometimes has to stand back and watch His children die.

OCTOBER

20

October

Each season of the year writes a message in nature that tells something of God's creative power. October is a month of change. In the northern part of the world its story goes something like this:

Yellow leaves
scuffling in the breeze
scatter rumpled memories
of summer's shade.
They whisper hints
of frosty winds
and powdery snow,
nudging thought toward skis
and conquest of
the distant slopes.

South of the equator October turns thoughts toward hot, summer days and Christmas on the beach.

No matter where you live—city or country—and no matter whether it's fall or spring, cold or hot, wet or dry, you can see signs of God's seasons. The colors you see, the sounds you hear, the textures you feel, the scents you smell, the flavors you taste, tell you that it's October.

Look out a window, if possible, for help in doing the following.

1. What are the three main colors that you see? ______

2. Give three or more sounds that you hear—use sound words to describe them. ______

3. If you were outside, what are three of the textures that you could feel—walls, tree trunks, etc.? Describe how each would feel to your hand. ______

4. What can you smell now? ______

5. What's your favorite fresh food—fruit or vegetable—that you can get to eat now? ______

Look back at your answers. Which are true only at this time of year? Which are caused strictly by God and nature? Are any of them caused by people alone? Which are the result of people working with something that God has created?

Using the words from your answers, create a poem or a song about October, or use the ideas to paint an October picture.

The heavens declare the glory of God; the skies proclaim the work of his hands. Psalm 19:1.

OCTOBER

21

When the Chickens Come Home

Let us acknowledge the Lord; let us press on to acknowledge him. As surely as the sun rises, he will appear. Hosea 6:3.

Marcelline looked puzzled when she heard the question. "When does the Sabbath begin?" she repeated. "Well . . ." She paused. She couldn't remember hearing about the exact time it began. In her home near the equator the days are always about the same length, and the sun goes down at about the same time each evening.

"Oh, I know," she said at last. "The Sabbath begins when the chickens come home to roost."

For those like Marcelline who live near the equator, keeping the Sabbath really is from even to even, because the sun sets at about the same time year round. They have no need for a sunset calendar to remind them of the Sabbath hours, because when the sun slides behind the horizon, darkness will fall quickly. The chickens know that too, and as soon as the light of the sun begins to slant from low in the sky, they hurry home.

Marcelline's right. The Sabbath hours do begin in her home on Friday evening when the chickens come home to roost.

The movement of the earth in its rotation on its axis and its path around the sun has been so constant throughout the centuries that scientists can tell within a fraction of a second when to expect the sun to rise or set at any place on any date. (The rotation of the earth on its axis is slowing down gradually, and every few years scientists must add a "leap second."

Marcelline has learned about that in school and about the lands within the Arctic Circle. But she can't imagine what it would be like to live where there's almost no night in midsummer and certainly not when there's almost no day in midwinter. She's never been where the weather becomes so cold that gardens can't grow or that the chickens can't go out. She's never seen snow nor felt the smooth coldness of ice.

She also knows that even though the time of sunrise and sunset can be precisely determined for any particular place in the world, two people living in the same area can have different amounts of sunlight on the same day. This depends upon the person and the conditions. One may live in a house on a hill, and the other in a house in a valley. One may spend most of the day indoors, and the other may work outside.

God is as sure as the sunrise and the sunset. He's as sure as the beginning of His Sabbath on each Friday evening. You may know about this as well as Marcelline knows about the land of the midnight sun. But do you know God?

OCTOBER

Judd Denis and the Second Coming

No one knows about that day or hour, not even the angels in heaven, nor the Son, but only the Father. Matthew 24:36.

Judd Denis was an ordinary man who lived on an ordinary street in an ordinary town. He worked hard, lived a more or less honest life, and went to church sometimes. He never had reached his dreams, though, of being rich and having a big house and a fancy car. Another year passed. It seemed he'd never have anything better. Then one day Judd Denis heard a radio preacher.

"The Lord has revealed his secrets to me," claimed the speaker. "He will return to this earth on August 1 of next year."

Judd Denis listened. Maybe the Lord had spoken. Maybe He was coming on August 1 and maybe that would give him, Judd Denis, the chance of his dreams. On January 2 Judd went to see his banker. He borrowed enough money to buy a fancy sports car and a beautiful big house with an enormous swimming pool. If the world was indeed ending in eight months, he would make those the best eight months he'd ever had. What's more, he would never have to pay for a thing, because he had signed a contract making the entire repayment due on August 15.

For eight months Judd Denis enjoyed his house and his pool and his car. He was so busy enjoying himself that he never bothered to think of what would happen when the Lord did come. Nor did he stop to think that possibly the Lord wouldn't come.

August 1 arrived, and it was a day like any other day.

Judd Denis went to bed that evening thinking it would be his last night on earth. On the morning of August 2 he woke up. Everything was still the same—the house, the pool, and the car.

"The Lord hasn't come!" he exclaimed. And suddenly Judd Denis felt worse than he had ever felt in his entire life.

The preacher had been wrong, and on August 15 he, Judd Denis, had to pay the bank hundreds of thousands of dollars.

The time of Jesus' second coming is the best-kept secret in the whole universe. On October 22, 1844, 150 years ago today, the first Adventists, like Judd Denis, expected Jesus to come. They hadn't been living for themselves, though, like Judd. Instead they'd been studying their Bibles and eagerly preparing to go to heaven. But they'd misunderstood the prophecy.

Are you waiting for Jesus to come? Are you using your waiting time to get to know Him better so that you will feel at home in heaven?

OCTOBER

23

Books

And that from childhood you have known the Holy Scriptures, which are able to make you wise for salvation through faith which is in Christ Jesus. 2 Timothy 3:15, NKJV.

Dianne and I both love books, and no matter where we go we'll find a bookstore just as quickly as a 5-year-old can spot a toy shop. So of course when we stopped at the visitors' center in the Great Smoky Mountains National Park, we found ourselves in the bookshop. Big books in full-color photo dust jackets stood temptingly on the shelves—but we'd come to browse, not to buy. Then I found a small, drab, olive-and-tan volume that seemed to have sneaked itself in among the fancier books. Even its title was plain—*Camping and Woodcraft*.

I like the outdoors, but I'm no camper. As I glanced through the book, though, I saw answers to questions I had wondered about for many years.

Dianne watched. "Do you want to buy it?"

"It has very useful information," I said while at the same time thinking of my bulging suitcase that was already at check-in maximum for going back to Africa. "Maybe it'd squeeze into my carryon."

She reached for it, taking the decision out of my hands, and went to the cash desk. "For your birthday," she said.

And so on the shelf by the desk in my writing room in Africa I have a camping handbook from the Great Smoky Mountains in America—an old book written more than 70 years ago that talks about outdated equipment. But the author was an outdoorsman who spent much of his time in the wilderness and knew what he was writing about. The basic information is still good anywhere in the world.

Dianne hadn't looked in the book, and she didn't know how old it was—she knew only that I wanted it.

Our friendship has a lot to do with books and writing. We became acquainted because she'd read an article I'd written, and then she wrote a letter to say how much she liked it. Since then we've become very good friends. We read and share a wide variety of books by many different authors, but nearly all those books have one thing in common—in one way or another each is about another book, a very old book that we both like best of all the books we've ever read.

That book, the Bible, was written a very long time ago by people who knew what they were writing about. Even though times have changed, the message is still good—in fact, it's the best news in the whole world.

OCTOBER

24

A Missionary Diary, Part 9

The wisdom of the prudent is to give thought to their ways. Proverbs 14:8.

Sunday. October 20, 1991—"The Belgians say we should be prudent today." The message Glynis just brought fits with what we've been hearing from the Americans. "In other words, if you have to go out, look before you drive," she explained. "Don't turn onto a side street without first checking to see that it's clear. They're expecting trouble, and you don't want to get caught in a mob!"

We've had other warnings to be prepared for full-scale trouble today or tomorrow. Lubumbashi is the main city in the country untouched by riots, and local folks want to keep it that way. This is the beginning of paydays, though, and if the promised raises aren't paid to the military, the teachers, and all the other government workers . . .

Monday—A very normal day with no problems.

Tuesday morning—very early (1:15 a.m.)—We've been up about two hours. Dr. Delgado's pounding on our door awakened us. He'd heard shooting in town. We're packed. There's some shooting, and cars are racing down our street toward the Belgian school. Racing? A heavy downpour ended just before the shooting started. I heard two cars hit the brakes for the stop sign at our corner, then slide across the intersection.

Two truckloads of soldiers just went by. According to the "net" (the missionary walkie-talkie network), looting is in progress in town with shooting both in the air and on the ground. Sporadic. Whether it's revenge for no pay or dissatisfaction with the government is not known at this point.

Date just came in from "circulating" around the mission with James and Martin. I'm washing clothes and boiling drinking water—we always boil water for drinking—and listening to the "net" to keep in touch with what's happening in town. Actually, I have three radios with three different broadcasts on—the net, the local radio station, and the BBC shortwave.

The local announcer just said, "If you're troubled with insomnia, we're here. A message from the governor's office says, 'Stay inside and keep calm. We're getting the situation under control.'

"Stay calm," the announcer repeats. She sounds calm, and her voice is reassuring. "Don't trouble your neighbor. There'll be a solution with the help of the Lord."

OCTOBER

25

A Missionary Diary, Part 10

Though you already know all this, I want to remind you that the Lord delivered his people out of Egypt. Jude 5.

Tuesday morning—continued. 1:35 a.m.—"Stay inside and stay calm," the Voice of Zaire radio announcer repeats. She goes on to compare these hungry and troubled times with the wanderings of the children of Israel in the wilderness when God sent them manna to eat and saved them from serpents. "The Lord will protect and help us, too," she says.

But how can anyone sleep tonight?

On the "net" two Zairians who work for the Methodist mission are downtown, watching from their windows, whispering reports to each other—sometimes in French, sometimes in Swahili. Soldiers with guns are chasing the guards away from the stores, clearing the streets, shooting open doors, breaking windows, and shooting into the air. Others are pushing inside, taking things—everything they can carry.

"I see a man with a mattress on his head," whispers one.

"Somebody's trying to open the gate of a mission house," says the other. "Wait. I'll go where I can see better." Silence. Then: "A soldier has come with a gun, and he's talking to the man. Now the man's leaving."

In the meantime the public radio announcer talks about loving our neighbors.

2:15 a.m.—Date and the others were just at the Belgian school. The officers encouraged everyone to come there till morning. We prefer to stay where we are since we're so close. Most of the Belgian soldiers are downtown—evacuating folks who are trapped there.

7:15 a.m.—According to the "net," the town is destroyed—stores emptied, shelves torn out, doors and windows broken, books and papers littering the streets. There's another peppering of shots. The Belgian troops are bringing more expats to the school. Around 4:00 this morning the Songa missionaries went over, and by 6:00 a.m. James estimated that at least 500 people were there. We spent the remainder of the night on couches in the living room—safer than in the bedroom.

Our Anglican missionary friends, the Nashes, are being brought now. They're in a tricky corner of town, and the soldiers gave them exactly five minutes to get their things and go.

My suitcase weighed more than 70 pounds, so I repacked, keeping just a sleeping bag and a few clothes and important papers. My little computer and printer are in a small backpack, so—if we have to leave—I'm ready to go.

OCTOBER

A Missionary Diary, Part 11

The Lord redeems his servants; no one will be condemned who takes refuge in him. Psalm 34:22.

Tuesday morning—continued. 10:00 a.m.—This is one of those days that seem to go on forever. There's still shooting—most of it sounds like a bunch of firecrackers popping off, except for the shots close by. The men say at least one tracer bullet came down on the mission during the night.

The Nashes just sent out a plea on "net"—does someone have a pair of shoes that might fit one of their little boys? In their hurried evacuation he came away in bare feet. Glynis called back that she has a pair that they're welcome to have.

10:35 a.m.—A single shot was just fired in front of the mission—scary! I was just with Mrs. Mwema, wife of the mission president, and her girls. Solva, her son, came by and told us about a little boy carrying a little box. He met the child coming down the street by the mission.

"You look tired," Solva said.

"I am," the boy said. "My parents sent me to get things from the stores, and I've worked hard and taken many things. But every time I got something, the older men would come and take it away from me. This is all I have left, and I'm very tired."

And he trudged on his way, carrying his one little box.

I'm tired too—from not sleeping.

Many parents have sent their children downtown to take whatever they can find. I'm not sure if they think of it as stealing now. Milliam has come to see what we're going to do. "I could never take anything, or send my little boy," she said. "That's not good."

A few billows of smoke mark where some stores have been set on fire. Otherwise, it's a very beautiful day—sunny and warm and the birds singing very loudly.

We've just been told that the Belgians are starting to fly people out of the country. If we want to leave, we must register now. They say it's not safe to stay. Date and I talk it over—it's time for us to go. I'll fly. Date'll drive—if the soldiers will escort vehicles to the Zambian border.

1:30 p.m.—We've just arrived at the Belgian school—the last missionaries to leave our mission. It's sad just to walk out and leave everything. Our things. Our African friends. We don't know if we'll ever see them again.

OCTOBER

27

A Missionary Diary, Part 12

Always give thanks for everything to God the Father. Ephesians 5:20, TEV.

Tuesday Afternoon—continued.

The huge tree scattered a comfortable shade over our group. Sometimes we talked, but a lot of the time we just sat. People passed—alone, in pairs, in clusters; adults, children. Others, like us, sat in shady places. Voices and children's laughter and footsteps on the walkways and a man talking on a loudspeaker blended to give a comfortable feeling like being at camp meeting. Only this wasn't camp meeting, and another staccato of gunfire reminded us of why we were there.

"Do you suppose you'll come back?" My question broke the silence that had settled over us again.

"It depends on what our people say, but I can't imagine not coming back." Gillian smiled, but it was the kind of smile that comes when you're tired and sad and wondering what to do.

It was still Wednesday. Gillian, Walter, and their two boys had come to the school with the Belgian soldiers before we arrived. Then local friends brought word that just after they'd left, their house was totally looted and the furniture and anything that couldn't be carried away was smashed and broken and their books and papers were torn and scattered along the road. Everything they now possessed was in the back of their car.

"What're we going to do?" asked 7-year-old Gavin.

"Well, we'll have to ask God about it," said Gillian.

"Of course that," returned Gavin, "but what else?"

The Belgians had assigned a classroom to each group, but they were very crowded, so that night Walter and Gillian pitched a borrowed tent under the tree where we sat. Other friends, the Bradfields, pitched a tent beside theirs, and we parked our camper beside the tents.

Gillian and Walter have taught the boys that they must always tell God thank You before they add a please to their prayers. The thank-You didn't come until the next night.

"I wish we hadn't lost all our stuff, God," prayed Gavin. "But thank You that we can have a real live adventure and sleep in a tent and have a picnic for every meal."

Do you remember to tell God thank You—even when things go bad? What unhappy thing has happened to you or your family recently? ____________________

____

What thank You can you tell God about it? ______

____

OCTOBER

28

A Missionary Diary, Part 13

I will come back and take you to be with me that you also may be where I am. John 14:3.

Wednesday

"Everyone listed for the first flight, please go to the parking lot."

The announcement came over the loudspeaker sooner than I'd expected. I pulled my suitcase out of the pickup, slipped on my backpack, and headed toward the parking lot. It was Wednesday morning. Date had gone to the mission to check on things. I hoped he'd be back so we could at least say goodbye.

We were loaded onto the back of three big, open trucks—armed soldiers on each. A pickup loaded with armed soldiers drove in front of us; another followed. Date did come before we loaded, and as we drove out through the school gates, he was filming us with his video camcorder.

As we turned onto the street, I saw Milliam standing by the side of the road. She was crying. We'd left food and money for her—there was nothing else we could do except pray for her safety.

"I'll be back!" I shouted. I clung to the rail as the truck picked up speed. "I'm coming back! I'm coming back!"

In a C-130 troop transport plane we were flown to Brazzaville, where we were able to arrange for commercial flights to our homes. Three nights later I landed in Washington, D.C., and spent the next four months with friends and family in North America. Date spent three weeks in Zambia and then went back to continue the ADRA work in Zaire. Our mission, our house, and our things were not harmed. Most of the other missionaries, including Walter and Gillian, were also able to return.

In John 14:1-3 Jesus tells His disciples that He's going to heaven but that He'll come back to get them. It's one of my favorite Bible promises. Researchers say it is probably the most favorite of all the Bible promises.

What are your favorite Bible promises? __________

____

Why? __________________________________

____

OCTOBER

29

The Goose Story

Your promises have been thoroughly tested, and your servant loves them. Psalm 119:140.

Rog leaned forward in his chair to listen better.

"By flying in a V pattern," the speaker continued, "geese gain 70 percent more speed. They often change leaders, each taking its turn so that one bird won't be worn out by always breaking the wind and setting the pace. Another marvelous fact is that if one is injured or sick and has to drop out of the group, two other geese will always go down to stay with it.

"For example, if one bird is shot by a hunter and falls, two others will go to its aid."

A question immediately formed in Rog's mind. Uncle George and his friends had taken him hunting. One of the men had shot a goose. When the bird fell, none of the others went to help. Instead they'd all scattered as fast as they could fly.

"Is it true that geese *always* take turns at being leader?" he asked Uncle George when he saw him later that week. "And do they really gain 70 percent speed by flying in a V instead of a straight line?" Uncle George worked in waterfowl conservation and knew lots about geese.

"I don't know that anyone has ever been able to follow a flock for a long enough distance to answer those questions for sure," Uncle George answered. "Some biologists think that geese change leaders when they fly, but they haven't been able to prove that's something they *always* do. Or if *all* the adult geese take turns."

"What about the speed?" Rog asked.

"Well, our office has nearly all the papers documenting research on geese. I've never seen any proof that they gain speed by flying in a V. Certainly not 70 percent, if they do at all. Where did you get these ideas?"

"A speaker at church used them to show something about God and creation. While he was talking, I thought about how you say a scientist needs to ask the right questions in the right places to see if things test true."

Uncle George nodded. "That's always a good idea," he said, "for everyone. Even when someone makes claims about God, check those claims. Always go to the Bible." He put his hand on Rog's shoulder. "Make sure you know the truth—especially the truth about God."

OCTOBER

30

The Story

Shemaiah has prophesied to you, even though I did not send him, and has led you to believe a lie. Jeremiah 29:31.

Gerry tilted the oak office chair back and propped his feet, oldtime newspaper-editor style, on the heavy wood desk. He was the youngest reporter on staff, but he thought of himself as an old-fashioned small-town newspaper reporter who someday would become a famous writer. Just then Jan walked by.

"Hey, Jan," he called, "I need your help."

"Sure, Gerry." She paused in the doorway.

"I've got this great story idea—something that will really catch the readers—but we need you to write it."

"What story?"

"About the witches' coven in town." Gerry smiled mischievously.

"Gerry!"

"It'd be a great joke to make folks think that we have our own witches right here—that a group has moved in from one of their exotic city places."

"Oh, no!" Jan gave Gerry one of her disgusted looks and shook her head emphatically.

"C'mon, Jan."

She shook her head again.

"All we need is to use your name."

"Gerry! What have you done?" she asked suspiciously.

"Nothing yet. But we need something to liven up the paper. Chick's got some pictures he'll doctor in the darkroom. I've got these great ideas for a make-believe interview. All we need is to use your name."

"My name, Gerry? Whatever for?"

"Well, when folks see your name by an article, they believe what they read. For some reason, they don't always believe what I write." He paused. "I don't know why."

"Sorry, Gerry, but folks have enough worries these days without our trying to make them believe lies like that. Besides, I don't want to be involved in any story that might make them doubt my name."

The story was never written.

Why do you think the newspaper readers did not always believe what Gerry wrote?

Why did Jan refuse to help him write the story?

OCTOBER

31

Halloween Traditions

And if you spend yourselves in behalf of the hungry and satisfy the needs of the oppressed, then your light will rise in the darkness, and your night will become like the noonday. Isaiah 58:10.

Halloween means hallowed or holy evening—the perfect name for an evening to go out and collect food and money to help the needy. But that's not how it got its name.

Halloween—or Allhallows' Eve—is observed only in the United States, Canada, and Great Britain. Many hundreds of years ago the pagan people of the British Isles ended their year on October 31 and had their New Year's Day on November 1. They believed that spirits of the dead were freed to visit their old homes on New Year's Eve. They also believed in witches. So they built huge bonfires to frighten away the witches and to light up the countryside to help visiting ghosts find their way home. In order to fool the real ghosts into thinking that they were ghosts too, the people wore weird costumes.

When missionary monks arrived from Rome, many of the people accepted Christianity. Their New Year's became Allhallows' or All Saints' Day in honor of the dead saints, and it was observed with big feasts. The poor Irish peasants began going out on Allhallows' Eve to beg for food and for money to buy special treats for their feast.

From these traditions came the idea for the costumes and trick-or-treating associated with our Halloween. The Americans added the idea of tricking. Black cats became a favorite Halloween decoration not only because they're considered unlucky, but also because the ancient Britons believed people were changed into cats as punishment for evil deeds. The Scottish made the first jack-o'-lanterns by hollowing out large turnips and putting faces on them. And an old Irish tale explains that a man named Jack couldn't go to heaven because of his stinginess. The devil didn't want him either, because of the practical jokes he played. So he was condemned to walk the earth with his lantern.

People today are fascinated with ancient traditions, and imitate practices of the past in an effort to come into contact with supernatural powers.

How much better to make contact with God, the greatest power in all the universe, and to follow His advice of "spending ourselves in behalf of the hungry."

The traditional Pathfinder activity of collecting canned goods for food hampers is one good way of doing this.

NOVEMBER

1

Big and Creepy

Sin is crouching at your door. It wants to rule you, but you must overcome it. Genesis 4:7, TEV.

Lanelle screeched and dashed for a can of spray. Dropping to her knees, she sent some wisps of insecticide under the cupboard where she'd seen a flat, leathery body disappear.

"Environmental friendly," she read on the label. "Well, I certainly hope it clears that—that—thing from my environment. It's big—and creepy!"

She shuddered.

Most people feel the same way as Lanelle does about cockroaches. They're ugly and disgusting. They're dirty, and they might carry diseases.

Cockroaches like dark, damp places and eat food, garbage, clothing, furniture, book bindings, and other insects. Even though they look enormous, their bodies are actually quite thin, and they can slide through tiny cracks and into surprisingly narrow hiding places. They're also very fast, and on their strong, equal-sized legs they can outrun almost every other insect.

At night when it's dark they like to roam about, clambering over cupboards and into anything that seems to be a good place to find food. They've been found inside refrigerators, microwave oven doors, and even in the microphone for a ham radio. But if they happen to be out and about and a light is turned on, they scurry for cover and quickly go into hiding.

Usually they can be kept out of the house by having everything clean and dry and by using roach killers in their favorite hiding places. But they're very hardy, very persistent, and very good at sneaking in along water pipes and then hiding out in cracks around sinks or other places where it's warm and moist. Sometimes they'll ride in on fruit or vegetables and then just hide any old place, and just when you're sure they've all been cleaned out, another one suddenly comes scurrying out of some unexpected spot.

I've never heard of any "save the cockroach" campaigns, nor have I read about the good they do, so why use an entire devotional page to talk about them? Well, they're like sin. They have a habit of showing up when you least expect them.

What are some other ways that cockroaches are like sin? What is the best way to deal with sin?

NOVEMBER

2

Princess and the Curtains

This calls for patient endurance on the part of the saints who obey God's commandments and remain faithful to Jesus. Revelation 14:12.

Princess had sleek tawny fur and was just plump enough to be cute. She had wise yellow-green eyes that often gave the idea that she knew something that no one else knew. She was intelligent, too, extremely intelligent—no one doubted that. And she was loving, very loving.

Whenever Laurel sat down to read or to watch TV, or just to rest, Princess would jump to the back of the couch and then step carefully down, so demure and so ladylike, paw by paw, to curl contentedly onto Laurel's lap. Then she would purr and purr and purr, giving the impression that there was not even a whisker of badness in her.

When anyone was around, Princess was good, very, very good—clean and tidy, never going where she was told not to go. She was the model pet.

But Laurel knew her cat better than that. As a kitten, Princess had found the joys of climbing the drapes. She loved to sink her claws into the thick fabric and then scamper quickly upward to where she could practice balancing as she walked elegantly back and forth on the thick, round rod.

Laurel scolded and spanked. Just as well as she knew how to purr, Princess knew she was not supposed to climb the drapes. But they were so tempting—their woven texture gave such excellent clawholds, and it was such fun.

As Princess grew older, she appeared to forget the drapes—at least she seemed to when Laurel was watching. One day, though, Laurel found some ugly telltale snags on one panel. They could be caused by only one thing—a cat's claws.

Laurel could not afford to have her drapes ruined, nor did she want to give up her pet, so she decided to have her cat's claws removed. Without claws, Princess wouldn't be able to climb anything, not even a tree for safety if a dog should chase her. Since she could not be trusted, she had to pay that price.

What we do when no one else is around to see us tells the kind of person we really are. What sort of person are you? Do you love God so much that you do right because it is right—even if no one is looking?

NOVEMBER

Hidden Forever

You may be sure that your sin will find you out. Numbers 32:23.

Many, many years ago a smuggler tried to sneak a shipload of tobacco into the United States. As his ship sailed toward land, one of his sailors pointed to something. "Look!" the sailor shouted. "A boat!"

The smuggler looked toward the horizon. A Coast Guard boat steamed toward them.

"Faster!" he ordered.

The sailors adjusted the sails, but they couldn't make the ship move any faster. As the smuggler watched, he saw that the Coast Guard boat was gaining on them. He knew that what he was doing was against the law, but in order to make some easy money he'd taken the chance. He also knew that if the officers on board that Coast Guard cutter caught him with the tobacco, he'd lose it and his ship—and he might even have to go to prison. To save himself and his ship, he had to do something fast.

"Throw the tobacco overboard!" he called to his men. "Hurry!"

At his orders, the men ran a sail up at the back of the ship so that the the Coast Guard officers wouldn't see what they were doing. Then they threw bale after bale of the dry tobacco leaves into the sea. The men worked hard, sweat pouring from them, as they hurried to get rid of all the tobacco before the Coast Guard boat would catch up to them. They knew that they'd all be punished if the officers found the tobacco.

"Look to see where the Coast Guard boat is now," the smuggler captain told one of the sailors when almost all the tobacco had been thrown overboard.

The sailor ran to the back of the ship and peered around the sail. His face turned white and his heart caught. He rushed back to the captain.

"Sir!" he exclaimed. "Sir! They won't sink!"

"What?" the smuggler demanded, and he hurried back to see for himself.

The bales of dry tobacco leaves floated on the water, scattered into a long, uneven line of big dark blocks that led from his ship right to the Coast Guard boat.

Have you ever tried to hide a sin, only to have it bob into plain view? The only way to hide a sin for sure is to confess it to God. If we confess our sins, He has promised to forgive them and to blot them out forever.

NOVEMBER

4

To Forgive

Forgive us our sins, for we also forgive everyone who sins against us.
Luke 11:4.

Do you know what Heidi said?" Ileana asked as she lowered her voice. "She said you . . ."

Fatima felt her cheeks go tight as Ileana repeated what she'd heard. "Why . . . Why . . ." Anger whipped her thoughts into a fury. "Those are lies! Nothing but lies! My family's good!" Fatima stamped her foot. More words wanted to boil out—hateful, disgusting words.

"I warned you," Ileana said. "You can't trust her!"

Whenever she thought of what Ileana told her, anger flared in Fatima's thoughts. *Just wait,* she promised herself. *I'll get even. I will.*

During morning worship as Dad was reading, a sentence hooked her attention. "From the prayer Jesus taught His disciples, we know that God can forgive us only if we forgive others."

"Even if someone does something really mean on purpose?" she asked her dad. "And says terrible things—do we have to forgive? Is that possible?"

"When Jesus was on the cross He asked God to forgive the ones who put Him there."

Fatima understood, and the idea mixed with others that had been bothering her. At last she decided she had to talk to Heidi in order to settle her thoughts. "Did you really say that?" she demanded.

Heidi nodded.

"But it's not true!" Fatima felt anger rising again.

"I'm sorry," Heidi said quietly. "It was mean. It wasn't true. It wasn't Christian. I don't know why I said it. I'm really sorry, Fatima."

"When Ileana told me, I was very angry." Fatima faced her classmate. "I still feel angry, and I don't want to forgive you."

Heidi looked worried.

"But that's not Christian either." Fatima felt herself begin to relax as she made herself say those words. "In worship yesterday we talked about how God can't forgive us if we don't forgive others. That's why I had to talk to you. I promised Jesus a long time ago that He could always stay in my heart, and there's no room for Him in my thoughts when I'm angry. I forgive you. I really do."

"Thanks," said Heidi. "I want to have Jesus in my heart, too."

NOVEMBER

Guy Fawkes

"Not by might nor by power, but by my Spirit," says the Lord Almighty. Zechariah 4:6.

Tonight's the night of skyrockets and firecrackers and watching the "guy" burn in Great Britain.

Bonfire Night is a time of family fun, but it's a reminder of the night more than 400 years ago when a young fellow named Guy Fawkes was caught with the fuse that he meant to use to light enough kegs of gunpowder to blow up the king of England and all the members of his government.

When Queen Elizabeth I died, her nearest living relative was the king of Scotland. He became James I of England and head of the official church. At that time there were three main groups of Christians—the Roman Catholics, who had the pope at the head of their church; members of the Church of England, who had made religion simpler and looked to the king as the head of their church; and the Puritans, who wanted Christianity purified of all its showy ceremonies and traditions, with neither a king nor a pope at the head of their church.

As king, James I became head of the Church of England, but a gang of Catholics plotted what they thought was a surefire scheme to seize control of the country. They talked a young soldier named Guy Fawkes into joining them. After renting a cellar under the House of Lords, the place where the king met with the nobles and religious leaders who were his advisors in running the country, the gang stocked it with more than a ton and a half of gunpowder. Then they waited for the government to meet.

Someone, though, sent a warning message. The cellars were searched, and Guy was caught with the fuse that he planned to light the next day. He and the other members of the gang were all sentenced to death.

Guy and the others involved in the Gunpowder Plot paid with their lives for trying to seize power by force. Their plot also caused problems for the ordinary people of the Catholic Church, and hatred boiled against them. Just as many Puritans fled to the New World because of religious persecution, so did many Catholics.

Satan knows that people trying to change other people's minds by force causes very bad feelings on both sides—hateful feelings that often lead to war—so he encourages them to be bossy and pushy to get others to do what they want.

God never forces anyone, but He does send His Spirit—the quiet Spirit of love and truth—to try to persuade you to follow His way. Have you asked for God's Spirit to come into your life?

NOVEMBER

6

Row Easy

For our struggle is . . . against the spiritual forces of evil in the heavenly realms. Ephesians 6:12.

Heavy rains had swollen the usually slow-paced river into an angry muddy-brown current. Tricia studied it. Close to the bank, where she'd tied her grandfather's rowboat, the water eddied calmly. But midriver . . .

Tricia took a deep breath. She had to get home. Sitting with her back to the bow, she flipped the rope free, settled the oars into their locks, dug them deep into the water, and pointed the boat toward the other side.

The boat skimmed across the calmer water, but then the current caught it. Tricia found herself being swept downriver. She dug the oars down and pulled hard, fighting with each stroke. She did not notice how the old wooden oars strained. Halfway across, caught in full current, she had visions of being swept out of control and carried toward the sea. In her hurry to get across that danger, she pulled each stroke with all her weight.

Suddenly her left arm jerked back, almost toppling her as the oar handle jumped free of the lock. She gasped as she saw the paddle blade swirl away.

The boat turned with the current, gaining speed. Terrified, Tricia dropped the broken shaft to the floor and hefted the good oar to the other side. With a solid sweep, she pointed the boat back toward home, but the boat rode the current faster and faster.

"In the bottom! Another oar!"

She turned. Her grandfather stood on the dock, motioning for her to look down. Under the floorboard she found an old oar. But its shaft was cracked.

"It's broken!" she yelled back.

"Shallow! Row shallow!" He forced his voice to be heard above the rush of the water. "Take short, quick strokes."

She fit the oar into the empty lock.

"Don't fight! Row easy! Keep your strokes shallow."

To her surprise, the boat began to move across the current. At last she was in the shelter of the far bank and could work her way up to the dock. "Sorry about your oar," she mumbled as she tied the boat.

"It's OK. I've got others." He was silent a moment, then said, "When a heavy current's running, don't fight. Row easy, and you'll make it fine."

Fighting and struggling, even against sin, often makes the situation worse. Learn to "row easy"—rely on Jesus.

The Name of God

What is the name of your God? What is He like? What sort of person is He?

Think about these questions. Then with one-word descriptions of God, fill in as many blanks as you can, using the letters that make up the name Amos calls Him—the Lord God Almighty.

T Teacher ____________ ____________
H Helper ____________ ____________
E Eternal ____________ ____________

L ____________ ____________ ____________
O ____________ ____________ ____________
R ____________ ____________ ____________
D ____________ ____________ ____________

G ____________ ____________ ____________
O ____________ ____________ ____________
D ____________ ____________ ____________

A ____________ ____________ ____________
L ____________ ____________ ____________
M ____________ ____________ ____________
I ____________ ____________ ____________
G ____________ ____________ ____________
H ____________ ____________ ____________
T ____________ ____________ ____________
Y ____________ ____________ ____________

Isn't God wonderful?

He's all of these good things—and more. And He wants you to become like Him.

He who forms the mountains,
creates the wind,
and reveals his thoughts to man,
he who turns dawn to darkness,
and treads the high places of the earth—the Lord God Almighty is his name.
Amos 4:13.

NOVEMBER

8

Twelve and His 13 Witnesses

Honest scales and balances are from the Lord; all the weights in the bag are of his making. Proverbs 16:11.

Twelve said it, and he has 13 witnesses who heard him say it."

Twelve—no one remembered just quite how he came to have that nickname—was usually at the center of things. He said that he had seen the math teacher talking with two suspicious-looking men at night on the street. He said that the men looked like thieves. He also said that because he saw them talking, the math teacher must belong to the gang organizing robberies at the mission.

"The math teacher's a thief." The rumor spread quickly through the school and into the community. "He belongs to the gang who stole the lab microscope. And a typewriter. Twelve has 13 witnesses."

"What's this?" the principal asked when he heard the accusation. "What proof does anyone have against the math teacher?"

"Twelve has 13 witnesses."

"Yes," agreed the principal. "Twelve has 13 witnesses. But 13 witnesses to what? Did those 13 witnesses see the math teacher talking to the men? Do they have any proof that those men are thieves? Do they know that the math teacher has anything to do with those men? Do they have any proof that the math teacher stole anything?"

The answer to each question was a quiet no.

"Before you make any judgments or lay any accusations," the principal warned, "be sure that you weigh the evidence carefully. Be sure you have enough facts. Be sure you use a just measure."

In Bible times, shrewd businesspeople used two sets of weights—a heavy one for buying, and a light one for selling. Both ways, they purposely cheated the other person.

In talking—and in listening—are you careful to use honest scales and balances?

Twelve tried to use the weight of his claim of having 13 witnesses to falsely accuse a teacher he did not like. The others let themselves be deceived by his clever words.

When you hear rumors, do you ask the right questions, as the principal did? Do you weigh the evidence honestly? Or could you let yourself be fooled by someone like Twelve with his 13 witnesses?

NOVEMBER

Just Call Me Sam

We did not follow cleverly invented stories when we told you about the power and coming of our Lord Jesus Christ, but we were eyewitnesses of his majesty.
2 Peter 1:16.

Just call me Sam," said William Samuel McGee, a road builder, when he arrived in Whitehorse during the Yukon gold rush of 1898. "There are too many other Wills and Bills around."

He tossed up a little log shack and went out to build roads and to do some prospecting. A little later a new bank teller moved into town and soon became known for the poems he wrote.

"Bank teller Service recited a poem about you the other night," Sam's friends told him when he came home from a prospecting trip.

Sam just laughed.

Several years later Robert Service's book, *Songs of a Sourdough*, with "The Cremation of Sam McGee" was published. And then Sam's friends really teased him.

"Give me some peace," he finally pleaded. "The 'Cremation's' a good story, but the tale's as tall as can be."

Tall though it may be, the story has some basis in truth. "Doc" Sudgen was called to help an old man lying sick in his shack on the shore of Lac LaBarge. By the time Doc arrived, the man had died. Since the frozen ground was buried under snow and since he was alone, Doc decided to dispose of the body by cremating it in the boiler of the nearby wreck of an old steamer called the *Alice May*.

By the time Robert Service heard that story, he'd already seen Sam's name in the bank ledger. Weaving everything together with a lot of imagination and making it all rhyme, he invented what was to become his most famous ballad—"The Cremation of Sam McGee"—the story of a prospector from Tennessee who'd come to seek his fortune but who could never get warm enough in the Yukon cold.

Of course, the real Sam McGee didn't come from Tennessee. He was a Canadian from Ontario, and his wife and children were members of the Adventist Church in western Canada. The real Sam did love to prospect, though, and discovered some valuable claims. Years later he returned to visit the Yukon. By then his old cabin had been turned into a tea room, and he had his picture taken in front of it under a sign that read, "Have a cup of tea with the ghost of Sam McGee."

Tall tales are entertaining and sometimes funny, but they're just stories. Faith needs to be based on truth. Put your faith in the eyewitness reports of Jesus in the Bible. They're true.

NOVEMBER

10

Freedom to Choose

So then, just as you received Christ Jesus as Lord, continue to live in him. Colossians 2:6.

Nathan had just moved into the neighborhood. Luke lived next door. The two of them walked to school together, and Luke invited Nathan to join his hockey team. The boys did other things together, and Nathan enjoyed having Luke as a pal—for a while.

"Don't forget your skates," Luke reminded him on hockey days. Then he started saying things like "Be sure to wear your red shirt tomorrow" and "Come to the mall with me after school." He didn't ask. He just said it as if he were in charge of what Nathan should do.

At first Nathan didn't mind, but the bossing continued to get worse.

"Bring a peanut butter sandwich in your lunch—and two cookies. . . . Start your piano practice at 4:30 p.m. so we can play before. . . . Use this new toothpaste like I got."

Nathan started to get tired of all Luke's orders.

"Ask Robyn over today. . . . Don't talk to Gabriel. . . . Wear your shoes tied like this. . . . Get some better notebook paper."

Nathan couldn't take it any longer. "Nothing's wrong with the paper I have!" he exploded. "I'm not your robot, and I'll talk to Gabriel if I like. And no, I'm not asking Robyn over this afternoon, because I have to go into town with my mom. And I'm tired of your telling me every move I should make."

Luke stared back at Nathan. "Do what I say or else!" he snapped back. But Nathan had already turned and was hurrying down the hall.

God gave everyone freedom to choose. Lucifer was free to rebel against God. The angels were free to follow Lucifer in his rebellion. Adam and Eve were free to sin. We're free to choose whether or not to follow God.

Nathan was free to choose Luke as a friend, but he rejected him because of his bossiness.

God wants to be our friend. Even though He has given certain rules, He knows that friends aren't bossy. "Do things My way and you'll be happier," He says. "Get to know Me, and you'll *want* to be like Me. If you're like Me, this is what you'll do."

Once you've learned what God is really like, you'll want to live His commandments.

NOVEMBER

I Thank God for Soldiers

Praise the name of the Lord your God, who has dealt wondrously with you. Joel 2:26, NKJV.

It was November 11, 1991. The sky was gray, the ground white, and the trees bare, but I was warm and snug in the house—and safe.

"I wish sometime we could go home for winter!"

Those words had come easily after we'd gone as missionaries to Africa—especially on those muggy November days where we live when the year is at its hottest, and I'd long for a cool, crisp Canadian November with icy-blue skies and new-fallen snow swirled in fluffy drifts across yards and draped on fences like marshmallow topping.

Now I had my wish, and I sat at a table in Joann's house in Edmonton, looking out the window at snow while the little computer that I'd brought with me on the plane in my backpack stared up with a blank screen. I made myself type a few words.

November 11 is the day to honor those who have defended the United States and Canada and protected the peace that I'd come to find.

I typed another line, but it was difficult to find the right words to say what I wanted about military people and winter and snow and family and friends and freedom and quiet days to work and God.

"Today I feel a special thanks for the soldiers who helped me come here, and for those who protected Date and the other missionaries when they drove out of the country."

"Thanks" really wasn't a big enough word. It was no holiday trip that brought me to North America for the winter. We'd been evacuated a couple of weeks earlier during rioting in Zaire. I remembered the Belgian soldier standing guard by the wall the night before I left, his battle uniform blending into the shadows, his beret businesslike on his head, his gun ready. Farther down, there were other soldiers. The evening was warm. Many people wandered about, others stood in groups, and a constant hum of voices filled the air. None of us knew what was going to happen—only that we'd been told to leave the country. Since the stories for this book had to be sent to the publishing house soon, I'd chosen to go to North America to find a quiet place to write.

A staccato of distant gunfire cut the evening, but I felt safe. The soldiers were there to protect us, and the next morning they guarded the way to the airport.

"God is our only true safety," I wrote, "but He uses people to keep other people safe. And today I praise Him for soldiers."

NOVEMBER

12

The Church and the Cows

The name of the Lord is a strong tower; the righteous run to it and are safe. Proverbs 18:10.

An old gray-brown brick church stands in a little village in the north of Holland. When it was first built nearly 450 years ago, the country was smaller, the sea closer, and the low-lying land of the village risked being flooded during winter storms.

Before building the church, workers, according to the wishes of the village council, followed the system used in other villages. They made a huge mound of dirt.

"Now our church will be a place of safety," the village leaders said, "and in times of flood, we can come here."

"What about our cattle?" someone asked.

"Plenty of room in the churchyard," suggested another.

"To just wander about? Would that be proper?"

"If we and our families can eat and sleep inside the church, surely our cows can come to the churchyard," argued another. "Would God be pleased if we saved ourselves and let His poor creatures drown?"

"I have an idea," said another villager. "We could set strong iron rings in the walls and tie our cows to them."

And so the church was built, and iron rings were set into the brick walls. Many years passed, and there was no big flood. Then one night a storm raged itself into a fury, scooping the waves higher and higher until they pounded against the dikes. In the middle of the night a messenger raced to the council head's house.

"Warn the people!" he yelled. "The dikes are breaking."

They rang the bell in the church tower, the signal of trouble, and soon flickering lanterns dotted the night. Mothers and big girls clutched bundles of bedding and helped small children. Fathers and older brothers herded cows. At last everyone was safe at the church. In the morning water covered all the farms, but the people and their cows were safe.

In the years since that flood, more dikes have been built and bigger and better pumps installed. The church still stands and the rings, now rusty with years, still stick out of the wall, but only a few people come to worship there these days. They no longer have to worry about floods as the folks did in years gone by, and they seem to have forgotten that the church was built as their place of safety where they could learn of God.

Do you find your safety in God?

NOVEMBER

Looking Upward

A man stood on the street corner, staring upward, his eyes fixed on the edge of the roof of the tall building across the street. He continued to stand there, his head tilted back, not moving his eyes from the spot that held his interest. Passers-by slowed and looked upward. Some stopped. And looked. Soon a small crowd of people stood around him looking up at the top of the building.

"What's up there?" someone finally asked.

The first man shrugged his shoulders, then turned and walked away. He had proved a point. If you seem to be looking at something interesting, others will want to see what you see.

The Bible has many texts about looking and watching. Here are five. Read them and then answer the questions.

"Jesus turned, saw them following him, and asked, 'What are you looking for?' " (John 1:37, TEV).

"We are looking forward to a new heaven and a new earth, the home of righteousness" (2 Peter 3:13, NIV).

"So then, dear friends, since you are looking forward to this, make every effort to be found spotless, blameless and at peace with him" (verse 14, NIV).

"Therefore I will look to the Lord; I will wait for the God of my salvation; my God will hear me" (Micah 7:7, NKJV).

"Let us keep our eyes fixed on Jesus, on whom our faith depends from beginning to end" (Hebrews 12:2, TEV).

1. What are you looking for? ________________
2. How do you "look" for God? ________________

____

3. Do you know someone who "looks" at Jesus in such a way that it makes you want to "look" at Him too?
4. What is it about that person that makes you want to look to Jesus? ________________

"If you have found Jesus, you will be a true missionary. You are to be enthusiastic in this matter, and let those know who do not appreciate Jesus that you have found Him precious to your soul, that He has put a new song in your mouth, even praise to God" (Ellen G. White, *Messages to Young People*, pp. 200, 201).

Do you look at Jesus in such a way that others will want to see Him too?

Look to Me, and be saved, all you ends of the earth! For I am God, and there is no other.
Isaiah 45:22, NKJV.

NOVEMBER

14

Know Him Well

You are . . . chosen to proclaim the wonderful acts of God.
1 Peter 2:9, TEV.

Christopher leaned against the fence and watched two old men as they walked toward the park bench.

"Notice details," Ms. Brillson said.

Christopher was doing just that. He paid close attention to how the two men walked, and how they talked to each other and laughed, and how one of them seemed to creak as he slowly sat down.

Christopher had been chosen to take the lead part of Grandfather Goode in the Christmas play.

"Watch some nice, grandfatherly men," Ms. Brillson suggested, "and remember that actors don't just see, they look at things in such a way that they'll remember exact details. You're going to create an old man on stage, and you'll do that better if you know how old men walk, sit, read, talk, laugh, and eat."

Since Grandfather Goode was a kindly old Christian gentleman who wanted to show his grandchildren the true meaning of Christmas, Christopher chose to watch people who appeared to be kind and happy.

"If you want the audience to believe what this play says," Ms. Brillson continued, "you're not going to have to just 'act' right, you're also going to have to believe what Grandfather Goode says and does. In this play, you are Grandfather Goode."

Jesus wants us to believe in Him and to study His Word so that we can learn to act like Him, but what He wants is something more than just playing a part like Christopher is learning to play the part of Grandfather Goode. Jesus wants us to know Him so well and believe in Him so much that we will actually become like Him.

How well do you notice things that are around you? These questions will help show how carefully you notice things.

1. What was your teacher/father/friend wearing yesterday?

2. What is on the bulletin board of your classroom? Of your Sabbath school room?

3. What one beautiful thing did you see on your way home from school Friday?

4. Describe every detail of the walkway that leads to where you live—size, color, what it's made of, how it feels, what's beside it, the sounds you hear, the odors you smell, etc. When you go out, try to find at least 10 details that you've never noticed before.

NOVEMBER

Lost to the World

It is the Lord your God you must follow, and him you must revere. Keep his commands and obey him; serve him and hold fast to him. *Deuteronomy 13:4.*

Have you ever tried that old trick of patting the top of your head with your right hand while at the same time rubbing your stomach around and around in a large circle with your left hand?

Or have you ever held your hand out flat and tried to make a V between your third and fourth fingers while you keep the second and third fingers and the fourth and fifth fingers tight together?

If you've never tried to do these tricks, try them right now.

Both of these tricks take lots of concentration if you're not used to doing them. When you first try them, you need to give all your attention to what you're trying to make your hands do. If not, they'll never do what you want them to do.

To concentrate means that you focus your mind completely on what you're doing and give that thing all your attention. Have you ever concentrated on anything so hard that you became so completely lost in your thoughts that you did not hear or see anything else that was going on around you?

If that has happened to you, we could say that at the time "you were lost to the world."

That's exactly what Jesus wants you to be—lost to the world. He wants you to give Him your thoughts and your actions, and pay such close attention to doing things His way that you will not even want to sin.

There are two main ways of giving your thoughts to Jesus—by studying the Bible and by praying. There's also a third way for followers of Jesus to do this—by sharing. But you first must know Jesus before you can share His love.

Messages to Young People says that doing good is good for both the giver and the receiver. If you forget yourself by doing good things for others, you'll feel better and even begin to think better.

It also says that the pleasure of doing good will make your face light up with cheerfulness. The faces of selfish folk, though, are gloomy and downcast, because "selfishness and self-love stamp their own image" upon the outward person (p. 209).

Wouldn't you like to have a happy face that shows that you're lost to the world?

NOVEMBER

16

Knocking

Here I am! I stand at the door and knock. Revelation 3:20.

There's a doorbell by the gate that opens into our mission yard. From inside the house we can't see who's at the gate, but very often we can tell who's there just by the way the bell rings. One of our friends has the habit of pushing the button two times very quickly. Another pushes it once very slowly. Others push it in other ways, and it rings differently for the different ways it's touched.

Actions do speak louder than words, and even the way you ring a doorbell or knock on a door tells something about you.

Try this experiment.

Pretend you are the person at the door in each of the following cases. Think about who each person is, where he or she is, what might have happened, and how he or she is feeling. Now knock (on the door, or wall, or table) as each of these people would knock.

1. An angry sister knocking on her brother's door.
2. A frightened first grade child who's been sent to the principal's office and is knocking on the door.
3. A friend stopping by to say hello.
4. A pizza delivery person knocking on the door of someone who's ordered a pizza.
5. A gossipy woman at her neighbor's door.
6. A nurse on hospital night duty knocking at a patient's door.
7. A passer-by knocking on the door of a house that has smoke pouring out of a basement window.

What was different about the way you knocked for number 1 and the way you knocked for number 6? ____

____

Did you knock harder for number 3 or number 5? __________ Or did you knock the same way for both? __________ Why? ____________________

What change did you hear between the way you knocked for number 2 and the way you knocked for number 7? ____________________

Jesus says He stands at the doors of our hearts and knocks. If He were knocking at the door of the house where you live, how might He knock? ____________

____

Would He knock like any of the above people?

____

Would you recognize His knock? __________

Would you let Him in? __________

NOVEMBER

Doing Things Because

"I am the resurrection and the life. Whoever believes in me will live, even though he dies." John 11:25, TEV.

Today we're going to do some speech exercises," Ms. Grable announced one afternoon without warning. "Susan, would you come up front?"

Susan looked up with surprise and started to open her mouth to object.

"Oh, you won't have to talk to the class," Ms. Grable said quickly. "All you need to do is to move around in front of the class and look at the floor."

It sounded quite simple, but after Susan walked back and forth a couple of times, looking down, she began to feel kind of stupid.

"Do you understand what I want you to do?" her teacher asked.

"No—I mean, not really," Susan stammered.

Ms. Grable smiled. "That's good!" she exclaimed.

Her reply made Susan feel even more confused until Ms. Grable turned to the class and explained what she meant.

"I haven't been fair with Susan," she said. "She has no idea why I asked her to look at the floor, and she doesn't know how she should look at it. If I'd have said, 'There's a secret trapdoor in our classroom floor, and I want you to find it so we can hide some money there,' she'd have known exactly what to do.

"Then if I'd said, 'Now pretend that Jayne's big brother has dropped a contact lens here in our classroom. Show us how you'd look for it.' Would she have kept looking at the floor in the same way?"

The children all shook their heads.

"Right now I want you all to pretend that you're looking for that contact lens."

In everyday life, when we know *why* we do things, it often helps us know *how* to do them. You do your chores carefully because you want your allowance, and you won't get it for a sloppy job. You floss your teeth because you want to keep them healthy. You tidy the living room because you want to impress your boyfriend. You take extra time to make your geography project neater because you want an A instead of a B.

Jesus also gives us "whys" for doing things His way. What are some of His whys? Do those "whys" help you love Him more?

NOVEMBER

18

Nehemiah's Sabbath Story

Then I commanded the Levites to purify themselves and go and guard the gates in order to keep the Sabbath day holy. Nehemiah 13:22.

Today we have another dramatic reading. This time it is from Nehemiah 13:15-22, TEV.

COMMENTATOR: When Nehemiah returned to Jerusalem, he was shocked to find that the people had forgotten God's Sabbath.

VOICE 1: At that time I saw people in Judah pressing juice from grapes on the Sabbath. Others were loading corn, wine, grapes, figs, and other things on their donkeys and taking them into Jerusalem; I warned them not to sell anything on the Sabbath. Some men from the city of Tyre were living in Jerusalem, and they brought fish and all kinds of goods into the city to sell to our people on the Sabbath. I reprimanded the Jewish leaders and told them,

VOICE 2: Look at the evil you're doing! You're making the Sabbath unholy. This is exactly why God punished your ancestors when he brought destruction on this city. And yet you insist on bringing more of God's anger down on Israel by profaning the Sabbath.

VOICE 1: So I gave orders for the city gates to be shut at the beginning of every Sabbath, as soon as evening began to fall, and not to be opened again until the Sabbath was over. I stationed some of my men at the gates to make sure that nothing was brought into the city on the Sabbath. Once or twice merchants who sold all kinds of goods spent Friday night outside the city walls. I warned them,

VOICE 2: It's no use waiting out there for morning to come. If you try this again, I'll use force on you.

VOICE 1: From then on they did not come back on the Sabbath. I ordered the Levites to purify themselves and to go and guard the gates to make sure that the Sabbath was kept holy.

VOICE 2: Remember me, O God, for this also, and spare me because of your great love.

COMMENTATOR: After that, the Jewish leaders never forgot the Sabbath. Instead they made more and more rules about what people could or couldn't do on the Sabbath day. And Satan was happy because the people began worrying so much about whether or not they were breaking the Sabbath rules that they forgot how to worship God.

But God didn't forget, and He sent Jesus to show us how to keep the Sabbath.

NOVEMBER

19

The Church That Didn't Fall

But everyone who hears these words of mine and does not put them into practice is like a foolish man who built his house on sand. Matthew 7:26.

Pastor Samuel slumped in the patio chair. "I have some very sad news," he said to Mrs. Brown.

"Oh?" The missionary replied.

"Yes. I wanted you to hear it from my very own lips."

Mrs. Brown waited for him to continue.

"You know the church we're building on the other side of town—you helped us buy roofing sheets for it."

Mrs. Brown nodded, wondering what had happened.

"Well, there's been a problem. When the people decided to put their church there, the builders told them to wait until they had enough money for a proper foundation. The land doesn't drain well, and the foundation should be of rock. The members were in a hurry to have a real church building," the pastor continued. "They had only enough money for an adobe brick foundation, but they built anyhow. And you know how heavy the rains have been."

The missionary nodded. "Is the church still standing?" she asked.

"Yes, the church still stands." As he spoke, Pastor Samuel sounded discouraged. "The walls have begun to sag, though, and they'll no doubt soon fall. We must put up braces to save the roof, but that is not the real problem. The members have many questions."

"Are they asking why?" Mrs. Brown asked.

"That's it exactly," replied Pastor Samuel. "They're asking why this is happening to their church, and they're wondering if the devil is stronger than God."

After a few moments Mrs. Brown said, "Isn't this a good time to remind them of Jesus' story of the wise man and the foolish man? The Bible says to listen to the counsel of the wise, but they wouldn't listen to the builders. Even things as good as a church must be built on a solid foundation."

"You're right," agreed Pastor Samuel. "Without putting the words of Jesus into practice, we will fall when the storms of temptation come." He began to smile. "This is not the end. We will brace the walls and dig a new foundation and put in rocks. If we are wise and put into practice the words of wisdom that we have received, our church will stand."

And it did.

NOVEMBER

20

A Famous Pot of Soup

He who comes to me will never go hungry.
John 6:35.

I'm starving. Give me some of that red stuff."

"OK, I'll trade you."

That trade made history. Esau got a pot of his younger brother's delicious red lentil soup—pottage, it's often called—and Jacob got all his older twin's rights as firstborn son. Esau was hungry, and he didn't care about God or future blessings, but Jacob wanted them. Many years later Jacob saw that what he did was mean and selfish and wrong. He repented, and God forgave and blessed him. Esau was later sorry that he'd lost the extra property and the right of being head of the family, but he never repented of trading away God's special blessings.

The meal Esau got in that trade has become one of the most famous pots of soup in all history.

When Jesus said that anyone who comes to Him will never go hungry, He was talking about spiritual food. Esau traded for Jacob's soup, and even though it was nutritious and filling, he needed to eat again the next day. He never did turn to God for that other food that will give eternal life.

Lentils, a small member of the pea family, are a favorite food in many parts of Asia, Europe, and America. People of the Middle East still eat pottage—a thick, nourishing soup made with red lentils, onions, garlic, rice, and olive oil. In other places a similar soup is made with dried peas. French Canadians use yellow peas, and the Dutch use green split peas.

In Holland it's a tradition to eat pea soup every week on cleaning day. Here's a recipe to try:

2 cups green split peas
9 cups water
1 large onion—chopped
3 large potatoes—peeled and chopped
3 large carrots—peeled and chopped
5 sticks of celery, including leaves, chopped
salt

Clean and rinse the peas. Put everything in a large soup kettle; bring to a boil. Skim off any scum. Cover and cook at a very low heat for about 1½ hours or until the peas are soft and the soup has thickened. (If your family uses a pressure cooker, this cooks in five minutes at full steam.) Salt it to taste. If you like, sprinkle Baco Bits® or croutons on top. It's a complete, nutritious meal by itself and is good served with toast or bread.

NOVEMBER

Sean's Prayer

For the eyes of the Lord are on the righteous and his ears are attentive to their prayer.
1 Peter 3:12.

Sean wanted a set of Lego® building blocks—not just any set, but one with knights and castles, just like Harry had. When they had visited Harry's family at Riverbend Mission, the two boys had played for hours and hours with Harry's Lego blocks.

"That's a super set!" Sean exclaimed to his mother. "I'd sure like one like that for my birthday."

"That's a very expensive set," his mother replied. "You know that we don't have a lot of extra money. And if we did, where could I buy you a set like that here at the mission? And we don't have any time to order one from Europe."

"Do you suppose God would hear if I would pray for a set?" he asked.

"I'm sure God would hear," his mother replied. "He hears all our prayers, but I'm not sure what His answer would be."

Sean nodded. "Do you suppose God would mind if I asked Him for that particular set?"

"I'm sure God wouldn't mind at all," his mother replied. "He likes us to tell Him everything that's on our hearts."

"Then I think I'll talk to Him about it."

And he did.

The days went by. Sean's birthday drew nearer. One day he said to his mother, "I think it would be very difficult for God to find me a set of Lego blocks like I want, but if He wants me to have a set, He'll take care of it. If not . . ." He shrugged his shoulders. "I really want some, but God knows best."

A few nights later they had some visitors, a family from one of the upland missions whom they hadn't seen in years but who had stopped by on their way home to Europe from the mission field.

After Sean had gone to bed, Donald, one of the bigger brothers of the visiting family, talked to Sean's mother. "I have a set of Lego blocks—a set of knights and castles. Would you mind if I gave it to Sean?"

"Mind?" Sean's mother exclaimed! "Not at all! In fact, that would be one of the nicest, happiest things that could happen for Sean, because, you see, he's been praying for that exact set. It'll be his birthday in a few days . . ."

And so Donald, to his own surprise, had become God's helper in answering Sean's prayers.

NOVEMBER

22

Paul and Silas in Prison

He then brought them out and asked, "Sirs, what must I do to be saved?" Acts 16:30.

This is a dramatic reading from Acts 16:25-39, NIV. (See instructions on page 28.)

NARRATOR: About midnight Paul and Silas were praying and singing hymns to God, and the other prisoners were listening to them. Suddenly there was such a violent earthquake that the foundations of the prison were shaken. At once all the prison doors flew open, and everybody's chains came loose. The jailer woke up, and when he saw the prison doors open, he drew his sword and was about to kill himself because he thought the prisoners had escaped. But Paul shouted,

PAUL: Don't harm yourself! We are all here!

NARRATOR: The jailer called for lights, rushed in and fell trembling before Paul and Silas. He then brought them out and asked,

JAILER: Sirs, what must I do to be saved?

NARRATOR: Paul and Silas replied,

PAUL and SILAS: Believe in the Lord Jesus, and you will be saved—you and your household.

NARRATOR: Then they spoke the word of the Lord to him and to all the others in his house. At that hour of the night the jailer took them and washed their wounds; then immediately he and all his family were baptized. The jailer brought them into his house and set a meal before them; he was filled with joy because he had come to believe in God—he and his whole family.

When it was daylight, the magistrates sent their officers to the jailer with the order:

OFFICERS: Release those men.

NARRATOR: The jailor told Paul,

JAILER: The magistrates have ordered that you and Silas be released. Now you can leave. Go in peace,

NARRATOR: But Paul said to the officers,

PAUL: They beat us publicly without a trial, even though we are Roman citizens, and threw us into prison. And now do they want to get rid of us quietly? No! Let them come themselves and escort us out.

NARRATOR: The officers reported this to the magistrates, and when they heard that Paul and Silas were Roman citizens, they were alarmed. They came to appease them and escorted them from the prison, requesting them to leave the city.

Real Freedom

So then, each of us will give an account of himself to God. Therefore let us stop passing judgment on one another. Romans 14:12, 13.

After the Pilgrims left for the New World, a civil war brought some religious freedom to those who stayed behind in England, and even though there were still just three main religious groups—Anglicans, Catholics, and Puritans—new churches were started.

One group was called the Levellers. They wanted complete religious freedom for everyone. Another group was called the Diggers. They thought that they could take land anywhere and farm it for themselves. Then there were the Seekers, the Ranters, the Family of Love, and others. Each of these groups thought it had found the only way to God, but none of them lasted long.

Other church groups such as the Presbyterians, Baptists, and Quakers also began during that period.

George Fox, a good Christian, saw that many people went to church on Sunday only because they were forced to attend. He thought people were just like a bunch of parrots when they repeated prayers from the church's prayer book, because they didn't understand the meaning of the words they said.

"Each person should be free to find his or her own way to God," he said. "They don't need bishops or priests to tell them what to believe." He encouraged the people to think deeply about God, to pray in their own words, and to read the Bible.

Many people liked what George Fox said, and soon he had quite a large following of people who believed that all human beings are created equal.

Back then the English used the words "you" and "your" and "yours" only when talking to someone they thought was equal or superior. When speaking to an animal, a child, or a servant, that same person would use the words "thee" or "thou" or "thine." To show what they thought of that system, the Quakers said "thee," "thou," and "thine" to everyone.

The Puritan leaders didn't like the idea of each person being able to worship God as he or she chose, and they passed laws based on their strict religion. People could be arrested for crimes such as eating a big Christmas dinner and then be cruelly punished so they'd learn to know the "love" of God.

Many years passed before the government gave freedom of religion to the people.

God's love isn't about force or punishment, but about freedom—and real freedom makes us responsible for our own choices.

NOVEMBER

24

A Thanksgiving List

As God's grace reaches more and more people, they will offer to the glory of God more prayers of thanksgiving. 2 Corinthians 4:15, TEV.

If you were to draw a picture of what Thanksgiving Day means, would you draw a picture of food, or would you draw a picture of someone praying?

Both pictures would be correct, because Thanksgiving Day is a day for giving thanks and for feasting.

What are you most thankful for today? ________

____

I asked myself the same question, only I was thinking of that Thanksgiving Day just after I'd been evacuated from Africa.

Friends, I decided. *I'm most thankful for the friends who helped me then.*

But the answer needed to be bigger and better than that, so I spelled out the word T-H-A-N-K-S-G-I-V-I-N-G, thinking I could make a fine thankfulness list with all those letters.

I named friends—Dianne, Pete, Linda, Dean, Jeff, Penny. Nobody's initials fit except for the *K*nights, who'd invited me to their place for *T*hanksgiving dinner. But Dianne had been in charge of a hotel, and she'd given me a quiet room where I could work. It had a *t*elephone, and I'd been able to *t*alk to my husband and learn that he was *s*afe. *N*ews from the mission was *g*ood—*n*one of our workers or things had been harmed.

Then there were the *a*irplanes I'd come on and the *a*irport where Linda and Jeff had met me. Of course, I put soldiers by *S*, and on the next line I added "*G*od's protection."

Before long all the blanks of my THANKSGIVING list were full, but I could have kept adding and adding to it.

See how quickly you can fill this THANKSGIVING list.

T ________________________
H ________________________
A ________________________
N ________________________
K ________________________
S ________________________
G ________________________
I ________________________
V ________________________
I ________________________
N ________________________
G ________________________

Use your list for a special prayer of thanksgiving to God.

NOVEMBER

25

Stand On Your Feet

Now get up and stand on your feet. Acts 26:16.

Folks were causing trouble, spreading stories and dividing the church. Saul didn't like that a bit. Those people were nothing but troublemakers, making absolutely absurd and ridiculous claims. They were wrong, absolutely wrong and should be stopped!

Being a man of action, Saul intended to go and stop them. He would not let them get away with disgracing God's church.

He went to the leaders and got official letters. Then he found some helpers and started off for Damascus. He would hunt down the troublemakers there, arrest them, and bring them back to Jerusalem. He intended to defend God's name.

As they neared Damascus. a bright light suddenly exploded around Saul. He fell, stunned.

Then a voice from heaven spoke.

A terrible feeling suddenly washed over Saul. "Who are You, Lord?" he asked.

The answer changed his life. "I am Jesus, whom you are persecuting. Now get up and stand on your feet. I have appeared to you to appoint you as a servant and as a witness of what you have seen of me and what I will show you."

Saul got up, but when he opened his eyes he couldn't see. His helpers had to lead him the rest of the way to Damascus. Three days later his eyes were miraculously cured, and he got up, was baptized, and began to preach that Jesus is the Son of God.

After Jesus had healed the demon-possessed man, the man begged to go with Jesus. But Jesus told him to go home to his family and to tell them what the Lord had done for him.

A miracle changed Saul the persecutor into Paul the apostle. An earlier miracle changed the demon-possessed man into a healthy, sound-minded person. Both men did as they were told and went and told others about Jesus.

Do you know anyone whose life has been changed by such a startling miracle? ________________________

I don't, but I do know people who have changed because they've chosen to follow God. Some of them have the gift of preaching. Others don't. But they all have this one thing in common—their lives show that they know God.

When you "stand on your feet," what do others learn about God? If you were the only Christian in all the world, what would the others know about God?

NOVEMBER

26

How Do I Know? Part 1

I have found David son of Jesse a man after my own heart; he will do everything I want him to do. Acts 13:22.

"But how do I know what God wants me to do?"

That's a good question, but even David, who was God's man, didn't always have the right answer. The Bible has several stories about what happened when he did what he felt like doing rather than stopping to ask what God wanted him to do.

God has three good answers to this question. He uses three ways to tell us what He wants us to do. They are:

1. His Word, the Bible.
2. His providential workings.
3. His Holy Spirit working on our hearts.

The number one way for you to know God's will is to read the Bible. It isn't important to God whether or not you read your entire Bible from cover to cover this year, but it is important that you spend time reading it. Reading the Bible is more than just reading words. It's taking time to stop and think about what it says.

When you read a Bible story, it is good to ask yourself questions like these:

1. What is the lesson of this story?
2. What does it tell me about God's way?
3. Is this a story that tells me what to do? Or does it tell me what not to do?

The story of Daniel in the lions' den gives an example of how God rewards faith and trust in Him. Samson and Delilah give us a good example of what can happen when we break trust with God and do the opposite of what He asks. The story of John the Baptist shows that things don't always go right even if we do just as God wants. Other stories such as the one Jesus told about the widow's mite show how important each one of us and what we do is to God.

Can you think of other stories that give us good examples of how God wants us to live? ______________

____

____

Now list some stories that show what *not* to do.

____

____

What other stories show how important we are and what we do is to God? ______________________

____

What Bible story has most helped you in understanding what God wants you to do? ______________

____

NOVEMBER

27

How Do I Know? Part 2

When two good friends spend time together, both talk. Sometimes one talks more than the other, but over a period of time each talks about half the time. They don't time themselves; they just know when it's time to talk and when it's time to listen. Otherwise they probably won't stay good friends.

It's the same when we spend time with God. If we do all the talking, how will we know what God has to say? How will our friendship have a chance to grow? In our prayers we need to spend time being quiet. This is one of the best ways of giving God's Spirit an opportunity to speak to our hearts. Remember, prayer is not just talking *to* God. It is talking *with* God.

Here are some suggestions of ways to listen for God during your prayers. Give Him a chance to talk to you.

TALKING TO GOD	LISTENING TO GOD
1. Thank you for ________ ____________________	1. Wait a moment. Let Him remind you of something else for which you could say "Thanks."
2. I'm sorry about ________ ____________________	2. Take time to accept His forgiveness.
3. Please give me ________ ____________________	3. Take time to really listen now. Are you asking according to His will?
4. I really am upset about ____________________	4. God likes us to tell Him everything—our complaints as well as our happinesses. When complaining, though, listen very carefully. Let Him give you ideas of what to do about the problem.
5. Please help__________ (name)______ to ________ ____________________	5. God is pleased when we pray for others. Give Him time to suggest ways to help this person.

And this is how we know that he lives in us: We know it by the Spirit he gave us. 1 John 3:24.

NOVEMBER

28

The Skating Championships

Set your hope completely on the blessing which will be given you when Jesus Christ is revealed.
1 Peter 1:13, TEV.

I just feel this is the right thing for me to do!" Farrah smiled, and excitement crinkled around her eyes. "I'm so excited!"

Her mother studied the piece of paper that Farrah had handed her. "I'm very proud of you. To think that you've been chosen to represent your skating club at the competition!" She spoke very carefully. "This is very important to you, I know."

Farrah's smile began to fade at the tone of her mother's voice. "This is my chance!" she exclaimed. "If I win, then I'm on my way toward the Olympics!"

"But it says all participants must be at all trials on Friday and Saturday."

"I know. But Mom, I've thought about that, and I feel that it's right for me to go. This is my chance, and you know what you say about using my God-given talents." She spoke quickly.

"I've also tried to help you understand that feelings don't tell you what God wants for you," her mother replied.

Feelings usually tell you what *your* will is.

Your *mind* tells you what *God* wants.

Farrah is an excellent figure skater, and she dreamed of one day representing her country in the Olympics. Farrah had also grown up believing in God and the Bible.

"This decision concerns your future," her parents finally told her about participating in the weekend competition. "We're not going to stop you from competing. The choice will be yours. We want you to pray about it, though, and think about it carefully before you decide. We'll also be praying."

They prayed. Farrah decided not to compete, but before she even had a chance to tell her coach, she announced that her events had been rescheduled for Wednesday and Thursday. Farrah placed in the group that went on to the regional championships, but she never scored high enough to become part of the Olympic team.

Have you ever had to choose between what your feelings told you was right and what you knew that God wanted you to do?

How did you know the difference? ______________

What did you choose to do? ______________

Why? ______________

NOVEMBER

Like Trees Walking

He looked up and said, "I see people; they look like trees walking around." Mark 8:24.

The man felt himself being pushed forward between other people. *I wonder if He'll really do anything?* he asked himself. His friends continued to guide him.

"Touch Him! Touch Him!" they called.

Instead of feeling Someone touch him, the man heard a different voice, one he'd never heard before, yet he knew whose it was.

"Come!" the voice said, and the One who spoke took his hand and started to lead him away.

Where's He taking me? What's He going to do? The man's thoughts stumbled with curiosity as he let himself be led away from the noisy crowd at the edge of the village of Bethsaida. *This isn't what they said He'd do.*

They stopped. And . . .

He's put spit on my eyes! The man's free hand flew up.

In that instant he felt the hands of the young Prophet touch him, and he heard the question "Do you see anything?"

Until that moment the man really hadn't thought about what was going to happen to him. Being here wasn't his idea at all—his friends had literally taken him by the hand and had led him to where the Prophet was passing through.

Then it was as if someone had suddenly lit an oil lamp in pitch-blackness. Forms appeared. And they moved. "I see people!" he exclaimed. He blinked his eyes and then looked again. The objects blurred as they moved—they didn't look as he expected they should. "They . . . they look like trees walking."

What's going on? he wondered to himself. *My friends said all this Prophet had to do was touch me and I'd be able to see as good as new. Well, He's touched me and, of all things, He's even rubbed saliva on my eyes, and now He's asked me if I can see.*

The man blinked his eyes again. He knew that he was looking at people, but they still looked like walking trees. At that moment he began to realize what was happening. *If this Jesus can do even this much for me, He can also make my eyes so that I can see as clearly as anybody else.*

Just then Jesus put His hands on the man's eyes again. When He lifted them, the man was amazed at how clear and distinct everything around him had become. He looked at Jesus.

"I can see!" he exclaimed. "I can see clearly!"

Do you have enough faith to see Jesus clearly?

NOVEMBER

30

Another Blind Man

"Go," said Jesus, "your faith has healed you." Mark 10:52.

Another blind man, Bartimaeus, lived down at Jericho, many miles away from Bethsaida, where the man in yesterday's story was healed. Bartimaeus made his living by begging at the roadside that led out of the city.

"What's going on?" he asked one day when he heard the sounds of a large crowd.

"Jesus of Nazareth is just leaving the city," someone said.

When Bartimaeus heard that it was Jesus, he began to shout. "Jesus!" he called out. "Son of David! Take pity on me!"

"Be quiet!" the people around him scolded.

Bartimaeus shouted even more loudly. "Son of David! Take pity on me!"

At the sound of his shouting Jesus said, "Call him."

"Cheer up, Bartimaeus," the people said. "Get up, He's calling you to come."

Bartimaeus threw off his cloak, jumped up, and went to Jesus.

"What do you want Me to do for you?" Jesus asked him.

"Teacher," he said, "I want to see again."

"Go," Jesus said. "Your faith has made you well."

And in that instant Bartimaeus could see—and he followed Jesus along the road.

Bartimaeus and the man at Bethsaida were both blind, and both were healed by Jesus, but the stories of their healings are very different, as these comparisons show.

1. The man of Bethsaida was brought to Jesus by his friends, but Bartimaeus sat by the road where Jesus passed by.

2. The friends of the man called to Jesus, but the people told Bartimaeus to be quiet.

3. Jesus took the blind man's hand and led him from the crowd, but He told the people to call Bartimaeus to come.

4. Jesus asked the blind man if he could see, but He told Bartimaeus that he was healed.

5. Jesus healed the blind man by an unusual two-step process, but He healed Bartimaeus immediately by just speaking to him.

Which man do you think was happier?

Jesus promises His healing love to each of us. Have you asked Him for it yourself? Or are you waiting for someone to lead you to Him?

DECEMBER

1

The Chancellor of Christmas

Today is December 1, the first day of the Christmas month, and you have just been made the chancellor of Christmas. In some ways this makes you the most powerful person in the world because Christmas is the most widely celebrated Christian holiday. As chancellor you are responsible for everything to do with Christmas, and you can make and change any laws about it that you choose.

Think about what this would mean if such a thing really were to happen. First, in your opinion, what are the most important or most common things that people do during the Christmas season?

1. ______
2. ______
3. ______
4. ______
5. ______
6. ______
7. ______
8. ______

Now let's suppose that you have decided to make three new laws that you think will make the Christmas season around the world happier than any Christmas has ever been, and because of that, the world will become a better place to live.

What three laws would you make?

1. ______
2. ______
3. ______

Do you think that most of the people would follow your new laws? ______

Why or why not? ______

______

Jesus came on that first Christmas so that everyone in this world could have a happier life, but He didn't find many people who wanted to do things His way. Why?

______

______

If suddenly it were announced today that you were going to be made the chancellor of Christmas and that on December 25 you would be placed in charge of the entire world for that one day, what three things would you plan to do that would make the world a better place for everyone to live?

1. ______
2. ______
3. ______

I have come in order that you might have life—life in all its fullness. John 10:10, TEV.

DECEMBER

2

When Good People Die

May your unfailing love rest upon us, O Lord, even as we put our hope in you. Psalm 33:22.

Cliff let his head drop onto his arms. Big sobs shook his body. Rob was dead. *Dead!* Cliff couldn't believe it. He didn't want to believe it. He should be able to go over to the phone and call Rob and ask him about the hike they'd planned for next weekend. But he couldn't. Rob wasn't there. He was dead. He would never be there again.

The sobs continued to shake Cliff's whole body. How could this have happened?

Where was God? Why hadn't He protected Rob? Rob hadn't done anything wrong! The accident wasn't his fault!

Why did Rob have to die?

Have you ever wondered where God is when good people die in bad accidents? Have you ever wondered about God's promises about deliverance when a good kid dies from AIDS? Or from some other sickness that has nothing to do with anything he or she did? Have you ever been angry with God because He didn't send His angels to keep someone you love from dying?

Job's three friends told him that he was suffering because of his sins, that God was punishing him.

Job argued. He didn't know why God wouldn't answer his prayers or why he had to suffer. He told his friends that he had been kind and fair and had done what was right before God, and that therefore he was not being punished.

In the end, God got after the three friends because they had not spoken of Him what is right as Job had.

The book of Job shows how far Satan will go to try to make a good person sin. Satan tried to make Job curse God, but he failed.

But what about the times that good people do die?

Think about it this way. What is the next thing that person will know? Won't it be the happiness of seeing Jesus come in the clouds? Can you imagine someone who's been killed in a car wreck telling God, "But I don't want to go to heaven now. I was on my way to . . ."

Cliff was left to carry the sadness of not having Rob here on earth anymore, and Satan would have been delighted to hear him blame God for his sadness. But Cliff knew that more than anything else, he needed to trust God's love.

DECEMBER

The Hidden Godhead

To him who overcomes, I will give the right to sit with me on my throne, just as I overcame and sat down with my Father on his throne. *Revelation 3:21.*

An old Hindu legend says that once upon a time all people on earth were gods. They lived together happily and at peace. And then one day they sinned, grieving the divine spirit of Brahman, the god of all gods.

Because of this, Brahman decided that the godhead should be taken from people and that it should be hidden in a secret place where human beings would never again find it. He asked the advice of the other gods. "Where shall I hide it?" he asked. "Where is the best place to put the godhead so that people will never find it again?"

"Bury it deep in the earth," said one. "No one will ever think to dig deep enough to find it."

Brahman shook his head. "No," he said. "That would not be good enough. Human beings are sure to think of looking there, and they will dig until they find it."

"Sink it into the deepest ocean," said another. "Surely they will never find it on the floor of the deepest ocean."

"No," said Brahman. "That would not be good enough. They would think to look there and dive until they find it."

"Hide it on the highest mountain," suggested the third.

Brahman shook his head again. "No," he said. "Humans would look there, too. They would climb and find it."

Others gave additional suggestions, but none were good enough. At last Brahman said, "I know what we can do. We'll hide it inside human beings themselves. They think they're clever, but they'll never think to look within. They will look and look for the godhead, but will never find it."

But the legend is wrong. God has not hidden Himself where we cannot find Him. He's not hiding on the highest mountain or in the deepest sea. Neither has He, as this legend suggests, hidden Himself inside people. Even so, what He wants more than anything is to be invited to live in each of our hearts.

That secret—the secret to having God living in our hearts—does lie hidden within each of us. That secret is the power we have called the *will*.

The will is that part of each person that is the power of choice. God has given each one of us the power of choice, and along with it He has given us the freedom to choose.

If you want God to live in your heart, it's up to you to choose to invite Him.

DECEMBER

4

Good News

How wonderful it is to see a messenger coming across the mountains, bringing good news, the news of peace!
Isaiah 52:7, TEV.

Isaiah lived when times were tough. There was lots of trouble and unrest in the country, yet he is the Old Testament writer who talks most clearly about the good news of Jesus' coming to save His people and set them right with God. Here is one of Isaiah's good news passages.

"How beautiful upon the mountains
Are the feet of him who brings good news,
Who proclaims peace,
Who brings glad tidings of good things,
Who proclaims salvation,
Who says to Zion,
'Your God reigns!'
Your watchmen shall lift up their voices,
With their voices they shall sing together;
For they shall see eye to eye
When the Lord brings back Zion.
Break forth into joy, sing together,
You waste places of Jerusalem!
For the Lord has comforted His people,
He has redeemed Jerusalem.
The Lord has made bare His holy arm
In the eyes of all nations;
And all the ends of the earth shall see
The salvation of our God"
(Isaiah 52:7-10, NKJV).

What's the best piece of news in this passage from Isaiah? ____________________

____

What good news have you received lately? ________

____

What words describe how you felt when you heard it? ____________________

____

What good news have you been able to tell someone else? ____________________

____

How did you feel to be the one who told the good news? ____________________

____

What good news do you have to share during this Christmas season? ____________________

____

DECEMBER

St. Nicholas

Everyone is the friend of a man who gives gifts. Proverbs 19:6.

The old Christmas song says that you'd better be good because, as the title states, "Santa Claus Is Coming to Town." But if Christmas is all about Jesus, where did we get the idea of a Santa Claus who brings gifts?

The answer to that question goes back to the year 300 and a man named Nicholas, who was the son of a wealthy Christian. When his parents died, Nicholas gave everything to the poor and became a priest. After he died, stories about the good and kind things he had done grew into legends about miracles. Eventually the Roman Catholic Church made him a saint, and December 6, the day of his death, became St. Nicholas' Day.

Sailors chose Nicholas as their special saint and carried his worship to many seaport cities, including Amsterdam, the capital of the Netherlands. The Dutch built several St. Nicholas churches, and in the 1500s St. Nicholas choir boys were given money and a holiday on December 6. Later students in convent schools were rewarded—or punished—on that day by a teacher dressed as St. Nicholas. He was dressed in a long, red bishop's robe, wore a red-and-gold miter on his head, and had a flowing white beard.

The idea spread until St. Nicholas' Day became a nationwide event in Holland, and his common name became Sinterklaas.

Dutch children believe Sinterklaas comes to Amsterdam on a ship from Spain with his milk-white horse and his servant Piet. Then, wearing his long, red robe, he rides his horse across the rooftops, stopping to listen at chimneys to hear if the children are good or bad. Piet scatters goodies through slightly open doors and leaves presents on December 5, St. Nicholas' Eve.

The Dutch brought their Sinterklaas traditions to the New World. These blended with notions of the fat, jolly Father Christmas of the English, and the name gradually changed to a legend of a Santa Claus who lives at the North Pole, drives a team of reindeer, stops on housetops, and clambers down chimneys to leave toys for the good children. Santa is still sometimes called St. Nicholas and remains a big part of the tradition of Christmas giving.

On the first Christmas God gave the greatest gift this world has ever received. He wants nothing more than for us to accept this gift and to be His friends.

DECEMBER

6

The Gifts of Christmas

And when they had opened their treasures, they presented gifts to Him: gold, frankincense, and myrrh. Matthew 2:11, NKJV.

Jasmin went over her list again. "Mom, Dad, Uncle Theo, Ms. Jensen, Sarah, Holly, Grandma." She read the names one by one. "And my two brothers and . . ."

She pressed her pen down hard as she added their names.

"I can't even afford to buy nice cards for all the people I want to give presents to."

Do you ever dream of what you could do if you had all the money you could possibly spend and could buy anything you wanted to buy? That's what Jasmin wished for when she again read over her list.

If you had all the money you could use, what special Christmas gifts would you buy? To whom would you give them? ______________________________

____

____

____

____

____

____

____

____

Jasmin knew that dreaming about what she'd do if she had enough money to buy gifts for everyone would not solve her Christmas problem.

"Give a wise man's gift," her grandma suggested.

"Wise man's gift?" Jasmin asked. "But those were very rich gifts."

Her grandma nodded. "Rich, but given to Jesus, not to just anyone. When Christmases come and I can't afford to give a fancy gift to someone special, I give a gift of prayer for that person instead. Sometimes I write a Christmas letter to let the person know that I've set aside a certain time to pray for him or her each week. Sometimes I keep it a secret."

Jasmin looked thoughtful. "Do you suppose it'd be OK if I'd make all the people cards and put in pictures of what I'd give them if I could, and then tell them that instead I'm giving them a gift of prayer?"

"I think that's an excellent idea," said her grandmother.

DECEMBER

7

The Creaky Old House

When you lie down, you will not be afraid; when you lie down, your sleep will be sweet. . . . For the Lord will be your confidence. Proverbs 3:24-26.

Once upon a long-ago time we lived in a weather-beaten gray two-story box of a house. When the blustery winds of the winter storms roared in from the coast, the old house shivered and shook and seemed to sway. Even when there were no storms, it still had a way of creaking and groaning, especially during the long winter evenings. Sometimes it sounded as though someone were crouching in the shadowy corners, even when there was nobody there. "What if someone's hiding up there?" I'd ask my mother when she announced that it was time for bed.

"Don't be silly," she'd say. "Come and I'll show you." And she'd get the big flashlight and climb the stairs with me and shine the light in all the corners—just to show me that no one was there. And I'd go to bed feeling safe.

On other nights, though, she'd just say, "Of course there's no one up there." And she'd shoo me off toward the stairs.

And I'd try to be brave.

Just to be safe, though, sock-footed I'd creep slowly up the long flight of stairs, keeping to the side so the steps wouldn't creak. When I reached the top, I'd bound across the large attic space, not daring to look toward the corners and forcing long, hurried strides toward my bedroom door. Then with a flying leap, I'd hurtle myself into bed. There I'd huddle, covers pulled tight, scarcely daring to breathe, hoping that whoever or whatever might be hiding in the shadowy corners would not get me.

My common sense told me that I was being foolish, yet I was afraid.

Do you ever feel frightened, even when you know there's no real reason to be afraid?

It's normal to be afraid sometimes. And it's comforting to have someone you trust by your side to show you that there really is nothing to fear.

When we get to know Jesus really well, He'll give us that kind of security.

DECEMBER

8

Can We Find Anyone Like This?

God will give Pharaoh the answer he desires. Genesis 41:16.

This is a dramatic reading adapted from Genesis 41:1-16, 25-27, 29-40. (See the instructions on page 28.)

NARRATOR: Pharaoh had two dreams that troubled him but that none of his wise men could interpret.

CUPBEARER: Today I am reminded of my shortcomings. Pharaoh was once angry with his servants, and he imprisoned me and the chief baker. . . . Each of us had a dream the same night, and each dream had a meaning of its own. Now a young Hebrew was there with us, a servant of the captain of the guard. We told him our dreams, and he interpreted them for us. . . . And things turned out exactly as he interpreted them to us: . . .

NARRATOR: So Pharaoh sent for Joseph, and he was quickly brought from the dungeon. . . . Pharaoh said to Joseph,

PHARAOH: I had a dream, and no one can interpret it. But I have heard it said of you that when you hear a dream you can interpret it.

JOSEPH: I cannot do it, but God will give Pharaoh the answer he desires.

NARRATOR: Then Pharaoh described his two dreams . . .

JOSEPH: The dreams of Pharaoh are one and the same. God has revealed to Pharaoh what he is about to do. The seven good cows are seven years, and the seven good heads of grain are seven years; it is one and the same dream. The seven lean, ugly cows that came up afterward are seven years, and so are the seven worthless heads of grain scorched by the east wind: They are seven years of famine. Seven years of great abundance are coming throughout the land of Egypt, but seven years of famine will follow them. Let Pharaoh appoint commissioners over the land to take a fifth of the harvest of Egypt during the seven years of abundance. They should collect all the food of these good years that are coming and store up the grain under the authority of Pharaoh, to be kept in the cities for food.

NARRATOR: The plan seemed good to Pharaoh and to all his officials. So Pharaoh asked them,

PHARAOH: Can we find anyone like this man, one in whom is the spirit of God?

NARRATOR: Then Pharaoh said to Joseph,

PHARAOH: Since God has made all this known to you, there is no one so discerning and wise as you. You shall be in charge of my palace.

A. Can we find anyone like this man?

B. The plan seemed good.

C. I am reminded of my shortcomings.

D. You shall be in charge.

E. ________ will not be remembered.

1. These phrases are exact words taken from the story of Pharaoh and Joseph. Choose one and think of a situation in which you would like to hear those words. Tell (or write) about it. *Or*

2. In 15 minutes, plan and act out an impromptu skit with your family or worship partners. Have it show a Christian moral. Be sure that at least one of the characters uses the exact words of one (or more) of these phrases. You may surprise yourselves with the good results and fun you can have doing this. You may even create something you'll want to share at Sabbath school or at a youth meeting. *Or*

3. Using one of these phrases as a theme, give a short, impromptu (spur-of-the-moment) worship talk.

DECEMBER

In Another Time and Another Place

God has shown you all this, so it is obvious that you have greater wisdom and insight than anyone else. I will put you in charge of my country. Genesis 41:39, 40, TEV.

DECEMBER

10

The Light in the Church

You are the light of the world. A city on a hill cannot be hidden. Matthew 5:14.

Kitenge village was big—and growing bigger. In fact, it had become the most important village in the chief's entire chiefdom. Only a few Adventists lived there, but they wanted to build a nice church, one that would honor God.

"You do the work, and we'll bring you the materials," the missionaries from a distant mission promised.

The Kitenge church members made bricks, laid the foundation, built the walls, and then waited. The missionaries had promised to bring wood for the rafters. They couldn't put the roof on without the wood.

Weeks passed. "Your missionaries have forgotten you!" their neighbors said.

The leader of a heathen group came to visit the pastor. "One of my men had a dream," he claimed. "In his dream he saw that the rains will soon come. When they come, they will make your church fall down."

The pastor listened patiently. In fact, he himself had begun to worry. The rains had started, and the missionaries still had not come. He called the members together to pray.

"Your church will fall down," more and more people said. "We don't need your church in our village."

"God will protect our church," the members replied. "You'll see. He'll protect our church."

"A witch doctor is making strong charms," someone else reported. "They'll for sure make the walls of your church fall."

Then another man visited the pastor. "Have your missionaries come?" he asked.

"Why do you ask?" replied the pastor.

"We saw a light in your church last night."

"No one's come. No one was in the church," said the pastor.

More nights passed, and there was more talk about a light in the unfinished Adventist church. The pastor investigated. There was no trace of anyone or anything that could cause a light.

"The witch doctor is afraid of the light in your church," others reported. "Is it the light of Jesus?"

The rain continued to fall, but the walls stood until the missionaries did arrive. In a few days the roof was on, and the church stood strong and ready. The members painted it a solid white, and then it stood like a light on the hill.

DECEMBER

11

Make the Strings Sing

Whatever your hand finds to do, do it with all your might. Ecclesiastes 9:10.

Lynne hunched over her cello, shoulders rounded, head down, eyes seeing nothing but the page of notes on the music stand. She clutched the bow timidly and sawed at the strings.

"Lynne," Ms. Fletcher said gently, "you must draw your bow in full, long strokes."

Lynne started again, but she still scuffed the bow across the strings so it made only hoarse, throaty sounds.

"Lynne," Ms. Fletcher spoke her name more firmly this time, "you must draw full, long strokes, and make the strings sing each note."

"But what if I make a mistake?" Lynne spoke more into the back of her cello than to her teacher.

"That's why I'm here, so I can help you learn how to play the hard parts."

"I don't want you to hear my mistakes."

"You can't hide your mistakes," Ms. Fletcher replied. "Even if you hunch over and don't play with a full bow. Even if you play very, very softly, I'll still hear your mistakes."

"I don't want them to be big and bad, though. I don't want to spoil the music." For the first time Lynne looked up at her teacher.

"Unless you draw the bow with confidence, you'll never be able to play pretty music. To make the music sound as it should, you must use long, full strokes." Ms. Fletcher laid her hand over Lynne's. "Like this. Long strokes. Strong strokes. Make the strings sing. Then, if a mistake happens, it stands out. You'll hear it easier yourself, and it will be easier for you to correct."

Lynne played a few practice notes. She looked up at her teacher. "Like this?"

Ms. Fletcher nodded and smiled. "Now, let's start again."

Have you ever met Christians who, like Lynne, seem to keep their heads down and shoulders hunched, afraid to admit who they are because they might make a mistake? Or because of what someone might think?

God is more interested in lives that sing with confidence in Him than He is in mistakes. He wants you to search for Him with all your heart and accept Him with confidence. Only as you live for God with your whole heart will your life for Him be beautiful.

DECEMBER

12

Some Magic Day

Do you truly love me? John 21:16.

"Are you ready for Jesus to come?"

Gabriel bit his lip. Pastor Smyth seemed to be looking straight at him. *I want to be ready,* he thought to himself. *I want to go to heaven.*

"Wanting to go to heaven's not enough," Pastor Smyth said as if reading Gabriel's thoughts. "You need to *know* that you belong to Jesus right this very minute." He emphasized the word *know*.

How can anyone know? Gabriel asked himself as he listened. *I'm a good person. I don't get in trouble for doing bad things. But how can I know if I'm good enough?*

"Deep in your heart *you know* whether or not you have given yourself completely to Jesus."

Gabriel felt a coldness grab at the pit of his stomach. *I'm a good person,* he told himself again. *That's what Christians are—good people.*

"Jesus came to this world so you could be set right with God and kept right, but He can't make you right unless you give Him every part of your life, every secret that you have tucked away inside your heart. He wants to be your best and closest friend. He wants you to be like Him. He . . ."

The coldness lay heavier in Gabriel's stomach, almost like a being-scared feeling. *But I don't feel anything special about Jesus*. The thought surprised him. Then he realized something else. *I don't even like reading the Bible. It's just something I've got to do*. He'd never let himself think such thoughts before. *But I'll keep reading it*, he told himself quickly, *and maybe someday I'll like it.*

Gabriel is not the only person who has surprised himself with thinking such thoughts. He didn't like the idea, but he knew that as scary as they were, his thoughts were true. He didn't know it then, but those very thoughts were an important step in his giving his heart completely to Jesus.

Many people make themselves read the Bible, and they say that they follow Jesus. Deep inside, though, they know that they're only doing that because they want to go to heaven. It's as if they're waiting for some magic day when something inside them will change and they'll automatically love Jesus and He'll become the most important person to them and they'll become excited about reading the Bible.

Are you waiting for some magic day like that, or do you truly love Jesus?

DECEMBER

13

Today

Listen! This is the hour to receive God's favor; today is the day to be saved!
2 Corinthians 6:2, TEV.

If you love Jesus, raise your hand."

Pastor Smyth's sermon was drawing to a close, and at those words Gabriel obediently raised his hand—as he'd always done ever since he could remember—to show that he loved Jesus.

But . . . but I don't know if I really love Him. His thoughts kept pulling him in that same surprising way, and he started to let his hand slip down. He looked quickly around. All his friends had their hands up. *Am I the only one who's not sure?* he asked himself, and for a horrible moment he had the idea that when Jesus came, he'd want to run and hide himself among the rocks while all his friends would be going to heaven.

Jesus! The word almost formed as a whisper on Gabriel's lips. *Jesus, take every part of my life. Set it right.*

Gabriel had never ever meant any words of any prayer as much as he meant those words, and in that instant the heavy, cold feeling that had been lying in his stomach was gone, and he felt warm and light and happy. He knew that Jesus had heard his prayer.

"For those of you who raised your hands, I want to remind you that it's not enough just to say that you love Jesus," Pastor Smyth continued. "You need to give Him ever part of your life, everything you like, everything you love. In exchange He'll fill your heart with His love, and you'll find that you'll want to spend more time with Him, praying and reading your Bible. The more you spend time with Him, the more you'll become like Him."

Gabriel had heard words like that before, but for the first time he found himself listening carefully.

"But it's not all easy." The pastor's voice became very serious. "The devil is going to try every trick he knows to discourage you. He's going to tempt you with too much television, or with sports, or even with too much of a good thing like homework—anything that will fill your mind so there'll be no room for Jesus. Being tempted, though, is not a problem as long as you stay close to Jesus. Learn to talk to Him any time and all the time, not just when you have your devotions. He'll be there to help you."

Pastor Smyth took off his glasses and laid them on the pulpit. "The Bible says that today is the day to be saved. Today," he repeated, and smiled, "let me remind you of a simple fact—each new day becomes today. If you keep your heart open to Him every day, Jesus will keep you right each 'today' as it comes."

DECEMBER

14

Tougher and Better

He has showed you, O man, what is good. And what does the Lord require of you? To act justly and to love mercy and to walk humbly with your God. Micah 6:8.

John Hornby was rather short, but he was strong. He always wanted to do things a little better than anyone else could. If someone worked hard, John would work harder. If others worked long days, John would work longer. If someone carried a heavy load, John would carry a heavier load. When he came to Canada from England, he decided to prove that he was tougher and could live in the wilderness better than anyone else.

Men of the north are good at hiding their feelings, so John tried never to show how he felt about anything. The Inuit or Eskimo people didn't talk very much, so John would go for days without saying a word. Even the Inuit hunters worried about this, because when they went out for a hunt, they always told others where they were going and when they planned to be back so if something should happen to them others would know where to look for them. But John never told his plans to anyone.

One time, though, when traveling down a river in the Northwest Territories with two other men, John suddenly seemed to become excited about something. Of course, he never said a word about what he saw.

John's sister came to Canada with her son Christian and Christian's friend. John invited the young men to go north with him, and he took them up the river to the place he'd seen that day. There were trees—John had never seen trees so far north—and a clearing that would make an ideal place for a cabin. Caribou passed that way, so he was sure they'd find plenty to eat. True to his ways, though, John never told anyone where they were going or when they'd be back.

They built a cabin and settled in for the long winter. That fall, though, the caribou didn't come, and John and his nephew found little other game. Before long their food supplies ran out.

No one was surprised when the three of them did not come back in the summer—that was like John. Several years passed, and still no one saw anything of them. Then the two men who had been in the canoe with John remembered the place along the river where he seemed to become excited. A plane flew over and found the cabin, but saw no one. Others went in by river. They saw the signs and found a diary Christian had written. It told the sad story of how they'd starved to death.

Do you try to prove that you're better than others, or do you walk humbly with your God?

DECEMBER

Protected

Put on the full armor of God so that you can take your stand against the devil's schemes. Ephesians 6:11.

"Look! Look!"

Baby Breanne waved her hands and started on galloping little steps toward the pretty butterfly that rested on a flower. But before she had gone six steps the butterfly flicked its bright blue wings and sailed off, flitting this way and that above the mission yard.

Off in the Central American forest, another bright, blue-winged butterfly floated along. Big, beautiful, and easy to see, it looked easy to catch, and a sharp-beaked bird swooped toward it.

Butterflies are one of the most delicate of God's creatures and have no way of fighting back when something attacks. But as the bird zoomed downward, the blue-winged butterfly suddenly started to fly very fast. Turning quickly and slipping from side to side, it dodged out of the way. Disappointed, the bird pulled out of its dive and flew off to find something else.

Many butterflies, like the blue butterfly in Breanne's yard and the other blue-winged butterfly in the forest, can speed up so quickly that they can outfly a bird, while others that can't fly so fast start zigzagging back and forth in such a way that the birds can't catch them. But not all butterflies can do that, and with 80 kinds of tropical birds that live by catching insects on the wing, how can these butterflies escape?

Well, some butterflies eat plants that make them taste bad—these include the monarch, which feeds on milkweed when it's a caterpillar. Most bad-tasting butterflies have similar bright colors that the birds learn to recognize and avoid. Some good-tasting butterflies also have these same color patterns, which helps them escape being eaten. Other good-tasting butterflies that can't fly well have the same color patterns as butterflies that are good fliers.

Another tasty butterfly never flies higher than a few inches above the forest floor, so that birds can't dive for it without crashing.

Birds learn to recognize the different color patterns, and they don't go after those that say "I taste bad," and seldom bother to chase those that say "You can't catch me!"

The devil, though, can't be fooled against snaring us with sin no matter how much we try to look like a good Christian. Are you protected with the whole armor of God? How?

DECEMBER

16

The Lost Sheep

Then Jesus told them this parable:

"Suppose one of you has a hundred sheep and loses one of them—what does he do? He leaves the other ninety-nine sheep in the pasture and goes looking for the one that got lost until he finds it. When he finds it, he is so happy that he puts it on his shoulders and carries it back home. Then he calls his friends and neighbors together and says to them, 'I am so happy I found my lost sheep. Let us celebrate!'" (Luke 15:4-6, TEV).

A. Using what you know about sheep, imagine what might have happened to the lost sheep and answer these questions.

1. Why did it get lost? ____________________
2. How did it get lost? ____________________
3. How did it feel when it realized it was lost?

____

____

4. What did it do then? ____________________
5. How long was it lost? ____________________
6. How did it feel when the shepherd finally found it? ____________________
7. What did the sheep do when it was back home? ____________________

____

Use your answers to tell a story about the sheep—or to write a story, poem, or song.

B. Have you ever felt like the sheep in your story? What made you feel that way? What happened to make you feel better?

C. Think of pictures you could make to show . . .

1. the sheep when it was lost.
2. the sheep when it was back home.

Now, answer these questions for each picture: Where would the sheep be? What would it look like? What other things would be in the picture? What colors would you use?

Draw or paint one of the pictures.

D. Several songs have been written about this story. Some are in *The SDA Hymnal*. To find them, look in the index entitled "Scriptural Allusions in Hymns" for songs that go with the story text (Luke 15:4-7).

Would any Christmas songs go well with this story? Play or sing some of these songs.

There will be more joy in heaven over one sinner who repents than over ninety-nine respectable people who do not need to repent. Luke 15:7, TEV.

DECEMBER

To Swallow a Camel

You blind guides! You strain out a gnat but swallow a camel. Matthew 23:24.

Whenever I read that text about swallowing a camel, I think of the silly words of the old nonsense song "I Know an Old Lady." The song says that the old lady swallowed a spider that wriggled and jiggled and tickled inside her. And then, to catch the spider, she went on to swallow all sorts of other living things until she finally swallowed a horse. It ends with a quick "She's dead of course!"

Jesus sometimes used hyperbole—exaggeration—to catch people's attention and get them to think about what they were doing.

No one could ever possibly swallow a camel. Of course Jesus knew that, and so did the scribes and Pharisees He was talking to. Those same scribes and Pharisees also had to admit that they used a linen or gauze cloth to strain anything they were going to drink. This was so that they would not, by accident, break the law by swallowing even the tiniest unclean insect.

In the Jewish law the gnat is on the list of unclean foods and therefore not to be eaten. So is the camel.

"Camels indeed!" harrumphed the Pharisees, annoyed that the people enjoyed the way this young Teacher had of putting them on the spot. No Pharisee would ever think of eating camel meat.

Jesus knew that, too, but He had other things in mind. He wanted them to see that while they were so careful and so bossy about the tiniest details of laws—the gnats—they'd become very unkind and unjust in their behavior and they'd just as well be eating camel meat.

Because of their laws, no one even dared carry a handkerchief in the usual manner on the Sabbath day because then it would be considered carrying a burden, working, and that person would charged with Sabbath-breaking.

Jesus wanted everyone to understand that it was more important to live God's love by being just and fair and gentle and considerate than to worry about how to carry some little thing on the Sabbath day without being guilty of working.

"The man's a sinner!" they raged. "He heals people on the Sabbath day—right in the synagogue even. And He had the audacity to tell one cripple to get up and walk and carry his bed—on the Sabbath day!"

They didn't—or couldn't—understand His love, and went right on swallowing their camels.

DECEMBER

18

The Parable of the Mice

If you are willing and obedient, you will eat the best from the land. Isaiah 1:19.

Once upon a not too-long-ago time, a little mouse lived in a cozy burrow in the corner of a very large field. He was a rather handsome little mouse, with a silky gray coat, a nose that was pointed just enough, a just-right tail, and whiskers that made him look very intelligent.

"Always respect that which belongs to others," warned wise old grandfather mouse. "Follow the counsel of those who are wise, and you will live a useful and happy life."

Little mouse dipped his nose politely.

"We mice belong to the order of those who gnaw," wise old grandfather said as he drew himself up straighter. "That is what our family name, 'Rodent,' means. Gnawing is a good and useful talent, but you must learn to gnaw only the right things."

Little mouse again dipped his nose very politely.

"Your house mouse cousins are in serious trouble. Many have even lost their lives—because they gnaw wherever they want. Some chew on electric wires and on matches and set horrible fires. Others chew through the frames of buildings, pull insulation from walls, and get into cupboards and food supplies. That has angered peoplekind, and they've made war against all of mouse-dom."

"Is war bad?"

"Very bad. And it will come to our field if we don't carefully obey the law of wisdom. Do you see those trees over there?" Old wise grandfather pointed with his paw.

Little mouse nodded.

"Never chew on the bark of those trees—they belong to humans."

"But isn't there anything we can eat without making them angry?" little mouse asked, not minding that he was interrupting.

"Certainly. We have many good trees and plants and seeds—more than enough."

"Then why should anyone want to eat what isn't ours?"

"Because many things look very good and are so tempting to try. But if we follow the law of wisdom, we'll live in peace and eat the good of the land that we have."

Satan makes sin look very good in order to tempt you and trap you into being a fighter on his side in his war with heaven.

In what ways might you "eat the good of the land" if you obey the law of wisdom that God has given?

DECEMBER

19

Almost Christmas and . . .

With righteousness he will judge the needy, with justice he will give decisions for the poor. Isaiah 11:4.

This is a group reading.

SOLO: My people are bent on turning away from me (Hosea 11:7). How can I consider a man pure with his loaded balances and his bag of false weights? The rich among you are full of violence, your citizens are liars every one (Micah 6:11, 12). The daughters of Zion are high and mighty, walking with their noses in the air (Isaiah 3:16). The young behave rudely towards the old (verse 5). You say, "When will the Sabbath be over so that we may offer our corn for sale?" (Amos 8:4).

CHOIR: How shall I come into the presence of the Lord? (Micah 6:6).

SOLO: You know well enough, O man, what is good! For what does the Lord require of you, but to be just, to love mercy, and to walk humbly with your God? (verse 8). Cease to do wrong, learn to do good, seek justice, restrain violence, defend the right of the orphan, champion the cause of the widow. Come, now, and let us settle the matter. . . . Though your sins are like scarlet, they shall be as white as snow; though they are red like crimson, they shall become as wool (Isaiah 1:17, 18).

CHOIR: He will come back, he will pity us, he will trample our sins under his feet. Yes, you will cast all our sins into the depth of the sea (Micah 7:19).

SOLO: Make yourselves ready to meet your God, Israel. Remember, it is the one who forms the mountains and creates the wind, and the Lord, God of hosts, is his name! (Amos 4:12, 13).

CHOIR: This is the Lord for whom we have waited; let us rejoice and exult in his deliverance! (Isaiah 25:9).

What about this Christmas season most reminds you of these Old Testament "sins"? ____________________

____

What good things are people doing now that make God happy? ____________________

____

This Christmas what are you doing to get ready to meet God? ____________________

____

What part of this reading gives you the most joy?

____

____

Which Christmas carols do you think best match this reading? ____________________

____

DECEMBER

20

Make Up Your Mind

Run in such a way as to get the prize.
1 Corinthians 9:24.

Talitha decided that she would like to play clarinet in the school band and that she wasn't going to be just any old kind of clarinet player who would always sit in the back row behind the others and be happy to play only easy music. She was going to become the very best clarinet player she could possibly be, and someday she would sit on the very front row on the very first chair that was for the best player.

Her parents bought her a nice new clarinet. Talitha opened the case and looked at the black pieces with the shiny silver keys. She took the two main pieces out of the case, held down the F-sharp ring on the one, just like the band director had shown her so the levers wouldn't jam, and carefully fitted the pieces together. Then she put on the bell, the barrel, and the mouthpiece.

"It sure looks nice," she told herself, and she set the clarinet on the top shelf of her bookcase. "Won't everyone be surprised when I take it to band tomorrow?"

Talitha left the clarinet lying on the shelf. She didn't practice placing her fingers on the keys to get the feel of where they should be, and she didn't try blowing through the mouthpiece.

Everyone knows that having a clarinet will not automatically make the person a good clarinet player, any more than owning a football will make anyone a good football player. It takes practice to become a good musician or a good athlete—lots of practice and training.

Talitha was serious about learning to play the clarinet, though, and she left her new instrument lying on the shelf just long enough to hurry down to the family room to get her music book. It had the instructions and the fingering chart that would show her how to play properly.

She practiced every day after school, but for many months she sat on the very last chair in the back row of the clarinet section. She didn't mind, though, because she knew that after she learned to play the easy parts, she could move on to the more difficult music—if she continued to practice.

She did. And one day she was ready to move to the first chair.

Have you made up your mind to one day have the prize of a crown that will last forever?

DECEMBER

21

Hannah Marie's Gift

We have different gifts, according to the grace given us. Romans 12:6.

"You do have a talent for growing flowers!" Hannah Marie's mother declared. "You've inherited your grandmother Hannah's green thumb along with her name."

"Growing flowers is too easy to be a talent," Hannah Marie said. "All you have to do is put a plant in some dirt in a pot, set it on a shelf, and take care of it."

Her mother smiled. "That sounds easy," she replied, "but I know some folks who put plants in pots of dirt, set them on a shelf, and water them, yet the plants never ever grow as they should."

"But each one needs a certain kind of soil and the right amount of light. Some like lots of water, and some like only a little."

"And some folks just don't know which likes what."

"It's easy to learn."

Easy if you like growing flowers.

Hannah Marie loved taking care of her flowers, and for Christmas she'd decided to share some of her nicest plants. Mrs. Falston, her teacher, would receive one of the best plants of all.

"It's an ivy geranium," Hannah Marie said when Mrs. Falston thanked her. "It'll grow rather quickly, and you'll need to transplant it soon. It'd be nice in a hanging basket—be sure to use some peat moss in the new soil. And be sure that it gets plenty of sun and that you don't overwater it." Hannah Marie spoke quickly when she got excited about explaining how to take care of plants.

Mrs. Falston listened carefully. "Oh, dear!" she exclaimed. "I hope I can remember all that. I'm happy to have a plant from your very own collection—you have such a gift for growing green things. I just hope it will do well for me."

"Oh, it'll grow easily," Hannah Marie said.

A few weeks later Mrs. Falston called Hannah Marie aside. "The plant that you gave me for Christmas isn't doing so well. Would it be all right if I brought it to school so you can show me exactly how to care for it?" She sounded a little ashamed. "I might be able to teach reading and arithmetic, but I need you to teach me about plants."

Hannah Marie smiled. She was beginning to understand that growing flowers was a special talent after all.

What gifts has God given you that you can share with others?

DECEMBER

22

The Lady in the Elevator

Blessed is he who is kind to the needy. Proverbs 14:21.

It was a dreary Oregon day many Decembers ago, wet and cold and soggy. Geraldine ducked her head and pulled her coat closer. Water squashed up from under her boots as she trotted beside her mother and brother toward the tall building on the corner.

"Can we look in a store after?" she asked.

"Not today." Her mother's voice was very businesslike.

Once inside, their steps took them straight toward the elevator. She giggled to herself—most of Garold's head was lost inside a huge blue stocking cap and in the long scarf their mother had wound round his throat and across his face.

"My brother's sick," Geraldine explained to the lady with pretty hair and a nice coat, who had entered the elevator with them. "We're taking him to the doctor. His throat's sore 'cause he has tonsils."

The lady smiled. "Oh!" she said.

"Tonsillitis," her mother corrected.

"That's too bad," said the lady. "And it's almost Christmas."

Geraldine nodded.

"What have you asked Santa Claus to bring you?"

Now, Geraldine knew perfectly well Santa Claus didn't bring their Christmas presents—and this year nobody would. "Oh, we won't be having any Christmas presents," she said politely.

"No presents!" exclaimed the lady. "Why ever not?"

" 'Cause my daddy's out of work."

Just then the elevator stopped, and the three of them hurried down the hall to the doctor's office. Garold got some medicine, and Geraldine forgot all about the lady in the elevator. The next day when they were listening to the radio, though, an announcement caught their attention.

"Would the mother of the little girl in the elevator whose father is out of work please contact this address?"

"Mama!" Geraldine exclaimed. "That lady from the elevator wants you to call her."

Her mother did.

On the day of Christmas Eve, a big box came with presents for all of them—a big blue truck for Garold, a doll and a pretty purse just the right size for Geraldine, some things for their parents, and even some food.

Geraldine has never forgotten the kindness of the lady in the elevator, who understood the true meaning of Christmas.

DECEMBER

23

A Special Gift

Santa's going to bring me a woodburning set for Christmas. He promised." Excitement skittered through Sue-Jean's words. "He promised, and I know he will." She hopped into the back seat of their old car. "I'm going to have a woodburning set. He promised."

"But you know that Santa is just a man wearing a red suit, who pretends to be a Santa," her mother began.

"But he promised," Sue-Jean insisted. "I told him all about how we would be at Grandpa and Grandma's. And he said that if they didn't have a fireplace, to just leave the door unlocked, and he could slip the woodburning set in." In her excitement she could hardly stop talking. "He did promise!"

"But you know that Santa is just pretend," her mother repeated. "He promises only those things that he thinks the mothers and fathers might get for their children."

"He said . . ."

Sue-Jean was not going to give up.

Two weeks after Christmas a big brown parcel arrived in the mail with Sue-Jean's name written on it. It came from the catalogue mail-order house. "It's something special for you," her mother said.

Sue-Jean eagerly tore the paper off, and inside she found exactly the woodburning set she had wanted. "See!" she exclaimed. "Santa did keep his promise."

Her mother shook her head. "Daddy and I ordered it for you," she explained.

It's easy for small children to believe in Santa Claus—especially when they get the gifts they ask for. It's also easy for those who are a little bigger to treat God like Santa Claus—to use their prayers only to ask Him to give them things they want.

God *does* want us to have good gifts, but in His love He also wants us to realize that being His child means more than just giving Him a selfish list of things we want.

What are some of the good gifts that God gives?
How can we keep our prayers from being selfish?
What is the best gift that God has ever given?
What are you giving God in return?

If you then, though you are evil, know how to give good gifts to your children, how much more will your Father in heaven give the Holy Spirit to those who ask him! Luke 11:13.

DECEMBER

24

The First Christmas

This child is chosen by God for the destruction and the salvation of many in Israel. Luke 2:34, TEV.

This is a dramatic reading from Luke 2:8-20, TEV. (See instructions on page 28.)

NARRATOR: There were some shepherds in that part of the country who were spending the night in the fields, taking care of their flocks. An angel of the Lord appeared to them, and the glory of the Lord shone over them. They were terribly afraid, but the angel said to them,

ANGEL: Don't be afraid! I am here with good news for you, which will bring great joy to all the people. This very day in David's town your Savior was born—Christ the Lord! And this is what will prove it to you: you will find a baby wrapped in strips of cloth and lying in a manger.

NARRATOR: Suddenly a great army of heaven's angels appeared with the angel, singing praises to God:

ANGELS: Glory to God in the highest heaven, and peace on earth to those with whom he is pleased!

[If you wish, sing "Hark the Herald Angels Sing."]

NARRATOR: When the angels went away from them back into heaven, the shepherds said to one another,

SHEPHERDS: Let's go to Bethlehem and see this thing that has happened, which the Lord has told us.

[Sing "O Little Town of Bethlehem."]

NARRATOR: So they hurried off and found Mary and Joseph and saw the baby lying in the manger. When the shepherds saw him, they told them what the angel had said about the child. All who heard it were amazed at what the shepherds said. Mary remembered all these things and thought deeply about them. The shepherds went back, singing praises to God for all they had heard and seen; it had been just as the angel had told them.

[Sing "Away in a Manger."]

DECEMBER

The Package Looks Right

Jesus answered: "Watch out that no one deceives you. For many will come in my name, claiming, 'I am the Christ,' and will deceive many." Matthew 24:4, 5.

Have you ever wanted something to happen so much that you would believe anyone who said it would happen?

I can remember the Christmas when I was 6 years old. I wanted nothing in the world more than a model farm with a big red metal barn. And lots of brown cows. And some horses. And a tractor and hay wagon. And a white rail fence that I could put all around. Not a day went by that I didn't tell anyone who would listen about the farm set that I wanted. I even showed them its exact picture in the Christmas catalog.

At last Dad brought home a tree. We trimmed it and set it in the living room. Soon a collection of prettily wrapped presents began to appear under it. Some were hard boxlike rectangles. Some were flat and floppy like clothes. Some had a card with my mom's name, some with my dad's, some with mine. Then one morning I saw it. A big present. Long. And just high enough to hold a barn.

"Is that my farm?" I asked Mom, not even bothering to check the tag.

She just smiled and said, "You'll have to wait till Christmas Eve to find out."

I asked Dad. He just shrugged his shoulders.

Then I asked my uncle. He smiled, and there was a mischievous twinkle in his eye. "It looks to be just the right size, doesn't it?"

That was all I needed to hear. I knew it was my farm. I could hardly wait until Christmas Eve. At last it was time to open our presents. I ripped off the paper and opened the big box and there it lay—the biggest, most beautiful *doll* I had ever seen, one that should have thrilled any little girl's heart. I felt the tears start to come. "But I wanted a farm. Uncle said . . ."

". . . that the package looked to be the right size," Mom finished for me.

I learned to love my dolly dearly. And I did get my farm set—later. But I remember the terrible disappointment that came from hearing what I wanted to hear.

Jesus warns us against being deceived by those who claim to be the Christ. We must be careful to check the evidence. Otherwise we could be fooled by a package that looks to be the right size.

DECEMBER

26

The Winning Team

Then choose for yourselves this day whom you will serve. Joshua 24:15.

Quin pulled his tuque (knitted cap) down over his ears, slipped his hockey stick through the handle of his gear bag, and hoisted it over his shoulder. "I'm going now," he called up the stairs. "Eon's on his way, and the other guys are coming."

"Make sure the ice is in good shape," his dad called back. "I'll be there at 2:00 for our game."

Each year on Boxing Day, as the day after Christmas is called in Canada, when the weather had been cold enough to get a good sheet of ice, they played "Old-Timers" against "All-Stars" on the school's outdoor rink. "You guys won't have a chance against us!" Quin called back.

His dad laughed. "We'll see!"

About an inch of snow had fallen overnight, and when Quin reached the school he could hear the scruffing of metal as it rasped across the ice. "Grab another scraper," Eon called.

As the boys worked—it was their job to keep the ice in good condition—they shared notes about the Christmas gifts they'd received. Most of them had gotten new hockey equipment, and they were eager to try it out. By the time they had the ice clean and ready for the game, the men had come and several other folks had gathered along the boards of the rink to watch the action. The pastor, as usual, would be referee.

Lots of the men hadn't been on skates since the past winter, but when their blades touched the ice, it was easy to see that they had grown up playing hockey. Quin watched his dad send the puck zinging into the net with his powerful wrist shot, and for a moment he wished that they could be on the same side. He no longer felt confident that he and his buddies would wipe the old folks out as easily as he'd bragged. They were in for a good game.

Both the Old-Timers and the All-Stars started off fast, but by midway in the second period, the men's experience began to give them the edge. The boys, though, had the advantage of earlier ice time as a team. The score seesawed, but when the pastor blew the final whistle, the Old-Timers had won 6 to 5.

In the game of life everyone has to play, and everyone can be on the winning side—if that's what's chosen.

Are you on God's winning team? If not, the rules allow you to change sides. You can be a winner. It's up to you to choose.

DECEMBER

27

Like the Swallow

How I love your Temple, Almighty God! How I want to be there!
Psalm 84:1, 2, TEV.

A big blue church stands solemnly at the side of the campus on Gitwe Hill in Rwanda, and on Friday nights and Sabbaths it is packed with worshipers. Birds, too, sometimes flit into the sanctuary briefly, then settle quietly, out of sight, on top of the back wall under the high-pitched roof. They never disturbed anyone, though, until vespers one Friday evening.

The church was packed as usual, and the singing seemed to have awakened a junior swallow. It swooped from its perch and winged its way toward the front. There it looped around the speaker's platform, flew toward the back, and slipped into a steep dive, but just before it crashed into the head of one of the students, it leveled and zoomed toward the front.

By this time the bird had caught the attention of many worshipers.

It circled back again, this time to swoop down and brush against the head of one of the ladies three rows in from the back. She jumped and swiped at the swallow.

The bird swooshed off, made a low pass over one of the young men a few rows farther ahead, then began a bobbing course, touching a head here, zooming close to an ear there.

Everyone was watching by now, but the bird seemed not to care that it had taken their attention away from the service. It continued to enjoy the new game it had invented to show off its flying skills. The young swallow became even bolder. Zooming toward another youngster, it slipped its wings into brakes-on position and landed.

The youngster didn't move, except to reach his hands slowly upward. Just as he about touched the bird, it soared off for another loop around the church and another series of quick head hops.

Finally as the swallow dived into a slow pass, one of the fellows snared it with his hands and carried the bird into the night.

When you're in church, do you keep your mind on what's being taught, or does it go hopscotching off—like the swallow ?

If you sit quietly with head forward, no one will guess that you're as unconcerned as the swallow about what's being said and that you're thinking about an exciting TV show you watched, or the pair of jeans you'd like to buy, or the party your group will be having New Year's Eve and about the special person you hope to be with. No one, that is, but God.

Do you love to be in God's temple?

DECEMBER

28

What Are You Doing?

I would rather stand at the gate of the house of my God than live in the homes of the wicked.
Psalm 84:10, TEV.

After she was baptized, Taylor's mom found a new job and moved to an apartment near a church school. When they had separated, Chanel's parents sent her to live with her grandmother because they both wanted her where she could have a Christian education. Kieland has lived in foster homes since he can remember, but because his mom has asked that he stay with Adventists, he's always gone to church.

Neither of Luke's parents are church members, but his parents send him to church with a neighbor and were pleased when he decided to be baptized.

Jessica's parents send her to a good public school. In the mornings the three of them have devotions together, and evenings she studies the special Bible lessons her parents got for her.

The parents of Taylor, Chanel, Kieland, Luke, and Jessica all want the best for their children. And that best includes going to church and having Christian training. No matter how often they go to church or how much good Christian teaching they get, though, each of these young people must decide what to do with what he or she learns.

What Christian training are you getting? Give yourself 10 points for each of the following that you usually do:

_______ go to church
_______ belong to Pathfinders or another Christian youth group
_______ attend a church school
_______ have family devotions
_______ watch Christian videos or Christian TV programs
_______ read the Bible each day
_______ read Christian books and magazines
_______ attend a baptismal class or other Christian study class
_______ take a Bible Study course (such as Junior VOP)
_______ listen to Bible story or other religious cassettes

How many points do you have? _______________

Even if you do all of the above and score 100 points, does that mean you'll automatically be ready for heaven?

If you could do only one of the above things, which do you think would be the most important to choose?

DECEMBER

The Red Herring

Reverence God and give glory to him; for the hour of his judgment has come! Revelation 14:7, Phillips.

"Don't be throwing any red herring in front of me!" Uncle Stan's voice had a ring of mock-sharpness.

"Red herring!" Kristine giggled.

"Exactly," he said. "You know very well that you're trying to sidetrack me so I won't say anything about the oil smeared on my workshop floor and the empty can.

"My bike chain needed oiling. I knew you wouldn't mind, but . . . there was an accident. I tried to clean it."

"So you tossed me a red herring so I wouldn't scold you."

"Red herring?"

"A dried, smoked herring. Sometimes in fox hunts they used to drag smoked—red—herring across the ground to destroy the scent and confuse the dogs. When someone brings up another topic to take attention away from the main issue, that's called a red herring.

Even though Christine knew her uncle probably wouldn't punish her, she still wanted to avoid talking about the wasted oil and the stain on his shop floor. What about you and God? When you make mistakes, do you want to talk to Him about them?

Some people worry about God and sins. Which of the following gives the best picture of how you think God treats sinners?

1. A stern judge who gives heavy punishments.

2. A scowling, thunder-voiced preacher, hunching over his pulpit and pointing His finger and yelling at everyone in His church to repent and change their ways so they won't be "lost!"

3. A police officer who pulls out a ticket pad and then says, "I won't give you a ticket this time."

4. A grandmother hugging a child who's just hurt himself.

Before making a final decision about these word pictures, think about this. With God there are no red herrings and no excuses, but because of Jesus' victory on the cross, Satan was judged and forever condemned. That same victory also judged you and offers to make you right with God. You can be made right with God this very minute if you choose to be.

Uncle Stan showed Kristine how to clean the oil stain from his shop floor, and she was happy to take the ugly stain away.

Jesus wants to take the stain of sin from your heart so that you can live happily with Him in heaven.

Now, which word picture is best? Can you make a better one?

DECEMBER

30

Satan Is a Sneak

Jesus answered, "It is written: 'Man does not live on bread alone, but on every word that comes from the mouth of God.'" Matthew 4:4.

Satan's number one wish is that we won't trust God or His Word. He tried to trick Jesus into jumping off the top of the Temple by reminding Him of the promise in Psalm 91:11, 12 that God would send His angels.

Jesus had learned the Scriptures as He was growing up, and He was ready for Satan's temptations. "Do not put the Lord your God to the test," He replied, quoting Deuteronomy 6:16.

Satan can't hold under his power anyone who honestly wants to know the truth. He still tries to trick us, though, and our best protection is knowing the Bible. God promises to send the Holy Spirit to help us understand the Bible if we study it prayerfully.

It's also interesting to learn about the Bible. The first Bible was translated into French in the year 1170, into German in the 1460s, and the first American edition was printed around 1750. Do you know who made the first complete English translation? ______________
In what year? ____________

Some Bible translations have strange names because of printing mistakes or because of old words that are no longer used. The Breeches Bible (1560) got its name from Genesis 3:7, which said that Adam and Eve "sowed figge-tree leaves together, and made themselves breeches." What does your Bible say they made? ______

____

Psalm 91:5 in the Bug Bible (1551) says "Thou shalt not be afraid of bugges by night." What does your Bible say?

____

In the Vinegar Bible (1717) the heading to Luke 20 reads "The Parable of the Vinegar." What should it be? _____

In the New King James Version, Ezra 7:21 has all the letters of the alphabet except J. "And I, even I, Artaxerxes the king, do issue a decree to all the treasurers who are in the region beyond the River, that whatever Ezra the priest, the scribe of the Law of the God of heaven, may require of you, let it be done diligently." In the Bible you use, how many different letters are there in that text?

____

What is the most important thing that you know about the Bible? ______________________________

____

(Answers are on page 381.)

DECEMBER

The Way

Jesus said to him, "I am the way, the truth, and the life. John 14:6, NKJV.

Adam snuggled into the big armchair beside his grandpa and listened. His eyes felt heavy, but he forced himself to keep them open. He intended to stay awake.

" 'I am the way, the truth, and the life,' " his dad read from the big family Bible. He looked around at the group sitting in the living room. "We've had a happy time this evening playing games and visiting," he said, "and in a few minutes we'll be beginning another new year. Our family welcomes the new year with a time of prayer and praise, but first my father will share a few thoughts on how we can make Jesus' way our way."

Grandpa slipped his arm around Adam and gave him a squeeze. "To follow Jesus, we need to understand about the will," he began. "That's the part of us that's our power of choice. When Adam and Eve chose to sin, they put their wills in Satan's control and lost the right to the tree of life. Ever since, Satan has been in control, and he does his best to sidetrack us from the way to heaven.

"Through Jesus we can win back the right to eat from the tree of life, but that means we must take our wills out of Satan's control and give them to God." Grandpa paused a moment. "You yourself must choose to belong to God and to obey Him. By yourself you can't change your heart, but you are in charge of your will, and in your heart of hearts you can decide to give it to God. When you choose to do this, God—Jesus—can set you right, and as long as you continue to choose His way, He'll keep you right."

Grandpa chuckled. "I'm talking from long experience, and after many mistakes I can tell you that when you choose God's way there'll be no miracles of not sinning anymore, because Satan will work his hardest to get you back under his control."

In the distance Adam heard the church bells begin to chime. Grandpa looked at his watch. It was exactly midnight. "Happy New Year, everyone!" he exclaimed. "Have a happy new year with Jesus!"

And Jesus said to ____________, "I am the way, the truth, and the life. Follow me." And ________________ got up and followed Him." Put your name in the blanks. Choose to follow Jesus' way.

Remember, it's not *what* you are but *whose* you are that counts, and *whose* you are will make you become *what* you are.

Answers

January 5:

1. Stand. 2. Look. 3. Ask. 4. Ask. 5. Walk.

January 10:

1. Amphipod, crustacean; pteropod, mollusk.
2. Snail, a mollusk. Psalm 58:8.
3. Pearls are formed within the shell of oysters and certain other mollusks.

January 12, 13:

A.—6. B.—3. C.—7. D.—1. E.—7. F.—4. G.—2. H.—5.

April 9:

Suggested answers—go to church, praise God in church, talk about ways we can please God, help someone who's sick, care for animals.

April 17:

10 texts for 36 school weeks = 360 texts; 8 texts for 16 vacation weeks = 128 texts. 128 and 360 = 488.

April 22:

The woman gave the man seven apples. He gave half of them plus half an apple (3 1/2 + 1/2) or four apples to the first man. That left him with three. He gave half of them plus half an apple (1 1/2 + 1/2) or two apples to the second man. That left him with one apple (1/2 + 1/2), which he gave to his wife.

April 25:

Proverbs 7:1; Matthew 18:35; Matthew 6:12; Luke 9:23; Proverbs 26:18, 19; Matthew 7:2; 2 Thessalonians 2:3

May 9:

Borrowed seed—1, 4, 5. Shared seed—2, 3, 6.

May 25:

He added the camel he loved to the 17 and that made 18. Then he was able to give

one half to his oldest son	=	9
one third to his second son	=	6
one ninth to his third son	=	2
total	=	17

There was one camel left—the camel the old man loved best. He was able to take it for himself.

May 28:

ANSWERS TO A QUIZ ABOUT THE BIBLE

1. Esther 8:9. It contains 90 words.
2. John 11:35. It says "Jesus wept."
3. 1,189. 929 in the Old Testament; 260 in the New Testament.
4. Psalm 117.
5. Mahershalalhashbaz (Maher-Shalal-Hash-Baz—Isaiah 8:1-4). This is the name that God told Isaiah to give his son, which is actually a Hebrew sentence meaning "Quick loot; fast plunder."
6. The Bible in the Algonquian Indian language in 1661. It was translated by John Eliot, a Puritan missionary, his two sons, and several Indian interpreters.
7. It is believed that all 66 books of the Bible were originally written in one of three ancient languages—Hebrew, Aramaic, and Greek.
8. The chapters and verses as we now know them appeared first in the Geneva Bible printed in 1557 (NT) and 1560 (OT). This was done to make the Bible easier to use. The idea was to break the text into separate sentences, but this does not always happen. Robert Stevens, one of the scholars who helped divide the chapters and verses, worked out his system while traveling from Lyons to Paris on horseback. Because of the awkward break between some verses, some scholars jokingly suggest that his horse must have stumbled a number of times along the way.
9. It comes from the ancient words meaning a collection of writings or book.
10. That's a matter of personal choice. Some scholars say Isaiah 40. Others suggest John 14:1-3. John and Psalms are the two individual books of the Bible that are most widely distributed.

June 3:

1. 588,000,000,000,000,000. 2. 5,280 feet; 6 feet = 880 people to a mile x 24,900 miles = 21,912,000 people.

June 26:

1. True. 2. True. 3. True. 4. False. 5. False. 6. Arctic.

June 28:

1. She's gone from a bad to a worse situation.
2. That's hardly worth anything.
3. We're selling things that don't have any value to their owners.

August 9:

Seek His kingdom first.

September 3:

All help.

December 30:

John Wycliffe completed the first translation of the Bible into English in 1382, but all copies were written by hand until it was first printed in 1450.

Genesis 3:7: "coverings" in NKJV, NIV, TEV, LB; "aprons" in KJV, RSV. Psalm 91:5: "terror" in KJV, RSV, NIV, NKJV; "dangers" in TEV, TLB. Luke 20 has the "parable of the vineyard." Ezra 7:21 has 25 letters in the KJV, fewer in NIV and TEV.

The most important thing to know about the Bible is that it teaches the truth about God.

SCRIPTURE INDEX